Re-Imagining Initial Teacher Education

RE-IMAGINING INITIAL TEACHER EDUCATION

Perspectives on Transformation

Edited by
Fionnuala Waldron, John Smith,
Maeve Fitzpatrick and Thérèse Dooley

The Liffey Press

Published by
The Liffey Press Ltd
Raheny Shopping Centre, Second Floor
Raheny, Dublin 5, Ireland
www.theliffeypress.com

A catalogue record of this book is
available from the British Library.

ISBN 978-1-908308-37-5

Printed in Ireland by Sprint Print.

Section Four: Language, Teaching and Learning in Initial Teacher Education

11. Learning Autonomy: Irish Language Education in Initial Teacher Education 245
Ríóna Ní Fhrighil, Coláiste Phádraig, Droim Conrach

12. Irish-medium Initial Teacher Education: Lessons from Self-evaluation 266
Eibhlín Mhic Aoidh, Jill Garland, Gabrielle Nig Uidhir, John Sweeney, St. Mary's University College Belfast

13. Irish and Modern Languages: A Collaborative Journey in Initial Teacher Education 285
Áine Furlong, Brendan MacMahon and Sinéad Ní Ghuidhir, Waterford Institute of Technology and NUI Galway

Section Five: Responding to Student Voices: Programme Reform and Transformation

14. Student Teacher Voice and School Placement: What We Can Learn if We Listen 307
Bernadette Ní Áingléis, Paula Murphy, Brian Ruane, St Patrick's College, Drumcondra

15. Developing 'Good' Post-primary Teachers and Teaching in a Reform Era: Cultural Dynamics in a Programme Level Study of the PDE 329
Paul F. Conway, Rosaleen Murphy, Michael Delargey, Kathy Hall, Karl Kitching, Fiachra Long, Jacinta McKeon, Brian Murphy, Stephen O'Brien and Dan O'Sullivan, School of Education, University College Cork

16. Inclusive Initial Teacher Education: The Case of Mature Students 349
Anne M. Dolan, Mary Immaculate College, Limerick

Acknowledgements

This book originated in an international conference on initial teacher education hosted by St. Patrick's College, Drumcondra. Our sincere thanks to the conference organising committee whose work ensured the conference was a resounding success: Michael O'Leary, Eithne Kennedy, Brian Ruane, Maeve Fitzpatrick, Pádraig Ó Duibhir, Aoife Myler, Thérèse Dooley, Dolores Corcoran, John Smith, Joe Travers, Maura Coulter, Daire Keogh and Fionnuala Waldron. Many other colleagues and friends contributed to the success of the conference and we thank them most sincerely. In particular, we are grateful to Pauric Travers, who, as President of St Patrick's College, gave valuable and significant support to the conference. We wish to express our gratitude to the speakers, facilitators and participants and hope that the book reflects the contributions and interests expressed over the three days of the conference. We are very grateful for the financial support given by the Research Committee of St. Patrick's College, without which this publication would not have been possible.

A special note of thanks to the artist, Eddie Kennedy, whose painting illustrates the cover of the book. The painting is entitled *Intentions* (oil on linen, 30cm x 35cm, 2003). We deeply appreciate his generosity in allowing us to use this image which captured our "intentions" so perfectly. You can view Eddie's work at the following sites: www.eddiekennedystudio.com; www.hillsborofineart.com; and www.jcacciolagallery.com.

Finally, we are deeply indebted to all those who agreed to contribute to the publication and those who gave of their time and expertise to review chapters. We trust that our combined efforts have resulted in a timely and valuable addition to the field of initial teacher education.

Notes on Contributors

About the Editors

Fionnuala Waldron is Dean of Education at St Patrick's College, Drumcondra, and Chair of the Centre for Human Rights and Citizenship Education. Her research interests include history and citizenship, human rights education and teacher education.

John Smith is a senior lecturer in Education and Director of the Graduate Diploma in Education (Primary Teaching) at St Patrick's College, Drumcondra, where he is also Coordinator of Online Teaching and Learning. His research interests include education policy and history as well as online pedagogies.

Maeve Fitzpatrick is Senior Administrator in the Education Department, St Patrick's College, Drumcondra. She is an expert in teacher education programme management, administration and change.

Thérèse Dooley is a lecturer in Mathematics Education at St Patrick's College, Drumcondra. She completed her PhD studies at the University of Cambridge. Of particular interest to her is the role of language and a conjecturing atmosphere in students' mathematical abstraction.

About the Authors

Chapter 1

Marilyn Cochran-Smith is the Cawthorne Professor of Teacher Education and Director of the Doctoral Program in Curriculum and Instruction at the Lynch School of Education, Boston College. She is a former president of AERA and an elected member of the National Academy of Education. Her research interests include teacher education research, practice and policy, social justice, and practitioner research. She has taught courses at St Patrick's College and presented keynote lectures in Ireland.

Chapter 2

John Furlong is a former Director of the Oxford University Department of Education and he is now an emeritus professor. John has researched and written on a wide range of different topics including the professional education of teachers. His most recent book, *Education – an anatomy of the discipline. Rescuing the university project?*, was published in 2013 by Routledge.

Chapter 3

John Smith – see *About the Editors* above.

Chapter 4

Liz Dunphy is a senior lecturer in Early Childhood Education at St Patrick's College, Drumcondra. Her research interests include young children's mathematics, early childhood pedagogy and the assessment of early learning. She contributed to the development of *Aistear: The Framework for Early Learning* (National Council for Curriculum and Assessment, 2009).

Chapter 5

Fred Korthagen is a Professor of Education at the Vrije Universiteit (VU University, Amsterdam) and Utrecht University, the Netherlands, and a co-founder of the Institute for Multi-level Learning (see www.corereflection.org). His specialisations are reflection and self-directed learning as key aspects of professional development, and the integration of theory and practice. Twice, in 2000 and in 2006, he received the *Exemplary Research Award* from the Division *Teaching and Teacher Education* of the American Educational Research Association (AERA).

Chapter 6

Dolores Corcoran is a lecturer in Mathematics Education at St Patrick's College, Drumcondra. Dolores was a teacher in primary schools for much of her life and has completed doctoral studies in the University of Cambridge. Dolores has also written chapters in edited books on Lesson Study and Teacher Knowledge of Mathematics.

Chapter 7

Zita Lysaght is a member of the Special Education Department at St Patrick's College, Drumcondra. Her teaching and her research portfolio reflect a broad range of interests including assessment, mixed-methods research design and evaluation, blended learning and collaborative/distributed teacher leadership.

Chapter 8

James Deegan is Professor of the Sociology of Education at Mary Immaculate College, Limerick. He is active in a number of fields including teacher education, doctoral education and qualitative research methods and is currently engaged in research on teacher educator knowledge. He also serves as Director of the Structured PhD (Education) and the International Research Methods Summer School (IRMSS) at Mary Immaculate College.

Chapter 9

Jones Irwin is a lecturer in Philosophy at St Patrick's College, Drumcondra. His research interests include philosophy of education, ethical-political theory and recent French thought. He has been working on alternative approaches to the teaching of ethics and religion in Irish schools. His most recent publication is the monograph, *Paulo Freire's Philosophy of Education: Origins, Developments, Impacts and Legacies* (Continuum: 2012).

Chapter 10

Maeve O'Brien is senior lecturer in Sociology, Coordinator of Human Development and Co-Director of the MA in Human Development at St Patrick's College, Drumcondra. Her research focuses on classed, gendered and affective inequalities and their relation to education. Her most recent book, *Pedagogy, Oppression and Transformation in a 'Post-Critical' Climate* (Continuum, 2011), draws on key Freirean ideas and interrogates the possibilities for transformation in education today.

Chapter 11

Ríóna Ní Fhrighil is a lecturer in the Irish Department at St Patrick's College, Drumcondra. Her research interests include Contemporary Poetry in Irish and English, Literary Translation, Second-Language Acquisition, Computer-Assisted Language-learning. Her most recent publications include a monograph on the poetry of Eavan Boland and Nuala Ní Dhomhnaill. She has also edited three collections of critical essays.

Chapter 12

Eibhlín Mhic Aoidh is a senior lecturer in Irish-medium Education at St Mary's University College, Belfast, and is currently Option Leader for Irish-medium MEd modules. She is completing an EdD at Queen's University Belfast and is researching assessment practices in Irish-medium early years settings. **Gabrielle Nig Uidhir** is senior tutor for Development at St Mary's University College, Belfast. She has researched and published on Irish-medium Education and recently collaborated with Dame Marie Clay in the development of an early literacy assessment tool for Irish-medium and Gaeltacht schools. **Jill Garland** was a senior lecturer in initial teacher education for Irish-medium primary education at St Mary's University College, Belfast, where she co-ordinated and developed a new PGCE course for the Irish-medium post-primary sector in partnership with Queen's University Belfast and the University of Ulster. **John Sweeney** is the senior tutor in St Mary's University College, Belfast, with responsibility for academic affairs and quality assurance. He is a former chairman of the Primary Committee of the Northern Ireland Council for the Curriculum, Examinations and Assessment. His research interests include the development of science and technology education in primary schools.

Chapter 13

Áine **Furlong** lectures in language education, French and intercultural communication at Waterford Institute of Technology. She holds a Doctorate in Applied Linguistics (TCD) and her research interests include CLIL, the relation of creativity to plurilingualism/culturalism and intercultural communication. **Brendan Mac Mahon** is a lecturer in Education and Programme Director of *An Dioplóma Gairmiúil san Oideachas* at NUI Galway. He holds a Doctorate in Education from Trinity College Dublin and his research interests include Disciplinary Literacy and Inclusion at second level. **Sinéad Ní Ghuidhir** lectures on the Dioplóma Gairmiúil san Oideachas (DGO), an initial teacher education programme through Irish at NUI Galway. She has a specific interest in active teaching, learning and assessment methods.

Chapter 14

Bernadette Ní Áingléis is Director of Teaching Practice at St Patrick's College, Drumcondra. Her research interests include collaborations with schools in teacher education, children's education and the law, and student teacher voice in learning, teaching and evaluation. Her professional background lies in primary teaching, leadership and administration, curriculum development, and evaluation. **Brian Ruane** is a lecturer in History Education and Citizenship Education at St. Patrick's College, Drumcondra, and programme leader in the Centre for Human Rights and Citizenship Education. Brian was previously Human Rights Education Manager with Amnesty International Irish Section. He has managed projects in Human Rights Education and published related materials, articles and manuals. **Paula Murphy** is a lecturer in Education (Drama) in St. Patrick's College, Drumcondra. She previously worked as a primary school teacher and as Education Officer for TEAM Educational Theatre Company. She has presented at a variety of national and international conferences and is a committee member of ADEI (Association for Drama in Education in Ireland). She is co-author of *Discovering Drama: Theory and Practice for the Primary School* (Gill & Macmillan, 2006).

Chapter 15

The authors of this chapter work in the School of Education, University College Cork (UCC). **Paul Conway** is a senior lecturer. He was Principal Investigator on the *Learning to Teach Study* (2008-10) and is Principal Investigator on the Irish Research Council-funded *Re-imagining Initial Teacher Identity and Learning Study* (2012-13). **Michael Delargey** is a college lecturer in ICT and Mathematics Education. He has research interests in mathematics curriculum reform. **Kathy Hall** is Chair of Education. She has worked in teacher education for 25 years. She served on the Teaching Council and was advisor to England's Department for Education on teacher CPD. **Karl Kitching** is a college lecturer. He is currently writing a book on the politics of racism in education and is Principal Investigator on the IRC-funded *Making Communion: Disappearing and Emerging Forms of Childhood in Ireland* study. **Brian Murphy** is a college lecturer in the areas of language teaching methodology, literacy and teaching studies and is also course leader for the MEd programme. **Fiachra Long** is a senior lecturer and is author of *Educating the Postmodern Child* (Bloomsbury: 2012). **Jacinta McKeon** is a college lecturer. Her research interests include second language learning and teaching. **Rosaleen Murphy** is a research fellow. She has been involved in several major research projects including the *Learning to Teach Study.* **Stephen O'Brien** is a college lecturer. His research interests include learning theory, educational policy and practice, multicultural education, inclusion, and curriculum and assessment. **Dan O'Sullivan** is a college lecturer. His principal research interests centre on inclusive education and the early-career learning of beginning teachers.

Chapter 16

Anne Dolan is a lecturer in primary geography in the Department of Learning, Society and Religious Education at Mary Immaculate College, Limerick. She has worked in teacher education, primary education, and adult education and has recently completed her doctoral studies as a part-time mature student.

Introduction

Re-imagining Initial Teacher Education: Perspectives on Transformation

Fionnuala Waldron
St Patrick's College, Drumcondra

In July 2011, the Faculty of Education in St Patrick's College hosted a conference to address the significant changes underway in initial teacher education in Ireland, which provided a forum for critical engagement with key issues and a shared space for envisioning future practice. This edited collection brings together a representative selection from the conference papers and seeks to capture the rich tapestry of ideas, research and scholarship that characterised the event. Presented in the book are sixteen chapters that range across significant sites of action within the field of teacher education, engaging with international and national policy trends and with the complex interaction of theory and practice characteristic of the sector. Informed by historical analysis, ideological critique, and empirical research, contributions explore questions relating to policy, practice, values, ethics and programme reform. The collection is structured around five key strands: policy trends and system change; conversations between theory and practice; navigating ideological spaces in initial teacher education; language, teaching and learning in initial teacher education; and responding to student voices in programme reform.

In addition, chapters are interlaced with multiple crosscutting and interwoven themes, ideas and imaginings such as the importance of collaboration, the challenges of diversity, the creative and transformative potential of renewal, the ethic of care, the agency of students, the centrality of relations, and the inherent complexity of the process of teaching. This web of possibilities is underpinned by two core principles – the fundamental relationship between education, teacher development and research and the importance of purpose.

Almost two decades ago, Marilyn Cochran-Smith and Susan L. Lytle argued for a reconceptualisation of the relationship between classroom teachers and research, which recognised the capacity of teachers to generate authentic knowledge about their practice (Cochran-Smith and Lytle, 1993). Crystallised in the phrase 'inquiry as stance' (Cochran-Smith and Lytle, 2009), the idea of practitioner research has since become synonymous with good practice in teacher development worldwide. The dynamic, critical and reflective relationship envisioned between teachers and their practice is generally set in a collaborative context of community. This new focus requires a shift in identity for many teachers away from the idea of the teacher as the authoritative and autonomous arbiter of classroom life, towards a more dynamic, less certain, and open process of continuous reconstruction. It is axiomatic that such practice has significant implications for how we work with students in initial teacher education and for the extent to which student-led research, enquiry-based learning, and critical reflection are given space to breathe.

The relationship between research and teacher education itself is multi-dimensional which perhaps explains the plethora of terms used to describe it, each of which captures particular dimensions. Whether one describes it as research-led, research-oriented, research-driven, or research-based, the elements of that relationship are generally recognised to include the following: a conceptualisation of teacher educators as research active and committed to the generation of knowledge; an expectation that they will draw on their own research and on the research of others to inform their teaching; commitment to an inquiry stance with regard to their own teaching and to the development of programmes that support students teachers as researchers, enabling them to grow into the kind of practice envisioned by Cochran-Smith and Lytle (1993, 2009) and by Corcoran, Ní Fhrighil and Lysaght in this volume. This is a complex and demanding role which requires institutional and systemic support and resourcing, support that may not be forthcoming, as discussed by John Furlong in chapter two. There can also be tensions within the system that militate against the kind of open-ended, enquiry-oriented practice envisaged by such conceptualisations. Teacher education in Ireland, for example, as elsewhere, has entered a period of increased surveillance and control and, as noted by Furlong, Smith, Deegan, O'Brien, and Conway et al. in this volume, there is concern that the discourse that has emerged around initial teacher education betrays some of the instrumentalism and reductionism characteristic of discourses elsewhere. Furthermore, where classroom practice is concerned, the relationship between research and practice all too often conceptualises teachers as consumers of models of 'best' practice generated elsewhere, and instances where the evidence-base is filtered, manipulated and commodified for teachers as prescriptive 'solutions' to generalised and decontextualised problems are evident in the Irish system, particularly in areas such as literacy and mathematics where system-wide responses are sought. In this kind of approach, the complex relationship between research and practice is reduced to the idea of 'what works' and, consequently, making choices within education, whether at the level of policy or at classroom level, becomes increasingly reductionist.

For student teachers, reducing choices about classroom practice to 'what works' is particularly problematic. What if the research-based practice endorsed by their initial teacher education programme doesn't work? What happens if student teachers or newly qualified teachers find themselves in contexts where that practice is challenged by the culture of the school, by challenging behaviour, by poor resources, by parents' expectations? What if 'what works' for the newly qualified teacher are precisely those traditional practices that characterised her/his 'apprenticeship of observation' (Lortie, 1975)? If 'what works' is your only measure for effective teaching then, when it fails to work, or when an alternative but less desirable practice works better, it is unlikely that newly qualified teachers will continue to practice in ways endorsed by initial teacher education programmes, a phenomenon sometimes described as a 'washing out' of the effects of initial teacher education. How can we ensure that the pedagogy developed by the student in the context of initial teacher education is robust enough to survive graduation, that the teacher identities constructed by student teachers are resilient?

In Chapter 5, Korthagen locates the person of the teacher at the heart of the theory/practice dynamic and argues for the need to align practice with mission. Unless the relationship between the 'how' and the 'why' of practice is one that includes a critical and living relationship with core values, the practice constructed is fragile in the face of challenge. It is tempting to say that the purpose of initial teacher education is simply to produce competent teachers who can teach well and who continue to develop their professional practice throughout their careers. Yet, as Paulo Freire has reminded us, education is never neutral; it is always political, and the perceived neutrality that underpins the idea of the competent professional is a deceptive one. And teachers themselves would be among the first to identify their roles as working towards a social good – a more just, caring and equal society, a better life for their students. As Michael Fullan said, 'teaching, at its core, is a moral profession. Scratch a good teacher and you will find a moral purpose' (1993, p. 12). Moreover, to reduce the purpose of initial teacher education to the development of competent professionals, even in the broadest and most holistic sense of that term, is to confuse purpose with function. 'Function', as David Hansen reminds us, 'is about maintenance; purpose, on the other hand, opens up the possibility of transformation' (2008, p. 23).

The idea that becoming a 'good' teacher extends beyond the idea of competencies and that initial teacher education should articulate a broader social purpose are common threads across several contributions to this collection – O'Brien's commitment to a justice-oriented ethic of care, Ní Áingléis et al.'s articulation of democratic practice, Irwin's exploration of the ethical space, Deegan's envisioning of education for transformation, are but four examples among many. It is increasingly common to find teacher education programmes endorsing social justice pedagogy or education for democratic citizenship perspectives. Moreover, as discussed by Cochran-Smith in chapter one, diversity has had a considerable impact on how teacher educators situate their practice nationally and internationally, and most programmes articulate some commitment to intercultural education or to a broader equality and democratic agenda. Writing in the context of teacher education in the US in 2009, Ken Zeichner states that 'it has come to the point where it is very difficult to find a teacher education program anywhere that does not claim that it has a social justice agenda and that it prepares teachers to work against inequities in schooling and society' (p. 25). In this context, Zeichner warns against the danger of sloganising and the loss of meaning that can accompany an over-generalised application of the term. Teacher education programmes that claim commitment to social justice perspectives, he argues, need to be clear about what is meant by social justice and about what student teachers are being prepared to do (2009, p. xvii).

Taking on a values-base in teacher education, then, requires teacher educators to go beyond a rhetorical commitment and to identify what it means in practice. The idea of educating student teachers for social justice, for example, encapsulates both critique and transformation, embodying Freire's two essential tasks of the educator, that of denunciation and annunciation. At the very least, therefore, it entails a commitment to critical engagement with the world and towards a conceptualisation of teachers as agents of social change. In this volume and elsewhere Maeve O'Brien and Marilyn Cochran-Smith have teased out some of the implications. Such a construction involves, among other things, engagement with issues of self, of power and of recognition – providing spaces for student teachers to interrogate their own perspectives, preconceptions and biases and helping them to recognise those perspectives as situated, as having an interest; enabling them to recognise power differentials and understand how they impact on society and on education at macro and micro levels. It involves helping them to recognise and challenge how inequalities play out in the classroom in terms of differential expectations, social relations, resources and discipline policies; to recognise all children as learners and to identify and challenge practices and beliefs that limit their development, such as approaches to literacy and mathematics that fail to engage them as creative and critical thinkers; to understand how the culture and experiences of children and their communities can be recognised and built on; to know how to engage with people from different backgrounds; to see diversity as an asset rather than an obstacle; to have the courage to challenge norms and practices that they identify as unjust and discriminatory (Cochran-Smith, 2004; Zeichner, 2009; Villegas and Lucas, 2002; Darling-Hammond and Bransford, 2005; Sleeter, 2008). These are difficult and complex tasks and are not amenable to easy solutions.

And yet, as Anne M. Dolan argues, the responsibility does not end there; at the institutional level, espousing social justice in teacher education includes a commitment to be proactive in widening access to teacher education and in facilitating participation of students from diverse backgrounds, to identifying systemic and institutional barriers, and practices and structures within teacher education that may be implicitly discriminatory. Commitment at programme level also implies coherence to the principles of social justice pedagogy across all programme elements, and ensuring that where claims to social justice pedagogy are made by a programme, it is accountable to those claims from a student perspective, providing them with the kinds of learning environments that will both challenge and support them, and that will engage with and extend their emergent understanding.

Indeed, a focus on social justice is generally found side by side with, or part of, a further commitment to education for democratic citizenship and is integral to the kind of citizenship education implied by the idea of thick democracy, one that is participatory, inclusive and critical (Gandin and Apple, 2002; Carr, 2008). Such a stance conceptualises education for democratic citizenship permeating all areas of education – structures, processes and relations – and explicitly addressing specific contexts and relations of domination (Apple, 2008, p. 106). If student teachers are to develop the capacity to educate for democratic citizenship, then they need to experience what that means in practice. Democratising practice in teacher education includes, but cannot be reduced to, student teachers participating in the decision-making structures of the programme and – to use Laura Lundy's insightful frame developed in relation to children's participation rights and exemplified in the writing of Ní Áingléis et al., in this volume – ensuring that their views are given space, voice, audience and influence (Lundy, 2007). It includes, also, the collaborative networks and relationships with partners envisaged by Furlong et al.

and Mhic Aoidh et al. (this volume) that democratise programme design. It suggests modes of teaching that are participative and dialogical, that engage students in deliberation on important issues, that provide opportunities for students to contest and to disagree, and that challenge them to listen to and engage with divergent views. If, as Dewey argues, 'democracy has to be born anew in each generation' (1916, p. 139) then education for democratic citizenship, like social justice education, takes on a transformative stance, envisioning and constructing the future, rather than maintaining the present.

Section One – Policy Trends and System Change: Global and Local Contexts

The first of the five sections in this book focuses on national and international policy trends and examines a range of key issues, contexts and movements that have proved influential in teacher education worldwide over the past few decades. Historical patterns, shared contexts and ideologies, policy borrowings and power elites are identified, analysed and critiqued, while the implications of state and European policy for reform in initial teacher education in key areas are teased out.

In Chapter 1, Marilyn Cochran-Smith presents a powerful and critical overview of current challenges in teacher education which are visible internationally across a range of contexts. The author addresses each in turn, identifying the ideological and political assumptions that underpin them. While few would dispute the idea that good teaching counts, the extent to which student performance is causally related to teacher quality is identified as the first challenge. If school success and failure is directly linked to the quality of teaching, then teacher education becomes the key policy site; teacher quality is redefined as a problem of policy rather than one of learning and the wider social contexts of schools and communities are ignored. This focus on teacher quality becomes even more problematic in the context of the growing accountability culture, identified by Cochran-Smith as the second challenge. The author argues that notions of accountability that see high-stakes test scores as appropriate measures of teacher and student performance ignore both the complexity of teaching and the wider social contexts of education, such as the growing diversity in school populations. The response of teacher education to that diversity represents the third challenge. Given the narrow demographic from which student teachers are generally drawn, the author argues the need for powerful teacher education to challenge the embedded assumptions and beliefs which can lead to a deficit view of diversity. However, the terrain of teacher education itself is an increasingly contested one and the growing number of alternative pathways into teaching is identified as the fourth challenge. Arguing cogently for university-based teacher education to articulate its value more explicitly, Cochran-Smith outlines the dangers inherent in the kind of diversification that has occurred, which has resulted in the proliferation of 'for-profit', online and school-based models. As her final challenge, the author problematises the conceptualisations of professionalism that find expression in different models of learning communities, and the views of the knowledge-practice relationship on which they are premised, and identifies the losses inherent in more instrumental models of community.

John Furlong returns to the question of university-based teacher education raised by Marilyn Cochran-Smith in Chapter 2, where he explores the uneasy relationship between teacher education and the university sector within the UK. Drawing on Newman's idea of the university, Furlong places the 'contestability of knowledge' at the heart of university-based education as a defining value. The author presents a critical analysis of the strengths and weaknesses of teacher education within the UK and of the impact of state policy on developments in teaching and research in the sector. He examines how characteristics specific to the field, such as the career pathways of teacher educators, funding sources, and institutional research cultures, can have a negative impact on research quality in the sector and argues that teacher education, despite its university setting, is bound to state agendas in both teaching and research. Furlong argues persuasively for a 're-tooling' of faculties of education and teacher education itself which embraces the 'contestability of knowledge' as a core value in teaching and research and eschews reductionist and instrumentalist views of teaching and teacher education. Indeed, Furlong sees the 'contestability of knowledge' as a foundational value across educational theory, research and practice and as fundamental to teachers' practice as critical educators. Given the decentralisation of knowledge production resulting from technological change and development, he argues that the university sector needs to develop new structures to support external partnerships which continue to embody the independence, criticality and quality deemed characteristic of the university. Highlighting the importance of critical scholarship, a vibrant research culture and ongoing dialogue between educational theory and practice, Furlong identifies the need for teacher educators to broaden their research focus to include areas with significant educational implications such as climate change and global poverty, reaching beyond the traditional boundaries of their field to pursue the complex issues of our time.

In Chapter 3, the Irish policy landscape in relation to teacher education is subjected to critical analysis by John Smith. Informed by international trends and set in the wider context of reform and rationalisation of the higher education sector in Ireland, the author tracks the evolution of policy in the sector over a ten-year period (2002-2012). Smith notes the contested nature of initial teacher education internationally and the prevalence of system-based reviews worldwide. Setting the current cycle of reform in Ireland within a more extended policy timeline, he sketches the domain of teacher education in the Republic as a policy site, identifying the main actors, policy networks and webs of influence. The chapter then turns to examine the policy agenda, identifying the key areas of reform at programmatic and structural levels. In an incisive critique of policy 'silences', Smith argues that, while policy reforms could realise significant change in the system, fundamental forces which have already prompted systemic change remain largely unproblematised. Smith identifies these forces as the privatisation of teacher education through for-profit provision and its impact on the health of the sector, the diversification of entry points into the teaching profession, the consequent importation of teacher education models from other jurisdictions, and the unconscious creep towards a graduate entry profession. In conclusion, Smith calls for a more thorough and open review of the sector that engages with the consequences, intended and unintended, of those policy silences.

The case for the centrality of early childhood education to primary pre-service teacher education is convincingly made by Liz Dunphy in Chapter 4. Dunphy outlines the current context for the early childhood education sector in Ireland, a context defined by diverse and uneven provision across the public and private sector, a growing but limited professionalisation of the workforce, and a rocky interface between the early childhood sector and the primary sector, where the majority of early childhood education continues to be located. Drawing on a wide range of international and national policy documents, Dunphy presents a compelling argument for the redesign of initial teacher education programmes to include a substantial focus on early childhood education and care. Dunphy's argument is based on the premise that primary schools remain rich sites for early childhood education, with access to teachers who are able to marry deep expertise in a range of key areas, including the creation of holistic and creative learning environments, the promotion of children's well-being, and pedagogical practice that is founded on a sound knowledge of children's learning. That such teachers and settings are best placed to ensure continuity and coherence between early childhood education and later primary education is also noted by the author. Welcoming recent frameworks developed to support children's well-being and learning in the sector, Dunphy notes the complex task facing teachers to marry existing practice with the more holistic integrated environments imagined by these frameworks. Dunphy's endorsement of primary schools as settings for early childhood education and of primary teachers as key facilitators of learning, development and care in that context, then, comes at a price – a restructuring of school contexts and infrastructure to take account of the needs of the sector and the prioritisation of early childhood education within initial teacher education. Rooting her recommendations in policy reviews of the sector and in new scholarship and research into early childhood, Dunphy challenges teacher educators and teacher education institutions to respond to current policy trends and to the needs of young children by placing early childhood education at the heart of reform.

Section Two – An Enduring Dynamic: Conversations Between Theory and Practice

The second section returns to a perennial challenge of teacher education – the marrying of theory and practice. While articulated generally as a problematic and, historically, as a failure, of teacher education, it also presents an interface which is dynamic, dialogical and richly nuanced, encapsulating the generative learning spaces and defining character of the sector. Chapters 5, 6 and 7 explore key dimensions of this problematic from different but complementary perspectives. All three chapters are informed by the possibilities for authentic learning offered by contingent moments embedded in the context of practice and enriched by theoretical insights through dialogue and meta-reflection, whether integrated at programme level through realistic teacher education and assessment for learning practices or through the lens of lesson study in the context of mathematics education.

In Chapter 5, Fred A. J. Korthagen demonstrates the potential of the 'realistic' approach to teacher education to generate authentic learning about teaching for student teachers. Korthagen begins by addressing the historical provenance of the theory-practice divide in teacher education and the assumption of a linear theory-to-practice relationship characteristic of traditional teacher education programmes. Setting out the key dimensions of the realistic approach, the author argues that it recognises the complex nature of teaching where decisions are made at an unconscious immediate level, drawing together both thought and emotions. Korthagen describes the process underpinning the 'one-to-one' element of the programme, where student teachers engage in teaching individual high-school pupils followed by structured reflection on the experience. Peer-to-peer discussion and interaction with the teacher educator provide an ongoing supportive environment for the student teacher, which includes access to appropriate theoretical moments to prompt progression and insight. Korthagen addresses the need to consider issues of belief, identity and mission as part of the reflective process. Using the *onion model* (Korthagen, 2004), he makes a persuasive argument for core reflection as an integrative process which promotes alignment between the personal and professional dimensions of teacher identity and supports teachers in ensuring that their practice remains rooted in and nourished by their core ideals and sense of purpose. Drawing on a range of studies that provide empirical support for the realistic approach to teacher education, the author examines the implications of this approach for the pedagogy of teacher educators and for the structure of teacher education programmes. Finally, he strikes a warning note with regard to any tendency to embed a new divide which simply reverses the traditional one, arguing that alternative programmes that endorse a 'practice first, theory later' model confuse socialisation with development and do nothing to promote the integration of theory and practice.

In Chapter 6, Dolores Corcoran argues that a closer examination of the opportunities offered in those unplanned 'contingency moments' when teachers have to improvise can provide rich learning in the teaching of mathematics. Corcoran begins by locating the teaching and learning of mathematics within a constructivist paradigm of human learning and argues that while initial teacher education programmes are underpinned by constructivist theories of learning, bridging the theory/practice divide is not unproblematic. Drawing on the Knowledge Quartet (Rowland, Huckstep, and Thwaites, 2005), which presents an analytical framework for teacher knowledge in mathematics, Corcoran develops the idea of 'the contingency dimension' as those moments when unexpected or unplanned for events, such as children's responses, and subsequent reflection on those moments, can provide multi-layered opportunities for learning for all participants – children, teachers and student teachers alike. The author draws on two studies, one with student teachers and one with classroom practitioners, to unravel and interrogate the rich possibilities for learning in the everyday exchanges characteristic of mathematics lessons, including the scaffolding that occurs when children build on each other's ideas. Corcoran draws attention to the emotional dimension of mathematics teaching and learning. Describing contingency moments as akin to 'an emotional tightrope', she notes the opportunities presented by such moments to affect learners' dispositions towards mathematics, both positively and negatively. Finally, the author argues for an approach to teacher education that provides student teachers with sustained experiences in mathematics learning communities where opportunities to recognise the complex processes whereby children construct meaning are married with reflection. Corcoran ends by repeating Shulman's call to 'make teaching public' (2005). In demonstrating how student teachers, teacher educators and teachers can deconstruct a teaching moment to reveal the possibilities for learning, this chapter exemplifies what such a collaborative public space could achieve.

The capacity to respond to contingent moments laden with the possibility of learning persists as a continuing thread through Chapter 7, which argues for the centrality of Assessment for Learning (AfL) as a generative element of teacher education and of classroom practice. In this chapter, Zita Lysaght begins from the premise that assessment is an integral part of teaching and learning and that AfL provides a strong model for progressing student teacher learning. Drawing from a broad range of international literature, the author considers the three recurring problems of teacher education – the need to interrogate pre-existing beliefs and perceptions of teaching and learning, the complexity of the practice of teaching and teacher education, and the integration of theory and practice in the moment of teaching. Lysaght argues that the concept of adaptive expertise (Hatano and Inagaki, 1986) provides us with a powerful and productive construct with which to engage with the complexities of classroom life where requirements of flexibility, adaptability and responsivity demand an expertise that includes, but goes beyond, the routine. Lysaght goes on to delineate the challenges in relation to knowledge transfer implicit in the idea of adaptive expertise and characteristic of classroom learning environments that espouse AfL. For example, the capacity to build on previous learning and to apply learning in new contexts that may or may not be familiar requires teachers and teacher educators to scaffold meta-cognitive awareness, conscious participation in learning, critical inquiry, and reflection. Drawing on recent international and national studies, the tensions between the learning environment and model of learning proposed by Lysaght and current practice in Irish education are clearly identified. In conclusion, Lysaght identifies the challenges for teacher education if student teachers are to develop their capacities to create learning environments that support the kinds of thinking and modes of engagement required by AfL. Like Corcoran, in Chapter 6, Lysaght calls on teachers to share their practice, to 'deprivatise' the classroom, and to articulate the principles that underpin their practice, a call that she extends to teacher educators in their quest to provide high quality teacher education.

Section Three – Navigating Ideological Spaces in Initial Teacher Education

The idea of complexity is found as a continuing thread in section three where the inherently ideological and political spaces where educational policy and practice are forged are deconstructed and critiqued. While all three chapters engage in critical analysis of the systemic impact of dominant ideologies and belief systems on the structures, practice and relations of education, the section is characterised by the articulation of the transformative possibilities of programme renewal.

In Chapter 8, James G. Deegan provides a complex and nuanced exploration of the possibilities offered by the current process of renewal in initial teacher education programmes in the Republic of Ireland. Beginning from a view of teacher education as a dynamic and iterative process of 'being' and 'becoming' and eschewing instrumentalist and reductive conceptualisations of becoming a teacher, Deegan characterises teaching and teacher education as a network of interrelated and iterative practices that are ongoing and relational, with learning and meaning-making occurring in contextualised and contingent spaces. Reviewing the historical timeline of policy change in teacher education in Ireland, the author reveals the influences, trends and discourses that marked the journey from a localised and inward-looking monologue focused on an imagined Ireland to the current contested space where, buffeted by the winds of international trends, the current reform process is being played out. Deegan highlights the dangers inherent in standards and accountability oriented discourses which currently dominate educational policy nationally and internationally, the influence of which can be seen in the recent conflation of policy change in teacher education and reform initiatives in literacy and numeracy. While such reform discourses privilege operational over conceptual frameworks of change, however, policy reform also offers teacher education opportunities for renewal and for re-imagining the process of becoming a teacher. The author argues for the renewal of teacher education programmes to be conceptualised as a 'project of choice' which is open-ended and transformative, a beginning rather than an end. Deegan articulates a vision of renewal which marries the deep transformative potential of threshold concepts with the dynamic holism of complexity theory and the opportunity to conceptualise teacher education as 'more than the sum of its parts'. Rather, the interconnected, dialogic, reflective and contingent learning spaces imagined by the author transcend traditional binaries and traverse the programme journey in recursive, dynamic loops. In conclusion, Deegan proposes 'bridging' as a metaphor which captures both the structural and agentic dimensions of 'being' and 'becoming' across the learning spaces of newly conceptualised programmes and, if systemic gaps and challenges are to be addressed for the twenty-first century, across teacher education itself.

The question of ethos, and more specifically, the teaching of ethics and religion, is identified in Chapter 9 as among the most complex and acute problems facing initial teacher education and education more generally in Ireland. Focusing in the first instance on what he terms meta-pedagogical issues, Jones Irwin notes the irredeemably ideological and political nature of the debate in the context of liberal democratic societies increasingly characterised by diversity. Irwin observes also the particularities of the Irish case, which include state funding of denominational faith-based schools as the dominant model of provision. Beginning with an examination of the distinction drawn by Alexander and McLaughlin (2003) between religious education from 'within' and 'without' a tradition, Irwin goes on to explore four ethical paradigms which inform moral education to varying degrees: character formation, moral development, care ethics, and genealogical critique. Drawing on the work of Nell Noddings and Michael Slote (2003), the author discusses each in turn, revealing their provenance and their ideological character, as well as the inter- and intra- paradigmatic strains and tensions. Addressing their application within an educational context, Irwin notes the interconnectedness between the liberal Kantian paradigm of moral development and progressive models of education, such as the child-centred model characteristic of Irish primary education. Irwin notes, also, the critique offered to the Kantian paradigm by communitarianism, which, as observed by Noddings and Slote (2003) finds expression in the idea of 'character education', a dominant model within moral education. The author goes on to address the challenge offered to both of those models by care theory and genealogical critique. Postmodernist in perspective, these alternative voices offer both a contestation and a critique of communitarian conservativism and Kantian universality and, crucially, in the context of growing diversity, suggest the possibility of transcending the binarisation of the ethical space proffered by ethics from 'within' and 'without'. In conclusion, Irwin makes a compelling argument for an opening up of debate in Ireland in relation to ethics and education, including the implications for teacher education, in the context of an increasingly diverse society.

The relationship between education and care theory is taken up again by Maeve O'Brien in Chapter 10. Arguing for the centrality of affect to education for human flourishing, O'Brien notes the corrosive impact of instrumentalist discourses of accountability and performativity on education as relational, caring and liberating, along with the growing commodification of education prompted by the drive towards competitiveness and privatisation. O'Brien draws on a wide range of feminist and interdisciplinary literature to examine the idea of a 'care praxis' that eschews the easy categorisation of care as either labour or love and recognises its emotional dimension, whether in the public or private, paid or unpaid domains. In the context of education, O'Brien critiques the current ideologically-based twinning of educational aims with the needs of a globalised economy, arguing instead for a focus on well-being as an explicit aim of education and for schools' contribution to student well-being to be included in the evaluation of schools and school systems, a development which would bring the caring dimensions of teachers' work and the relational nature of teaching and learning into sharper focus. Drawing on Noddings (2003) distinction between caring *for* and caring *about*, and on Freire's idea of humanising education, the author examines the complex and potentially radical dynamic between teachers' concern with relations, emotions and affect (caring *for*) and their commitment to social justice and transformative educational practice (caring *about*) in the context of a holistic educational practice. O'Brien recognises the challenges faced by teachers and by teacher educators in seeking to develop such a practice, including those posed by the binarisation of cognition and emotion and the dominance of technical-rational outcomes-oriented models of education. In conclusion, O'Brien argues that if teacher educators are to engage student teachers in the kind of caring relational and dialogic practice necessary to enable them to develop as caring, responsive and critical teachers committed to holistic and humanising education, then teacher educators themselves need to develop a transformative, ethical and caring praxis.

Section Four – Language, Teaching and Learning in Initial Teacher Education

In Section Four, teacher education is considered through the prism of the relationship between education and the Irish language, a significant particularist dimension of initial teacher education on the island of Ireland. While the immediate context is local, however, collectively and individually the chapters speak to broader narratives and wider constituencies – models of immersion education characteristic of multilingual systems worldwide, second-language learning in European and other international contexts, the potential of information and communication technologies (ICT) to unlock opportunities for student autonomy and for student-oriented learning experiences, and the creative synergies that can emerge through collaboration.

In Chapter 11, Ríóna Ní Fhrighil examines how computer-assisted language learning can promote learner autonomy in the context of second-language learning. Ní Fhrighil locates her discussion within current national and European language policy and with reference to the role of ICT in developing learner autonomy. Drawing on key literature in the field of language learning, Ní Fhrighil critiques the concept of learner autonomy, highlighting the scaffolding role played by teachers, particularly through the provision of expert feedback, along with the demands which learner-centred approaches make on learners and teachers alike. In the case of learners, such approaches require them to be proactive in their engagement with learning, while for teachers, responsivity to the needs of learners places high demands on their linguistic capabilities. In addition, taking responsibility for one's own learning includes the capacity to reflect on the process. Such reflective activity, however, implies meta-awareness of language and of language-learning which, Ní Fhrighil argues, is supported by integrated language approaches which encourage transferable skills and competencies across languages. Ní Fhrighil goes on to present the findings of a small, exploratory case study which looked at the use of Wimba Voice Tools – an asynchronous voice technology – to support language learning in a context characterised by learner autonomy. While such approaches offer expanded opportunities for language use, the author concludes that for learner autonomy to develop, it needs to be embedded in the wider language-learning discourse. Finally, the author argues that implementing a learner-centred communicative curriculum at primary level requires teachers who are linguistically competent and who understand the principles of learner autonomy. Moreover, it requires an approach to initial teacher education that provides opportunities for content and language integrated learning.

The role of immersion education in ITE in meeting the needs of the Irish language community is addressed in Chapter 12 by Eibhlín Mhic Aoidh, Jill Garland, Gabrielle Nig Uidhir and John Sweeney. Drawing on a range of national and international literature in immersion education and on the findings and process of a self-evaluation study, the authors identify key issues and approaches in the area. Recruitment of teachers emerges as the critical problem for immersion education worldwide, demonstrating the need for improved provision in initial teacher education. The complexities of teaching in an immersion context extend beyond language proficiency and the authors make a strong case for the need to provide student teachers themselves with the experience of immersion in the context of teacher education. Mhic Aoidh et al. continue by outlining the genesis and development of the immersion initial teacher education programme in their institution, which was the first of its kind on the island of Ireland. The main components of the programme, along with its key areas of emphasis and its responsivity to state policy, are also addressed. The chapter moves on to focus on the self-evaluation of the programme which was prompted by state requirements for continued recognition. Based on an agreed framework common to all initial teacher education providers, the programme team engaged in a critical and collaborative process of review. The process itself proved to be a creative and positive one, identifying good practice as well as areas for development across the three key quality indicators of leadership and management, achievements and standards, and quality of provision for learning. The authors go on to address two issues of specific relevance to immersion education in terms of the learning gained from the evaluation process – promoting the linguistic competence of students and the importance of partnership with schools and organisations. In conclusion, the chapter argues that self-evaluation processes are to be welcomed as opportunities for both celebration and critique, offering both the affirmation of good practice and the promise of renewal and development.

In Chapter 13, Áine Furlong, Brendan MacMahon and Sinéad Ní Ghuidhir focus on the idea of content and language integrated learning (CLIL) and its importance in the context of teacher education for subject specialists at second-level. Highlighting the need for greater development at programmatic level and the dearth of resources for the sector, they present an innovative inter-institutional collaboration which brings together second-level teacher educators working in Irish-medium teacher education and specialists in CLIL to develop and implement a joint module. The authors situate their chapter within the contested terrain of Irish language education where public discourse on the language is dominated by a range of well-rehearsed educational and quasi-educational issues which, in many cases, ignore both the broader social and political contexts in which Irish language learners are situated as well as the complexity of the educational landscape itself. Furlong et al. locate their approach within the broader context of the role of language in the learning process. Drawing on the work of Vygotsky and others, they argue that the inseparability of thought, language and learning provides a clear rationale for language sensitive approaches to teaching and learning, such as that demonstrated in CLIL. The chapter surveys the growing literature surrounding the CLIL approach and outlines the local context in which the collaboration was forged. It goes on to provide a comprehensive account of the practice underpinning the collaboration and its reforming impact on traditional practices in relation to assessment. Located firmly within the European policy context, the collaboration places Irish at the heart of the European project, combatting latent or residual feelings of isolation on the part of Irish-medium student teachers and demonstrating the potential for renewal which interdisciplinary synergies and collaboration present.

Section Five – Responding to Student Voices: Programme Reform and Transformation

The final section of the book challenges teacher educators to respond to the voices of student teachers in the reform project. Drawing on empirical research around school placement at primary and second-level and on the voices of mature students in relation to their experiences of undergraduate initial teacher education programmes, these chapters demonstrate the potential contribution which research into student experiences can make to programme renewal and reform.

Chapter 14 is set in the context of school-university partnerships as settings for the experiential school-based learning that occurs during school placement. Locating such partnerships within a democratic frame, it constructs a welcome space in which student teachers articulate their experiences of working in schools. Through giving voice to student teachers' experiences, the authors provide a powerful lens through which to explore the dynamic interplay of power, trust and agency in the complex relational context of school-based learning. This chapter draws on data generated by the *Partnership with Schools Project*, a significant action research project which has had a strong influence on policy regarding the role and nature of school placement in pre-service teacher education in the Republic of Ireland. Informed by the philosophical discourse of theorists such as Dewey, Buber, Freire and Foucault, and located within a 'communities of practice' frame (Lave and Wenger, 1991), the authors present a nuanced analysis of student experience which addresses questions of relationships, processes and structures. The analysis underlines the possibilities offered by the partnership model for supporting student teacher learning. It suggests, for example, that the nature of the student/teacher relationship has a definitive influence on the quality of the learning process. Where the relationship was characterised by mutual respect and premised on dialogue and openness, school placement was experienced as a positive learning-oriented process characterised by collaboration and community. Moreover, the structures and processes that underpinned the model provided student teachers with an holistic experience as members of a school community. In addition, the changing role of the classroom teacher in the context of partnership suggests an evolving role for the university-based tutor whose capacity to provide an overarching context for the particular experiences of the student was identified as necessary and valuable. In conclusion, student voice was facilitated both by the model under investigation and by the research process itself, which demonstrated the value of conceptualising student teachers as partners in the project of renewal and reform in initial teacher education.

In Chapter 15, Conway et al. draw on student teachers' experiences and voices to explore key issues in initial teacher education and to identify potential avenues of change. The authors begin by revisiting the idea of the 'good' teacher as the core dynamic in public and policy discourses around the quality of education – already raised by Cochran-Smith in Chapter 1 – noting that the assumptions that underpin common sense understandings of teacher quality tend to focus on the person of the teacher and marginalise the role of initial teacher education in the process of becoming a teacher. The chapter draws on the findings of the *Learning to Teach Study*, a recent research project undertaken by researchers in the School of Education, University College Cork. Premised on a sociocultural approach which recognises the situated and relational nature of teacher education and the cultural and political dimensions of learning to teach, the study focuses on the cultural dynamics that shape the experiences of student teachers in the post-primary teacher education context. The student teachers whose voices inform this significant Irish study were participants in the university's initial teacher education programme in 2008-2009. The authors present key findings from the study and examine their implications for student learning. They identify the relative absence of opportunities for observation and professional dialogue during school placement and discuss the potential impact on student teachers' learning, including their capacity to move beyond their own experiences as learners in the system and embrace reform-oriented practice. Furthermore, while students recognised the need for inclusion and differentiation in their planning and teaching, the study found that the conceptualisation of inclusive practice as integral to teaching rather than as an add-on posed a significant challenge to some students. In conclusion, Conway et al. examine a range of questions prompted by the findings relating to school partnership, collaboration and dialogue, and the promotion of broader conceptions of competence which have the potential to generate renewal in initial teacher education programmes.

In Chapter 16, Anne M. Dolan draws on the voices of mature students, as expressed through national and international research, to problematise their access to and experiences of initial teacher education. Dolan begins by sketching the policy landscape for widening participation in higher education, with particular reference to mature students. Locating the question of mature student entry into higher education in the context of lifelong learning, the author differentiates between issues of access, such as flexible policies for admission, and issues of accessibility, which are concerned with how institutions meet the needs of their mature students once they have gained entry. Ireland has made substantial progress in improving access for mature students. Yet, participation rates are lower than the EU average and there is low provision of part-time and flexible higher education options for mature students. Drawing on a number of Irish and international studies, Dolan examines the factors that limit mature students' capacities to engage with higher education in general and initial teacher education in particular, such as financial constraints and family responsibilities, and their intersection with issues of gender and class, as well as with the internal structures and practices of institutions and programmes. In particular, the author raises the issue of whether the wealth of experience and prior learning which mature students bring with them to higher education is sufficiently recognised and valued. Drawing on the voices of mature students themselves to illuminate feelings of isolation and difference, Dolan argues for the development of flexible initial teacher education programmes at undergraduate level that are specifically designed to meet the needs of mature students and identifies both the structural and cultural changes needed to progress such reforms.

Conclusion

The ideas, arguments and questions contained in these sixteen chapters are indicative of the growing national and international discourse around teacher education. Critical, reflective, at times provocative, the chapters are also characterised by hope and the promise of renewal. Standing as we are at the brink of a new era in initial teacher education in Ireland, we need to ensure that our re-imagined programmes develop in student teachers the knowledge, skills and capacities that characterise good classroom practice and that they nurture the kinds of dispositions that support lifelong learning. We also need to ensure, however, that the idea of professional competence is not set in false opposition to a broader vision of education and that their teaching is informed by a strong sense of purpose. Recent research with Irish teachers in early career stage by Morgan et al. (2010) attests to the impact of positive affective classroom experiences on teachers' motivation and resilience, the desire to 'make a difference' made manifest in repeated micro-encounters in the classroom. Christopher Day talks about 'a passion for teaching' as embracing the intellectual and emotional commitment that characterises good teachers (Day, 2004). Initial teacher education should enable student teachers to develop their passion for teaching, to root their desire to 'make a difference' in a strong and resilient sense of purpose that will survive the challenges they will inevitably face as beginning teachers. Surrounded, as we are, by the language of competency, learning outcomes, and accountability, it is timely to remind ourselves of the need for passion.

References

Alexander, H. and McLaughlin, T.H. (2003). Education and spirituality. In N. Blake, P. Smyers, R. Smith and P. Standish (Eds.), *The Blackwell guide to philosophy of education*. Oxford: Wiley-Blackwell.

Apple, M. (2008). Is deliberative democracy enough in teacher education? In M. Cochran-Smith, S. Feiman-Nemser, D. J. McIntyre and K. E Demars (Eds.), *Handbook of research on teacher education: Enduring questions in changing contexts* (3rd ed.) (pp. 105-110). New York: Routledge.

Carr, P. (2008). Educating for democracy: With or without social justice. *Teacher Education Quarterly*, Fall, 117-133.

Cochran-Smith, M. (2004). *Walking the road: Race, diversity, and social justice in teacher education.* New York: Teachers College Press.

Cochran-Smith, M. and Lytle, S.L. (1993). *Inside/outside: Teacher research and knowledge.* New York: Teachers College Press.

Cochran-Smith, M. and Lytle, S.L. (2009). *Inquiry as stance: Practitioner research in the next generation.* New York: Teachers College Press.

Darling-Hammond, L. and Bransford, S. (Eds.). (2005). *Preparing teachers for a changing world: What teachers should learn and be able to do.* San Francisco: John Wiley and Sons.

Day, C. (2004). *A passion for teaching.* London: Routledge.

Dewey, J. (1916). *Education and democracy.* New York: Free Press.

Fullan, M.G. (1993). Why teachers must become change agents. *Educational Leadership, 50*(6), 12-17.

Gandin, L.A. and Apple, M. (2002). Challenging neo-liberalism, building democracy: Creating the citizen school in Porto Alegre, Brazil. *Journal of Education Policy, 17*(2), 259-279.

Hansen, D.T. (2008). Values and purpose in teacher education. In M. Cochran-Smith, S. Feiman-Nemser, D.J. McIntyre and K.E Demars (Eds.), *Handbook of research on teacher education: Enduring questions in changing contexts* (3rd ed.) (pp. 10-26). New York: Routledge.

Hatano, G. and Inagaki, K. (1986). Two courses of expertise. In H. Stevenson, H. Azuma and K. Hakuta, (Eds.), *Child development and education in Japan* (pp. 262–272). New York: Freeman.

Korthagen, F.A.J. (2004). In search of the essence of a good teacher: Towards a more holistic approach in teacher education. *Teaching and Teacher Education, 20*(1), 77-97.

Lave, J. and Wenger, E. (1991). *Situated learning: Legitimate peripheral participation.* Cambridge: Cambridge University Press.

Lortie, D.C. (1975). *Schoolteacher: A sociological study.* Chicago: University of Chicago Press.

Lundy, L. (2007). 'Voice' is not enough: Conceptualising Article 12 of the United Nations Convention on the Rights of the Child. *British Educational Research Journal*, 927-942.

Morgan, M., Ludlow, L., Kitching, K., O'Leary, M. and Clarke, A. (2010). What makes teachers tick? Sustaining events in new teachers' lives. *British Educational Research Journal*, *36*(2), 191-208.

Noddings, N. (2003). *Happiness and education*. Cambridge: Cambridge University Press.

Noddings, N. and Slote, M. (2003). Changing notions of the moral and of moral education. In N. Blake, P. Smyers, R. Smith and P. Standish (Eds.), *The Blackwell guide to philosophy of education*. Oxford: Wiley-Blackwell.

Rowland, T., Huckstep, P. and Thwaites, A. (2005). Elementary teachers' mathematics subject knowledge: The knowledge quartet and the case of Naomi. *Journal of Mathematics Teacher Education, 8*(3), 255-281.

Shulman, L. (2005). Signature pedagogies in the professions. *Daedalus, 134*(3), 52-59.

Sleeter, C.E., (2008). Preparing white teachers for diverse students. In M. Cochran-Smith, S. Feiman-Nemser, D.J. McIntyre and K.E Demars (Eds.), *Handbook of research on teacher education: Enduring questions in changing contexts* (3rd ed.) (pp. 559-582). New York: Routledge.

Villegas, A. M. and Lucas, T. (2002). Preparing culturally responsive teachers: Rethinking the curriculum. *Journal of Teacher Education*, *53*(1), 20-32.

Zeichner, K. (2009). *Teacher education and the struggle for social justice*. New York: Routledge.

Section One:

Policy Trends and System Change: Global and Local Contexts

Chapter 1

Trends and Challenges in Teacher Education: National and International Perspectives

Marilyn Cochran-Smith
Boston College

There is no question that teacher education is a major concern worldwide. My focus in this chapter is on five major trends and challenges in teacher education and on their underlying assumptions and tensions: (1) unprecedented attention to teacher quality; (2) shifting notions of accountability; (3) meeting the needs of increasingly diverse school populations; (4) mounting questions about who should teach, who should teach teachers, where and how; and (5) competing conceptions of teacher professionalism. Clearly these five do not encompass all the challenges facing teacher education, but they touch on some of the most important and far-reaching issues confronting the field today. Although my focus will be primarily the US context, many of the challenges that face teacher education in the US are also challenges in many other nations worldwide. Of course these play out differently depending on national agendas and histories.

Unprecedented Attention to Teacher Quality

In many places around the world, there is unprecedented attention to teacher quality, defined primarily in terms of student achievement.

There is now a broad consensus that teacher quality makes a significant difference in schoolchildren's learning and in overall school effectiveness (e.g., Cochran-Smith, 2005a; Furlong, Cochran-Smith and Brennan, 2009).

Teacher Education as a Policy Problem, Not a Learning Problem

Politicians, policy makers and researchers of all stripes now assume that teachers are a critical influence (if not the single most important influence) on how, what and how much students learn (Darling-Hammond, 2010; McKenzie and Santiago, 2005; Organisation for Economic Co-operation and Development (OECD), 2005). In keeping with this assumption, in many nations there are now extremely high expectations for teacher performance, and questions about how a nation's teachers are recruited, prepared and supported are among the hottest topics in the public and academic discourse regarding education (Cochran-Smith, 2005a; Cochran-Smith and Fries, 2011).

In one sense, of course, this is good. It is high time that the value of teachers' work was acknowledged. However, when it becomes self-evident that teacher quality, and the quality of teachers' education, determine school effectiveness, then teacher education is treated as what we have called a 'policy problem' (Cochran-Smith and Fries, 2005) to be solved by high-level leaders in the business and policy worlds (Oakes et al., 2006) with the assumption that getting the right policies in place will drastically improve teacher quality and thus students' achievement, often as indicated by national and international comparisons (Cochran-Smith, 2005a; Kennedy, 1999). The downside here is that treating teacher education as a large-scale policy problem assumes a more or less linear relationship between policy, teacher quality and students' achievement. The assumption is that these will automatically be improved when policy makers correctly manipulate the broad policy parameters governing teaching and teacher preparation (Kennedy, 1999). In the US, this means policies regulating things like coursework and licensing requirements for teachers, required college majors, teacher tests, quality and quantity of time spent in classrooms prior to teaching, how teacher education programmes are evaluated, and what routes and pathways into certification and teaching are allowed (Michelli and Earley, 2011). In Ireland, this is reflected in the current move to change the length of the teacher preparation period from 3 to 4 years and in discussions about targeting literacy and numeracy education more directly.

While policies are certainly important, large scale policies regarding teacher education generally do not adequately account for the contexts and cultures of schools, which vary widely, nor for how these cultures support or constrain teachers' abilities to use knowledge and resources. In addition, the policy approach downplays the importance of teacher education as a 'learning problem' (Cochran-Smith and Fries, 2005), which is influenced by large scale policies, but also – and as importantly – has to do with teachers' thinking and interpretations, decision making and growth and development as professionals in local communities of practice. From this perspective, the premise is that good teaching depends primarily on teacher learning over time, and on teachers' knowledge, skills, beliefs, attitudes and values (Cochran-Smith and Lytle, 2009). The current tendency in the US and in many other nations is to foreground policy regarding the preparation and credentialing of teachers and to push to the background teachers' learning. From my outsider's perspective, Ireland seems to me to be at a crossroads in terms of whether it will construct teacher education primarily as a policy problem or as a learning problem, or whether it will find some appropriate balance between the two.

Teachers as Saviours and Culprits

The second tension here is a paradox that I and others have noted before (Cochran-Smith, 2001, 2004). When policy discussions about educational improvement focus on school issues only, the assumption is that teachers are both saviours and culprits. That is, the assumption is that teachers are the most intractable problem educational policy makers must solve because, it is alleged, it is teachers' meagre knowledge and skills that are the cause of the failure of the schools in the first place and, at the same time, that teachers are the best solution to that problem because, it is assumed, improved teacher quality is the cure for all that ails the schools. A US report by The Teaching

Commission, which was chaired by the former CEO of IBM, was particularly straightforward on this point. The report said:

> Bolstering teacher quality is, of course, not the only challenge we face as we seek to strengthen public education... But the Teaching Commission believes that quality teachers are *the* [emphasis added] critical factor in helping young people overcome the damaging effects of poverty, lack of parental guidance, and other challenges.... In other words, the effectiveness of any broader education reform ... is ultimately dependent on the quality of teachers in classrooms. (2004, p. 14)

A report on the state of teaching and teacher education across OECD participating nations, which was titled Teachers Matter, had a very similar theme (OECD, 2005). These same ideas are reflected in many of the policy commentaries presented by the leaders of departments and ministries of education in the US as well as in many European and other nations.

As I noted above, of course teachers matter, but there is a major concern here. Teachers (and teacher education programmes) alone cannot fix the worst schools and improve the life chances of the most disadvantaged students in any nation without simultaneous investments in resources, capacity building and enhancing teachers' professional growth, not to mention changes in students' and families' access to housing, health and jobs (Cochran-Smith, 2005a; Economic Policy Institute, 2008). The irony here is that in the US, making a statement like the one I just made sometimes gets construed by critics of teacher education as an 'excuse' for teacher education or as evidence of its low expectations for its own teachers (e.g., Haycock, 2005; Hess, 2005). In my view, this is wrongheaded. Acknowledging that the problems of a nation's schools include, but go far beyond, teachers and that the problems of a nation include, but go far beyond, the schools, is not an excuse. It reflects complete acceptance of the goal of equal and high quality education for all students as well as rejection of the idea that holding teachers and teacher educators accountable for everything will fix everything without attention to other much larger problems.

The Purpose of Education

The third tension that is part of the current heavy emphasis on teacher quality and teacher effectiveness has to do with the larger goals and purposes of education – and with whether the bottom line is the economy or the future of our democratic societies. Nearly worldwide, it is now assumed that education and the economy are inextricably linked (Furlong et al., 2009). That is, it is taken for granted that the health and robustness of the economy are tied to the quality of teachers and the ways they are prepared and educated. The idea here, informed by what Spring (2011) calls the 'human capital paradigm', which is a neoliberal derivative, is that teachers are responsible for producing a labour force with the array of knowledge and skills needed to thrive in the 'knowledge society', thus enabling the nation to compete and to either maintain or boost its position in the global economy.

A recent speech by President Obama illustrates the tight link between education and the economy. He said:

> America will not remain true to its highest ideals – and America's place as a global economic leader will be put at risk – unless we … do a far better job than we've been doing of educating our sons and daughters; unless we give them the knowledge and skills they need in this new and changing world. For we know that economic progress and educational achievement have always gone hand in hand in America. (Obama, 2009)

The point behind this kind of discourse, which is very common in Ireland as well (e.g., Conway, 2012), is the economic need for an educated (and thus competitive) work force, rather than the larger social need for everybody to have access to teacher quality as a fundamental human right in a democratic society (Sleeter, 2009).

The challenge for teacher education, then, in many but not all countries (and there are several intriguing exceptions, including Finland), is to make sense of and respond to these two competing agendas: to educate teachers who can teach all students to participate in a democratic society, on one hand, or to educate teachers who can teach all students to compete in the global economy, which may primarily benefit the elite. It is not clear whether these can be thought of as complementary rather than competing agendas, but this is part of the challenge facing us.

Shifting Notions of Accountability

The second major challenge facing teacher education, which is closely related to and intertwined with the first, emerges from shifting notions of accountability with a focus on outcomes and quantification (Cuban, 2004). In teacher education, changing notions of accountability have been referred to as a shift from inputs to outcomes (Schalock and Imig, 2000). Prior to the mid-1990s, at least in the US, the emphasis in teacher education was not on outcomes (Cochran-Smith, 2005b). It was primarily on process – how prospective teachers learned to teach, how their beliefs, attitudes and identities as teachers changed over time, what contexts supported their learning, and what kinds of content, pedagogical and other knowledge they needed. The assessment of teacher education focused on what is now retrospectively referred to as 'inputs' – institutional commitment, qualifications of faculty, content and structure of courses and fieldwork experiences, and the alignment of all of these with professional knowledge and standards. The shift in teacher education from inputs to outcomes was part of a larger sea change in how we think about educational accountability writ large (Cuban, 2004). In response to comments like those in the previous paragraph, some people pose the question: So what's the problem with accountability? My response to this is simple – nothing and everything.

Reductionist View of Teaching and Learning

Despite agreement about the need for accountability for the work of teaching and teacher education, the problem is that increasingly we are dealing with reductionist views of teaching and learning. The accountability bottom line – higher scores on standardised student achievement tests of literacy and numeracy and/or strong performances on international comparisons of achievements in these areas—is increasingly the singular focus of discussions about the impact and improvement of teacher education. In other words, increasingly teaching quality and students' learning are equated with high-stakes test scores. It is this simplistic equating that is problematic rather than the larger notion of accountability itself (Cochran-Smith, 2002).

Oddly enough, a book about writing – Anne Lamott's *Bird by Bird: Some Instructions on Writing and Life* – is helpful. In one chapter, Lamott advises writers to avoid simple oppositions in their development of plots and characters. She says:

> I used to think that paired opposites were a given, that love was the opposite of hate, right the opposite of wrong. But now I think we sometimes buy into these concepts because it is so much easier to embrace absolutes than to suffer reality. [Now] I don't think anything is the opposite of love. *Reality is unforgivingly complex* [emphasis added]. (1994, p. 104)

In her book, Lamott goes on to tell writers to embrace the complexity of real life and write about its biggest questions. This aligns well to our work as teacher educators. My point here is that, like reality, teaching is unforgivingly complex. It is not simply good or bad, right or wrong, working or failing, well or poorly planned. Although dichotomies like these are popular in the headlines, they are limited in their usefulness. A major challenge for teacher education, which is reflected in the Teaching Council of Ireland's 2011 report on the continuum of teacher education, is to embrace the complexity of teaching and learning even in the age of accountability.

Value-Added Measures

In many countries, the heavy emphasis on outcomes accountability is bringing heightened attention to the continuous monitoring of students' progress and teachers' performance. In the US, this is playing out in the form of value-added assessments of teacher education, which are intended to evaluate individual teacher education programmes in terms of how much value they add to the achievement of the eventual students of the teachers prepared in that programme.

As is well known, value-added assessments are statistical procedures for estimating school and teacher effectiveness using student-level test score records from year to year. In August of 2010, the *Los*

Angeles Times newspaper commissioned a study using data from the Los Angeles Unified School District (LAUSD) to obtain value-added estimates for nearly 6,000 elementary school teachers. Their results were debuted with a picture of a classroom teacher standing in front of his students and this headline: 'GRADING THE TEACHERS, Who's teaching LA's kids? A *Times* analysis, using data largely ignored by LAUSD, looks at which educators help students learn, and which hold them back.' The caption under the picture said, 'Over seven years, John Smith's fifth-graders have started out slightly ahead of those just down the hall but by year's end have been far behind.' It is important to note here that the newspaper picture identified and portrayed the actual teacher, John Smith, and his students (whose backs faced the camera), as well as their school and its location.

Not surprisingly, this story prompted a huge flurry of responses – both enormously negative and enormously positive – including some talk of a boycott of the *LA Times* by the teachers' union. There was also a news story a few weeks later about a teacher who committed suicide, which was attributed by family and friends, at least in part, to the teacher's shock and despondence over his low rating, announced in the newspaper.

Partly in response to the LA situation, a group of education scholars authored a cautionary piece, published by the Economic Policy Institute, about the uses of value-added assessments (Baker et al., 2010). Their report said there was broad agreement among statisticians, psychometricians and economists that student test scores alone are not sufficiently reliable and valid indicators of teacher effectiveness to be used in high-stakes personnel decisions, even when sophisticated statistical applications such as value-added modelling (VAM) are employed. They made it clear that researchers currently doubt whether VAM methodology can accurately identify more and less effective teachers. This is partly because there have been dramatic fluctuations in value-added estimates across statistical models, years and classes that teachers teach. For example, they indicated that one large study found that for teachers who were ranked in the top 20 per cent of effectiveness in the first year, fewer than a third were in that top group the next year, and another third moved all the way down to the bottom 40 per cent. They pointed out that this runs counter to most people's notions that the true quality of a teacher is not likely to change much over time and raises questions about whether what is measured is largely a 'teacher effect' or the effect of a wide variety of other factors. They added that one study even found that students' fifth grade teachers were good predictors of their fourth grade test scores. Inasmuch as a student's later fifth grade teacher cannot possibly have influenced that student's fourth grade performance, this curious result suggests that value-added results are based on factors other than teachers' actual effectiveness (Baker et al., 2010).

It seems fair to say to say that the valued-added assessment approach is complicated, controversial and suspect in terms of its application to individual high-stakes decisions. Nevertheless, a number of states in the US are now developing state-wide, longitudinal data systems that link students' test scores with data about their teachers and the institutions that prepared them. There is now federal funding available as an incentive for states to develop these systems. In Louisiana, the state-wide Value-Added Teacher Preparation Assessment Model, which is consistently lauded by US Secretary of Education Arnie Duncan as an exemplar of responsible teacher education (e.g., Duncan, 2009), evaluates the effectiveness of preparation programmes throughout the state based on the test scores of the students of teachers who graduated from the various institutions. This system identifies exemplary programmes as well as programmes that do not measure up or lead to continuous improvement.

Meeting the Needs of a Diverse School Population

The third major challenge facing teacher education takes us in a different direction – preparing teachers to meet the needs of the increasingly diverse school population, which in many nations involves growing disparities in the school opportunities and outcomes of minority and majority groups. Although this challenge is complex and far-reaching, I take up just three aspects here.

Changing Population Patterns

The first aspect of this challenge involves recognising changing demographic and immigration patterns. In many nations throughout the world, there is increasing diversity in the school population as well as increasing recognition of the challenges posed by diversity (Banks, 2009; Castles, 2009; OECD, 2006).

Although the situation has changed in Ireland and some other countries since the global economic recession that began in 2008, many nations have experienced major changes in migration flow over the last two decades, with the result that in a number of countries the total number of people entering the country has far exceeded the number leaving. Countries in this category include, but are not limited to, the United States, Canada, England, Scotland, Ireland (prior to 2008), most of the countries in western and northern Europe, Australia, New Zealand and Singapore (OECD, 2006).

In the US, the issues are intense. There have been enormous increases in immigration over the last decade, bringing large numbers of students whose first language is not English into the public schools and as well as heightened awareness of diversity. This has added to a situation where, in response to the Civil Rights movements of the 1960s and 1970s, inequities based on the marginalisation of indigenous and formerly enslaved minorities have been brought into the foreground (Banks, 2009). The racial and ethnic characteristics of the school population in the US have changed dramatically over the last several decades – from 78 per cent White students (that is, from European American backgrounds) and 22 per cent students of colour (that is, African American, Hispanic, Asian, or indigenous Native American) in 1972 to 55 per cent White students and 45 per cent students of colour in 2008 (National Center for Education Statistics, 2003, 2010a). Demographers predict that by 2035 the majority of school students in the US will be from these minority groups (Hodgkinson, 2002).

Another way to think of the diversity in US schools is in terms of the number of those whose first language is not English – often referred to as English language learners (ELLs), though some prefer 'multilingual learners' to emphasise multiple language capacity as a strength not a deficit. The number of multilingual learners increased from 3.8 million in 1979 to 10.9 million almost 20 years later (National Center for Education Statistics, 2010b). In addition, the number of students with disabilities who receive special education services, many of whom spend much of their time in regular education classrooms, increased from just over 4 million in 1981 to more than 6.5 million in 2008 (National Center for Education Statistics, 2009).

Interestingly, even in countries that have long been considered homogeneous in language, ethnicity and culture, the situation has changed (Banks, 2009; Castles, 2009). In Japan, for example, the current trend is that there are more people coming in to the country than going out. This includes Japanese returnees as well as newcomers from African and South American countries (Hirasawa, 2009). This means that in Japan there is an increasing number of students in schools – especially primary schools – with limited Japanese language skills. And of course, Ireland was long considered a culturally, ethnically and religiously homogeneous nation. Now, however, it is estimated that as many as 10 per cent of students in Irish schools are from diverse countries, cultures and language groups (Taguma et al., 2009), and 70-75 per cent of these students do not speak English as a first language.

Persistent Disparities in Opportunities and Outcomes

Globally, new population patterns have heightened awareness in many nations of the challenges posed by diversity and foregrounded the inequities in achievement and other school-related outcomes that persist between majority and minority groups or between immigrant and settled groups. I want to be clear here that the challenge for teacher education is not that there is an increasingly diverse student population. In fact, many people in teacher education and other fields actively value diversity and welcome its impact on teachers and students in terms of enlarged world views, richer perspectives on the human condition, and the ability of all people to participate in a diverse democratic society.

But there are severe and important disparities related to diversity. Commonly referred to in the US as 'the achievement gap', it is now widely known that there are marked disparities among the achievement levels of student groups that differ from one another racially, culturally, linguistically, socioeconomically and geographically (Ladson-Billings, 2006). Specifically, it is now well documented that White and Asian students consistently score higher than their African American and Hispanic counterparts on standardised tests of reading and mathematics skills. African Americans and Hispanics also have higher rates of dropping out of high school and lower rates of high school graduation and college attendance than White and Asian students. This, then, is the 'demographic imperative' – the urgent need to reduce the persistent association between demographic diversity, on one hand, and disparities in school achievement and other outcomes, on the other hand (Economic Policy Institute, 2008).

There are similar patterns in some other countries. In Japan, there are current achievement gaps between inherited social class groups. In New Zealand, schools do not produce comparable achievement results for their Maori and Pacific Island students (New Zealand Ministry of Education, 2011). And in Ireland, students from immigrant groups, from socially disadvantaged backgrounds, and from the Traveller community are most likely to fail (Department of Education and Skills, 2010).

Preparing Teachers to Teach Diverse Populations

In the US, even though the student population has become increasingly diverse, the teacher population has continued to be primarily white European American (Villegas and Lucas, 2001). Like the issue of diversity itself, the fact that teachers and students are different from one another demographically is not necessarily in and of itself a problem, but we know from years of research that unless they have powerful and ongoing teacher education experiences that help them do otherwise, many White middle class teachers understand diversity as a deficit and tend to have lower expectations for minority students (Goodwin, 2000; Irvine, 1990).

In the US, especially since we now have a black president, it is easy for some people to assume that we now live in a race-less or 'colour-blind' society. This is clearly not the case. A major challenge for teacher education is to create contexts where teacher candidates (and teacher educators themselves) interrogate and rethink fundamental assumptions about colour blindness, meritocracy, white normativity and assimilation as the major purpose of education. Like teacher educators in Ireland, teacher educators in the US are working on these issues, but we are far from succeeding at these challenges.

In teacher education in many parts of the world, we are now faced with the challenge of preparing teachers to help close these achievement and opportunity gaps by developing coursework, community experiences and clinical experiences that help teachers develop cultural competence, use culturally sensitive interpretive perspectives, establish and maintain caring relationships with diverse students that support their learning, and work respectfully with colleagues, families, communities and social groups. We also have to teach prospective teachers specific practices for working with English language learners so that they gain language and literacy skills and also learn rich academic content in mathematics, social studies, the sciences and the arts. For students with special needs, this means ensuring that they have access to the general curriculum through differentiated instruction and other specific strategies. These are huge challenges with much more to be said than space allows.

Who Should Teach, Who Should Teach Teachers, Where and How?

The fourth big issue facing teacher education has to do with mounting questions about who should teach, who should teach teachers, where and how. These are questions that are increasingly asked in the US, although they are by no means unique to that country.

Multiple New Providers of Teacher Education

Questions about who should teach and who should teach teachers are very visible in debates about so-called 'alternate' routes to teacher certification and teacher licensure and in the proliferation of teacher education providers that target different populations. Unfortunately, the term 'alternate', which in the US is often juxtaposed to the term 'traditional', is not used at all consistently (National Research Council, 2010). Sometimes the term, 'alternate', is used to include every initial teacher preparation programme or pathway into teaching that is not a four year undergraduate college or university based programme. Of course this would deem all post-baccalaureate programmes 'alternate'. However, much of the time, the language of 'alternate' routes is used to refer to entry pathways into teaching that are greatly streamlined, including some that bypass colleges and universities altogether.

In the US, so-called 'alternate' certification programmes, which exist in nearly all states, now produce a third of the nation's teachers, according to Emily Feistritzer's National Center for Education Information report (2011). These programmes differ dramatically in terms of who they target as prospective teachers. For example, Teach for America (TFA) , the best known of the 'alternate' certification programmes, recruits recent college graduates from top institutions who complete a six week training session prior to their placement in high needs schools and then participate in professional development throughout their two year commitment. In Urban Teacher Residency programmes, many of which are school-district rather than college or university initiated, the target is finding teachers in shortage areas, such as science, math, special education and/or working with English language learners. Candidates complete a master's degree through the auspices of a partner university while working for a full year in classrooms alongside teacher-mentors. In the US and some other places, there are also for-profits, like the University of Phoenix, and completely online teacher programmes, like the American Board for the Certification of Teachers (ABCTE), which is a test-only online programme. Now approved as a route to teacher certification in ten states, the test targets career changers who want a fast 'cost effective' certification route.

New providers of initial teacher education which challenge the role of colleges and universities are not unique to the US. In Ireland, Hibernia College, an online programme, prepares over 700 teachers per year. Teach First, which is modelled after TFA and supported enthusiastically by the business and corporate worlds, is a thriving programme in England. In 2007, TFA and Teach First launched Teach for All to support entrepreneurs who are building local TFA-type programmes in Germany, Estonia, India, Pakistan, Israel, China, Norway, New Zealand and other places.

What Do Universities Do Well?

Underlying the rise of so many alternate pathways into teaching are serious questions about who should teach and who should teach teachers which pose many challenges to colleges and universities as the primary providers of teacher education. In my view, universities and colleges have not done a very good job of making it clear what they are in a unique position to provide, given their unparalleled knowledge resources, their research expertise, and their potential for interdisciplinary collaborations. Regardless of the proliferation of new models, new providers and new partnerships, colleges and universities are uniquely positioned to help prospective teachers learn to do a number of very important things. A few of these are: understanding the social and historical patterns that created the existing system and the aspects of the system that perpetuate inequities; learning about the relationships of culture and schooling; examining their most deeply held beliefs and expectations about children, the work of teaching and the purposes of education; understanding how people learn in various contexts; and developing research- and theory-informed teaching strategies and practices in specific subject areas and in areas related to meeting the needs of diverse school populations.

It is difficult to imagine that knowledge and skills like these can be learned through programmed modules, at for-profit training centres, or by passing a test. In the US, and perhaps in other nations as well, I believe that teacher educators, myself included, have not made a compelling argument for why learning these kinds of things is so important and why colleges and universities are uniquely positioned to teach them.

Alignment vs. Critique

This concern is related to a second issue, which I refer to as alignment versus critique. Behind some of the questions about who should teach teachers – particularly in school-based programmes – is the intention to tighten the alignment between teacher preparation and school standards, curriculum, procedures and assessments. Even though teacher education certainly needs to be closely linked and attentive to what is going on in schools, there are issues here.

These are reflected in comments made by Grover Whitehurst when he was Director of the Institute of Education Sciences. At a White House conference, Preparing Tomorrow's Teachers, Whitehurst (2002), was charged with outlining the results of scientific research related to teacher preparation. At the end of his presentation of research that showed considerable variation in teachers' effectiveness at raising pupils' test scores, he continued his comments about alignment:

> We would not tolerate a system in which airline pilots varied appreciably in their ability to accomplish their tasks successfully, for who would want to be a passenger on the plane with the pilot who is at the 10th percentile on safe landings. Yet the American system of public education is built on ... the ethic of ... autonomous teachers who close the doors to their classrooms and teach what they wish as they wish. ('Putting it all together', para. 2)

Whitehurst went on to say that tighter alignment between teacher education and school assessments and standards could eliminate unwanted variation among teachers.

There is a telling irony in comparing teachers to airline pilots to make the case for alignment. To a great extent, flying a plane is a technical activity wherein following a tight script for standard operating procedures (e.g., maintaining safe altitude levels) and accomplishing identical objectives (e.g., smooth landings) are aspects of successful performance that are both concrete and uncontested. Granted, pilots exercise professional judgment in certain unusual and emergency situations, but generally speaking, airplane operating procedures are uniform and how a pilot flies a plane really has nothing to do with who is on board, what they are carrying with them, whether or not they have previously been airplane passengers, or where they are going after they land. This is not like teaching, which has everything to do with who is in the room (and in the school and community), what cultural and linguistic resources they bring with them, what and how much previous school experience they have had, and how much of what the school counts as important knowledge and experience they can draw on.

In addition, tight alignment of teacher preparation with school procedures and testing programmes undermines completely the historical and essential role of the university to critique the current system. It has long been part of the university's responsibility in democratic societies to raise questions about school practices and labels and to challenge aspects of curriculum and teaching that reinforce inequities.

Competing Conceptions of Professionalism

The fifth challenge facing teacher education today is what I refer to as competing conceptions of professionalism. This relates to several of the other challenges I have addressed. I take up two issues here.

Knowledge-Practice Relationships

The first issue is what I have written about collaboratively with my colleague and co-author, Susan Lytle, as knowledge-practice relationships (Cochran-Smith and Lytle, 1999). Our argument, greatly simplified here, is that underlying all programmes and initiatives related to teachers' education – whether initial, early, or ongoing – are particular assumptions about knowledge and professional practice and how these are related to one another in teachers' work.

In some countries, and certainly in the US, the emphasis of many initiatives is on what we have called a 'knowledge-for-practice' conception of the relationship between knowledge and practice. By this I mean that it is assumed that outside researchers generate what is commonly referred to as formal knowledge or best practices for teachers to faithfully implement inside their classrooms and schools. The assumption here is that teachers will teach better when they know the formal knowledge base and they implement externally-certified practices and procedures in practice.

This vision of how to improve teacher education in order to improve teaching and learning is primarily an individualistic one, even when it is carried out at the whole-school level. The goal is for each teacher to enact empirically-certified best practices, as laid out in the scientifically research-based curriculum and assessment standards and frameworks approved by the state. From this perspective, wherein the 'knowledge-for-practice' conception of the relationship between knowledge and practice is operating, the professional teacher is a practitioner who knows the formal knowledge base and implements state of the art practices in his or her classroom. The 'knowledge-for-practice' conception contrasts sharply with the relationship between knowledge and practice that we have called 'knowledge of practice.' From this perspective, it is assumed that the knowledge teachers need to teach well is generated when they treat their own classrooms and schools as sites for intentional investigation and when they treat the knowledge and practices produced by others as generative material for interrogation and interpretation. From this perspective, professional teachers are regarded as those who draw on, but also question and critique the research and strategies produced by others to generate local knowledge of practice. They work with others throughout the professional lifespan to theorise and construct teaching that is finely tuned to local communities but also connected to larger social, cultural and political issues.

This latter conception of the teacher as a professional is one who is always raising questions, always uncertain in a sense. This means that professional teachers have doubts and raise questions, not because they are failing, but because they are learning. These different ideas about knowledge-practice relationships are linked to conceptions of professionalism that sometimes compete with one another. They also relate to, but sometimes compete with, ideas about the communities in which teachers learn and the work that learning communities do.

Teacher Communities

Over the last decade or more, there has been a great deal of emphasis in the US and many other countries on teacher groups with labels including 'professional learning communities', 'teacher learning communities', 'practitioner inquiry communities', 'teacher and administrator research communities', as well as 'teacher research groups', 'practitioner research communities', and 'practitioner and community member collaborative groups'. These have been promoted as important – and cost effective – levers for educational reform. It is important to emphasise that these terms and labels are not consistently used, and one cannot be at all sure about what a group does or how it functions, let alone its intellectual legacy or historical roots, from its label.

At the risk of inappropriately generalising and for heuristic purposes only, I want to discuss briefly two of the most common labels for these groups – professional learning communities and inquiry communities (for a more detailed discussion see Cochran-Smith and Lytle, 2009). Professional learning communities and inquiry communities have a lot in common. Both focus on: inquiry (or question and problem posing), using the data of practice, establishing and supporting communities of new and experienced teachers (including sometimes administrators), making teachers' and students' learning central, complex school cultures and equity agendas. Both recognise the central role of teachers in shaping the life of schools and as agents in transforming the work of schools. But similarities can also mask differences in the competing views of professionalism that these approaches have.

The roots of practitioner inquiry are in several social movements and research traditions that challenge the traditional knowledge base for teaching because it has failed to account for the knowledge generated by teachers. The major roots of professional learning communities, on the other hand, are in school effects research on how schools produce academic achievement and other desired outcomes. With practitioner inquiry, communities are both means toward larger ends and ends in themselves. In communities, teachers jointly build knowledge, but they also interrogate their own assumptions, construct new curriculum and engage with others in a search for meaning in their work lives. With professional learning communities, there is a more instrumental view of community, understood as a lever for school reform and a way to increase performance on achievement tests, decrease absenteeism, or produce other school outcomes.

With practitioner inquiry, the point is for teachers to develop rich and deep understandings of the how, where, why and what of students' learning. Because teachers' work is intellectual rather than technical, it is assumed that richer teachers' learning is linked to richer students' learning. With professional learning communities, the focus is on teachers learning how to select or construct 'local best practices' based on careful analysis of their own and other schools' test and other data, interpreted from a diagnostic/prescriptive perspective. With practitioner inquiry, there is a very broad and, some would say, loose definition of data – including students' work of all kinds as well as observations of students in and out of school, practitioners' plans and journals, school artefacts and classroom talk. With some professional learning communities, there is an almost exclusive emphasis on assessment data, particularly tests. Here practitioners learn how to generate questions about test data and how to rectify discrepancies or close achievement gaps. With practitioner inquiry, learning communities are not necessarily school-based. Rather there are multiple contexts where practitioners deepen their understandings and learn new strategies. With professional learning communities, schools are the fundamental unit of change, and it is assumed that meaningful reform must take place at school level. To generate change, students' learning needs are held up to the yardstick of standards and expectations. Commitment and capacity are assumed to increase when data indicate that learning is lagging behind.

Finally, with practitioner inquiry, the larger project is generating deeper understandings of how students learn – from the perspective of those who do the work. This project is rooted in a deep and profound sense of accountability for students' learning and their life chances. This is about equity, but it critiques, and thus works both within and against the current accountability regime. The more instrumental focus of professional learning communities locates them inside the prevailing accountability frame, and the equity agenda is defined as closing the achievement gap, which may unintentionally retain the current structures of power and privilege rather than challenge dominant values about the purposes of schooling, the relationships of researchers and the objects of research, and the educational questions that are most worth asking.

Conclusion

Teacher education is demanding work. Professionals engaged in teacher education practice, policy and research face many challenges, including the five I have discussed here. I believe that teacher education – particularly college and university teacher education – is at a crossroads. But the crossroads looks different and is about different issues in different places. In the US, the crossroads is about whether university-based teacher education will even continue to exist as we know it in the next few decades. In Ireland, with what may be 'duelling agendas' on the table, there is perhaps a different kind of crossroads and a different kind of opportunity to rethink teacher education, teacher learning over the lifespan, and the role of teachers in the future of democratic societies in a global era. My hope is that this discussion has contributed to the directions people take at the crossroads.

References

Baker, E., Barton, P., Darling-Hammond, L., Haertel, E., Ladd, H., Linn, R., ... Shepard, L. (2010). Problems with the use of student test scores to evaluate teachers. Washington, DC: Economic Policy Institute.

Banks, J. (2009). Multicultural education: Dimensions and paradigms. In J. Banks (Ed.), *The Routledge international companion to multicultural education* (pp. 9-32). New York: Routledge.

Castles, S. (2009). World population movements, diversity, and education. In J. Banks (Ed.), *The Routledge international companion to multicultural education* (pp. 49-61). New York: Routledge.

Cochran-Smith, M. (2001). The outcomes question in teacher education. *Teaching and Teacher Education, 17*(5), 527-546.

Cochran-Smith, M. (2002). The unforgiving complexity of teaching: Avoiding simplicity in the age of accountability. *Journal of Teacher Education, 54*(1).

Cochran-Smith, M. (2004). The report of the Teaching Commission: What's really at risk? [Editorial]. *Journal of Teacher Education, 55*(3), 195-200.

Cochran-Smith, M. (2005a). The new teacher education: For better or for worse? *Educational Researcher, 34*(6), 181-206.

Cochran-Smith, M. (2005b). Teacher education and the outcomes trap. *Journal of Teacher Education, 56*(5), 411-417.

Cochran-Smith, M. and Fries, K. (2005). Researching teacher education in changing times: Paradigms and politics. In M. Cochran-Smith and K. Zeichner (Eds.), *Studying teacher education: The Report of the AERA Panel on Research and Teacher Education*. Mahwah, NJ: Lawrence Erlbaum Associates.

Cochran-Smith, M. and Fries, K. (2011). Teacher quality, teacher education and diversity: Policy and politics. In A. Ball and C. Tyson (Eds.), *Studying diversity in teacher education*. Washington, DC: American Educational Research Association.

Cochran-Smith, M. and Lytle, S. (1999). Relationship of knowledge and practice: Teacher learning in communities. In A. Iran-Nejad and C. Pearson (Eds.), *Review of research in education* (Vol. 24, pp. 249-306). Washington, DC: American Educational Research Association.

Cochran-Smith, M. and Lytle, S. (2009). *Inquiry as stance: Practitioner research for the next generation*. New York, NY: Teachers College Press.

Conway, P. (2012, April). *The politics of teacher education reform in Ireland: From contentment to concern*. Paper presented at the American Educational Research Association, Vancouver, British Columbia.

Cuban, L. (2004). Looking through the rearview mirror at school accountability. In K. Sirotnik (Ed.), *Holding accountability accountable* (pp. 18-34). New York: Teachers College Press.

Darling-Hammond, L. (2010). *The flat world and education: How America's commitment to equity will determine our future*. New York: Teachers College Press.

Department of Education and Skills. (2010). *Better literacy and numeracy for children and young people*. Dublin: Author.

Duncan, A. (2009, October). *Teacher preparation: Reforming the uncertain profession*. Speech delivered at Teachers College, Columbia University, New York. Retrieved from http://www.ed.gov/news/speeches/teacher-preparation-reforming-uncertain-profession.

Economic Policy Institute. (2008). *A broader, bolder approach to education*. Retrieved from the Broader Bolder Approach to Education website http://www.boldapproach.org/

Feistritzer, C. E. (2011). *Profile of teachers in the US.* Washington, DC: National Center for Education Information.

Furlong, J., Cochran-Smith, M. and Brennan, M. (Eds.). (2009). *Policy and politics in teacher education: International perspectives.* London: Routledge, Taylor and Francis.

Goodwin, A. (2000). Teachers as (multi)cultural agents in schools. In R. Carter (Ed.), *Addressing cultural issues in organizations: Beyond the corporate context* (pp. 104-114). Thousand Oaks, CA: Sage.

Haycock, K. (2005). Choosing to matter more. *Journal of Teacher Education, 56*(2).

Hess, F. (2005). The predictable, but unpredictably personal, politics of teacher licensure. *Journal of Teacher Education, 56,* 192-198.

Hirasawa, Y. (2009). Multicultural education in Japan. In J. Banks (Ed.), *The Routledge international companion to multicultural education* (pp. 159-169). New York: Routledge.

Hodgkinson, H. (2002). Demographics and teacher education. *Journal of Teacher Education, 53*(2), 102-105.

Irvine, J. (1990). *Black students and school failure.* New York, NY: Greenwood Press.

Kennedy, M. (1999). The problem of evidence in teacher education. In R. Roth (Ed.), *The role of the university in the preparation of teachers* (pp. 87-107). Philadelphia: Falmer Press.

Ladson-Billings, G.J. (2006). From the achievement gap to the education debt: Understanding achievement in US schools. *Education Researcher, 35*(7), 3-12.

Lamott, A. (1994). *Bird by bird, some instructions on writing and life.* New York: Anchor Books.

McKenzie, P. and Santiago, P. (2005). *Teachers matter: Attracting, developing and retaining effective teachers.* Paris: Office for Economic Co-operation and Development.

Michelli, N. and Earley, P. (2011). Teacher education policy context. In P. Earley, D. Imig and N. Michelli (Eds.), *Teacher education policy in the United*

States: Issues and tension in an era of evolving expectations (pp. 1-13). New York: Routledge.

National Center for Education Statistics. (2003). *Status and trends in the education of Hispanics* (Publication No: NCES 2003-008). Retrieved from http://nces.ed.gov/pubs2003/2003008.pdf

National Center for Education Statistics. (2009). *Number and percentage distribution of 3 to 21-year olds served under the Individuals with Disabilities Education Act (IDEA), Part B, and number served as a percentage of total public school enrollment, by type of disability: Selected school years, 1976–77 through 2007–08*. Retrieved from http://nces.ed.gov/fastfacts/display.asp?id=64

National Center for Education Statistics. (2010a). *Racial/ethnic enrollment in public schools: Indicator 4*. Retrieved from http://nces.ed.gov/programs/coe/indicator_1er.asp

National Center for Education Statistics. (2010b). *The condition of education 2010* (Publication No: NCES 2010-028). Retrieved from http://nces.ed.gov/fastfacts/display.asp?id=96

National Research Council. (2010). *Preparing teachers: Building evidence for sound policy*. Washington, DC: Committee on the Study of Teacher Preparation Programs in the United States, Center for Education. Division of Behavioral and Social Sciences, and Education.

New Zealand Ministry of Education. (2011). *Reading literacy achievement: primary schooling*. Retrieved from http://www.educationcounts.govt.nz/indicators/main/education-and-learning-outcomes/748

Oakes, J., Lipton, M., Rogers, J. and Renée, M. (2006, July). *Research as a tool for democratizing education policymaking*. Paper presented at the International Invitational Symposium on Figuring and Re-configuring Research, Policy and Practice for the Knowledge Society, Dublin, Ireland.

Obama, B. (2009, March 10). *Taking on education*. Speech presented at the US Hispanic Chamber of Commerce, Washington, DC.

Organisation for Economic Co-operation and Development (OECD). (2005). *Teachers matter: Attracting, developing and retaining effective teachers*. Paris: Author.

Organisation for Economic Co-operation and Development (OECD). (2006). *International migration outlook.* Paris: Author.

Schalock, D. and Imig, D. (2000). *Shulman's union of insufficiencies +7: New dimensions of accountability for teachers and teacher educators.* Washington, DC: American Association of Colleges for Teacher Education.

Sleeter, C. E. (2009). Teacher education, neoliberalism, and social justice. In W. Ayers, T. Quinn and D. Stovall (Eds). *The handbook of social justice in education* (pp. 611-624). New York: Routledge.

Spring, J. (2011). *The politics of American education.* New York: Routledge.

Taguma, M., Moonhee, K., Wurzburg, G. and Kelly, F. (2009). *OECD reviews of migrant education*: Ireland. Paris: OECD.

The Teaching Commission. (2004). *Teaching at risk: A call to action.* New York: Author.

The Teaching Council. (2011). *Policy on the continuum of teacher education.* Dublin: Author. Retrieved from http://www.teachingcouncil.ie/_fileupload/Teacher%20Education/FINAL%20TC_Policy_Paper_SP(1).pdf

Villegas, A.M. and Lucas, T. (2001). *Preparing culturally responsive teachers: A coherent approach.* Albany, NY: SUNY Press.

Whitehurst, G. (2002, March). *Scientifically based research on teacher quality: Research on teacher preparation and professional development.* Paper presented at the White House Conference on Preparing Tomorrow's Teachers, Washington, D.C.

Chapter 2

The Universities and Teacher Education: Where Are We Now and Where Should We Be?

John Furlong
University of Oxford

Introduction

> Education is the second largest discipline under consideration and perhaps one of the most complex. Structural, historical and institutional factors affect all disciplines in different ways but in Education their impact has been quite profound (Mills et al., 2006, p. 44).

In this chapter I want to consider three fundamental questions about the current position of education in general and teacher education in particular within our universities. I want to ask 'Where are we?', 'How did we get to be where we are?', and 'Where might or should we be?' In answering these questions I will be referring primarily to experience within the English policy context, although some of the data I draw on are based on figures for the UK. I leave it to you to consider the relevance and implications of what I have to say for your own countries; I suspect, however, that there are many similarities although there may also be some key differences.

To begin…

I think that the first question we need to consider is 'What is a university anyway?' Of course the 'idea' of a university is a highly contested concept. The traditional notion, derived from Newman's ideas that it is an institution that is dedicated to the pursuit of 'truth' – that its aim, in the words of Matthew Arnold (1869), is to 'the best that has been thought and said'. This idea has been hard to maintain in a world of relativist conceptions of knowledge; and yet for me there is still an important and essential truth in Newman's ideas. Universities may no longer be institutions where truths are disseminated; none of us have that confidence in the knowledge that we hold any more. However, universities are I believe still distinctive in society in that they are places that make a commitment to the 'pursuit' of truths; they are institutions that make a commitment to a certain sort of process. And at the heart of that process is a fundamental commitment to what I will call the contestability of knowledge. It is this commitment to the idea that all knowledge can and should be contested through the application of 'reason' that is at the heart of our teaching, at the heart of our scholarship and at the heart of our research. This is what makes universities distinct in our society. There are no other contemporary institutions where the 'contestability of knowledge through the application of reason' is such a core value.

But of course the field of education itself has always had a very fragile relationship with universities. In England, there has been a 100 year history of a slow and often deeply contested institutional integration into the higher education sector; Ireland has a similar history. In England today, faculties of education are now almost universally integrated into the university system. Yet despite this, I would argue that integration is in many ways still very fragile. Indeed, one might argue that integration into the core values of higher education (encapsulated, as I have said, as 'the contestability of knowledge') may well be weaker today than it was, say, 20 years ago.

Faculties of Education – Where Are We Now?

I now want to look at a number of factors that help us characterise the shape and size of the field, as it is currently constituted. Again, the data is from the UK, but it does I think illustrate broad international trends.

Individuals and Institutions

In trying to understand the current position of education as a field we should perhaps begin by recognising that it is very large: it is currently the second largest social science discipline within the university sector in the UK. The Economic and Social Research Council (ESRC) demographic review (Mills et al., 2006) demonstrates this clearly – education, with around 5,000 academic staff, is second only to business studies and management in terms of size. Other disciplines are much smaller in number – psychology has under 3,000 staff (about the same number as physics) and sociology about 1,200. Disciplines such as anthropology and social work are smaller still.

The ESRC demographic review also gives us some important evidence on the current make-up of the field. In terms of age it is clear that education has an ageing population with over 50 per cent of academic staff over 50 years of age (based on 2003/4 data) – indeed, it is the subject area with the largest percentage of staff over that age. Education is also a highly feminised field and the percentage of women has been increasing over time. In 1995/6, 46 per cent of education academics were female; by 2003/4 the figure had risen to 59 per cent. Such a finding could well be linked to a further fact – that salaries are substantially lower than in other disciplines, with education staff having one of the lowest proportions of staff on higher salaries.

The ESRC demographic review also provides evidence on nationality and ethnicity. The number of non-UK nationals employed in the field is, at 4 per cent, the lowest of all of the social sciences (every other subject has figures in the mid-teens). It is also a predominantly white field with the lowest proportion of non-white staff – 4 per cent.

Where Do Educationalists Come From?

Another distinctive feature of our field is that education academics have shorter careers than many others. Evidence from Taylor (2002) suggests that staff typically have a dual career, switching into higher education after a teaching career. As a result, university careers are much shorter.

We can also put together some important data on the relative 'purity' of different disciplines. As Mills (personal communication, 2007) has shown, education is a very 'impure' field compared with, say, psychology, anthropology or economics. Only 50 per cent of education staff, it would seem, undertake their highest level qualification within the discipline. Overall, therefore, education as a field is a significant 'importer' from other disciplines.

One further factor that marks education out from other disciplines is the very low proportion of staff with doctorates as their highest qualification. According to Higher Education Statistics Agency (HESA) data, the percentage of education academics with a doctorate is currently 25 per cent; in psychology, the equivalent figure is over 60 per cent.

Institutional Differences

As a field of higher education, education is therefore very different in many ways from other disciplines. But of course it is not a unified field; there are important institutional differences that we need to be aware of as well. In the UK, amongst the pre-1992 university sector, there are some universities and departments that increasingly characterise themselves as the 'research elite' while others might be seen as the 'research insecure'. Twenty years of the Research Assessment Exercise (RAE) has had an enormous impact on differentiating the sector. Amongst the post-1992 universities there are also substantial institutional differences. There are the ex-polytechnics – mainly urban and highly diversified universities, often serving a regional community. And there are the ex-teachers' colleges which are themselves increasingly diversifying – some into relatively small liberal arts, teaching-only universities, others (what we might call 'the new entrepreneurs') are growing and diversifying rapidly. Each of these different types of university itself has a different history, a different trajectory and sets up very different 'lived realities' for their staff and their students.

Teaching and Research – Where Are We Now?

Teaching

For the majority of education departments, much of our core teaching remains focused on initial teacher education – the Bachelor of Education (BEd) and the Postgraduate Certificate in Education (PGCE) – although many departments also have a strong programme of Continual Professional Development (CPD) work with a growing focus on masters degrees. Additional programmes, which vary substantially in their significance between different universities, include Master of Science (MSc), Doctorate in Education (EdD), PhD and then a range of specialist professional courses such as EdPsych and TEFL degrees. As I will argue below, these additional, non-initial teacher training (ITT) courses are of particular significance within education departments' economies.

But it remains the case that in almost every education department in England, initial teacher education is a key component. This is highly significant in that initial teacher education in England is funded and managed by the government through the TDA – the Training and Development Agency for Schools. Since its establishment in 1994, the TDA has come to define course structure and course content – expressed in the form of 'standards'. And it has worked in collaboration with Ofsted – the inspectorate – to undertake course inspection within an agreed framework; the results of those inspections produce course and institutional league tables. Perhaps most significantly of all, the English government, through the TDA, has insisted that there are multiple providers of initial teacher education. There are currently 32 different routes into teaching with almost 20 per cent of entrants being prepared through employment-based routes. In other words, although 80 per cent of trainee teachers do enter the profession through a higher education based course, for the English government, higher education has no *essential* contribution to make to professional education. Teacher education, as defined by the TDA, is an entirely instrumentalist activity. Many universities may and do run courses that are far from instrumentalist in their approach to professional education but it remains the case that, in terms of what is formally expected, and particularly in terms of what is formally inspected, the government's model of professional education is predominantly instrumentalist.

Strengths and Weaknesses

Overall, if we critically examine teaching in our main area of work – initial teacher education – we can see that in England, as it is currently constructed, the sector has both strengths and weaknesses. There is strong evidence that over the last 15 years teacher education courses in England have become more consistent and, if Ofsted evidence is to be believed, of higher quality (94 per cent are now rated 'good' or 'outstanding' by Ofsted, (Ofsted, 2011)). There is also strong evidence that student teachers are far more satisfied with their professional preparation than a generation ago, as indeed are their head teachers in their first posts. Recruitment into initial teacher education is also more consistently strong than in the past. These are real success stories. There are, however, real weaknesses I would suggest which come about because of the domination of government imposed instrumentalism. The highly practical focus of almost all forms of initial teacher education has had a major impact on theory, on research, on the topics that education departments are allowed to teach and on staffing – on who is recruited and on what sorts of staff development opportunities are made available to them. On all of these issues, I would argue that the English government's instrumentalist agenda has reduced and narrowed the scope and the culture of university education departments.

Research

> There is much to be done to increase research capacity in such a large discipline, and no quick-fix solutions. Education, more so than all other disciplines, is vulnerable to changes in policy legislations, affecting schools and Higher Education alike. The variety of types and locations for educational research

> also make communication difficult and work against the creation of a proactive research agenda that addresses both educational theory and practice (Mills et al., 2006, p. 45).

In trying to understand the current state of education research we should perhaps begin by recognising that education is a field, not a discipline. Lynn Yates, the Australian educationalist, published a highly popular book a few years ago called *What Does Good Educational Research Look Like?* (Yates, 2004). In it she emphasises how much educational research is differentiated. It is differentiated: in terms of methodology – from randomised controlled trials to action research; in terms of theory – from atheoretical positivism to post modernism; and in terms of purposes – policy research, applied and practice based research, blue skies research. On all of these counts, she argues, there is substantial variation across the field. As a result, educational research becomes highly vulnerable to critique, to fashion and, particularly important in England, to government intervention. One is perhaps left wondering if, in other social science disciplines, it would be necessary to write a book with such a title. In most disciplines, things are much clearer, there is more consensus as to what good research is than there currently is in Education.

One important factor influencing the current nature of our research culture is the source of funding. Overall, funding levels for educational research in the UK have been strong in the last 10 years. However, the sources of funding are perhaps different from other social science disciplines. For example, educational research is three times more likely to be funded by government than by research councils; it has relatively low funding levels from industry and EU but has a strong profile of funding from charities. And the impact of these different funding sources is not neutral. Government bodies are often far more instrumental in their approach to research than other funders. And neither charities nor government bodies expect that same social scientific rigour that is demanded by research councils or the EU; peer review also often means something different for these funding bodies. Despite the high levels of funding overall, therefore, these factors have a significant impact on the character and quality of research in our field.

It is also important to recognise the highly differentiated nature of the system. As the Organisation for Economic Co-operation and Development (OECD) observed in its 2002 report on educational research in England, while there are at least 100 separate institutions conducting educational research, 80 per cent of the funding from government, charities and research councils goes to just 22 institutions (CERI, 2002). As a consequence, the ESRC demographic review noted that 'A mid-range of institutions (graded 4 or below in 2001) ... with a substantial community of research active staff ... are finding it virtually impossible to attract significant funding for research' (Mills et al., 2006, p. 44). This in turn has an impact on research cultures.

Strengths and Weaknesses

Overall in terms of research, it is clear that there are currently some important strengths as well as weaknesses in our achievements. On the positive side there are many examples of very high quality work – both academic research and policy research. There are individuals and institutions with research profiles that would compare well with the very best in the rest of the social sciences. Educational research is also widely influential internationally with a strong profile of ISI citations from our best researchers. And we should not forget that we have a very large number of successful research active academics.

But there do remain some significant current weaknesses. In terms of bidding for ESRC grants, in England, education is currently 11th out of 17 social science disciplines; given the size of our discipline this is not a measure of success. There are also weaknesses in terms of our recruitment base. While there are clearly advantages in recruiting 'second careerists' into an applied field such as education, this can only be a benefit if there are appropriate training and development opportunities for staff in order to develop them as researchers; too often this is not the case. Probably as a direct consequence of this fact, we know that the quality of some research is not strong and that the range of methodologies employed is often narrower than it should be; we have a particular weakness in capacity for the use of quantitative methodologies. A final weakness is the growing separation of research in education from other disciplines – despite the obvious overlap with fields such as psychology, sociology, philosophy and economics, educational research has far less contact with these disciplines than it did a generation ago (Furlong and Lawn, 2010).

Why Are We Where We Are?

> As higher education and science became increasingly important instruments of national economic policy ... the relationships between higher education and the state were redefined. Higher education institutions and their members were subject to unprecedented government steerage and scrutiny but also had to locate themselves and compete in various forms of market (Henkel, 2005, p. 159).

As I have argued, in England, it took nearly 100 years for teacher education to become fully embedded in the university system. In recent years, similar journeys have been undertaken in many countries around the world and today, internationally, teacher education is predominantly a university based activity. But in England, the movement of teacher education into the university sector was a pyrrhic victory. Throughout the twentieth century, the aspiration of many teacher educators to join universities was so that they might enjoy the freedoms of self-governance and the commitment to research and critical scholarship that had been the hallmark of the university system. But by the late twentieth century, when the amalgamations were complete, universities themselves had begun to change.

In trying to understand the current position of the field of education in the university sector in England and indeed internationally, we therefore need to recognise the changing parameters of higher education itself. Increasingly, I would suggest, universities have come under the influence of neoliberal policies expressed as the coming together of human capital theory and economic rationalism. As Simon Marginson (2007) has observed, these changes have resulted in a redefined internal economy for universities, in which under-funding drives a 'pseudo-market' in fee incomes, soft budget allocations for special purposes and contested earnings for new enrolments and research grants. Increasingly, therefore, higher education 'managers' (deans and heads of department) find themselves having to compete in internal and external markets in order to maintain the position of their departments. This has major implications for both teaching and research.

In terms of research, for example, as we have already observed, 20 years of the RAE have now established a highly differentiated sector and the English government has now made it clear that it no longer sees research as an essential ingredient of higher education. As a consequence, England's first 'teaching only' universities (which included faculties of education) were established recently and, with the potential growth of more private universities, more are on the way. At the same time, the government has also made an explicit attempt to harness research in the pursuit of global competitiveness – in science, technology and indeed in education. Government over the last decade or so therefore established a 'new social contract' for research (Demeritt, 2000) – increased funding for all forms of research, including educational research, in return for increased accountability and greater government specification of research topics and methodologies. Education has been drawn into these neoliberal policies along with every other discipline within the university sector.

Teaching has also become fundamentally influenced by neoliberal policies. Human capital theory has encouraged the massification of higher education so that as many young people as possible have access to the credentialism that universities offer. However, there has been insufficient funding to cover the costs of the major expansion of the sector. Once again, university managers increasingly have found themselves having to compete for external funding in a highly competitive environment. As we have already noted, the dominant 'market' in terms of teaching for university education departments in England is TDA-funded forms of teacher education. What has become increasingly clear in recent years is that those institutions that are entirely dependent on TDA funding are particularly vulnerable to government intervention. If all of a department's teaching is funded by the TDA with its current instrumental focus, then this has major consequences for the staff that are recruited, for the professional development opportunities they are offered and for the type of research culture that is developed. Again, as Marginson says, 'The paradox of this new openness to outside funding and competition is a process of 'isomorphic closure' through which universities with diverse histories choose from an increasingly restricted menu of commercial options and strategies' (Marginson, 2007, p. 4).

Cochran Smith (2008) makes a similar point: 'Many people, myself included, have argued for years that good teacher education focuses on an expansive rather than narrow notion of practice' (p. 18). However, both in the US and in England, university teacher education has become increasingly instrumentalist as universities, in search of funding, compete to take on the government funding and with it, government agendas. As a result, Cochran Smith argues, the 'ends' question – debates about the purposes of teaching and learning in school – is closed.

By contrast, those institutions that have access to alternative sources of teaching funding – those offering non-ITT undergraduate courses, those with a significant stake in the international postgraduate market – it is these institutions that have a degree of insulation from the demands of government. As a consequence, they are able to use their positional advantage to recruit and support the development of a broader range of staff. This in turn has major implications for the types of research and scholarly culture they are able to develop.

As a result of neoliberal policies, therefore, the differentiation within the higher education sector has dramatically increased in recent years. In England, a small number of well positioned universities are able to maintain their independence and their commitment to the core traditional values of higher education (the contestability of knowledge) while the majority, in both teaching and research, have found themselves increasingly bound to government agendas.

Where Should Education Be in the Knowledge Society?

In the final section of this chapter I want to look at three key issues – professional education, knowledge production and research. In each case I argue that the departments and faculties of education in general and teacher education programmes in particular, must be 're-tooled' if they are to meet the needs of contemporary society.

'Re-tooling' for Professional Education

However persuasive arguments such as those put forward by Cochran Smith and others might be to those of us in the university sector – that teacher education should be based on an expansive rather than a narrow notion of practice – it would seem to me that such arguments are, in themselves, unlikely to be persuasive to governments. The view that teacher education should be narrow and functionalist, focused primarily on forms of training relevant to current government objectives, is now deeply embedded in England and increasingly elsewhere. To argue otherwise is too easily written off as no more than special pleading.

If we are to persuade government that it needs to invest in a richer form of teacher education, one that can draw strength from the traditional values of university based education, then it would seem to be more appropriate to address the argument 'from below'. We need to construct an argument about the forms of school education needed in contemporary society. What does it mean to prepare young people for 'learning in an uncertain world'? What forms of education are needed in a world where there are increasing uncertainties in relation to technology, in relation to knowledge and in relation to a society with ever increasing international mobility, diversity of values and cultural conflict? In this sort of world I would argue that, more than ever before, we need to educate young people to think critically about knowledge and about values, to recognise differences in interpretation, to develop the skills needed to form their own judgements in a rapidly changing world. This in turn has major implications for professional education. If those who teach are to be 'critical educators', then part of their own professional education must be based on the same approach to teaching and learning. Teachers themselves must learn to take 'the contestability of knowledge' as a core value in their own professional learning. And of course, as I have already argued, this is the essential purpose of university based education.

Such an approach to professional education has major implications for the university sector. It means that we must maintain our commitment to 'the contestability of knowledge' in all our teaching. That in turn means that every lecturer must be a participant in a 'scholarly culture' – able to contribute to the 'conversations at the forefront of their discipline' (Furlong, 1996). And in turn that means universities must support and expect all of their lecturers to undertake some form of personal research and scholarship – the essential ingredient for maintaining that 'scholarly culture'.

However, this cannot be an argument for going back to the past where universities remain distant from the world of practice. We do need forms of professional education that are more than instrumental, that debate 'ends' as well as means, but if we have learned anything from the last 20 years of 'the turn to the practical' it is that we also need high quality practical training that is relevant both to the needs of schools and to the nation. The university must be a key contributor to the professional education of the future but not as it was in the past. Far more than before, we need universities and schools to work in forms of 'complementary partnership' (Furlong et al., 2000), where each contributes from its own strengths, its own 'essential purposes' and neither is in the lead. Developing these sorts of partnership is highly challenging for both schools and universities but is essential, I would argue, if we are to develop forms of professional education and indeed forms of schooling relevant to the twenty-first century.

'Re-tooling' for New Forms of Knowledge Production

One of the major challenges facing the university sector overall is that growing numbers of institutions, including educational institutions, are starting to recognise that they can engage in forms of knowledge development on their own – without the involvement of universities at all. In a world that is increasingly technically sophisticated, in a world where a majority of the population is being university educated, innovation and development is increasingly decentralised. 'Mode 2' knowledge production (Gibbons et al., 1994) is increasingly seen by governments and industry as a key contributor to the further development of industry and civil society more generally. Moreover, the development of Web 2.0 and other forms of social media is now pushing this 'democratisation' of innovation and development forward at a dramatic rate. Increasingly, therefore, the educational system, including schools, is asking hard questions about what the university sector has to contribute to their long term development; increasingly, encouraged by government, schools and local authorities are starting to take responsibility for their own learning and development. As I said, this has major implications for the whole of the university world, including those of us in education faculties.

In the past, education has not responded well in adapting itself to the needs of its own 'industry' – the school system. With the honourable exception of the Action Research movement – exemplified in the work of Stenhouse, Elliott and others – educational research has remained largely separate from the world of schools – defining its own research agendas, seeing its primary audience as other academics rather than the world of policy and practice itself.

The development of a more complex and more confident educational system poses major challenges here. So much so that I believe that it is time to think again about institutional structures for applied fields such as education. Conventional university departments may not be the most appropriate organisation form to ensure that universities can continue to provide high quality research-based knowledge that is relevant and accessible to the educational system.

In recent years I have been interested in following the fortunes of the Bristol-based Futurelab (http://www.futurelab.org.uk/) – an organisation devoted to research and development in the field of new technologies and learning. Futurelab is a not-for-profit organisation, working in partnership with a range of others in order to: incubate new ideas, taking them from the lab to the classroom; share hard evidence and practical advice; support the design and use of innovative learning tools; communicate the latest thinking and practice in educational technology; and provide the space for experimentation and the exchange of ideas between the creative, technology and education sectors. In short, it is involved both in basic and applied research and in knowledge transfer. In order to achieve these ends Futurelab has been set up with a particularly interesting constitution that is to my knowledge unique in the field of education. It has strong links with Bristol University but is not part of it; it has core government funding with close links with the Department of Education and it has close links with industry – both hard and software manufacturers and the creative industries. All three groups – university, government and industry – are key partners with Futurelab but not in charge of it. Close links to government mean that research remains close to current policy agendas; close links to the university ensure high quality independent research; close links to industry mean access to the latest technical developments and opportunities for commercial exploitation. However, all research, even when funded by industry, is widely disseminated; it is all in the public domain.

I am not suggesting that Futurelab is necessarily a model for the future of all or indeed any other research institutes in the field of education. Nevertheless, its highly successful 10-year history does, for me at least, raise questions as to whether, in a rapidly changing world, we need to rethink the shape and constitution of at least some of our university-based activities. And there is evidence that the English government itself is now accepting this argument. In its recent 2010 White Paper it argued that in the future, university schools of education should develop more on the lines of Teaching Hospitals; they should become University Teaching Schools, with a school embedded within them (Department of Education, 2010). As our Minister for Schools, Nick Gibb, said in November this year:

> In the NHS, teaching hospitals have become centres of excellence in their local areas by training current and future generations of doctors and nurses while also providing excellent medical care.... We want teachers to have the same opportunities so teaching schools will work with other schools and with universities [emphasis added] to deliver excellent initial teacher training, ongoing professional development and leadership development, while also providing an excellent education to pupils. (Gibb, 2010, 'A culture of collaboration', para. 16)

Knowledge transfer does not happen without the right sort of infrastructure and, it would seem to me, we have been significantly unsuccessful in the past in building that infrastructure on our own – that is why schools and other educational institutions are increasingly 'going it alone'. Maintaining our values for independent critical research and scholarship while also ensuring their relevance is a real challenge in our changing world and this, I would suggest, must encourage us to look quite fundamentally at how we are currently organised.

'Re-tooling' for Research

The final area where we need to 're-tool' for the twenty-first century is in relation to research itself. What I have tried to demonstrate is that it is quite inappropriate to think about 'research capacity' as something that is separate from teaching. We don't simply increase our capacity for high quality research by laying on more and more courses in research methods training – however valuable that might be. If university departments and teacher educators want to have a vibrant research culture then they urgently need to think hard about the type of teaching that they undertake. This means that deans and heads of departments need to insist that all of their teaching programmes are based on 'the contestability of knowledge'. Whether or not government bodies define teacher education in narrowly instrumental terms, it is incumbent on those leading our university departments to remain committed to the core values that make universities distinctive. Not to do so, it seems to me, lays us open to the question – increasingly asked in England – as to whether or not universities are important at all in professional education.

As I have tried to show, maintaining our commitment to critical education is not only important for those we educate, it is also vital for ourselves. Research cultures can only grow in contexts where the commitment to the core values of the university system is taken seriously. In undertaking the analysis for this chapter, I was shocked to learn that only 25 per cent of academic staff working in education in the UK have a doctorate. As I have said publically in England on a number of occasions, this is something that is our responsibility; this is something that those leading departments and faculties of education need to see as a major priority if we are to continue to maintain our position within higher education. At the present, it is not something that government itself will prioritise; it is however something that we must prioritise.

As a community, we also need to take responsibility for improving the quality of our research – across the full range of research methods available. A rich and vibrant research culture would have access to a wide range of theories and methods and would be able to deploy those confidently in relation to the wide range of educational questions that demand our attention. In my view there is now some evidence that as a community we have begun to take this responsibility but there is much more to be done.

But not all of our university departments are in an equal position to contribute to the further development of the field. In a world of highly differentiated institutions, some institutions – the research elite – I believe, have particular responsibilities here. Because of their differential funding, they also have the resources to do so. One area where I believe those privileged institutions need to take responsibility is in relation to the maintenance of the foundation disciplines of education. Current government policy in the UK has meant that it has been increasingly difficult for the majority of university education departments to employ specialists in the psychology, history, sociology and philosophy of education. Yet, often indirectly and in complex ways, these disciplines do remain vitally important for the health of our discipline. If our better-off research based university departments do not take responsibility for maintaining these disciplines then they will die – indeed, as I have argued elsewhere (Furlong and Lawn, 2010), given the current demographic challenges we face with an ageing population, there is an urgent need for those institutions that can to take the renewal of the disciplines as a serious priority.

There is one other issue that I believe is important in the area of research and that is to do with our research agenda. Partly because of the nature of our teaching, and its consequent impact on the staff we recruit, the vast majority of our research is focused on the school population. In recent years, higher education has started to emerge as an important topic for research as well, although in many institutions this takes place as much outside education departments as inside them.

However, if education departments are to have a secure position in the university of the future then they rapidly need to broaden their research agenda. Issues of teaching and learning in the school system are important to study but in the modern world, educational questions are emerging in an ever increasing range of contexts and teacher educators have an important contribution to make. It is now widely accepted that there are important educational questions that need to be asked in relation to: climate change; social equality; the economy;

world poverty; and social change – particularly the fact that we have a rapidly ageing society. However, it is salutary to reflect that, although there is wide recognition that there are educational dimensions involved in all of these major issues, few governments or other funding bodies would turn to university education departments to contribute to research and advanced teaching in relation to them. Not surprising, if so much of our research and expertise remains so firmly rooted in the compulsory school system.

If we are to maintain our position in the university system, I therefore believe that we urgently need to find ways to broaden our research agenda. None of the issues I have defined above are purely educational ones. Developing a research profile in them will therefore demand that those involved in teacher education become much more collaborative than they have been in the past. There is growing evidence that some bodies in the UK and in particularly in Europe now recognise that in addressing complex social issues of the future, interdisciplinary teams of experts – economists, political scientists, conservationists as well as educationalists – all need to work together. If we as experts in education do not take up this challenge, if we don't learn how to work in multi-disciplinary teams, then there is a strong chance that we will be increasingly marginalised from key policy debates.

Conclusion

This has been a broad ranging chapter in which I have inevitably spent more time raising questions and challenges than in providing answers. However, in conclusion, I would like to emphasise that in thinking about the future of our field in the twenty-first century, in the 'knowledge society', we need to begin by going back to our essential purposes; we need to build our future by recognising what it is we are and what it is we are not. We are not training institutions, certainly in the narrow sense of that term, focused only on instrumental agendas defined by others. Nor are we 'think tanks', focused only on new ideas rather than the careful assessment of evidence. We must recognise that in a future that is already becoming increasingly complex and increasingly unpredictable, new forms of knowledge production demanding more and more interdisciplinary work will be essential. If we are to take our proper place in that world then we need to ensure that in all of our work – our teaching, our research and our scholarship – we keep what I have called 'the contestability of knowledge' at its heart. This is our 'truth'; this is what we have, in partnership with others – practitioners, policy makers, industry and academics from other disciplines – to contribute to the development of the field of education in the modern world.

References

Arnold, M. (1869). Culture and anarchy. In R. Super (Ed.) (1965), *The complete prose works of Matthew Arnold*, Vol V. Ann Arbor: University of Michigan Press, 1960-1977.

CERI/OECD. (2002). *Educational research and development in England: Examiners' report* (CERI/CD 2002/10 Sept).

Cochran Smith, M. (2008). The new teacher education in the United States: Directions forward. *Teachers and Teaching: Theory and Practice, 14*(4), 271-282.

Demeritt, D. (2000). The new social contract for science: Accountability, relevance, and value in US and UK science and research policy. *Antipode 32*(3), 308 – 29.

Department of Education. (2010). *The importance of teaching: The schools white paper 2010.* London: Stationery Office.

Furlong, J. (1996). Do student teachers need higher education? In J. Furlong and R. Smith (1996), *The role of higher education in initial teacher training*. London: Kogan Page.

Furlong, J., Barton., L., Miles, S., Whiting, C. and Whitty, G. (2000). *Teacher education in transition: Re-forming teaching professionalism.* Buckingham: Open University Press.

Furlong, J. and Lawn, M. (Eds.). (2010). *Disciplines of education: Their role in the future of education research.* London: Routledge.

Gibb, N. (2010, Nov). *Speech by Nick Gibb to the SSAT National Conference, Birmingham, UK.* Retrieved from http://www.education.gov.uk/inthenews/speeches/a0068867/nick-gibb-to-the-ssat-national-conferenc

Gibbons, M., Limoges, C., Nowotny, H., Schwartzman, S., Scott, P. and Trow, M. (1994). *The new production of knowledge: The dynamics of science and research in contemporary societies.* London: Sage.

Henkel, M. (2005). Academic identity and autonomy in a changing policy environment. *Higher Education, 40*(1-2), 155-176.

Marginson, S. (2007, May). *Are neo-liberal reforms friendly to academic freedom and creativity? Some theoretical and practical reflections on the constituents of academic self-determination in research universities.* Presented at Ideas and Issues in Higher Education Seminar, University of Melbourne Centre for the Study of Higher Education.

Mills, D., Jepson, A., Coxon, A., Easterby-Smith, M., Hawkins, P. and Spencer, J. (2006). *Demographic review of the social sciences* (Report commissioned by the Training and Development Board of the Economic and Social Research Council (ESRC)).

Ofsted (2011). *The annual report of Her Majesty's Chief Inspector of Education, Children's Services and Skills 2010/11.* London: Author.

Taylor, C. (2002). *The RCBN consultation exercise: Stakeholder report.* Cardiff: ESRC Teaching and Learning Research Programme, Research Capacity Building Network.

Yates, L. (2004). *What does good educational research look like?* Buckingham: Open University Press.

Chapter 3

Initial Teacher Education in Ireland: Transformation in the Policy Context

John Smith

St Patrick's College, Drumcondra

> The emphasis needs to be on asking the important questions – and constructing the problem of teacher education in thoughtful, appropriate ways (Cochran-Smith and Fries, 2008).

Initial teacher education in Ireland is undergoing its most significant transformation since achieving degree status and university recognition in the 1970s. Currently, the system is subject to aggressive, ambitious programme and structural reform agendas as set by the Teaching Council (2011a, 2011b), the Department of Education and Skills (DES) (2011a, 2011b) and the Higher Education Authority (HEA) (2012b). The climate for change is shaped by global policy trends as well as by local economic, social and cultural conditions that appear aligned to favour reform but also rationalisation agendas at this particular time. At such a juncture it seems apposite, from a policy perspective, to reflect on: the prevailing contextual factors; the policy network – the actors and how they interrelate; the issues that have (or have not) arisen for attention and how these have been constructed as policy problems.

Against a background of programme and structural change, this chapter sets out to see how we are 'constructing the problem' of Irish teacher education and examines some of the policy issues and policy shifts of the last decade. It looks at transformation in the policy context and landscape over that time. In doing this, it describes national and international factors, focuses on the notions of policy sites and policy moments, and explores the teacher education policy network. Analyses and data are drawn mainly from the realm of initial teacher education (ITE) in the Irish primary sector though there is increasing overlap with early childhood education and second level in the agenda for policy reform. Having first considered contextual factors and noted gradual momentum in Irish teacher education policy from 2002 to 2012, the chapter explores teacher education as a policy site with an evolving policy network centred on the newly established Teaching Council. Finally, whilst noting the thrust of emergent programme and structural reform agendas, the chapter highlights some critical policy *silences* involving the impact of for-profit provision, the importation of teacher preparation models and the accidental transformation towards a graduate entry profession.

The Evolving Context for Reform

The context for policy intervention arises from constantly shifting societal, economic and political forces. Whilst the important shaping forces may well be local, there is an increasing tendency towards globalisation of policy trends in education. In Ireland, while we may observe international influences in the gradual momentum towards teacher education policy reform over the last decade, the recent context for Irish education policy-making is dominated, in many respects, by negative local economic conditions. In this context, teacher education cannot be considered apart from an overall reform agenda aimed at enabling Irish higher education to 'successfully meet the many social, economic and cultural challenges that face us over the coming decades' (DES, 2011a, p. 4). With such a strong imperative for rationalisation, the challenge now facing teacher education policy makers is to identify the opportune and resist opportunistic programme and structural reforms.

Global trends in teacher education reform can help illuminate local practice and there are valuable lessons to be learned from international research and review. Authorities pursuing recent and ongoing teacher education reform in jurisdictions such as Scotland, Wales, Northern Ireland, England, New Zealand, Queensland, Ontario, Singapore and the United States have commissioned system reviews to help inform policy direction. These reviews present recurring themes such as: local context; recruitment; demand and supply; quality of provision; regulation and standards; phases of teacher education; partnership, and strategic planning (e.g., Cauldwell and Sutton, 2010; Englert, 2012; Donaldson, 2010; Furlong, Hagger and Butcher, 2006; House of Commons, 2010; National Institute of Education, 2009; Ontario College of Teachers, 2006; Rivers, 2006). These examples show that the fundamental concepts of how, where and when teachers are educated are contested in restructuring teacher education models worldwide. In current Irish circumstances care will be required to ensure that resultant changes serve the good of teacher education as well as contributing to broader policy objectives. There is evidence too of international policy creep towards a homogenisation of professional standards within teacher education (Menter et. al., 2010) whilst, at the same time, a reinforcement of the great variance in ideological emphasis for teacher education ranging from technical to professional preparation (Furlong, Cochran-Smith and Brennan, 2008). In places, the English and US systems especially, reform is consistently accompanied by strenuous efforts to measure and quantify using narrowly defined standards and competences, holding schools, teachers and teacher educators to account using *policy technologies* (Ball, 2008) inspired by neoliberal, new public management and market ideologies. Reassuringly, recently restated 'guiding principles' and broader Teaching Council policy statements (2011a, p. 10; 2011b) suggest that Ireland is taking an enlightened view of teacher professionalism that has much in common with systems like Scotland's which identifies successful teacher education as doing 'more than seek to attain particular standards of competence and to achieve change through prescription. They invest in developing their teachers as reflective, accomplished and enquiring professionals' (Donaldson, 2010, p. 4). Ireland, whilst reflecting many of these reform motifs and being influenced by globalising policy trends, presents a unique setting where over the past decade review, critique, structural and legislative changes, economic and social conditions have converged to open a policy window for the transformation of teacher education.

Contrasting styles of system review bookend a decade in Irish teacher education. In 2002, reports at primary and second level – *Preparing Teachers for the 21st Century: Report of the Working Group on Primary Preservice Teacher Education* (Kellaghan, 2002) and the *Report of the Advisory Group on Post-Primary Teacher Education* (Byrne, 2002) – were the result of lengthy and broad consultation following on the successful partnership model that had been established in Irish education during the 1990s (Walshe, 1999). Their terms of reference covered both programme and structural concerns. However, in spite of broad representation, lengthy deliberation, recommendations on critical systemic issues and grass roots support from teacher educators (Burke, 2009), they failed to have any significant influence on policy at the time. Some of their key ideas, such as, for example, the extension of the BEd programme (Kellaghan, 2002), have echoed down the decade and resurfaced at the core of recent initiatives. In contrast, in 2012 Sahlberg's report, *A Review of the Structure of Initial Teacher Education Provision in Ireland* (DES, 2012), commissioned under the auspices of the HEA (2012b), had a much narrower focus. It urged 'regard to the recommendations of the National Strategy for Higher Education to 2030 in relation to smaller institutions ... [that] would include providers of teacher education' and sought to guide rationalisation of teacher education provision within broader higher education policy objectives. Its terms of reference excluded programme review, now considered the concern of the Teaching Council (Hyland, 2012) which had commenced programme reform without reference to a formal system review. It is interesting to note the contrast in resultant reforms arising from these two distinct approaches to review as a precursor to change. There are complex reasons as to why there should be momentum in 2012 and not in 2002. These no doubt include changed political context and leadership as well as social and economic factors; but there is also the sense that the momentum has been gradually building through the decade.

System review has been one facet of an emerging critique of teacher education sustained throughout the last decade from within– as well as from without. Starting with Kellaghan (2002) the teacher education community has been critical of the system – especially in repeated calls for programme reform including the restructuring and lengthening of ITE programmes (e.g., Burke, 2002, 2009; Kellaghan, 2002, 2009). The DES, through its Inspectorate, published a number of reports that contributed to a critique of teacher education at all levels of the continuum. Two such reports – *Beginning to Teach: Newly Qualified Teachers in Irish Primary Schools* (DES, 2005) and *Learning to Teach: Students on Teaching Practice in Irish Primary Schools* (DES, 2006) – made specific critical findings and recommendations relating to teacher education programmes. The National Council for Curriculum and Assessment (NCCA) has likewise shone a critical light on performance (2005, 2008). In the lead up to recent policy proposals, Coolahan (2007) and Conway, et al. (2009) helped further synthesise the Irish teacher education context. The provision of research and discussion fora through the auspices of the Standing Committee on Teacher Education North and South (SCoTENS) and the Colleges of Education Research Consortium, respectively, has also been significant in stimulating critique.

From without, the widely influential *Teachers Matter* (Organisation for Economic Co-operation and Development, 2005) can be read alongside a number of European Union policy directives (European Commission, 2005, 2007, 2010) in further framing the teacher education reform context in Ireland, as elsewhere. These affirm the importance of good teachers and teaching – as key policy levers in ensuring economic well-being and the promotion of a 'knowledge society' – as well as promoting homogenisation (*ergo* transferability) of qualifications and standards. Hogan (2010) considers the combined policy impact of their stated principles and approaches to teacher competences identifying 'fresh opportunities ... for teacher education to join [the] debate with policy-makers on a more favourable footing (p. 141)' and concludes that:

> When viewed from an educational practitioner's standpoint ... such forces are clearly more benign than the doctrines of

> the free market that gained an international ascendency in educational quarters during the 1990s (p. 144-145).

In addition to review, critique and international influence there are structural forces at work in extending the contours of Irish teacher education. In particular, the unprecedented level of continuous professional development (CPD) activity generated by the implementation of the Primary School Curriculum (NCCA, 1999) has been transformative in a number of respects. These include the emergence of a phalanx of new agencies with teacher education or professional development activities within their remit. Due to the completion of the curriculum rollout and shrinking resources many of the agencies have since contracted or merged but a legacy of this period may include the future contesting of teacher education provision across the continuum between these new agencies and traditional providers. During this curriculum rollout phase a cadre of teachers has emerged who were variously seconded and contracted to the provision of CPD in schools. Many of these teachers pursued postgraduate studies and have sought to continue within teacher education/CPD roles where opportunities arise. Their presence, with their knowledge, skills and experience, represents a largely latent capacity within the teacher education system. Finally, the curriculum reform dynamic had an impact on Irish education policy discourse and formation. Some senior figures from the resultant agencies have gone on to hold key positions in the teacher education network. This is especially true of Áine Lawlor who moved from being National Director of the Primary Curriculum Support Programme (PCSP) to being the first Director of the Teaching Council.

Structural and personality changes within the administration too have been factors in creating the conditions for reform. The current Minister for Education and Skills, Ruairí Quinn, has had a concerted impact on teacher education since coming to office in 2011. He was seen as keen on reform and prepared to instigate 'major change … [and] … restructure the teacher training colleges … sooner rather than later' (*Irish Times*, 2011). He has had the dubious political *advantage* of economic and social conditions conducive to the pursuit of rationalising reforms where counter argument from the establishment can easily be cast as self-interest. Beyond ministerial influence, there have been changes within the permanent administration that have better enabled management of policy issues. In 2004 a new Teacher Education Section (TES) was formed and this has resulted, arguably, in a more focussed approach towards teacher education within the DES under the leadership of Dr Alan Wall who has an informed knowledge of Irish teacher education policy nurtured by his study of, and early role in, the Teaching Council (where he served as Deputy Director for a period). Most significantly, from a systemic and structural perspective, there has been a legislative hand over of regulatory responsibility for teacher education to the Teaching Council. Within this evolving context of review, critique, structural change and global influence, the Teaching Council has provided a new platform for the teacher education policy community. Its subsequent close attention to teacher education matters and a raft of associated policy measures have created far reaching reform agendas in the realms of programme design, sector regulation and accountability.

The Teaching Council

The establishment of the Teaching Council in March 2006 was a landmark in the long pursuit of professional identity for the teaching community. Its genesis can be traced back to the establishment of the Scottish Teaching Council in 1965 and attempts to follow suit here in Ireland during the 1960s and 1970s (INTO, 1994). The Council's widespread functions and powers encompass the governance, regulation and promotion of the teaching profession – though it remains ultimately subject to ministerial control (Government of Ireland, 2001). Its significance as a policy site in initial teacher education derives from its wide ranging regulatory remit in relation to, *inter alia*, the establishment, review and accreditation of programmes as well as the setting of entry requirements and qualification standards for students. It represents a new forum, a network where teacher education is represented alongside other stakeholders, and where policy actors select issues, set agendas, negotiate, share power and ultimately form policy. It has clearly signalled its intent in relation to teacher education regulation and reform:

> … the accelerating pace of societal and legislative change and educational reform, coupled with the increasingly complex and demanding role of teachers, necessitate a thorough and fresh look at teacher education (Teaching Council, 2010, p. 5).

In brief, the Council consists of 37 members. The majority (22) are teachers – 16 elected and six teacher union nominees. The Minister for Education and Skills nominates five members, two of whom are nominated by the Irish Congress of Trade Unions and the Irish Business and Employers Confederation, respectively. Currently, the three others are drawn from the DES Inspectorate, the Irish Primary Principals' Network, and the for-profit teacher education provider, Hibernia College, even though legislation – *Teaching Council Act 2001 (Amendment of Nominating Bodies) Order 2012* – has been enacted allowing for Hibernia College to take representative turns among nominees from teacher education. The school management bodies have four members and parents' bodies for both primary and second-level get one each. State-funded teacher education is represented by four nominees from the sector.

From a policy analysis perspective the composition of the Council is interesting as a measure of teacher education influence in the network. Though concepts of size and power may not reliably be conflated in the policy network context generally, the relative position of teacher educators is of particular interest here. Over time, teacher educators would appear to have lost influence in the evolving education network. Whereas today they occupy four of 37 positions (c. 10 per cent) on the Council, an earlier proposal would have given them nine of 28 positions (c. 33 per cent) (INTO, 1994). Meanwhile, others–management bodies, parents' bodies and business/employers groups–have gained ground. Teachers have achieved a majority status. Wall (2009), in his account of the negotiations leading up to the establishment of the Council, suggests that:

> … one group has been, in retrospect, excluded in some degree from the process, that is teacher educators … they were not explicitly represented during the talks on the format of the body in question.… One of the reasons this might be the case is that, in relation to the broader issues of teacher educa-

> tion, they did not feature as bodies with which the Department consulted (this would mean that it is more a question of policy style/who belongs to the policy community) (p. 97).

Elsewhere, he lists important groups as:

> ... four main groupings: the Government represented by the Department of Education and Science; the three teacher unions; the School Management Bodies and policy brokers (p. 50).

Teacher educators would thus appear to have missed out on an opportunity to participate more fully in contesting and debating the policy agenda that led to the establishment of the Council and the teacher education sections of the accompanying legislation. Indeed, it would seem from Wall's analysis that teacher educators were not influential at that time within the wider education policy network. Given the comprehensive teacher education remit eventually awarded to the Teaching Council, and events thereafter, this leaves teacher educators at a potential disadvantage in negotiating future teacher education policy direction.

The Teaching Council fits within definitions of policy networks and communities (Holloway, 2009). Although its working might be explored in terms of (social) partnership mechanisms, it is perhaps most usefully conceived of as a *mandated network* – typical of public sector networks set up in pursuit of particular goals and through consensus oriented policy development, supporting multilateral co-operation and coordination (Provan and Kenis, 2008). Policy networks such as the Teaching Council present settings for complex interrelationships between actors who maintain multi-layered links within and beyond the network itself. Thus, although organisations such as the NCCA and the DES Inspectorate do not formally nominate members to the Council, we can assume that their influence is nonetheless felt. Such policy networks are typically active across the policy lifespan in the definition of issues, the setting of agendas as well as policy formation and implementation. Their focus is on networked governance in a policy domain through collective action, self-regulation and negotiation, and they represent the reshaping of hierarchy and bureaucracy. However, as Wall (2009) has observed in the case of the Teaching Council, the assumption should not be made that the emergence of such a mandated, self-regulating network entails a stepping back by the state. Of course, ITE providers continue to negotiate with the DES in relation to many issues – fiscal resources, staffing and student intake, in particular – with key facets of ITE policy-making thus remaining outside the direct control of the Teaching Council and its associated policy network. Writing in the Irish context, MacCarthaigh (2012) notes that within such newly adopted governance regimes politicians struggle with the complexity of 'strategic rather than detailed operational control' and with the 'delegation of tasks to agencies and a retreat of the core state from functions and from policy areas in which it had previously been involved' (p. 27). Can the significant teacher education policy impacts of the literacy and numeracy strategy, *Literacy and Numeracy for Learning and Life* (DES, 2011b), be read as an attempt at reclamation of power to the centre? Whatever the case, whilst the central administration retains control of strategic policy levers, the teacher education sector essentially answers to two masters. Nonetheless, the Council has introduced a new dynamic to teacher education policy-making and provided a forum for the evolving policy network. Part of the transformation in context between 2002 and 2012 is that ITE is now an active policy site where network actors and their agendas can be more readily accommodated and articulated. Against this contextual and policy-making backdrop then, what are the policy issues that have (or have not) arisen for attention and how have they been problematised?

What is on the Policy Agenda? What is Not?

Here we look briefly at how programme and structural reform is being framed before going on to raise questions about the lack of policy emphasis regarding a number of emergent systemic trends. After decades of gradualism the ITE community is now busied with ambitious reforms including the hastened review, redesign and accreditation of programmes. For the first time, Irish teacher education programmes are being prescribed in terms of 'mandatory elements' and 'learning outcomes'. Programme guidelines have emerged that 'set out the criteria and guidelines which providers of programmes of ITE *are required to observe*' (Teaching Council, 2011a, p. 6, my emphasis). As noted earlier, and in spite of the Teaching Council's strong remit regarding ITE programmes, the DES has intervened strongly in programme reform through its literacy and numeracy strategy (DES, 2011b), an intervention that can be read, to some extent at least, as a political response to the furore over disappointing national results in the *Programme for International Student Assessment* (PISA) tests in 2009 (Perkins et al.). In the strategy document the DES seeks to take advantage of a policy window where the:

> ... period of development and change in teacher education and professional development that lies ahead presents an excellent opportunity to ensure that we provide teachers with the skills and knowledge that they need to teach the fundamental skills of literacy and numeracy in the best ways possible (DES, 2011b, p. 33).

'To ensure the development of teachers' skills in literacy and numeracy teaching,' the report recommends a range of actions including, most significantly, the extension of ITE programmes to four and two years in the cases of the BEd and the Graduate Diploma in Education (GDE) programmes, respectively (p. 34). Thus, the most sought after programme reform in teacher education has arrived rather suddenly but in a very specific and tightly circumscribed context and with aggressive timeframes for change. Whilst the proposed programme reforms have been broadly welcomed, the new guidelines, the Council's formal review and accreditation structures, and the continued involvement of the DES and its Inspectorate, combined, provide for unprecedented levels of regulation, evaluation and accountability in teacher education.

In March 2012, with ITE providers reeling from the implications and ramifications of programme reform, the Minister for Education and Skills commissioned a review of the structure of initial teacher education provision. This review was designed to dovetail with broader higher education reforms and had a narrow scope with structural rationalisation a primary focus (HEA, 2012b). It was conducted by a three-person international panel under the auspices of the DES/HEA with written submissions from individual institutions on their 'future role in teacher education' and brief direct representations invited from nominated, clusters of teacher education institutions – a novel mode of consultation for the sector but echoing higher education policy priorities (DES, 2011a; HEA, 2012a). Expediently completed and made public in September 2012, the report's major recommendation was the reconfiguration of the 19 state funded providers of teacher education into six 'centres for teacher education' (DES, 2012). Teacher education providers were identified as already responding to the rationalisation agenda and the suggested clusters will not have come as a surprise. It remains to be seen how effectively the sector can recast itself and whether or not there will simply be a shifting of the deck chairs. The issue of governance in a merging sector will be an obvious point of interest and in this respect the Minister for Education and Skills, Ruairí Quinn, strongly supports the removal of denominational influence from education. The reviewers were tightly constricted in their remit but they did find some room for general comments on aspects of the system beyond institutional realignment, for example noting the importance of retaining the exceptionally high calibre of entrants to teacher education (DES, 2012, p. 19). However, whilst laying heavy emphasis on the importance of university-based teacher education in determining teacher quality and citing the need for closer attention to issues of supply and demand in a quality context, the report, nevertheless, failed to comment overtly on the potential structural impact of a significant proportion of newly qualified teachers emerging through a non-university, for-profit setting.

It is too early to offer a critique of the outcomes but the scale and pace of current programme and structural reforms are remarkable in a sector used to long-term, incremental change and the impact of these reforms will significantly affect how and where Irish teachers are educated for decades to come. However, there are strong, emergent systemic forces at work that are already changing the nature of teacher education. At a time of unprecedented reform these remain largely *unproblematised* in the policy setting. In setting forth the issues of privatisation, the importation of teacher education models, and the changing undergraduate/graduate profile of teacher entry, this chapter is asking why these transformational forces are being ignored?

Privatisation and For-profit Provision in Irish Initial Teacher Education

In August 2003, the then Minister for Education and Science, Noel Dempsey, sanctioned an ITE course to be provided by online education company, Hibernia College. Initially approved in response to a crisis of unqualified teachers in primary schools, this commercial initiative has grown to become the largest single programme in initial teacher education – now responsible for one-third of all entrants to teaching at primary level. In spite of the obvious systemic impact of this alternative entry programme the resultant issues have remained stubbornly unproblematised in the policy debate. A reluctance to create a dialogue that includes consideration of the implications of this new system dynamic may stem, in part, from the controversy that surrounded the initiative initially and that has resulted in a certain *balkanisation* within the teacher education community – perhaps exacerbated by the intimacy of the policy network. However, any analysis of the transformation of teacher education policy in Ireland must attempt to explicate some of the issues that arise as a consequence of such a fundamental policy shift – particularly in light of '*a thorough and fresh look at teacher education*' (Teaching Council, 2010, p. 5).

A factual account of events surrounding this unique departure in Irish teacher education may be gleaned from the contributions of parties, including the DES, the Higher Education and Training Awards Council (HETAC), Irish National Teachers' Organisation (INTO), the heads of the Colleges of Education and Hibernia College, who were invited to address an Oireachtas (Parliament) education committee in a series of sessions (Joint Committee on Education and Science, 2003, 2004a, 2004b, 2004c). In summary, whilst differentiating for the varying standpoints and emphases of different parties, these accounts indicate a series of events stemming from a contributory crisis where the DES came under pressure from the INTO to provide a modular course to address the issue of unqualified teachers employed in the primary school system. In January 2003, the DES was approached by Hibernia College in regards to the provision of such a course. Subsequently, the DES contacted state Colleges of Education with regards to their potential provision of such a course but progress by them towards course proposals appears to have been slow. In the event, Hibernia College succeeded in having its programme accredited by HETAC in July 2003 and approved by the DES with the involvement of staff from the state's Primary School Support Programme (PCSP) considered essential to the successful development and delivery of the courses (Rowland, 2004, para. 152-153). The course was the subject of much comment at the time; not least in respect to the expedition of its approval which was set in contrast to the general torpor that beset teacher education policy at a time when the results of a major system review had just become available (Coolahan, 2007). At the time neither Hibernia College nor HETAC had any track record or experience in the provision of teacher education programmes. The decision of the DES to approve the course for ITE purposes marked a significant policy shift. The systemic impact has gone far beyond the initial policy intent assumed to have been to eliminate the deployment of unqualified teachers in schools. In hindsight, teacher educators, as Wall (2009) depicted them in relation to the Teaching Council negotiations, appear to have been strategically naive in not reading the urgency and potential implications of developments in 2003. If they were naive then they were matched, if not exceeded, by the DES and the INTO in their failures, at the time, and it would seem since, to recognise the potential impact of this *policy decision* on the system.

Initial vocal opposition from the teacher education establishment to for-profit provision of programmes has receded to be replaced, at times, with a discourse of derision towards state providers in some subsequent media coverage of teacher education. The repeated thrust of the rhetoric has been to suggest that the for-profit company has had to battle against the conservative mainstream whilst providing an innovative and equivalent teacher education service 'at no cost to the state' and to represent the traditional colleges as suspicious, reactionary, protectionist and anti-innovation (see, for example, Holden, 2006, 2008, 2010; Flynn, 2012; *Irish Times*, 2012). The current

Minister for Education and Skills, Ruairí Quinn, has been 'robust' in defending the example of the 'free' Hibernia College course whilst discussing reform in the teacher education and higher education sectors (see, for example, *Irish Times*, 2012; Quinn, 2012). The implicit threat to state-funded teacher education colleges at a time of review and rationalisation is thinly veiled.

However, beyond the rhetoric and the political posturing, the discourse surrounding for-profit provision of initial teacher education has failed to mature and continues to ignore an analysis of legitimate policy concerns including: teacher demand and supply; the return of non-university accredited ITE; the ability of the state to ensure quality and standards in corporate provision; the role of state apparatus in supporting or promoting for-profit enterprise; the impact on the state's own teacher education apparatus; the destiny for teacher education in any future scenario not favourable to profit-making.

Ball (2009) has characterised circumstances involving similar for-profit provision in education as:

> ... experimental and evolutionary policy 'moves' which involve the reinvention of public sector institutions and a reformation of the overall institutional architecture of the state and its scales of operations ... part of ... [a] shift from government to governance in which... new forces are able to colonise spaces opened up by the critiquing of existing state organisations (p. 100).

Figures provided in the background paper to the *Review of the Structure of Initial Teacher Education Provision in Ireland* help capture a snapshot of provision in 2011 (Hyland, 2012).[1] For-profit provision now accounts for 37 per cent of all newly qualified primary teachers educated in Ireland – 78 per cent of graduate entrants. Cognisant of the worrying global trends identified in the proliferation of 'alternate' teacher education provision (Cochran-Smith, this volume), this policy silence needs to be broken and the systemic impact of evolving dynamics openly assessed. Perhaps all is well, but, with the Teaching Council's cycle of programme review currently in abeyance, only a few long-standing programmes have been subjected to its accountability regime as we continue to rely on a commercial operation to supply one-in-three of our primary teachers. Nor is this the only systemic issue that escapes the current agenda as a further 20 per cent of all newly qualified teachers now comes from abroad.[2]

Importing Teachers and Models of Teacher Education

Due to consistently high demand for limited teacher education places in Ireland, and a sustained interest in teaching as a career choice, substantial numbers of students go abroad, principally to the countries of the UK, to gain access to preparation programmes. When qualified, under EU regulations, these teachers then present their qualifications to the Teaching Council in Ireland for adjudication and registration. With 20 per cent of new teachers now using this route an important systemic trend has been established representing another 'alternative' entry route and an *accidental* importation of teacher education models from elsewhere. Though not necessarily the intention of regulators to adopt teacher education policies, models, or standards from elsewhere, the cumulative number of teachers involved and the ongoing nature of the effect leads to the *de facto* importation of teacher education models, facets of which may be at distinct odds with the guidelines and mandatory programme elements being prescribed and accredited by the Teaching Council. Inevitably, such a trend will lead to a dilution of whatever vision of teacher education Teaching Council guidelines and programme reforms may aspire to.

Whilst employing large numbers of teachers educated in other jurisdictions we should understand that models elsewhere are designed and regulated in response to local and national needs in the same way that the Teaching Council works towards local guidelines for Irish providers. For example, the dominant model of teacher education in England and Wales – popular destinations for Irish students seeking teacher education – is at variance with the Irish model in that it is often more oriented towards technical competence and, as such, has been subject to criticism (see for example, Furlong, this volume; Hulme and Mentor, 2008). Looking at UK teacher education programmes there is a wide range of possible courses (1400) and models from a range of providers that includes universities, colleges, employment-based initial teacher training and school-centred initial teacher training (Graduate Teacher Training Registry, 2012). Programmes are also in a constant state of flux with regards to entry and programme requirements and the teacher education project generally is subject to continual tension, conflict and radical reform efforts (McNamara and Menter, 2011). We cannot assume equivalence to programmes in Irish institutions. It would seem an impossible logistical task for the Teaching Council to moderate for perceived programme shortfalls in their assessments of returning teachers' qualifications. Thus we currently have a situation where one in five new teachers in our primary schools is being prepared abroad using models of teacher education that may or may not be aligned with Irish requirements or guidelines and over which we have no regulatory or evaluative control.

There is a third system dynamic that arises primarily from the growth of these two 'alternate' routes to teacher qualification. Because those taking up the Hibernia College course are graduates and those seeking courses abroad are primarily graduates and because, combined, these routes now account for one in two new primary teachers, the net effect is to have begun a transformation towards a graduate entry profession. Reading from figures analysed by Hyland (2012, p. 12), 48 per cent of primary ITE entrants in 2011 were postgraduates and 52 per cent undergraduates (this does not account for the large proportion of the c. 500 returning teachers who will have been graduate entrants to teacher education in the UK). By contrast, in 2002, 20 per cent were postgraduates and 80 per cent undergraduates (Burke, 2002, p. 161). Movement towards a graduate entry profession or towards more balance between undergraduate and graduate entrants may well be welcome. The point being made here is that this fundamental shift in teacher selection policy is not a considered change; rather it is the knock-on effect of powerful, underlying system dynamics that fail to be considered in the policy agenda even though Irish teacher education is paused (momentarily) at a significant crossroads and supposedly taking stock of the factors required to ensure future quality provision.

Conclusion

In the decade from 2002 to 2012 there has been a transformation of the Irish teacher education policy context. Contrasting approaches to programme and structural renewal have played a part, as have the influences of global trends and local conditions. Economic, social and general higher education policy factors have combined to create a unique policy context and a window of opportunity for reform in teacher education, with the Teaching Council presenting a new form of governance in the sector – a new mode of policy 'control through calibration and other steering mechanisms' (Ball, 2009, p. 103) – though centralised fiscal and resource policy levers remain well-tuned. There are also other significant, though perhaps accidental, policy shifts and system dynamics that have occurred in the areas of for-profit provision, the importation of teacher education and the resultant increase in graduate entry to teacher preparation. As teacher education embraces reforms, many of which are welcome, has it taken enough stock to confidently move forward assured of enhancing quality? In taking advantage of the opportunity and anxiously seizing the moment has the agenda been crafted too narrowly? Is the teacher education voice being heard in policy negotiation and debate? Is the teacher education community itself ignoring some of the critical issues and powerful system dynamics? Does the continued, combined impact of private provision and teacher importation indicate a policy failure? What is the potential longer term impact of the lowering of entry standards on the high status of Irish teachers and teaching? Should current fundamental reform of teacher education not be based on a more thorough review, or at least acknowledgement, of all aspects of teacher education? Are we really taking '*a thorough and fresh look at teacher education*' and, if so, are we '*asking the important questions – and constructing the problem of teacher education in thoughtful, appropriate ways*'? (Teaching Council, 2010, p. 5; Cochran-Smith and Fries, 2008)

Endnotes

1. The percentages are based on the table produced in Hyland's background paper. Institutions might query the exact figures attributed therein. Notwithstanding minor adjustments the overall picture is representative of the trends. The figures for Montessori trained teachers are not counted.

2. An analysis of the statistics on the number of teachers taking the requisite Irish language competency exam, *An Scrúdú le hAghaidh Cáilíochta sa*

Ghaeilge (SCG), provides a good estimate of the impact on the system. Since 2006 on average 573 persons per annum have applied to sit the exam. The sole purpose of the exam is to fulfil requirements of teachers returning from teacher education programmes in other jurisdictions. It seems reasonable, therefore, to assume that 500+ teachers have been entering our teaching cohort each year having prepared elsewhere. Statistics available at: http://www.ilrweb.ie/ILR_SCRUDU.html

References

Ball, S. J. (2008). New philanthropy, new networks and new governance in education. *Political Studies, 56*(4), 747-765.

Ball, S. J. (2009). Academies in context: Politics, business and philanthropy and heterarchical governance. *Management in Education, Vol 23* (Issue 3), 100-103.

Burke, A. (2002). *Teaching: Retrospect and prospect* (2nd ed.). Dublin: Brunswick Press.

Burke. A. (2009). The BEd Degree: Still under review. *Oideas, Vol 54*, 30-67.

Byrne, K. (2002). *Report of the Advisory Group on Post-Primary Teacher Education*. Dublin: The Stationery Office.

Cauldwell, B. and Sutton, D. (2010). *Review of teacher education and school induction project*. Retrieved from the Queensland Government website: http://education.qld.gov.au/students/higher-education/services/projects/review.html

Cochran-Smith, M. and Fries, K. (2008). *Researching teacher education in changing times: Paradigms and politics*. In M. Cochran-Smith, S. Feiman-Nemser and D. J. McIntyre (Eds.), *Handbook of research on teacher education: Enduring questions in changing contexts* (Third ed., pp. 1050-1093). New York: Routledge/Taylor and Francis Group and The Association of Teacher Educators.

Conway, P., Murphy, R., Rath, A. and Hall, K. (2009). *Learning to teach and its implications for the continuum of teacher education: A nine-country cross-national study*. Dublin: The Teaching Council.

Coolahan, J. (2007). *A review paper on thinking and policies relating to teacher education in Ireland*. Paper prepared for the Teaching Council.

Department of Education and Science (DES). (2005). *Beginning to teach: Newly qualified teachers in Irish primary schools*. Dublin: The Stationery Office.

Department of Education and Science (DES). (2006). *Learning to teach: Students on teaching practice in Irish primary schools*. Dublin: The Stationery Office.

Department of Education and Skills (DES). (2011a). *National strategy for higher education to 2030: Report of the strategy group*. Dublin: The Stationery Office.

Department of Education and Skills (DES). (2011b). *Literacy and numeracy for learning and life: The national strategy to improve literacy and numeracy among children and young people 2011-2020*. Dublin: Author. Retrieved from http://www.education.ie/en/Publications/Policy-Reports/lit_num_strategy_full.pdf

Department of Education and Skills (DES). (2012). *Report of the International Review Panel on the structure of initial teacher education provision in Ireland*. Dublin: Author.

Donaldson, G. (2010). *Teaching Scotland's future: Report of a review of teacher education in Scotland*. Edinburgh: The Scottish Government.

Englert, L. (2012). *Report of the Teacher Education Implementation Taskforce. Queensland: Queensland Government*. Retrieved from http://education.qld.gov.au/students/higher-education/resources/taskforce-report.pdf

European Commission. (2005). *Common European principles for teacher competences and qualifications*. Retrieved from http://ec.europa.eu/education/policies/2010/doc/principles_en.pdf

European Commission. (2007). *Improving the quality of teacher education*. Retrieved from http://ec.europa.eu/education/com392_en.pdf

European Commission (2010). *Improving teacher quality: The EU agenda* (Brussels: Directorate-General for Education and Culture, Lifelong Learning: policies and programme, EAC.B.2 D(2010) PSH).

Flynn, S. (2012, May 15). Surprise at decision to invest €40m in St Patrick's teacher training college. *Irish Times*. Retrieved from http://www.irishtimes.com/newspaper/ireland/2012/0515/1224316130488.html

Furlong, J., Cochran Smith, M. and Brennan, M. (Eds.). (2008). Politics and policy in teacher education: international perspectives. Special Edition of *Teachers and Teaching: Theory and Practice*, 14(4/5)

Furlong, J., Hagger, H. and Butcher, C. (2006). *Review of initial teacher training provision in Wales.* Wales: Welsh Assembly Government.

Government of Ireland. (2001). *The Teaching Council Act.* Dublin: The Stationery Office.

Graduate Teacher Training Registry. (2012). *Entry requirements.* Retrieved from http://www.gttr.ac.uk/students/beforeyouapply/entryrequirements/ (16th July, 2012).

Higher Education Authority. (2012a). *Towards a future higher education landscape.* Retrieved from http://www.hea.ie/files/TowardsaFutureHigherEducationLandscape.pdf

Higher Education Authority. (2012b). Terms of reference for 'A Review of the Structure of Initial Teacher Education Provision in Ireland'. Unpublished. Circulated to stakeholders by HEA on 26th April 2012.

Hogan, P. (2010). *The New significance of learning: Imagination's heartwork.* Routledge.

Holden, L. (2006, November 28). Anyone for cyberschool? Has online teacher-training confounded its critics? *Irish Times*, p. 13.

Holden, L. (2008, November 25). The hibernian shaking it up. *Irish Times*, p. 14.

Holden, L. (2010, November 23). Overtaking the mainstream. *Irish Times.* Retrieved from http://www.irishtimes.com/newspaper/education/2010/1123/1224283929126.html

Holloway, D. (2009). Reforming further education teacher training: a policy communities and policy networks analysis. *Journal of Education for Teaching: International Research and Pedagogy*, Vol 35, Issue 2, 183-196.

House of Commons. (2010). *Children, Schools and Families Committee: Training of teachers* (Fourth report of Session 2009–10, Volume I Report, together with formal minutes). Retrieved from http://www.publications.parliament.uk/pa/cm200910/cmselect/cmchilsch/275/275i.pdf

Hulme, M. and Mentor, I. (2008). Learning to teach in post devolution UK: A technical or an ethical process? *Southern African Review of Education*. Special Issue, Teacher Education. *14*(1-2), 43-64.

Hyland, A. (2012). A review of the structure of initial teacher education provision in Ireland: Background paper for the International Review Team, May 2012. Dublin: Higher Education Authority.

INTO (1994). Comhairle Múinteoireachta – A Teaching Council: accessible, accountable, autonomous. Dublin: Author.

Irish Times (2012, January 31, p. 15). Teacher's Pet: Quinn puts boot into teacher training.

Irish Times (2011, May 3, p. 13). Teacher's Pet: An insider's guide to education.

Joint Committee on Education and Science. (2003, 23 October). EU Directive 99/42/EEC: Presentations. Ireland: Oireachtas. Retrieved from http://debates.oireachtas.ie/EDJ/2003/10/23/00003.asp

Joint Committee on Education and Science. (2004a, 15 July). On-Line primary teaching courses: Presentations. Ireland: Oireachtas. Retrieved from http://debates.oireachtas.ie/EDJ/2004/07/15/00003.asp

Joint Committee on Education and Science. (2004b, 29 July). Primary teaching courses: Presentation. Ireland: Oireachtas. Retrieved from http://debates.oireachtas.ie/EDJ/2004/07/29/00003.asp#N50

Joint Committee on Education and Science. (2004c, 30 September). On-line Training Courses for Primary Teachers: Presentations. Ireland: Oireachtas. Retrieved from http://debates.oireachtas.ie/EDJ/2004/09/30/00003.asp

Kellaghan, T. (2002). *Preparing teachers for the 21st. century: Report of the working group on primary preservice teacher education*. Dublin: The Stationery Office.

Kellaghan, T. (2009). The future of the teacher education continuum in Ireland: Opportunities and challenges. *Oideas, Vol 54*, 14-29. Dublin: Department of Education and Skills.

MacCarthaigh, M. (2012). Politics, policy preferences and the evolution of Irish bureaucracy: A framework for analysis. *Irish Political Studies*, *27*(1), 23-47.

McNamara, O. and Menter, I. (2011). 'Interesting Times' in UK teacher education. Research Intelligence: News from the British Educational Research Association. Issue 116, 9-10. Retrieved from http://www.education.ox.ac.uk/wordpress/wp-content/uploads/2010/07/Research-Intelligence-116.pdf

Menter, I., Hulme, M., Elliot, D. and Lewin, J. (2010). *Literature review on teacher education in the 21st century*. Government of Scotland.

National Council for Curriculum and Assessment. (2005). Primary curriculum review, phase 1 Final report with recommendations. Retrieved from http://www.ncca.ie/en/Publications/Reports/Primary_Curriculum_Review,_Phase_1_Final_Report_with_recommendations.pdf

National Council for Curriculum and Assessment. (2008). Primary curriculum review, phase 2 Final report with recommendations. Retrieved from http://www.ncca.ie/en/Publications/Reports/Primary_Curriculum_Review,_Phase_2_Final_report_with_recommendations.pdf

National Institute of Education. (2009). *A teacher education model for the 21st century*. Singapore: Author.

Ontario College of Teachers. (2006). *Preparing teachers for tomorrow*. Ontario: Author.

Organisation for Economic Co-operation and Development (OECD). (2005). *Teachers matter: Attracting, developing and retaining effective teachers*. Paris: Author.

Perkins. R., Moran. G., Cosgrove. J. and Shiel. G. (2009). *PISA 2009: The performance and progress of 15-year-olds in Ireland – summary report*. Dublin: Educational Research Centre.

Provan, K. and Kenis, P. (2008). Modes of network governance: Structure, management, and effectiveness. *Journal of Public Administration Research and Theory*, *18*(2), 229-252.

Quinn, R. (2012, 25 January). Joint Committee on Jobs, Social Protection and Education. Debate: Teaching Council Act 2001 (Amendment of Nominating Bodies) Order 2012: Motions, p. 4. Retrieved from http://debates.oireachtas.ie/FAJ/2012/01/25/00004.asp

Rivers, J. (Ed.). (2006). *Initial teacher education research programme: A summary of four studies*. New Zealand: Ministry of Education.

Rowland, S. (2004, 30 September). On-line training courses for teachers: Presentation. Oireachtas, Joint Committee on Education and Science. Retrieved from http://debates.oireachtas.ie/EDJ/2004/09/30/00003.asp

Teaching Council. (2010). *Draft policy on the continuum of teacher education - Background report: Teacher education in Ireland and internationally*. Dublin: Author.

Teaching Council. (2011a). *Policy on the continuum of teacher education*. Dublin: Author.

Teaching Council. (2011b). *Initial teacher education: Criteria and guidelines for programme providers – in accordance with section 38 of the Teaching Council Act, 2001*. Dublin: Author.

Wall, A. (2009). External influence or internal politics – the perception and reality of policy formation in Irish education: How do the main actors perceive that policy leading to the establishment of the teaching council was derived? Unpublished, D.Gov., QUB.

Walshe, J. (1999). *A new partnership in education: From consultation to legislation in the nineties*. Dublin: Institute of Public Administration.

Chapter 4

At the Heart of Change: Early Childhood Education and Initial Teacher Education in Ireland

Liz Dunphy
St Patrick's College, Drumcondra

Introduction

Statutory school starting age in Ireland is 6 years of age. In practice, however, it has been traditional for most children to begin school considerably earlier. In fact, until recently about half of all 4-year-old children and the majority of 5-year-old children were enrolled in primary schools. So called Early Start classes in primary schools have, for a number of years, afforded targeted educational provision for some 3-year-old children (1,600) identified as 'at risk' because of economic and social disadvantage. In January 2010 the government introduced a free preschool year for all eligible 3 to 4-year-old children in the year before they attend primary school. This consists of three hours each day, five days a week for 38 weeks of the year (September to June). It is provided by a range of providers, in varied types of accommodation. Providers include private enterprise, community playgroups and Irish-language preschools. To qualify for the grant-aid by the Department of Education and Skills, providers must ensure that there is one person on site with a Level 7 qualification in early education (this is equivalent to a pass degree). Approximately 400 primary schools now have a preschool on campus, some managed by the school authorities but most run, for now, by private enterprise.

In order to bring Ireland into line with other countries, the likely future of early childhood education is one of increased participation by children in the age range birth to 6 years. Depending on economic considerations, children's participation in early childhood education will be funded to a greater or lesser degree by the State. However, already in the United Kingdom (UK), which is our nearest neighbour and which has an education system structurally similar to that in Ireland, there is provision for all children aged 3 to 5 to attend preschool; this is to be extended to children aged 2 who are deemed to be in disadvantaged circumstances. Recently, the Early Years Foundation Stage (for children from birth to 5/6 years) has been recognised as the first stage in education in the UK.

Here in Ireland, as in a number of other countries, there are welcome moves to develop the workforce for early childhood care and education. The growth in demand for Early Childhood Care and Education (ECCE) degrees as offered in many Institutes of Technology and some universities is evidence that there is considerable interest in this area of study. The free preschool year initiative will likely fuel the demand for ECCE courses as employment possibilities in the sector become apparent. The enhanced roles that primary teachers and primary schools in Ireland can play, alongside these new professionals, in the newly configured and emerging early education sector is an issue that needs serious consideration at this juncture.

In this chapter I argue that pre-service provision in early childhood education for primary teachers should be significantly strengthened as part of the reimagining of initial teacher education. I examine a number of issues which support the argument for the extension of provision in pre-service teacher education. The first issue raised relates to the interface between the preschool and primary education sectors which may become increasingly contested as new policies and structures to support early childhood education are developed in the years ahead, including a growing awareness of the need for primary education to build seamlessly on the early education provision that is provided in preschool/out of school settings. The second issue raised is the recognition at policy level of the need to align developments in early childhood education with reform of primary pre-service teacher education programmes. The third issue discussed relates to developments in the research base relating to early childhood and the emerging consensus regarding the range of knowledge, skills, attitudes and dispositions that teachers now need in order to engage effectively in the work of early childhood education in primary schools. The fourth issue is the development, in recent years, of national frameworks for early childhood education in Ireland and the consequent demands that these frameworks place on teachers in terms of curriculum organisation and pedagogy and on the primary education system at an infrastructural level. Finally, the chapter problematises the issue of staff appropriate to the initial teacher education sector and argues for faculty that bring both academic rigour and experience in a diverse range of ECCE settings to their teaching and research, along with greater institutional commitment by initial teacher education providers to the early childhood sector. In summary, this chapter explores the current national and international contexts within which early childhood education as a component of teacher education can be viewed and the consequent argument for review and reform of the relative emphasis on early childhood education in initial teacher education.

The Interface between Early Education and Primary Education

The recent *Cambridge Primary Review* suggested that, in England, the notion of a Foundation Stage to age 6 and a Primary Stage from age 6 to age 11 was worthy of detailed discussion (Alexander, 2010, p. 491). The report drew attention to the fact that England was out of step with many other countries in the practice of enrolling children of 4 or 5 years of age in schools, since, on average, only 16 per cent of 5-year-old children in the European Union are in formal schooling. This critique applies equally to Ireland since, as noted above, about half of all 4-year-old children and almost all 5-year-olds are enrolled in primary schools. Given that Ireland often looks to the UK in terms of policy and given that the structural features of the two educational systems are closely aligned, the question of school starting age will almost certainly become an issue for consideration and debate here in

Ireland in the very near future. Such a debate will once again throw the spotlight on current provision and on the level of preparedness of teachers to provide high quality early childhood education in primary schools.

The fact that in Ireland there is now an emerging early childhood profession, i.e., graduates who have obtained degrees in ECCE and who are specially prepared for work with children from birth to 6 years, could be seen to strengthen any arguments that the well-being and education of children of 6 years of age and below should be undertaken only by these professionals. It should be noted however that these graduates represent only a small fraction of the current workforce in settings providing the free preschool year. It should also be noted that the extent to which this workforce has had sufficient opportunities to engage with the study of key aspects of early learning such as language development, early literacy and mathematics is likely to vary greatly. Furthermore, the recent *Workforce Development Plan* for the early childhood care and education sector in Ireland (Department of Education and Skills (DES), 2010) does not endorse the need for degree-level education for all educators working with young children, nor does it mandate degree status. This is despite the fact that, internationally, the level of educators' qualifications is generally considered to be a key factor affecting the quality of the provision (e.g., Bowman, Donovan and Burns, 2001; Saracho and Spodek, 2007). It also flies in the face of the argument that education should matter for early childhood educators as much as it matters in other professions including primary teaching (e.g., Early et al., 2007).

In responding to any challenge regarding the suitability of schools as sites for early childhood education, teacher educators, schools and teachers will of course argue that state provision for early childhood education in schools should be maintained and extended to include children in the age range 3 to 6 years. Latterly, teacher education has moved to implement many of the new perspectives on early childhood education, while recent policy initiatives have included early childhood education as a mandatory element of initial teacher education (Teaching Council, 2011, p. 14); re-imagined programmes, then, can seek to build further on these advances, incorporating the latest thinking in terms of early learning and development. Based on current programmes, and reinforced by the possibility of enhanced provision enabled by recent policy changes, there is a strong argument that early childhood education should continue to be located in primary schools where young children are guaranteed to interact on a regular basis with teachers well versed in issues of learning, skilled in matching effective teaching strategies with the characteristics of young learners, sensitive to ways in which learning environments are created for children of different ages and for diverse learners, and with a well-developed pedagogical content knowledge across the various areas of learning. No such guarantee is available for children attending other settings, nor are there any indications that this will be the case in the foreseeable future. Primary teachers are also in an ideal position to address issues of continuity between early learning experiences and later approaches, and to ensure a gradual progression for children from informal foundational experiences to more specific discipline-based learning in key areas such as literacy and mathematics. These are issues that we now know are crucial for optimal learning and development and for later academic success (e.g., Neuman and Dickinson, 2011; Clements, Sarama and Di Biase, 2004).

Moreover, the role of the primary sector in ensuring equality of access to ECCE was highlighted in the report of *The National Economic and Social Forum on Early Childhood Care and Education* (NESF, 2005) which proposed a policy framework for ECCE. The framework was based on a number of key principles, one of which was that of universal access for all children to early childhood care and education. The Forum envisaged that the key role of primary schools in early care and education would be further developed. It was recommended that serious consideration should be given by education authorities to campus style developments wherein the range of ECCE services could be provided. However, in order for schools to fulfil an enhanced role, it was advised that:

> … significant reforms of the present primary school system are also urgently needed, particularly if it is to accommodate the needs of preschool children but also because it currently provides only for 4-5 year olds. The key changes needed are in

> relation to the physical infrastructure and reduced adult/child ratios (ibid., p. 81).

Given the requirement for systemic reform at school level articulated by the NESF report, it is not surprising that there is broad acknowledgement of the importance of early childhood education among key stakeholders. The challenges presented to teachers and to schools by developments in early childhood education and care, both at home and elsewhere, are well recognised by the teaching profession, and there is on-going debate about enhanced provision for early childhood education in primary schools and on the alignment of pedagogy and provision with current theories and research findings (e.g., Irish National Teachers' Organisation (INTO), 2005).

The Policy Context of Early Childhood Education for Pre-service Teachers in Ireland

Over a decade ago there was a clear recognition at policy level of the need for a further strengthening of the study of early childhood education at pre-service level for all teachers. The report, *Preparing Teachers for the 21st Century,* made a number of specific suggestions regarding the range of courses with which pre-service teachers should engage. Specifically it concluded that early childhood education would become 'an increasingly important part of teacher preparation for all students as the key role in laying the foundations of education for all children is more clearly recognised' (DES, 2002, p. 129).

The *Thematic Review of Early Childhood Education and Care Policy in Ireland* (Organisation for Economic Co-operation and Development (OECD), 2004) recommended 'a thorough reassessment of teacher training for the early childhood classroom'. It went on to state that:

> Teachers working with young children should have considerably more exposure to research-based ECEC pedagogy.... The OECD review suggests that reviewing the three-year B.Ed. teaching degree, with a possible lengthening of it to four-years, but above all ensuring a focus on ECEC-related theories and methodologies are included in all three (four) years of training. (ibid., p. 84)

Critical of existing practice in the early years' classrooms, the report also asserted that teacher education provision was:

> ... totally inadequate to change the predominant teaching model.... On a long-term basis, an education degree course, with the possibility of specialising in early childhood education and care (covering the age-group 0 to 8), may be more appropriate to the needs of the field (ibid., p. 84).

The OECD report (2004) further suggested a possible role for teachers who attain a high level of specialisation in early childhood education. It proposed a redevelopment of the infant school at local level with specific management responsibilities given to a senior teacher. It delineated the responsibilities of such a manager/leader and included the range of issues related to the education and well-being of children in the infant school. According to the report, these should include responsibility for the education and well-being of children attending preschool on the school campus.

As policy makers recognise, then, any reform of the primary school system, particularly one which is aimed at extending the role of schools in ECCE, requires concurrent reform of primary pre-service education in order to prepare teachers for their enhanced roles in the ECCE sector. While the recent inclusion of early childhood education as a mandatory element in initial teacher education is a step in the right direction (Teaching Council, 2011, p. 14), it does not go far enough, saying little, for example, about the depth or character of that provision within the newly conceptualised programmes. A survey of recent developments in the research-base of early childhood education offers some insights.

Developments in the Research-base in Early Childhood Education: A Question of Pedagogy?

Recent research (e.g., Bowman et al., 2001) has revealed a great deal about the nature and extent of early learning and how it can be influenced by context, culture and interactions. Research has also revealed the consequences of variations in quality for children's well-being and their future life chances (e.g., Pianta et al., 2009). Such research makes it imperative that early childhood education is addressed at pre-service level in an even more comprehensive way than heretofore and that it embraces a thorough study of all aspects of children's learning from birth.

In making the case for a more in-depth study of early childhood education it is important to clarify some of the ways in which this aspect of education may be conceptualised as different to that undertaken by education students generally. Moyles (1995) sees the major difference between the pedagogy of early childhood and that which characterises work with older children as being one of *emphasis*. She argues that some elements of pedagogy (e.g., play, first-hand experiences, language and communication, observation) need to be foregrounded for early learning, while other elements may have a lesser role. Language development, for example, is crucial to development in early childhood and is based on a type of intentional responsiveness by the adult to the child. This is something which is acknowledged to be 'impossible to script procedurally and dependent on well-tuned responsive conversational inputs to children; it needs to feature open-ended questions, expansions, advanced linguistic models and recasts' (Pianta et al., 2009, p. 76).

Katz (2003) argues that the emphasis in early childhood education should be on intellectual rather than on academic goals. She describes intellectual goals as goals which emphasise reasoning, the process of reflection, the development and analysis of ideas and the creative uses of the mind. In contrast, she sees academic goals as ones that emphasise learning of skills rather than the deepening of understanding. Munn (1994) characterises early childhood as the period in which children develop their metacognitive frameworks in relation to literacy and mathematics, i.e., their general understandings of what these aspects of human activity are all about. Recent research in the field of both literacy (e.g., Neuman and Dickinson, 2011) and mathematics (e.g., Cross, Woods and Schweingruber, 2009) emphasise how the origins of both are located in the foundational experiences of early childhood and how the nature of these are crucial for later learning and development. An understanding of the continuities between children's earliest experiences (including play) and later literacy and mathematics is vitally important for early childhood educators. In addition, leading early childhood educators emphasise the development of positive dispositions as a critical outcome of early childhood education (e.g., Bertram and Pascal, 2002). The task of fostering such dispositions has now become a crucial area of concern for early education (e.g., Carr, 1999).

In making the case for enhanced provision, pedagogy represents a second important area. Indeed, recent theoretical developments offer us considerable insight in terms of understanding how best to support early learning (e.g., Vygotsky, 1978; Rogoff, 1998). The type of early childhood pedagogy arising from theory is both dense and detailed (e.g., Pelligrini, Galda and Dresden, 1991; Katz, 1997; Edwards, Gandini and Forman, 1998; Siraj-Blatchford et al., 2002). From the point of view of practice, recent research in the UK (e.g., Siraj-Blatchford et al., 2002; Moyles, Adams and Musgrove, 2002; Adams et al., 2004) clearly indicates the nature of the pedagogy necessary to ensure optimal learning during the early years. According to this research, the effective early childhood educator is: skilled in the use of a range of pedagogical strategies; can use them as appropriate; is knowledgeable about current learning theory; appreciates the processes through which young children learn; appreciates the central role of teaching in early childhood education; and is highly skilled in responding to children and in interacting with them to promote learning and development. However, in addition to the above emphases, the research further suggests that teachers working with children of 6 years and under must also incorporate further strategies to promote optimal learning and development (Dunphy, 2008). They must, as a matter of routine:

- be able and willing to take cognisance of a child's perspective on the learning environment;
- plan in a flexible manner to ensure that children's emerging interests, concerns and needs are addressed;
- ensure a balance between adult-led interactions and child-led interactions;
- use discussion and dialogue with children to promote higher-order thinking;

- create opportunities for extending child-initiated play and teacher-initiated group work;
- ensure that children have opportunities to work individually with the teacher, in small groups and occasionally in larger groups;
- provide opportunities for play and for intervening in children's play as appropriate;
- ensure a balance between play and teacher-planned activity; and
- ensure that children have opportunities to pursue specific interests.

While many of these pedagogical emphases are ones that are shared with teachers working with older children, one of the key differences resides in the way in which effective interactions and reciprocal communications are established and managed with young children. This is a particularly challenging task given that early childhood is the period during which most children are still acquiring skills in these areas. Recent years have seen an ever-increasing emphasis on the ways in which educators interact with children since it is now recognised that 'effects of organised curricula on children's skills are mediated and/or moderated by teacher-child interactions … these interactions must be a central focus …' (Pianta et al., 2009, p. 76). This implies that one of the greatest challenges facing teacher education is the preparation of teachers who, on the one hand, ensure children's engagement in deliberate and planned instruction in key areas such as literacy and mathematics (e.g., Ginsburg, Lee and Boyd, 2008) and who, on the other hand, ensure a classroom environment that is not overly structured or controlled (e.g., Pianta et al., 2009).

Two Frameworks for Early Childhood Education in Ireland

Síolta: The National Quality Framework for Early Childhood Education (Center for Early Childhood Development and Education (CECDE), 2006) and *Aistear: The Early Childhood Curriculum Framework* (National Council for Curriculum and Assessment (NCCA), 2009) are two frameworks designed over the last decade as supports to educators working with children across the age range birth to 6 years. Such frameworks are now a feature of the educational provision in a number of developed countries, indicating a growing international recognition of the need to pay close attention to the early learning experiences of children, both in terms of promoting a good childhood and promoting children's optimal learning and development into the future. Premised on a set of principles for the provision of high quality early childhood education, *Síolta* focuses on all aspects of quality within early education settings. *Aistear*, on the other hand, guides adults in relation to the provision of appropriately challenging, rewarding and enjoyable learning experiences for children from birth to 6 years.

Aistear is a framework to support all adults who engage with children in the age range birth to 6 years. Sociocultural perspectives on learning, teaching and, to a lesser extent, assessment, are clearly discernible in the *Aistear* documentation. It describes learning and development through the four interconnected themes of *Well-Being, Identity and Belonging, Communicating and Exploring and Thinking*. It is envisaged that the *Aistear* framework will be used by teachers, together with the *Primary School Curriculum* (DES, 1999) and *Síolta*, to guide their work in planning, teaching and assessing early learning.

It is a considerable challenge for teacher education to ensure that pre-service teachers have a variety of opportunities over time to engage deeply with the various elements of these, in particular with *Aistear*. Pre-service teachers will need to explore the tensions and relationships between the philosophical and pedagogical emphases in Aistear and those of *The Primary School Curriculum*. In particular, differences such as those related to the presentation of learning (themes versus subjects), the aims, goals and/or objectives for learning, and the central place of play in the *Aistear* framework, are all issues that are complex to work with for both pre-service teachers and those already in practice. Differences in the documents in relation to concepts of curriculum and curriculum planning and development are key issues that also need to be taken into consideration. *Aistear* brings the work of teachers in the junior classes in primary schools into sharper focus. Its significance for teacher education relates to the potential demands that it makes on teachers of young children in relation to pedagogy and the ways in which teachers will use it in the future to support, extend and rethink practice as outlined in *The Primary School Curricu-*

lum (DES, 1999). While *The Primary School Curriculum* is organised around quite specific outcomes (detailed objectives) delineated for each of eleven subjects, *Aistear* foregrounds a responsive approach with an emphasis on co-constructing the curriculum with the children based on their interests, concerns and working theories. For teachers of the youngest children, it involves developing what Wood refers to as 'an integrated pedagogical approach' which she describes as 'one in which teachers are involved with children in planning for play and child-initiated activity, based on their observations and interactions' (2010, p. 12). This focus on co-constructed and responsive curricula represents a fundamental shift in teachers' practice and in how the primary school curriculum is mediated currently. It involves, among other things, moving away from teaching practices which dichotomise play and work or which emphasise teacher-directed didactic approaches over child-initiated learning. Other key changes lie in understandings of the nature of curriculum itself; the need to interrogate how adults support children's learning and the nature of adult-child relations, all of which are important in relation to the practice of early childhood education.

The recent policy paper, *Literacy and Numeracy for Life and Learning: The National Strategy to Improve Reading and Writing Among Children and Young People 2011-2020* (DES, 2011) clearly prioritises the role of Aistear in the work of educators in supporting early learning in all settings, including primary schools. There is a clear recognition of the role of informal learning, including play, in providing the foundations for later learning in both literacy and mathematics.

The Way Forward

The *Cambridge Primary Review* (Alexander, 2010) raised the issue of the suitability of the concept of the generalist teacher and the ability of that teacher to meet the range of challenges likely to arise in the course of work in schools. A debate on this issue here in Ireland would almost certainly result in the case being made for specialisation to teach children of 6 years of age and under. Primary teachers must be equipped to take on any challenge in this regard. The key issue in relation to quality provision really focuses on the kinds of curriculum and learning experiences children have and the kinds of pedagogy they encounter, as opposed to where early education is sited. Educationalists will need to argue *for* school settings as prime sites for early education under the guidance of primary teachers.

The BEd degree in Ireland has recently been restructured in order to update initial teacher education and to ensure that teachers in the future are competent to meet the various challenges which they may face and to adapt as necessary (Teaching Council, 2011). While early childhood education has in practice been studied by most, if not all, teacher education students since the early 1970s, it is now, as noted earlier, a mandatory area of study. This is a welcome development. There is now considerable scope within the new structures for increased attention to early education by all students and for providing the choice to specialise in early childhood education for some. However, increased attention requires increased supports, particularly in the form of additional specialised staff.

In the United States a recent study of a large sample (approximately 20 per cent) of the 1,200 colleges offering early childhood teacher education at pre-service level offered interesting insights into questions relating to the quality of these courses. The authors sought the perspectives and recommendations of early education faculty on quality improvement in early childhood teacher education (Hyson, Tomlinson and Morris, 2009). A key issue investigated was the kinds of supports required by early childhood teacher education programmes. A number of these were identified, some of which are predictable, such as resources and time. Less predictable perhaps, but of key importance, were supports such as: institutional recognition of the value of the programme; institutional understanding of the context of early childhood education; and professional development opportunities for staff. Critically, the study demonstrated the need to look at the profile of those teaching on early childhood education degree courses since this was found to be problematic. The authors concluded that it was essential that course lecturers should have academic expertise in the area of early childhood care and education and should also have recent direct experience in early education settings. In the Irish context, this implies that universities and colleges seeking to offer credible programmes need to employ faculty who have experience in settings besides primary schools, i.e., in settings which provide early childhood education and care for children from birth to 3 years of age.

Conclusion

Informed by an international focus on enhancing the quality of pre-service teacher preparation, the recent review of initial teacher education in Ireland and the new national frameworks for early childhood education present a confluence of factors facilitating a renewed focus on the nature and extent of pre-service provision relating to early childhood education. Recent policy developments, new knowledge and insights generated by research into early childhood education, along with increased understanding of its complexity and importance, provide a rationale and context for substantially enhanced provision within primary teacher education. In the past, pre-service teacher education has not engaged systematically with the education of all children from birth to 6 years. Renewed and extended focus on early childhood education at pre-service level, including opportunities for specialised study, will place early education where it should be – at the core of teacher education and at the heart of reform.

References

Adams, S., Alexander, E., Drummond, M. and Moyles, J. (2004). *Inside the foundation stage: Recreating the reception year.* London: Association of Teachers and Lecturers.

Alexander, R. (Ed.). (2010). *Children, their world, their education: Final report and recommendations of the Cambridge Primary Review.* UK: Routledge.

Bertram, T. and Pascal, C. (2002). Assessing what matters in the early years. In J. Fisher (Ed.), *The foundations of learning* (pp. 87-101). UK: Open University Press.

Bowman, B., Donovan, S. and Burns, S. (Eds.). (2001). *Eager to learn: Educating our preschoolers.* (Report of Committee on Early Childhood Pedagogy, Commission on Behavioural and Social Sciences and Education National Research Council). Washington DC: National Academy Press.

Carr, M. (1999). Being a learner: Five learning dispositions for early childhood. *Early Childhood Practice, 1*, 82-99.

Centre for Early Childhood Development and Education (CECDE). (2006). *Síolta: The national quality framework for early childhood education.* Dublin: CECDE.

Clements, D., Sarama, J. and DiBiase, A. (Eds.). (2004). *Engaging young children in mathematics: Standards for early childhood mathematics education.* Mahwah, NJ: Lawrence Erlbaum and Associates.

Cross, C., Woods, T. and Schweingruber, H. (Eds.). (2009). *Mathematics learning in early childhood: Paths towards excellence and equity.* (Report of Committee on Early Childhood Mathematics, National Research Council of the National Academies). Washington, DC: The National Academies Press.

Department of Education and Science (DES). (1999). *The Primary School Curriculum.* Dublin: The Stationery Office.

Department of Education and Science (DES). (2002). *Preparing teachers for the 21st century: Report of the working group on primary pre-service teacher education.* Dublin: The Stationery Office.

Department of Education and Skills (DES). (2010). *A workforce development plan for the early childhood care and education sector in Ireland.* Dublin: Author.

Department of Education and Skills (DES). (2011). *Literacy and numeracy for learning and life: The national strategy to improve literacy and numeracy among children and young people 2011-2020.* Dublin: Author. Retrieved from http://www.education.ie/en/Publications/Policy-Reports/lit_num_strategy_full.pdf

Dunphy, E. (2008). Developing pedagogy in infant classes in primary schools: Learning from research. *Irish Educational Studies, 27*(1), 55-70.

Early, D, Maxwell, K., Burchinal, M., Alva, S., Bender, R., Bryant, D… Zill, N. (2007). Teachers' education, classroom quality, and young children's academic skills: Results from seven studies of preschool programs. *Child Development, 78*, 558-580.

Edwards, C., Gandini, L. and Forman, G. (1998). *The hundred languages of children: The Reggio Emilia approach: Advanced reflections* (2nd ed.). Greenwich, UK: JAI Press Ltd.

Ginsburg, H., Lee, J. and Boyd, J. (2008). *Mathematics education for young children: What is it and how to promote it* (Social Policy Report Volume XX11, 1). Retrieved from Society for Research in Child Development website: www.srcd.org/

Hyson, M., Tomlinson, H. and Morris, C. (2009). Quality improvement in early childhood teacher education: Faculty perspectives and recommendations for the future. *Early Childhood Research and Practice, 11*(1). Retrieved from http://ecrp.uiuc.edu/v11n1/hyson.html

Irish National Teachers Organisation (INTO). (2005). *Leading early years education: Proceedings of November '05 Consultative Conference on Education.* Dublin: Author.

Katz, L. (1997). *Fostering social competence in young children: The teacher's role* Washington, DC: National Association for the Education of Young Children.

Katz, L. (2003). The right of the child to develop and learn in quality environments. *International Journal of Early Childhood, 35*(1), 13-22.

Moyles, J. (Ed.). (1995). *Beginning teaching: Beginning learning in primary education.* Buckingham: Open University Press.

Moyles, J., Adams, S. and Musgrove, A. (2002). *SPEEL: Study of pedagogical effectiveness in early learning* (Research Report No. 363). London: Department for Education and Skills.

Munn, P. (1994). The early development of literacy and numeracy skills. *European Early Childhood Education Research Journal, 2*(1), 5-18.

National Council for Curriculum and Assessment (NCCA). (2009). *Aistear: The early childhood curriculum framework.* Dublin: Author.

National Economic and Social Forum (NESF). (2005). *Early childhood care and education* (Report 31: July 2005). Dublin: Author.

Neuman, S. and Dickinson, D. (Eds.). (2011). *Handbook of early literacy research.* Vol. 3. New York: The Guilford Press.

Organisation for Economic Co-operation and Development (OECD). (2004). *OECD Thematic review of early childhood education and care policy in Ireland.* Dublin: The Stationery Office.

Pelligrini, A., Galda, L. and Dresden, J. (1991). A longitudinal study of the predictive relations among symbolic play, linguistic verbs, and early literacy. *Research in the Teaching of English*, *25*(2), 219-235.

Pianta, R., Barnett, S., Burchinal, M. and Thornburg, K. (2009). The effects of preschool education: What we know, how public policy is or is not aligned with the evidence base, and what we need to know. *Psychological Science in the Public Interest*, *10*(2), 49-88.

Rogoff, B. (1998). Cognition as a collaborative process. In W. Damon, D. Kuhn and R. Siegler (Eds.), *Handbook of child psychology: Vol 2. Cognition, perception and language* (5th ed., pp. 679-744). New York: John Wylie.

Saracho, O. and Spodek, B. (2007). Early childhood teachers' preparation and the quality of program outcomes. *Early Child Development and Care*, *177*(1), 71-91.

Siraj-Blatchford, I., Sylva, K., Muttock, S., Gilden, R. and Bell, D. (2002). *Researching effective pedagogy in the early years* (Research Report 356). London: Department for Education and Skills.

Teaching Council. (2011). *Initial teacher education: Criteria and guidelines for programme providers*. Dublin: Author.

Vygotsky, L. (1978). *Mind in society: The development of higher psychological processes*. Cambridge, MA: Harvard University Press.

Wood, E. (2010). Developing integrated pedagogical approaches to play and learning. In P. Broadhead, J. Howard and E. Wood (Eds.), *Play and learning in the early years* (pp. 9-26). London: Sage.

Section Two:

An Enduring Dynamic: Conversations between Theory and Practice

Chapter 5

Linking Practice, Theory and Person in Teacher Education[1]

Fred A.J. Korthagen
VU University, Amsterdam

Introduction

Research reveals a big theory-practice divide in teacher education programmes. Hence, doubts have surfaced concerning their effectiveness. In this chapter, I describe the so-called 'realistic approach' to teacher education, which aims at overcoming the gap between theory and practice. It shows a new direction in the pedagogy of teacher education and leads to significant conclusions about the need for careful programme design, an elaborated view of the intended process of teacher learning, specific pedagogical strategies, and a focus on the professional development of teacher educators.

Since formal teacher education came into existence, the relationship between theory and practice has remained its central problem (Lanier and Little, 1986). As psychological and pedagogical knowledge grew during the twentieth century, academics wanted to provide this knowledge to teachers in order to promote the use of scientific insights in schools. Hence, it seemed logical to teach important theories to teachers, who could then apply this knowledge base to their teaching. Following Carlson (1999), I call this the theory-to-practice approach which was often exemplified by teacher education programmes consisting of a collection of isolated theoretical courses. Clandinin (1995) refers to it as 'the sacred theory-practice story'. Wideen, Mayer-Smith and Moon (1998, p. 167) put it like this:

> ... the implicit theory underlying traditional teacher education was based on a training model in which the university provides the theory, methods and skills; the schools provide the setting in which that knowledge is practiced; and the beginning teacher provides the individual effort to apply such knowledge.

Schön (1983, p. 21) calls this the technical-rationality model and states that this model is based on the notion that 'professional activity consists in instrumental problem solving made rigorous by the application of scientific theory and technique.' In fact three basic assumptions are implicit in this view. One is that theories help teachers to perform better in their profession. Another is that these theories must be based on scientific research. Finally it suggests that teacher educators should make a choice concerning the theories to be included in teacher education programmes.

Many studies have shown that this traditional theory-to-practice approach has little influence on the practices of novice teachers. Zeichner and Tabachnick (1981), for example, found that the theories presented to student teachers during their preparation for the profession seemed to be 'washed out' as soon as they started teaching, although these authors also suspect that these theories may in fact have had little or no impact on student teachers in the first place (compare Cole and Knowles, 1993; Veenman, 1984). As a result, the impact of teacher education on students' practice is limited, as Wideen, Mayer-Smith and Moon (1998) conclude in their thorough and extensive review of the international research on the outcomes of teacher education. A similar conclusion was drawn by the American Educational Research Association (AERA) Research Panel on Teacher Education in a meta-analysis of North-American research (Cochran-Smith and Zeichner, 2005). They cite several studies that show how beginning teachers struggle for control and experience feelings of frustration, anger and bewilderment. The process they go through is more one of survival than of learning from experiences.

Realistic Teacher Education

An approach to teacher education aimed at overcoming the gap between theory and practice is the 'realistic approach', which was originally developed at Utrecht University in the Netherlands. Its key principles are formulated by Korthagen, Kessels, Koster, Lagerwerf and Wubbels (2001) as follows:

1. The approach starts from student teachers' practical experiences in authentic contexts.
2. It aims at the promotion of systematic reflection by student teachers.
3. It builds on the personal interaction between the teacher educator and the student teachers and on the interaction amongst the student teachers themselves.
4. The teacher educator adds, not so much theory with a capital 'T' (the knowledge from academic textbooks), but practical insights and guidelines that fit in with the concerns and questions of the student teachers at that moment (theory with a small 't').

Brief theoretical modules are offered only in the final part of the programme so that the student teachers also develop the ability to view learning and teaching from a theoretical stance.

The Sources of Teacher Behaviour

Why is a realistic approach to teacher education more promising than the traditional theory-to-practice model? The reason has to do with the sources of teacher behaviour.

The traditional practice of transferring theories to teachers might work if, during their teaching, these teachers were guided by their rational thinking. Nowadays we know that this is not the case. During a lesson many things happen simultaneously, and there is a continuous pressure on teachers to act. These factors make it almost impossible for teachers to be consciously aware of everything that plays a role at the moment of action (Clark and Yinger, 1979; Eraut, 1995; Schön, 1987). As a result, teachers take few conscious decisions during classroom teaching. Much teacher behaviour is what Dolk (1997) has named *immediate behaviour,* i.e., behaviour involving little reflection. Epstein (1990) states that such behaviour is mediated by the so-called *experiential system* in humans, which makes rapid information processing possible, mostly through the use of images and emotions. This experiential system is linked to physical responses and automatised processes. It functions in a holistic way, which means that the world is perceived in terms of conglomerates, in which separate entities are unified into wholes that direct one's behaviour. This often takes place subconsciously (Lazarus, 1991) and on the basis of simple fight, flight or freeze mechanisms which develop at a young age (Rothschild, 2000). Epstein's theory clarifies that there are strong interrelations between thinking, feeling and behaviour. His theory has been confirmed by brain specialists, such as Immordino-Yang and Damasio (2007), who have concluded that much of our human functioning takes place through processes in which thinking and emotions are strongly linked. They also found that we are often unaware of these links. Similar insights are discussed by Hargreaves (1998) and Korthagen (2010) in the context of teachers. The above is summarised in Figure 1. It shows that when we think about the sources of teacher behaviour, we may be inclined to focus on the upper left corner but in reality the three other areas in Figure 1 are perhaps even more important.

	Rational	**Non-rational**
Conscious		
Unconscious		

Figure 1: The Intrapersonal Sources of Teacher Behaviour

An Example of a Programme Element: The One-to-One

If we take these insights seriously, there are consequences for the way in which teacher educators work with student teachers and also for the way student teachers reflect. For example, when discussing or reflecting on practical experiences with teaching, it makes quite a difference whether the focus is solely on a rational analysis of what happened or also includes the role played by emotional and motivational aspects in the student teacher and/or the pupils. Korthagen et al. (2001) discuss such consequences for coaching and reflection and elaborate on a pedagogy of teacher education that builds on this broader view of teaching. For the purpose of the present chapter, we will now focus on one example of a programme element, namely the *one-to-one*. This makes it possible to connect the ideas described above with the concrete practice of teacher education.

The one-to-one has been developed in response to the fact that teaching a whole class on a regular basis appears to be a complex experience for beginning student teachers, an experience that tends to foster concerns related to 'survival'. This is why the first teaching period in the programme has been simplified. Each student teacher gives a one-hour lesson to one high school pupil once a week for eight weeks (key principle 1 of realistic teacher education, see above). Neither the university-based teacher educator nor the mentor teacher is present during the actual one-to-one lessons, but there are coaching sessions and seminar meetings during the one-to-one period. The lessons are audio-recorded and are subsequently the object of detailed reflection by the student teacher (key principle 2). This reflection is structured by means of the ALACT model (named after the first letters of the five phases, see Figure 2). The fifth phase is again the first phase of the next cycle, which means that the model is a spiral one: the realistic approach aims at an ongoing process of professional development.

During the one-to-one period, the student teachers form pairs. Of the eight one-to-one lessons, four are discussed by the student teachers within these pairs and four lessons are discussed by the pair and the teacher educator, thus creating a 'community of learners' (key principle 3). The teacher educator can then offer small theoretical notions fitting in with the process which the student teacher is experiencing (key principle 4). After both types of discussion, the student teacher writes a report on the most important conclusions he or she has reached.

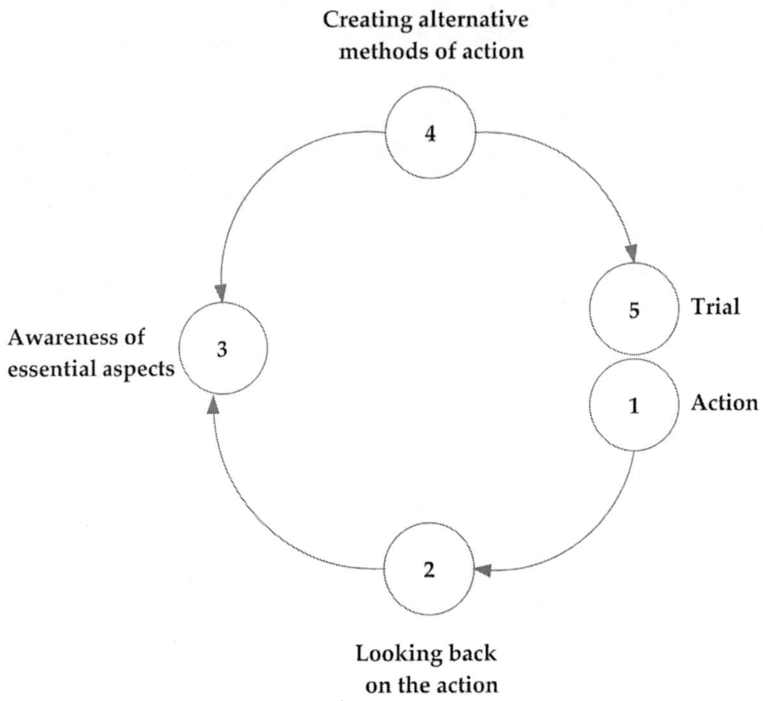

Figure 2: The ALACT Model of Reflection, Named after the First Letters of the Five Phases

A general finding is that by listening to the audio-recordings, the student teachers rapidly discover that they failed to listen to what the pupil was saying, or started an explanation before the problem was clear to the pupil. As one of our student teachers put it, 'The one-to-one caused a shift in my thinking about teaching, from a teacher perspective to a pupil perspective.' This quote is representative of the learning processes of most student teachers in the one-to-one. However, there also appear to be considerable differences between student teachers in what is learnt during such a one-to-one arrangement. To mention some examples, one student teacher focused on the lack of self-confidence in the pupil with whom she worked and started to search for ways to improve the child's self-image, while another student teacher was confronted with her own tendency to explain things at a fairly abstract level. As a consequence, she aimed to include more concrete examples in her teaching. In sum, the one-to-one gives student teachers many opportunities to learn on the basis of their own experiences and the individual concerns they develop through these experiences. They learn not so much by being taught by their teacher educators, but by structured reflection on their experiences and discussions with peers and small theoretical elements that the teacher educator links to the student teachers' experiences. In this way, the student teachers begin to reflect on their initial views of teaching and learning and often start to question these views. Of course, later in the programme student teachers teach whole classes, but the focus here is also on their individual professional growth and their personal strengths and struggles. Furthermore, their development is supported by a growing competence in self-directed learning and reflection, in other words on personal ownership of the developmental process. Hence, it is important that the student teachers learn how to use the ALACT model autonomously, which is a goal receiving continuous attention throughout the programme.

The Professional and the Personal

The ALACT model is a process model and does not say much about the possible contents of reflection. In this respect, the so-called *onion model* (Korthagen, 2004) may be helpful (Figure 3). It distinguishes between six content levels of reflection and demonstrates that an exclusive focus on competencies in teacher development is too limited.

A teacher can reflect on the environment (the first level), for example a specific class or pupil, his or her teaching behaviour (second level), or competencies (third level). The reflection starts to deepen when there is a focus on underlying beliefs (fourth level) and on how the teacher perceives his or her own (professional or personal) identity (fifth level). Finally (on the sixth level), the teacher can reflect on his or her place in the world, on his or her personal mission as a teacher. This is a transpersonal level (sometimes referred to as the level of spirituality, see e.g., Dilts, 1990), as it has to do with meanings that reach beyond the individual. It is the level that refers to the teacher's personal inspiration, to ideals, to the moral purposes of the teacher. At the deeper levels, people's personal qualities, called *core qualities*, emerge. For example, a mission to help pupils develop self-confidence is often connected to core qualities such as sensitivity, empathy and/or steadfastness. Professional learning deepens when teachers become aware of their core qualities and use them intentionally and systematically. This idea leads to a more person-oriented view of educating teachers than a mere competency-based approach, which is often based on standard lists of competencies.

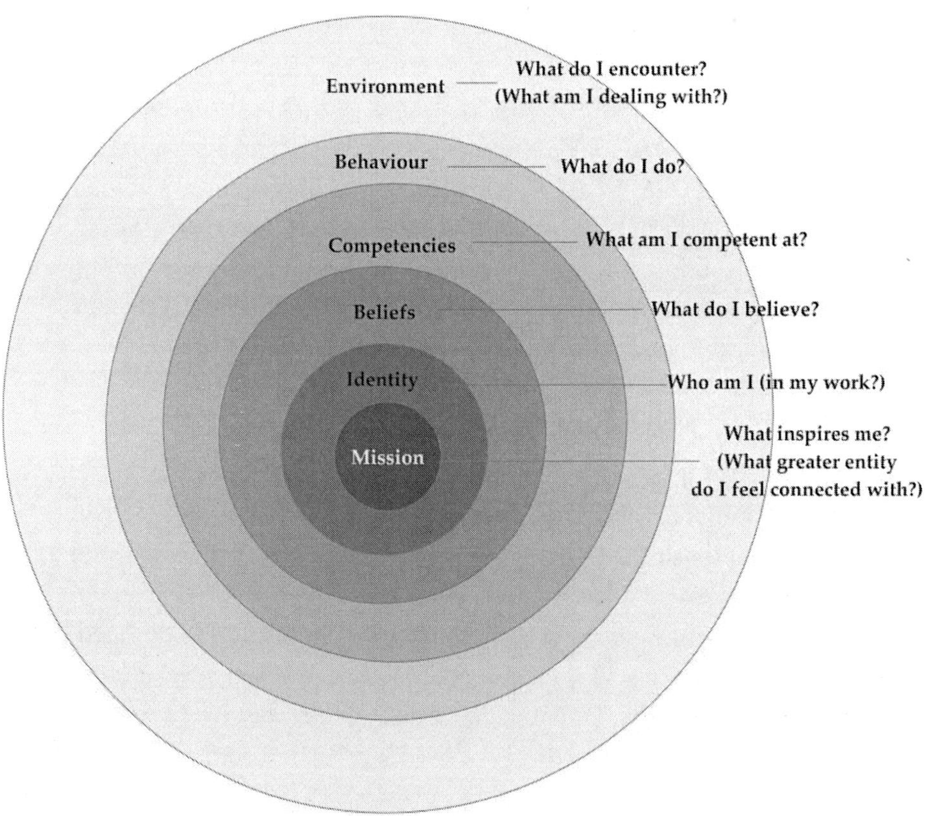

Figure 3: The Onion: A Model of Levels in Reflection

The levels of the onion model are all interrelated, and professional reflection is deepened by a search for the connection between these levels. A discrepancy between the levels (for example, a tension between one's beliefs and one's behaviour, or a felt distance between one's mission and the environment in which one is working) is experienced as a problem. Reflection on the levels can help to foster *alignment* between these levels, which is experienced as inner harmony and effectiveness. Struggles on the level of behaviour or competencies, for example, obtain a different meaning when they are considered from the point of view of one's commitment to a long-term aim on the sixth, transpersonal level, and the development of personal core qualities needed for this long-term growth process. If the levels of identity and mission are included in the reflection, we speak of *core reflection* (Korthagen, 2004; Korthagen and Vasalos, 2005), because these levels lie nearer to the core of the person, and because this kind of reflection brings people into contact with their core qualities.

Comparable with the change from a focus on the conscious and rational sources of teacher behaviour towards the other cells in Figure 1, we can now also see another change taking place. For quite a long time the attention of researchers was focused on the three or four outer levels of Figure 3, and the focus of the promotion of reflection by teachers was generally in line with this. However, there is now growing attention on the need for teacher reflection on the levels of identity and mission (e.g., Beijaard, 1995; Kelchtermans and Vandenberghe, 1994). For example, Palmer (1998, p. 10) says: 'Good teaching cannot be reduced to technique; good teaching comes from the identity and integrity of the teacher.' It is my view that this principle should change traditional practices in teacher education and that attention to the inner levels of the onion model is a prerequisite for a balanced integration of the personal and the professional in teaching. Tickle (1999, p. 136) states that 'the teacher as a person is the core by which education itself takes place', and both researchers and teacher educators increasingly acknowledge this notion.

Related to this is an interesting study by Tigchelaar, Brouwer and Korthagen (2008) into the development of second-career teachers, which showed that people who change careers and go into teaching often do this on the basis of a deepened understanding of their personal identity or a strong commitment to some personal goal. However, the study also revealed that teacher educators responsible for the education of these second-career teachers seldom ask questions about these more personal aspects. Rarely do they use them as a springboard for professional development as a teacher. In other words, the levels of identity and mission are often simply ignored, even in cases where they are of high personal importance to the student.

Many teachers choose their profession because of some deeply felt inner mission, but the personal goals and commitments of a large number of teachers seem to be frustrated by institutional pressures and by the lack of support from school leaders–and even close colleagues–to translate inner missions into concrete behaviours in specific environments. As one of the in-service teachers with whom I worked stated, 'Everyone who decides to work with people must have ideals. Everyone has that "level" inside, but at a certain moment you can decide to close the hatch.' Such a quote reveals a sad phenomenon in education. Teacher shortages have received a great deal of attention, and in many countries teacher educators are investing in specific curricula in order to attract more people into teaching. Perhaps it is no less important to support those already teaching in implementing their ideals, for research has shown that the loss of ideals and lack of support in their realisation have a great impact on the development of burnout and decisions to leave the profession. As Palmer (1998) says, finding answers to the question 'What's the sense of it all?' is not a luxury, but a necessity, if teachers are to continue to put their hearts and souls into their work. We have developed professional development courses for teacher educators and mentor teachers to support their ability to promote core reflection (Korthagen and Vasalos, 2005). Core reflection requires specific coaching competencies, but it thoroughly deepens reflection in teachers.

Empirical Support for the Realistic Approach

Contrary to many other approaches in teacher education, the realistic approach is well researched. For example, a national evaluation study of all Dutch teacher education programmes preparing for secondary education and carried out by an external research office (Luijten,

Marinus and Bal, 1995; Samson and Luijten, 1996), showed that 71 per cent of a sample of graduates of the Utrecht programme (n=81) rated their professional preparation as 'good' or 'very good'. This is a remarkable result, as, in the total sample of graduates from all Dutch teacher education programmes preparing for secondary education (n = 5135), this percentage was only 41 per cent ($p < 0.001$). In the light of the present chapter, a fundamental question is whether the realistic approach succeeds in reducing the gap between theory and practice. Several studies have focused on this more specific question. For example, an evaluative overall study among all graduates of the Utrecht University programme showed that 86 per cent of the respondents considered their preparation programme as relevant or highly relevant to their present work as a teacher (Koetsier, Wubbels and Korthagen, 1997). Hermans, Créton and Korthagen (1993) conducted an in-depth study with a group of twelve student teachers in which all the principles of realistic teacher education described above were incorporated. All twelve student teachers reported a seamless connection between theory and practice. Quotes from student teachers' evaluations include: 'The integration theory/practice to my mind was perfect'; 'Come to think of it, I have seen and/or used all of the theory in practice'; and 'The things dealt with in the course are always apparent in school practice.'

An extensive longitudinal study by Brouwer and Korthagen (2005) focused on the relationship between programme design and effects of 24 teacher education curricula in use at Utrecht University during the years in which the realistic approach was introduced. Quantitative and qualitative data were collected from 357 student teachers, 31 teacher educators and 128 mentor teachers at various moments during these programmes and during the first two years in which the graduates worked as teachers. Concrete learning effects on the work of the graduates during their first professional year (measured by means of 14 criterion variables) appeared to depend primarily on the degree to which theoretical elements in their preparation programme were perceived by the student teachers as being functional for practice during their student teaching and on the cyclical alternation between school-based and university-based periods in the programme. In addition, a gradual increase in the complexity of activities and demands on the student teachers appeared to be a crucial factor in integrating theory and practice. As far as core reflection is concerned, several studies have now been carried out that provide evidence of the strong impact of this type of reflection on teacher development. These studies are brought together in Korthagen, Kim and Greene (2013).

Implications for Teacher Education

In sum, we may conclude that teacher education can make a difference, but that this may require careful programme design based on:

- an elaborated view of the intended process of teacher learning,
- specific pedagogical strategies, and
- an investment in the professional development of the teacher educators (Korthagen, Loughran and Russell, 2006).

In the development of a programme based on the principles of realistic teacher education, each of these components may take much time and energy, especially because they require teacher educators to assume a special, and often unconventional, role. For example, they must be able to create suitable learning experiences for student teachers, which on the one hand should not trigger too many 'concerns for survival', but on the other hand should be sufficient to provoke questions and concerns that could serve as a basis for the next step. Teacher educators must also be competent at promoting further awareness and reflection by student teachers on their experiences. It is often helpful to take one concrete, recently experienced, and relatively brief teaching situation as a starting point for reflection, a situation which still evokes some concern or question in the student teachers. Furthermore, they must be able to offer theoretical notions from empirical research in such a way that these notions fit into the student teachers' reflections. The crux of 'theory with a small t' is that the student teachers start to 'perceive more' and are able to act upon this sharper perception (*pedagogical sensitivity*).

A very obvious consequence is that student teachers' needs, feelings, emotions, concerns, values and so forth, should be taken seriously as a starting point for professional development. These are certainly not only of a cognitive nature! All these teacher educator competencies imply the need for professional development and training of teacher education staff and mentor teachers, an issue often overlooked (Koster and Korthagen, 2001). This is especially the case if one wishes to deepen professional learning processes in teacher education by using core reflection.

Of course, we should realise that many teacher educators have to work with large cohort groups in which close personal coaching of student teachers is not always possible. In order to address this problem in the Utrecht programme, we have developed structural methods in which student teachers do as much of the coaching as possible *together*. This so-called *peer-supported learning* (Tigchelaar and Melief, 2000) aims at structuring the intended five-step individual reflection process about concrete teaching experiences through a series of questions, as well as promoting reflective discussion of the teaching experiences in groups of three to four student teachers. For this purpose, the student teachers are trained in coaching skills, which of course is also helpful to their work with pupils. Moreover, the small group discussion takes place according to a pre-structured format, leading to a written report on concrete issues and questions. The teacher educator can, to a large extent, react to these reports in meetings with the cohort as a whole. Apart from the fact that such a method saves staff time, it prepares student teachers for peer-supported learning in communities of practice during the rest of their careers.

Organisational Consequences

The realistic approach to teacher education has consequences both for the types of interventions teacher educators should use to promote the intended learning process in the student teachers and for the organisation of teacher education curricula. First of all, linking theory and practice with the aid of the ALACT model requires frequent alternation of school teaching days and meetings aimed at the deepening of teaching experiences. Secondly, in order to harmonise the interventions of the school-based mentor teachers and institute-based teacher educators, close cooperation between the schools and the teacher education institute is necessary, which fits in with the international trend towards school-based teacher education. Not every school may be suitable as a practicum site: the school must be able to offer a sound balance between safety and challenge and a balance between the goal of serving student teachers' learning and the interests of the school. Thirdly, the approach advocated here implies that it is impossible to make a clear distinction between different subjects in the teacher education programme. The realistic approach is not compatible with a programme structure showing separate modules such as 'subject matter methods', 'general education', 'psychology of learning', and so forth. Relevant and realistic teacher learning is grounded in concerns created during teaching experiences. Such experiences are not as fragmented as the programmes of many teacher education institutes would suggest.

Finally, a warning has to be given regarding an extreme elaboration of the realistic approach. In many programmes, the traditional approach of 'theory first, practice later' has been replaced by the adage 'practice first, theory later.' Alternative programme structures have been created in which novice teachers sometimes receive very little theoretical background, hence teacher education becomes more of a process of guided induction into the tricks of the trade. In many places in the world, this trend is also influenced by the need to solve the problem of teacher shortages. Although this development may satisfy teachers, politicians and parents, there is a great risk involved. The balance seems to shift completely from an emphasis on theory to reliance on practical experiences. Such an approach to teacher education does not, however, guarantee success. Dewey (1938, p. 25) once said that 'the belief that all genuine education comes about through experience does not mean that all experiences are genuinely or equally educative' (see also Loughran, 2006, p. 22). As already discussed above, teaching experience can be a process of socialisation into established patterns of practice, rather than an opportunity for professional development (e.g., Wideen, Mayer-Smith and Moon, 1998). Hence, there is a risk that in a 'practice first approach' the basic question, namely *how to integrate theory and practice*, will still not be solved. There is sufficient evidence that in this respect, the realistic approach provides a fruitful new direction, which may lead to a new view on the goals and practices of teacher education worldwide.

Endnotes

[1] This chapter is an adapted version of the following publication: Korthagen, F.A.J. (2010). How teacher education can make a difference. *Journal of Education for Teaching*, 36(4), 407-423.

References

Beijaard, D. (1995). Teachers' prior experiences and actual perceptions of professional identity. *Teachers and Teaching: Theory and Practice, 1*(2), 281-294.

Brouwer, N. and Korthagen, F. (2005). Can teacher education make a difference? *American Educational Research Journal, 42*(1), 153-224.

Carlson, H. L. (1999). From practice to theory: A social constructivist approach to teacher education. *Teachers and Teaching: Theory and Practice, 5*(2), 203-218.

Clandinin, D.J. (1995). Still learning to teach. In T. Russell and F. Korthagen (Eds.), *Teachers who teach teachers* (pp. 25-31). London/Washington: Falmer Press.

Clark, C. M. and Yinger, R.J. (1979). Teachers' thinking. In P. L. Peterson and H. J. Walberg (Eds.), *Research on teaching: Concepts, findings and implications* (pp. 231-263). Berkeley, CA: McCutchan.

Cochran-Smith, M. and Zeichner, K.M. (Eds.). (2005). *Studying teacher education: The report of the Panel on Research and Teacher Education.* Washington, DC: American Educational Research Association/Mahwah: Erlbaum.

Cole, A.L. and Knowles, J. G. (1993). Teacher development partnership research: A focus on methods and issues. *American Educational Research Journal, 30*(3), 473-495.

Dewey, J. (1938). *Experience and education.* New York: Macmillan.

Dilts, R. (1990). *Changing belief systems with NLP.* Cupertino: Meta Publications.

Dolk, M. (1997). *Onmiddellijk onderwijsgedrag* [Immediate teaching behaviour]. Utrecht: WCC.

Epstein, S. (1990). Cognitive-experiential self-theory. In L.A. Pervin (Ed.), *Handbook of personality, theory and research* (pp. 165-192). New York: The Guilford Press.

Eraut, M. (1995). Schön shock: A case for reframing reflection-in-action? *Teachers and Teaching: Theory and Practice, 1*(1), 9-22.

Hargreaves, A. (1998). The emotional practice of teaching. *Teaching and Teacher Education, 14*(8), 835-854.

Hermans, J.J., Créton, H.A. and Korthagen, F.A.J. (1993). Reducing the gap between theory and practice in teacher education. In J.T. Voorbach (Ed.), *Teacher Education 9: Research and developments on teacher education in the Netherlands* (pp. 111-120). De Lier: Academisch Boeken Centrum.

Immordino-Yang, M.H. and Damasio, A. (2007). We feel, therefore we learn: The relevance of affective and social neuroscience to education. *Mind, Brain and Education, 1*(1), 3-10.

Kelchtermans, G. and Vandenberghe, R. (1994). Teachers' professional development: A biographical perspective. *Journal of Curriculum Studies, 26*, 45-62.

Koetsier, C.P., Wubbels, Th. and Korthagen, F.A.J. (1997). Learning from practice: The case of a Dutch postgraduate teacher education programme. In M.I. Fuller and A.J. Rosie (Eds.), *Teacher education and school partnerships* (pp. 113-132). New York, NY: Edwin Mellen Press.

Korthagen, F.A.J. (2004). In search of the essence of a good teacher: Towards a more holistic approach in teacher education. *Teaching and Teacher Education, 20*(1), 77-97.

Korthagen, F. (2010). Situated learning theory and the pedagogy of teacher education: Towards an integrative view of teacher behavior and teacher learning. *Teaching and Teacher Education, 26*, 98-106.

Korthagen, F.A.J., Kessels, J., Koster, B., Lagerwerf, B. and Wubbels, T. (2001). *Linking practice and theory: The pedagogy of realistic teacher education.* Mahwah, NJ: Lawrence Erlbaum Associates.

Korthagen, F.A.J., Kim, Y.M. and Greene, W.L. (2013). *Teaching and learning from within: A core reflection approach to quality and inspiration in education.* New York/London: Routledge.

Korthagen, F., Loughran, J. and Russell, T. (2006). Developing fundamental principles for teacher education programs and practices. *Teaching and Teacher Education, 22*(8), 1020-1041.

Korthagen, F. and Vasalos, A. (2005). Levels in reflection: Core reflection as a means to enhance professional development. *Teachers and Teaching: Theory and Practice, 11*(1). 47-71.

Koster, B. and Korthagen, F. (2001). Training teacher educators for the realistic approach. In F.A.J. Korthagen, J. Kessels, B. Koster, B. Lagerwerf and T. Wubbels, *Linking practice and theory: The pedagogy of realistic teacher education* (pp. 239-253). Mahwah: Lawrence Erlbaum Associates.

Lanier, J. and Little, J.W. (1986). Research in teacher education. In M.C. Wittrock (Ed.), *Handbook of research on teaching* (3rd ed) (pp. 527–560). New York: MacMillan.

Lazarus, R.S. (1991). *Emotion and adaptation.* New York/Oxford: Oxford University Press.

Loughran, J. (2006). *Developing a pedagogy of teacher education.* London: Routledge.

Luijten, M.C.G., Marinus, J.E. and Bal, J.M. (1995). *Wie gaat er in het onderwijs werken?* [Who is going to work in education?]. Leiden: Research for Beleid.

Palmer, P. J. (1998). *The courage to teach.* San Francisco: Jossey-Bass.

Rothschild, B. (2000). *The body remembers: The psychophysiology of trauma and trauma treatment.* New York: Norton and Co.

Samson, L. and Luijten, R. (1996). *Wie gaat er in het onderwijs werken?* [Who is going to work in education?] (part of the report specifically focusing on the Utrecht programme). Leiden: Research voor Beleid.

Schön, D.A. (1983). *The reflective practitioner: How professionals think in action.* New York: Basic Books.

Schön, D. A. (1987). *Educating the reflective practitioner.* San Francisco, CA: Jossey-Bass.

Tickle, L. (1999). Teacher self-appraisal and appraisal of self. In R.P. Lipka and T.M. Brinthaupt (Eds.), *The role of self in teacher development* (pp. 121-141). Albany, NY: State University of New York Press.

Tigchelaar, A., Brouwer, N. and Korthagen, F. (2008). Crossing horizons: Continuity and change during second-career teachers' entry into teaching. *Teaching and Teacher Education, 24*, 1530-1550.

Tigchelaar, A. and Melief, K. (2000). Peer supported learning for students on paid practice: Student teachers learn to supervise one another. In G.M. Willems, J.H.J. Stakenborg and W. Veugelers (Eds.), *Trends in Dutch teacher education* (pp. 185-195). Apeldoorn/Leuven: Garant.

Veenman, S. (1984). Perceived problems of beginning teachers. *Review of Educational research, 54*(2), 143-178.

Wideen, M. Mayer-Smith, J. and Moon, B. (1998). A critical analysis of the research on learning to teach: Making the case for an ecological perspective on inquiry. *Review of Educational Research, 68*, 130–178.

Zeichner, K. and Tabachnik, B.R. (1981). Are the effects of university teacher education washed out by school experiences? *Journal of Teacher Education, 32*, 7-11.

Chapter 6

Constructivism Made Visible in Contingency: Learning to Teach Mathematics in a Community of Practice

Dolores Corcoran
St Patrick's College, Drumcondra

Introduction

Constructivism has come to be widely accepted as a grand theory of human learning (Cobb et al., 2003). It is based on the principle that 'learning is not a passive receiving of ready-made knowledge but a process of construction in which the students themselves have to be the primary actors' (Glasersfeld, 1995, p. 120). As an epistemology, constructivism constitutes 'a framework within which to address situations of complexity, uniqueness and uncertainty and to transform them into potentially solvable problems' (Cobb, Wood and Yackel, 1991). These scholars argue that the value of constructivism as a theory in the field of mathematics education depends on whether 'this way of sense making, of problem posing and problem solving, contributes to the improvement of mathematics teaching and learning in typical classrooms with characteristic teachers' (pp. 157-8).

In this chapter I propose to focus on constructivism in the service of mathematics teacher development and suggest that in the existing initial teacher education (ITE) context, while student teachers are exposed to various propositions of constructivism in their studies, these may be difficult to conceptualise in practice since student teachers rarely get an opportunity to 'see' constructivism in action in classrooms. An analytical framework known as the Knowledge Quartet (KQ) can be used to highlight the various dimensions along which the mathematical knowledge of the teacher impacts the lesson. Fourth among the KQ dimensions is contingency which identifies practitioners' ability to think on their feet when lessons do not go according to plan. I will develop here the notion that contingency moments are important sites of learning for student teachers and others and they are to be welcomed for the insights they give into pupils' construction of mathematical ideas.

Mathematics teaching has long been recognised as complex and 'different' because of the dual nature of mathematics itself: its deep conceptual structures (the content of mathematics); and the surface structures (form) – the words and symbols used to communicate content (Skemp, 1982). Commenting on this special characteristic of mathematics education, Steinbring (1998) contends that the relationship between the words and symbols and the ideas they represent is 'subject to developments and changes' (p.162) as learners progress with 'making meaning' of the mathematical concepts and procedures they meet in school. It is intended that mathematics education should lead to students 'constructing' increasingly connected networks of mathematical ideas which they can apply in different problem situations.

This notion of learning mathematics resonates with Piaget's key idea of learning as a cyclical process of assimilation and accommodation (Block, 1982). It also has a strong sociocultural provenance, based on Vygotsky's notions of spontaneous and scientific concepts and the process of internalisation, which originate in and are supported by social interaction (Rogoff, 1990). Constructivism is always associated with a reform agenda, since 'constructivist theories focus on the processes by which learners build their own mental structures when interacting with an environment' (Wenger, 1998, p. 279) and applies to all participants in the learning community, pupils and teachers alike. Constructivist theories of learning form the basis of many teacher education foundation courses, and student teachers, when they engage in teaching practice, are offered 'situated learning' opportunities to bridge the theory/practice divide. However, these constructivist processes may be difficult to instantiate in classroom settings where student teachers are learning to forge an identity as teacher. A theory of constructivism, whether active or passive, describes internal activity on the part of the learner, and the direction and depth of this learning may go unnoticed by the teacher (Anthony, 1996). The contingency dimension, however, occurs at the interface between teaching and learning and has the potential to allow the teacher an insight into how concepts are being constructed by learners. An awareness of contingency moments in teaching would help to maximise the opportunities for learning about mathematics teaching afforded by classroom practice.

Constructivism in the Irish Primary School Curriculum

Reform approaches to teaching mathematics in Ireland were introduced in the 1999 Primary School Curriculum. Constructivism is central to the preamble to the mathematics curriculum documents (National Council for Curriculum and Assessment (NCCA), 1999a, 1999b) but is undermined somewhat by the technical approach taken to layout of content objectives. In addition, constructivist notions concerning the processes of communication and learning, the nature of information and knowledge, and interaction with others, were telescoped in Irish curricular terms into an 'emphasis on talk and discussion' (Primary Curriculum Support Programme (PCSP), 2012). This appears to have created interpretive challenges for teachers because, as Glasersfeld (1995) points out, in order to adopt a constructivist way of thinking, certain key concepts underlying educational practice need to be radically refashioned. Such refashioning appears to have been largely rhetorical in terms of primary mathematics teaching.

Teaching to develop mathematical thinking skills implies a huge change of classroom culture, a change of classroom organisation, and ultimately a change of understanding of what it means to do mathematics as pupil and as teacher. However, the curriculum appears to have had little impact on Irish classrooms. Concern about the manner in which certain aspects of the mathematics curriculum are implemented is never far from the surface and has resulted in policy changes concerning the teaching of mathematics at first and second level and in teacher education (Shiel et al., 2006; Eivers et al., 2010; Department of Education and Skills (DES), 2011). Eivers et al., (2010) refer particularly to constructivism being insufficiently understood by practicing primary mathematics teachers.

Theoretical Framework: The Knowledge Quartet

The Knowledge Quartet (KQ) highlights the various dimensions along which the mathematical content knowledge of the teacher impacts a lesson (Rowland, Huckstep, and Thwaites, 2005). The four dimensions of the KQ, grounded in the study of mathematics teaching, were devised in a linear fashion with the *foundation* dimension – that which is learned primarily in the teacher education institution – believed to form the basis for the next two dimensions; *transformation*, the teachers' choices by which the mathematics to be taught is made available to learners; and *connection*, the manner by which mathematical ideas are synthesised into a coherent curricular whole. Fourth among the KQ dimensions is *contingency*, which demonstrates practitioners' ability to think on their feet when lessons do not go according to plan. Each of the four superordinate dimensions of the KQ has arisen from a systematic observation and video recording of mathematics lessons and is based on multiple contributory codes.

The Contingency Dimension

The contingency dimension was initially identified with three indicative codes: responding to students' ideas; the use of unplanned-for opportunities; and teacher's deviation from the lesson agenda. Further research has added two more codes: teacher insight, and responding to the (un)availability of tools and resources (Rowland, Thwaites, and Jared, 2011). This research has illustrated three types of situations or events that can act as triggers for contingency moments in teaching. These triggers may be the students in the classroom, the teacher him/herself, or pedagogical tools and resources. Turner (2009), in her study of pre-service and beginning teachers, found that when participants' reflection was directed post hoc towards their contingent actions, they were afforded opportunities for development of mathematical content knowledge for teaching. I wish to develop the notion that contingency opportunities during mathematics lessons – particularly in response to students' ideas – are important sites of learning for student teachers, both in-the-moment and in retrospect, which are to be welcomed for the insights they give into pupils' construction of mathematical ideas. Likewise, they are important sites of learning for the researchers and teacher educators who analyse them.

The Studies

This premise arises from two studies, one conducted with student teachers (2006/07) and one conducted with practising teachers (2010/11). The first arose through engagement in a community of practice with student teachers who took an education elective course called *Learning to Teach Mathematics Using Lesson Study* (Corcoran and Pepperell, 2011). My research question in that instance concerned how student teachers' mathematical knowledge for teaching could be developed. To seek answers, six third year Bachelor of Education students and I, as course tutor, engaged in lesson study – a deceptively simple protocol that has been found to influence personal and communal learning in sophisticated ways (Hart, Alston, and Murata, 2011). The Knowledge Quartet (KQ), with its initial eighteen contributory codes, was introduced to the student teachers as a shared language to talk about mathematics teaching. During the practice of lesson study, student teachers began to focus on children's responses to the mathematics lessons they had planned and taught. From these contingent moments, their attention moved towards the connection and transformation dimensions of their teaching. While concentrating on connection opportunities in a lesson, transformation issues were raised and vice versa. Thus, since mathematics teaching is a dynamic sociocultural pursuit, the above three dimensions of the KQ could be said to arise from, be informed by, and in turn, crucially transform, the primary dimension – teachers' foundation knowledge for teaching mathematics. This foundation knowledge includes mathematical content knowledge, theoretical underpinnings of pedagogy, and beliefs about mathematics teaching and learning.

The first contingency scenario comes from the lesson study research. The next two scenarios are taken from a study of the use of Realistic Mathematics (RME) materials. The research questions in the second study related to the impact of RME curriculum materials on classroom practices and children's learning and the support needs of teachers implementing the RME curriculum materials (Corcoran and Moffett, 2011). Each of nine lessons was observed and video-recorded. Immediately afterwards, I wrote a brief descriptive synopsis of the lesson. The lessons were later transcribed and converted to DVD. In the scenarios discussed in this chapter, the participants each engaged with others in a community of practice to discuss and review the lessons. These post-lesson review sessions were audio-recorded. I now offer three instances where there was potential to 'see' children constructing mathematical ideas in the classroom. Each was handled differently by the teacher.

Contingency Scenario 1: Finola's Lesson on Weight

Finola opted to participate in the *Learning to Teach Mathematics Using Lesson Study* elective course. She acknowledged her negative relationship with mathematics and was anxious to change that in order to become a better teacher of mathematics. The lesson in which this contingency scenario arose was one of two on the topic of weight which had been prepared collaboratively by the lesson study group. It was taught on a 'dive-in' basis in a school near the college where the principal and class teacher had agreed to allow the visiting student teachers to teach and observe a 'research lesson.' Written parental and pupil consent had been sought to video record the lesson for educational research purposes. Finola volunteered to teach the research lesson and, as this was the first lesson study cycle, she was understandably nervous. As a designated disadvantaged school with low pupil-teacher ratios, there were fewer than twenty 9/10-year-old children present in the classroom. During the planning phase, Finola had expressed a broad goal for the lesson which was that children would know 'What is a kilogramme? How does it feel? How heavy is it?' In line with a sound pedagogical principle in relation to teaching measurement – focus on the attribute – the lesson plan commenced with the recommended weight of school bags as an introductory problem. Finola's opening of the mathematics lesson was invitational:

> *Finola*: This morning, I'm going to start by giving you a problem, so today, you, we really have to think and try and sort this problem out. It's about school bags, now. (Here, she put both hands out in front of her in a balancing gesture.) Your school bag should be, it should be about three and a half kilogrammes. Now it's, so that's supposed to be what your school bag should be. That's about one tenth of your body weight. It shouldn't be any heavier than that. Do you think that's, how heavy do you think? Mmm. Do you think that means your school bag should be heavy or what weight your schoolbag should be?
>
> *Child*: It should be only about a quarter of your weight.
>
> *Finola*: One tenth of your body weight. OK. A quarter of your body weight. OK. But we'll see, because that's what we have to think about today.

The child's interjection that it 'should be only about a quarter of your weight' shows how Finola's introductory problem engaged this boy's attention and provided a classic contingency opportunity. Her lesson was planned to explore weight from the Measures strand of the curriculum. However, fractions are an important element of the Number strand on the fourth class mathematics curriculum and integral to measurement activities. Finola had focused on weight by introducing the idea that a school bag should typically be 3.5 kilogrammes and flagged that as being 'about a tenth of your body weight'. In this contingency moment the child challenged what Finola had said, offering the fractional relationship of 'about a quarter of your body weight.' Finola might have questioned his understanding of a quarter or of his body weight, or she might have invited him to consider and compare the relative values of a quarter and a tenth. Instead, Finola stayed with her prepared lesson plan and asked other children, 'So how heavy do you think you are and how heavy then is your school bag?'

I conclude from this lesson transcript that the question relating to the weight of school bags which children were invited to investigate was introduced merely as a 'faux' problem to catch the attention of the class and focus it on the topic of weight. Whatever her intentions, the mathematical potential of the problem context was not realised in the introductory phase of the lesson because Finola did not pursue the child's suggestion. It is not unreasonable to suppose that she was prepared for questions and comments relating to 'about 3.5 kilogrammes' as the weight of a school bag and the ten times greater 'about 35 kilogrammes' as the body weight of a child in fourth class. She appeared nonplussed by the unexpected mention of a quarter and moved quickly to the planned weighing and benchmarking exercises. Thus, by failing to respond to this child's idea about a quarter as opposed to a tenth of his body weight, Finola lost an opportunity to 'see' the child constructing fraction concepts and a potentially valuable teaching moment may have been lost.

Contingency Scenario 2: Phoebe's Lesson on a Ratio Table

The next two scenarios occurred in lessons taught by teachers, each with more than 5 years' experience. Phoebe and Liam were teacher participants who were engaged in teaching a series of lessons on fractions from a Mathematics in Context (MiC) textbook, *Some of the Parts* (Van Galen et al., 2006). In Phoebe's case, I observed and recorded her teaching three of these lessons and in Liam's case, four. The lesson plans were outlined in some detail in the *Teacher's Guide* (Webb et al., 2006) and had been discussed with the teachers in advance of their being taught to children aged 10/11 years, in mainstream classes matched for socioeconomic status and school size.

The context for Phoebe's lesson was a recipe for eight servings of Chicken and Tortilla Casserole. A ratio table was provided and children were asked to complete the table for four and then two servings. In the *Teacher's Guide* she was advised to '...bring students to the board or overhead and have them share how they found half of half and a half of a third' and to have them 'draw pictures to explain their reasoning' (ibid., p. 21).

Figure 1. Chicken and Tortilla Casserole Recipe

Number of Servings	8		
Number of Chicken Breast Halves	8		
Jars (1 lb) of Salsa	1		
Cups of Light Sour Cream	1		
Cups of Half-and-Half	1/2		
Number of Tortillas	12		
Cups of Shredded Cheddar Cheese	4		
Cups of Grated Parmesan Cheese	1/3		

As children were working in pairs to fill in an activity sheet (see Figure 1), Phoebe drew the ratio table on the board and then invited individual children to fill in the amounts of ingredients required in the appropriate columns. Phoebe encouraged children to justify why they each wrote a particular amount and the filling of the table progressed steadily and without apparent difficulty on any pupil's part. The contingency moment arose at Turn 3 of the following transcript when a girl was called to fill in the last amount in the third column (a half of one sixth or a quarter of one third). The excerpt begins where the fourth row of the third column had been filled correctly.

> *Teacher*: [Turn 1] So you have gone from a half to a quarter to an eighth. Are you all happy with an eighth? Again, an eighth being half of a quarter. Don't be shy, don't be afraid to say to the class when you come up how come this number is happening. OK. *The next two amounts were entered by pupils and justified as 'three is half of six' and 'one is half of two'.*

Teacher: [Turn 2] And now the cup of Parmesan? Zita.
Zita (incorrectly) entered a ninth in the third column as half of a sixth.

Zita: [Turn 3] One ninth.

Teacher: [Turn 4] So ... *(moving to stand beside Zita)*

Zita: [Turn 5] You just halve the sixth.

Teacher: [Turn 6] So think, so if you halve the sixth and you get half of that ... *Zita erased the nine and (correctly) entered a twelfth as half of a sixth.*

Teacher: [Turn 7] Good. Lovely. Are you happy with that?

I perceived Zita's writing of a ninth as a contingency moment where Phoebe could have probed the thinking that led to applying a third, sixth, ninth pattern instead of the expected third, sixth, twelfth. It appears that Zita was attempting to follow the previous pattern of fractions she had noticed on the table – that is half, quarter, eighth – without understanding its significance. Zita might have benefited from having acknowledged the fact that in a ninth, she had found a third of a third rather than half of a sixth. Had Phoebe responded to her initial idea by probing where the answer of a ninth had come from, then Zita – and those of her classmates who may well have thought as she did – would have been afforded an opportunity to explain her reasoning and thus explore the different meanings of the two sequences, as she constructed conceptual understanding of division by two as multiplication by a half.

Contingency Scenario 3: Liam's Lesson on the Ratio Table

Liam also taught the Chicken and Tortilla Casserole lesson (Van Galen et al., 2006) and it was while watching his lesson unfold that I became aware of the potential for 'seeing' constructivism in action as children were encouraged to verbalise their reasoning and reflect and comment on their solution processes. The following transcript concerns Liam questioning children as he observed them work at filling in the ratio table for two servings. There were numerous contingency opportunities in this lesson where I became aware of the 'unveiling' of children's construction of mathematical ideas. The contingency moment I wish to discuss here occurred at Turns 8 and 9.

> *Teacher*: [Turn 1] Dermot, you've come up with a little, you've seen a pattern, you were telling me. Do you want to explain to us what the pattern was? Go on, what was the pattern you came up with?
>
> *Dermot*: [Turn 2] Add the, well, six and six is twelve so twelve is there at the bottom.
>
> *Teacher*: [Turn 3] So it was a sixth for one measurement so you've just added six onto the bottom and you get a twelfth. Was there any other one like that?
>
> *Dermot*: [Turn 4] There was one quarter.
>
> *Teacher*: [Turn 5] And you added four to get half that. You were just doubling the bottom number really weren't you? Did anybody else notice that?
>
> *Chorus*: [Turn 6] Yeh (*hands went up around the room*).
>
> *Teacher*: [Turn 7] So is everyone happy with that? Yeah, Amy? (*to girl with a perplexed expression*)
>
> *Amy*: [Turn 8] Do you know what Dermot said, I think this might be the same as what he said, I didn't really get that, but three and three is six, that means there's two threes in a sixth. That means there's two sixths in a third. Is that what he was saying?
>
> *Teacher*: [Turn 9] Say that again Amy.
>
> *Amy*: [Turn 10] You know in your number thing (*holding up the activity sheet*), there's two threes in a six, so there's two sixths in a third isn't there?
>
> *Teacher*: [Turn 11] Yes, there's a pattern there, you've seen a pattern developing.

This piece of transcript is interesting for a number of reasons. Other researchers might look to the face-saving speech on Amy's part (Turn 8), where she draws attention to Dermot's idea while protecting herself by declaring that she 'didn't really get that.' Such vague language is characteristic of evolving mathematical thinking, documented by Dooley (2011), where, given rich mathematical tasks, classmates build on each other's ideas in whole-class conversation. Earlier in the same lesson, there had been an acknowledgement of pattern spotting when Liam had questioned Joe about the number of cups of 'half-and-half' for four servings.

> *Teacher*: How do you find out what a half of a half is? Anyone able to help me there?
>
> *Donal*: A quarter.
>
> *Teacher*: How did you know it was a quarter?
>
> *Donal*: Because if, I don't know, I just came up with it.
>
> *Teacher*: Joe, how did you come up with it?
>
> *Joe*: I was just looking at the sheet and if you go two quarters make a half, but if you were to halve a half you get a quarter.

No further comment was made on this way of working at the time, but it may well have influenced the thinking of Dermot and Amy. Liam appeared to regard Donal's first answer of 'a quarter' as a contingency opportunity but his 'How did you know?' question did not appear to yield a productive result. He then turned to Joe for further detail and appeared satisfied with the answer. Observing this lesson I became aware that an unusual classroom dynamic appeared to be at work here. Children appeared to be thinking out loud and the pace was such that, while the lesson was structured by the mathematical material being presented – recommended problem questions from the *Some of the Parts* textbook – the classroom culture appeared to be investigative. Contingency moments kept cropping up, articulation of children's ideas was invited, and Liam appeared to respond to each contribution in an inquiring non-evaluative manner.

Discussion of the Three Scenarios

These three scenarios occurred in Irish classrooms where constructivism as a theory of learning mathematics is explicit in the curriculum. There is no claim to evaluate the lessons. Rather, my interest is in highlighting the potential for 'seeing' children's thinking inherent in contingency opportunities. A crosscutting feature of the three scenarios is that children are responding to the lesson, as orchestrated by the teacher, in unexpected and unplanned for ways. In Finola's case she was nonplussed and appeared torn between acknowledging and ignoring the child's suggestion. It might be supposed that because Finola was a student teacher she could not be expected to be aware of contingency opportunities. Such facility might come with experience. Phoebe, however, was an experienced teacher, and her response to a contingency moment appeared to be embarrassment for the girl making the error, which 'mistake' Phoebe quickly sought to correct. In each case, there was 'affect' or emotions and 'identity work' at play in these classrooms (Mendick, 2006). In Finola's class, the boy may have wondered why his suggestion had been ignored. He may have felt frustrated that his interest in fractions, which the problem had piqued, was not pursued. He may have felt disempowered in that this mathematical problem appeared opaque and impenetrable. The data do not tell us what he was feeling but we might conclude that the incident may not have been a positive experience for him. Finola, as co-researcher in the lesson study community of practice, reflecting later on this scenario, resolved to acquire the teaching knowledge and skills necessary to equip her to deal more productively with contingency opportunities in future.

The data do not tell us about 'emotions' in Phoebe's classroom either. We do not know how Zita actually felt, but she may have sensed the teacher's unease at her performance. She may have been embarrassed to have been seen to have been publicly 'wrong' without discovering how or why. The contingency dimension of the KQ initially sought to pinpoint the teacher's mathematical knowledge-in-action, with researcher learning occurring according to how these situations were handled and potential for improvement of teaching by reflecting on the event in retrospect. None of these lessons was analysed from a discourse perspective (Wells, 2007), nor does the KQ framework include an 'affect' code, yet this study suggests that the contingency dimension of mathematics lessons is an emotional tightrope, and since contingency moments can occur at any time then the teaching of mathematics is always an emotional space. This fact may be implicit in the first 'aim' listed for primary mathematics teaching, namely, 'to develop a positive attitude towards mathematic and an appreciation of both its practical and its aesthetic aspects' (NCCA, 1999a, p. 12). Contingency moments are opportunities to fulfil this aim, either positively or negatively.

In Liam's classroom and in contrast to the other two lessons, the mathematics might be said to belong to the children rather than the teacher, with a potential increase in positive attitudes to mathematics. All three participants were teaching problem-based lessons. Both Phoebe and Liam were following the same lesson plan but only Liam appeared to be engaged in 'exploratory teaching' (Steffe and Thompson, 2000, p. 274). The concept of exploratory teaching is a prerequisite of a teaching experiment where the learners' mathematical thinking is the object of study (Dooley, 2011). When conducting a teaching experiment, it is also recognised that the researchers, both teacher and observer(s), are learning about teaching mathematics from different vantage points, and consequently different learning opportunities are available to each (Steffe and Thompson, 2000). It was while observing this lesson that I became aware for the first time that I was actually 'seeing' children 'constructing' mathematical ideas. I have been involved as researcher in lesson study for a number of years and heretofore I was interested in contingency moments only for the challenges they present to teachers.

Lesson study, with its collaborative preparation and review phases and its teaching and observation of the 'research lesson', also constitutes a form of teaching experiment with research potential for all participants. This includes opportunities for children to learn from each other's ideas as articulated in class but also to become conscious and cognisant of their own thinking processes as they strive to construct meaning in mathematical situations. Such awareness involves knowledge about one's cognitive functioning and knowledge about one's motivation and emotions. Awareness of self in relation to mathematical learning and problem solving is part of the 'mathematical disposition' which good mathematics teaching strives to engender (DeCorte, 2004). How contingency opportunities are handled can influence this growth in self-awareness.

Conclusion

The Irish primary mathematics curriculum lists the communication and expression of mathematical ideas, processes and results in oral and written form as one of the six mathematics skills to be developed through the teaching of content (NCCA, 1999a, pp. 38; 62; 86). A superficial interpretation of this would be to value only the communication of fully formed, correct mathematical ideas. Too often the teacher is the arbiter of these and, where the communication of mathematical ideas is encouraged, it is most often in a teacher-centred 'explanation, invitation, response, evaluation (EIRE)' format (Nic Mhuirí, 2011). In this chapter I argue for another way of teaching mathematics. By recognising children's contributions to lessons as opportunities for learning about their thinking in a non-evaluative manner, the teacher is setting the scene for future teaching. Glasersfeld (1995) has given the term 'conceptual analysis' to the process of looking behind what students say and do. To engage in conceptual analysis, the teacher needs to build an understanding of possible meanings that lie behind students' language and actions (Steffe and Thompson, 2000, p. 277). Advocating a framework for orchestrating mathematical discussions in classrooms, Stein et al., (2008) propose the anticipation and monitoring of students' responses as a prerequisite for fostering productive mathematical talk. An important starting point for mathematics teacher development might be that student teachers learn first to recognise, then come to welcome, unexpected contingency opportunities as zones of actual construction of mathematical ideas by the participating pupils.

Schön's (1983) metaphor of the swamp for professional practice has been invoked when discussing constructivism in terms of mathematics teaching (Cobb, Wood, and Yackel, 1991). Much as theorists might wish to drain the swamp, the reality of practice remains 'messy' and both reflection-in-action and reflection-on-action are called for as beginning teachers – and their more experienced colleagues – grapple with the highly complex task of anticipating and responding to children's embryonic mathematical ideas. The KQ has proven useful in framing analysis of lessons and as part of the shared repertoire for discussing the analysis of teaching. The KQ is also useful to student teachers in thinking about planning for teaching and in reflecting on lessons taught or observed. Were it to remain a 'reification' (Wenger, 1998), its eighteen contributory codes could become a sterile checklist and its value would be limited to the different interpretations taken from each code by parties using it. In order to vivify any dimension of the KQ, student teachers need to negotiate the meaning in practice. This contention places strong emphasis on the need for teacher preparation to pay greater attention to the utterances and gestures integral to the practice of mathematics teaching. It requires that 'clinical practice' of mathematics teaching becomes central to teacher education (Grossman, Hammerness and McDonald, 2009). It presupposes not just the collation by teacher educators of numerous contingency opportunities as 'cases' for study (Shulman, 1986) but the sustained immersion of student teachers in mathematics learning communities (Hufferd-Ackles, Fuson and Sherin, 2004). When studying teaching in practice, the contingency dimension of the KQ offers opportunities to foster the collective development of mathematical knowledge. Engagement with responding to children's ideas enriches the personal knowledge base on which individual teachers draw in developing practice. The ephemeral nature of any lesson has been documented (Lewis and Tsuchida, 1998), and collaborative in-depth study of research lessons through lesson study has been offered as a means by which teachers can engage meaningfully and productively with enhancing their mathematics teaching (Fernandez, 2005).

This research confirms that the practice of collectively studying teaching with an openness to addressing contingency opportunities affords teachers and co-researchers an invaluable insight into how children are learning and to their thought processes as they construct and connect mathematical ideas in classroom settings. I have come to view mathematical knowledge for teaching primary mathematics in new ways and, in consequence, think differently about how mathematical knowledge can be developed or stifled by classroom experiences. As a result of studying how best to prepare people for professional practice, a call has been made to 'make teaching public' (Shulman, 2005). This challenge gets to the heart of teacher education where researchers have been asking what are the 'core practices' that student teachers and teacher educators need to learn. Participation in a community of practice dedicated to learning about how children's mathematical thinking gives rise to unexpected contingency moments during lessons would be a useful place to start. Such opportunities frequently occur in primary classrooms and constitute invaluable learning opportunities for teachers who are willing to embrace them.

References

Anthony, G. (1996). Active learning in a constructivist framework. *Educational Studies in Mathematics, 31*(4), 349-369.

Block, J. (1982). Assimilation, accommodation, and the dynamics of personality development. *Child Development, (53)2,* 281-295.

Cobb, P., Confrey, J., diSessa, A., Lehrer, R. and Schauble, L. (2003). Design experiments in educational research, *Educational Researcher, 32* (1), 9-13.

Cobb. P., Wood, T. and Yackel. E. (1991). A constructivist approach to second grade mathematics. In E. von Glasersfeld (Ed.), *Radical constructivism in mathematics education* (pp. 157-176). Dordrecht: Kluwer.

Corcoran, D. and Moffett, P. (2011). Fractions in context: The use of ratio tables to develop understanding of fractions in two different school systems. In C. Smith (Ed.), *Proceedings of the British Society for Research into Learning Mathematics, 31*(1), pp. 23-28.

Corcoran, D. and Pepperell, S. (2011). Learning to teach mathematics using lesson study. In T. Rowland and K. Ruthven (Eds.), *Mathematical knowledge in teaching*. London: Springer.

De Corte, E. (2004). Mainstreams and perspectives in research on learning (mathematics) from instruction. *Applied Psychology: An International Review, 53*(2), 279-310.

Department of Education and Skills (DES). (2011). *Literacy and numeracy for learning and life:* The national strategy to improve literacy and numeracy among children and young people 2011-2020. Dublin: Author.

Dooley, T. (2011). RBC epistemic actions and the role of vague language. In B. Ubiz (Ed.), *Proceedings of the 35th conference of the International Group for the Psychology of Mathematics Education* (Vol. 2, pp. 281-288). Ankara: PME.

Eivers, E., Close, S., Shiel, G., Millar, D., Clerkin, A., Gilleece., L. and Kiniry, J. (2010). *The 2009 national assessments of Mathematics and English Reading.* Dublin: The Stationery Office.

Fernandez, C. (2005). Lesson study: A means for elementary teachers to develop the knowledge of mathematics needed for reform-minded teaching? *Mathematical Thinking and Learning,* 7(4), 265-289.

Glasersfeld, E. von, (1995). *Radical constructivism: A way of knowing and learning.* London: Falmer Press.

Grossman, P., Hammerness, K. and McDonald, M. (2009). Redefining teaching, re-imagining teacher education. *Teachers and Teaching. 15*(2), 273-289.

Hart, L., Alston, A. and Murata, A. (2011). *Lesson study research and practice in mathematics education: Learning together.* USA: Springer.

Hufferd-Ackles, K., Fuson, K. C. and Sherin, M. G. (2004). Describing levels and components of a math-talk learning community. *Journal for Research in Mathematics Education, 35*(2), 81-116.

Lewis, C. and Tsuchida, I. (1998). A lesson is like a swiftly flowing river: Research lessons and the improvement of Japanese education. *American Educator, 22*(4), 14-17 and 50-52.

Mendick, H. (2006). *Masculinities in mathematics.* London: Open University Press.

National Council for Curriculum and Assessment (NCCA). (1999a). *Primary school mathematics curriculum.* Dublin: The Stationery Office.

National Council for Curriculum and Assessment (NCCA). (1999b). *Primary school mathematics teacher guidelines.* Dublin: The Stationery Office.

Nic Mhuirí, S. (2011). Look who's talking now: The role of talk in relation to mathematical thinking and problem solving. In T. Dooley, D. Corcoran and M. Ryan (Eds.), *Proceedings of fourth national conference on research on mathematics education.* Dublin: St Patrick's College.

Primary Curriculum Support Programme (PCSP). (2012). *Main changes of emphasis.* Retrievable from the PCSP Archive website: http://www.ppds.ie/pcsparchive/ma_intro.php. Originally accessed 30 April, 2010 from www.pcsp.ie

Rogoff, B. (1990). *Apprenticeship in thinking, cognitive development in social context.* New York, NY: Oxford University Press.

Rowland, T., Huckstep, P. and Thwaites, A. (2005). Elementary teachers' mathematics subject knowledge: The knowledge quartet and the case of Naomi. *Journal of Mathematics Teacher Education, 8*(3), 255-281.

Rowland, T., Thwaites, A. and Jared, L. (2011). Triggers of contingency in mathematics teaching. In B. Ubuz (Ed.), *Proceedings of the 35th conference of the International Group for the Psychology of Mathematics Education* (Vol 4, pp. 73-78). Ankara, Turkey: PME.

Schön, D. (1983). *The reflective practitioner.* New York: Basic Books.

Shiel, G., Surgenor, P., Close, S. and Millar, D. (2006). *The 2004 National Assessment of Mathematics Achievement.* Dublin: Educational Research Centre.

Shulman, L. (1986). Those who understand knowledge growth in teaching, *Educational Researcher, (2),* 4-14.

Shulman, L. (2005). Signature pedagogies in the professions. *Daedalus, 134*(3), 52-59.

Skemp, R., (1982). *Mathematics in the primary school.* London: Routledge.

Steffe, L. P. and Thompson, P. W. (2000). Teaching experiment methodology: Underlying principles and essential elements. In R. Lesh and A. E. Kelly (Eds.), *Research design in mathematics and science education* (pp. 267-307). Hillsdale, NJ: Erlbaum.

Stein, M. K., Engle, R. A., Smith, M. S. and Hughes, E. K. (2008). Orchestrating productive mathematical discussions: Five practices for helping teachers move beyond show and tell. *Mathematical Thinking and Learning, 10*(4), 313-336.

Steinbring, H. (1998). Epistemological constraints of mathematical knowledge in social learning settings. In A. Sierpinska and J. Kilpatrick (Eds.), *Mathematics education as a research domain: A search for identity* (pp. 513-526). Dordrecht : Kluwer Academic Publishers.

Turner, F. (2009). Developing mathematical content knowledge: The ability to respond to the unexpected. In M. Tzekaki, M. Kaldrimidou and H. Sakonidis (Eds.), *Proceedings of the 33rd conference of the International Group for the Psychology of Mathematics Education* (Thessaloniki, Greece. July 19-24, 2009).

Van Galen, F., Abels, M., Burrill, G., Spence, M.S. and Hedges, T. (2006). Some of the parts. In Winconsin Centre for Education Research & Freudenthal Institute (Eds.), *Mathematics in context.* Chicago: Encyclopaedia Britannica.

Webb, D., Hedges, T., Dekker, T. and Ables, M. (2006). Some of the parts: Teacher's guide. In Winconsin Centre for Education Research & Freudenthal Institute (Eds.), *Mathematics in context.* Chicago: Encyclopaedia Britannica.

Wells, G. (2007). The mediating role of discoursing in activity. *Mind, Culture, and Activity, 14*(3), 160–177.

Wenger, E. (1998). *Communities of practice.* UK: Cambridge University Press.

Chapter 7

The Professional *Gold Standard*: Adaptive Expertise through Assessment for Learning

Zita Lysaght
St Patrick's College, Drumcondra

Introduction

This chapter is anchored in the work of Hatano and Inagaki (1986) in relation to adaptive expertise and the application of this concept by Hammerness, Darling-Hammond and Bransford (2007) to initial teacher education. According to Hammerness et al. (2007), helping prospective teachers become adaptive experts, i.e., professionals with the ability to balance efficiency with innovation in day-to-day teaching, is not something that can be achieved by engaging in a theoretical exploration of the concept. Rather, if initial teacher education is conceived as part of a continuum of lifelong learning that builds on students' personal school experiences and sets them on their career paths as professional educators, teachers must be given opportunities to overcome three key challenges. They need to divest themselves of the preconceptions about teaching, learning and assessment developed during their 'apprenticeship of observation' years (Lortie, 1975). Second, they must embrace the 'problem of enactment' (Kennedy, 1999) so that they begin, not only to think like teachers, but to put their intentions into action in classrooms. Finally, they need to accept and respond creatively to the 'problem of complexity' by developing meta-cognitive knowledge and skills of self-regulation (Flavell, 1976; 1979; Lampert, 2001).

In wrestling with each of these challenges, pre-service teachers have to come to grips with assessment, given its irreducible relationship to teaching and learning. In response, this chapter seeks to highlight weaknesses in Irish education in relation to assessment in order to signal the need to optimise and exploit opportunities to provide pre-service teachers with focused and sustained support in this area. In doing so, the chapter does not seek to imply or address weaknesses in current courses in assessment offered by initial teacher education programmes in Ireland; the dearth of evaluation research on teacher education in Ireland currently prohibits such review or analysis at this time. Rather, the rationale for foregrounding Assessment for Learning (AfL) at pre-service level is two-fold: first, research has demonstrated repeatedly that, when implemented as intended, AfL can effectively double the rate of student learning (Wiliam, 2007); second, AfL is a pedagogy of contingency that acknowledges the complexity of classroom life. Hence, its use supports the development of metacognition and self-regulation, learning practices that are closely associated with adaptive experts. Moreover, in keeping with the definition of AfL as 'any assessment for which the first priority in its design and practice is to serve the purpose of promoting pupils' learning…' (Black et al., 2002, p. 2), AfL promotes a social constructivist, progressive approach to teaching and learning. As such, it seeks to knit assessment into the fabric of teacher-student and student-student engagement 'minute-by-minute, day-by-day' (Leahy et al., 2005), such that evidence of learning is shared and used collectively to drive learning forward. Learning environments of this kind, that actively embrace and promote the 'spirit' of AfL, challenge teachers and learners to assume increasing flexibility in knowledge and power and, *ipso facto*, roles and responsibilities. At its best, then, AfL promotes adaptive, flexible and innovative instruction (shared by teachers and students) that responds in timely fashion to the evolving needs of learners, individually and collectively.

The chapter is in three parts. The first reviews briefly the triad of challenges that pre-service teachers face. This is followed by consideration of the allied concepts of adaptive expertise and knowledge transfer and a review of the kinds of learning environments and teaching, learning and assessment practices that promote the development of such expertise. Premised on the belief that the development of adaptive expertise is consistent with an assessment for learning approach to teacher education, this section seeks to highlight how engagement in AfL-mediated learning contexts at pre-service level prepares teachers to expose, in turn, their own students to opportunities to innovate and discover solutions to novel problems routinely. The chapter concludes by highlighting key challenges facing initial teacher education providers in light of findings from recent Irish studies regarding assessment practices in schools and students' adaptive expertise.

The Triad of Challenges Facing Teachers

The idea that teachers tend to teach as they were taught has long been attributed in the literature to the 'apprenticeship of observation' (Lortie, 1975) that takes place in their school-going years. Reflecting on the influence of this apprenticeship, Pellegrino (2006) comments that it serves to develop preconceptions, belief systems and prior knowledge in students that frequently reflect '… faulty mental models about concepts and phenomena' (p. 3). As observed (e.g., Berry, 2004; Flores, Cousin and Diaz, 1991), these mental models of teaching and learning – referred to by Flores et al. (1991) as 'habitudes' – are typically resistant to change (Pajares, 1992) and, if left unexamined and unchallenged, can exert significant, and potentially undesirable, consequences on how young teachers think and act.

Coupled with the challenges arising from this apprenticeship are problems of enactment and complexity. In keeping with the extensive corpus of literature questioning the efficacy of programmes of teacher professional development both internationally (e.g., Borko, 2004; Cochran-Smith and Lytle, 1999) and nationally (e.g., Loxley et al., 2007), reviews of the impact of pre-service teacher education have reported unpredictable and apparently indirect outcomes (e.g., Berry, 2004). A recurring concern in this literature, one shared by teacher educators, is the variability in the preparedness of graduate teachers to assume the role of competent adaptive professionals. Fairbanks et al. (2010), for example, highlight the fact that although graduates of education programmes may be 'technically competent', it does not necessarily follow that they are 'particularly responsive to students or situations' despite teacher educators' belief that 'it is such responsiveness that constitutes thoughtful teaching and lies at the centre of teacher effectiveness' (p. 161).

Concerns of this kind parallel a shift in focus in teacher education research from conceptualising models of continuing professional development (e.g., Cochran-Smith and Lytle's (1999) seminal framework of teacher knowledge *for-*, *in-* and *of-* practice) to consideration of how best to strike a balance in teacher education between efficiency and innovation, as highlighted by Schwartz, Bransford and Sears (2005). Such interest is spurred by the realisation that the art of teaching is as Shulman (2004) describes it, the 'most demanding, subtle, nuanced and frightening activity that our species ever invented…' (p. 504). In response, teacher education is increasingly understood as a lifelong process aimed at supporting practitioners to habitually 'adapt and invent strategies, manage competing agendas, interrupt and construct subject-specific and interdisciplinary curriculum and build classroom and school cultures within conditions that are ultimately uncertain' (Cochran-Smith and Lytle, 2002, p. 2).

Reflecting on the increasing reference to terms such as 'adaptive expertise' and 'adaptive metacognition' in educational research, Fairbanks et al. (2010) remark that this reflects a growing acceptance that 'routine expertise' is necessary but no longer sufficient in a world in which 'the sheer magnitude of human knowledge renders its coverage by education an impossibility' (Bransford, 2001, p. 3). Arguably, the concept of adaptive expertise is also gaining currency because it provides educators with an impetus and framework for reconceptualising how educators can manage and apply their knowledge and skills optimally in their day-to-day professional lives. As noted by Bransford, Darling-Hammond and Le Page (2007), increasingly, teacher education programmes must '… consider the demands of today's schools in concert with the growing knowledge base about learning and teaching if they are to support teachers in meeting these expectations' (p. 2). Such reconceptualisations of teacher education, it is argued, are necessitated by the complex interplay of a range of factors including expectations that, despite increasingly complex student profiles resulting from changing demographics and inclusive education policies, a growing percentage of young students will emerge from schools with attitudes and skills that equip them for lifelong learning and membership of an international workforce that is flexible, mobile and sufficiently adaptive to manage and respond creatively to an ever-changing world.

Expectations of this kind are reflected in the introduction of international benchmarks of student achievement, one of the most influential of which is the Organisation for Economic Co-operation and Development's (OECD) Programme for International Student Assessment (PISA) which asks: 'Are students well prepared for future challenges? Can they analyse, reason and communicate effectively? Do they have the capacity to continue learning throughout life?' In response, it is asserted that PISA '… answers these questions and more, through its surveys of 15-year-olds in the principal industrialised countries' (OECD, 2011, para. 1) as they near completion of compulsory education. While one might question this assertion – as Eivers (2010) does with reference to the most recent performance of Irish students on PISA – the intended prioritisation of adaptive expertise over routine expertise and knowledge is undisputable. This throws up questions, such as those raised by Bransford et al. (2007), about how teachers may be prepared to create learning environments for students that foster the development of such skills through learning that supports inquiry, application, production and problem solving.

Answers to such questions are not immediately forthcoming, however. Barron and Darling-Hammond (2008) note the 'checkered history' that such approaches to teaching (e.g., those associated with social constructivism) have enjoyed to date which they attribute, in part, to the fact that implementing them requires '… simultaneous changes in curriculum, instruction and assessment practices

– changes that are often foreign to teachers as well as students' (p. 13). Reflecting on these challenges, Pellegrino (2006) makes three interesting observations. First, he notes that increasingly sophisticated understanding about the nature of competence and the development of expertise across core areas of the curriculum has not been used optimally to inform curricular goals, instructional processes or modes of assessment. Second, he observes that because teaching requires a 'unique form of expertise above and beyond knowledge of a given discipline' (p. 2), teaching graduates must themselves have the opportunity to develop and hone their skills as adaptive practitioners in the domain of daily classroom instruction. Third, he argues that there is a serious mismatch between contemporary models of learning and most current approaches to curriculum, instruction and assessment.

Pellegrino's (2006) observations serve to highlight the fact that although teachers are widely acknowledged as linchpins to educational reform, and, *ipso facto*, improved student performance (e.g., Hattie, 2005; Tharp and Gallimore, 1988), apparent inconsistencies within and across teacher education programmes pose significant obstacles to the overall reform of teacher education, and to the coherence and quality of programme design and implementation in particular. Such inconsistencies, it is suggested, include a lack of alignment between what is known about the nature of expertise and how such expertise may be developed in key knowledge domains and the extent to which this is reflected in learning outcomes, teaching and learning pedagogies and assessment tools and procedures. As noted previously (Barron and Darling-Hammond, 2008), fundamental differences among teacher educators in philosophical stances towards such core issues as teaching, learning and assessment are often rooted in the unexamined paradigms that underpinned the teacher education programmes to which they themselves were exposed as undergraduates. Untangling this issue, Shepard (2000) argues that what is really at issue here is the need to replace the once dominant twentieth century paradigm of social efficiency, behaviourist learning theories and scientific measurement with a paradigm based on social constructivism and sociocultural theories which prizes the development of adaptive expertise to use knowledge innovatively over the accumulation of knowledge facts. To unpack these issues further and to examine the import of such changes for educators, the focus turns now to the allied concepts of adaptive expertise and knowledge transfer.

Adaptive Expertise and Knowledge Transfer

First coined by Hatano and Inagaki in 1986, the construct of adaptive expertise has been examined and reviewed by many prominent educators over recent decades (e.g., Bransford and Schwartz, 1999; Holyoak, 1991; Schwartz, Bransford and Sears, 2005). The following quotation from Lin, Schwartz and Bransford (2007) provides a useful deconstruction of the core ideas. Adaptive experts, they say, possess:

> . . . procedural fluency that is complemented by an explicit conceptual understanding that permits adaptation to variability. The acquisition of adaptive expertise is fostered by educational environments that support active exploration through three tiers. The first tier highlights the variability inherent to the task environment. The second tier highlights the variability permitted in the individual's procedural application. The final tier highlights the variability of explanation permitted by the culture, such that people can share and discuss their different understandings. (p. 66)

For a thorough account of the concept, the reader is referred to Lin et al. (2007); however, for the purposes of this chapter, some brief deconstruction is offered at this point, beginning with the ideas of procedural fluency, explicit conceptual understanding and adaptation to variability.

Schwartz, Bransford and Sears (2005) propose that adaptive expertise may be viewed in terms of two opposing but complementary dimensions – innovation and efficiency (Figure 1). Innovation skills represent the knowledge-building skills associated with expanding knowledge in pursuit of solutions to novel problems and, as such, contrast sharply with efficiency skills which represent the collection of knowledge and experiences (schemas) experts leverage for solving routine problems quickly and efficiently. Emphasising the centrality of both routine knowledge and expertise in this process, Hatano (1982) argues that:

> . . . flexibility and adaptability seem to be possible only when there is some corresponding conceptual knowledge to give meaning to each step of the skill and provide criteria for selection among possible alternatives for each step within the procedure (p. 15).

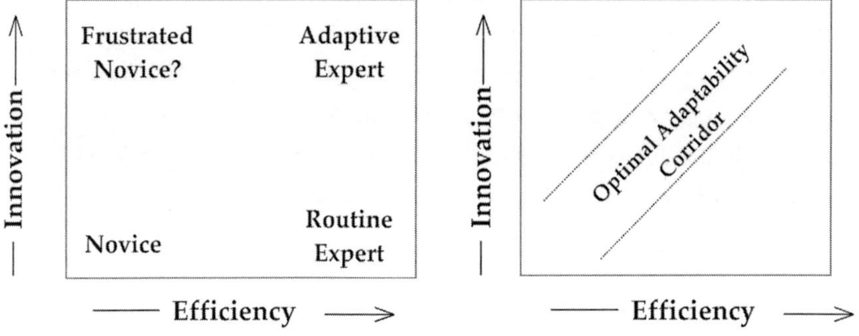

Figure 1. The twin elements of adaptive expertise (Schwartz et al., 2005)

Distinguishing between these skill-sets, Schwartz et al. (2005) caution that the development of adaptive expertise is not something that happens after people develop routine expertise in a 'capstone course'. Rather:

> The path toward adaptive expertise is probably different from the path toward routine expertise. Adaptive expertise involves habits of mind, attitudes and ways of thinking and organising one's knowledge that are different from routine expertise and that take time to develop. We don't mean to imply that 'you can't teach an old routine expert new tricks'. But it's probably harder to do this than to start people down an 'adaptive expertise path' to begin with, at least for most people. (Bransford, 2001, p. 3)

Hence, the recommendation that instead of adopting a *skills first-application later* approach, students should be encouraged to innovate and discover solutions to novel problems as a matter of routine, depicted by the optimal adaptability corridor in Figure 1.

Knowledge Transfer

An underlying tenet of contemporary learning theory is the need to elicit and build on students' prior knowledge to ensure teaching for understanding (Bransford, Brown and Cocking, 1999; Shepard, 2000). With reference to teacher education, this idea may be traced back to Feiman-Nemser (1983) who urged the need to engage the beliefs, knowledge and experiences that prospective teachers bring with them into teacher education programmes. More recently, Darling-Hammond and Bransford (2005, p. 284) have urged that '... novice teachers need to understand the role of prior knowledge in enabling, and sometimes, impeding, new learning.' In keeping with this principle, adaptive expertise assumes the ability to build on previous learning (transfer in), in addition to the capacity to apply learning to new situations (transfer out), which may be familiar (requiring near/specific transfer) or new (requiring far/general transfer). General or far transfer, as one might anticipate, presents much greater challenges for the learner as he/she is expected to identify and select from a bank of knowledge the most appropriate approach to adopt, and knowledge to apply, to a novel challenge or context. For general knowledge transfer to occur, students – be they pre-service teachers following a Bachelor of Education degree course or students in primary or post-primary schools – must engage as a matter of course with authentic learning situations that actively seek to develop their ability to approach novel contexts creatively; such approaches to learning (and teaching) contrast sharply with those that emphasise the memorisation of information and procedures, through repetition, to the point of automaticity. As elaborated later in this chapter, teaching/learning contexts underpinned by an assessment for learning pedagogy offer such opportunities.

To this end, research highlights four core factors that impact students' ability to develop this skill including: (1) the kind of learning experience(s) to which the student is originally exposed; (2) the various contexts in which knowledge is gained and applied; (3) students' ability to apply meta-cognitive skills to discern similarities and differences between and across subjects and knowledge domains; and (4) students' readiness to engage in critical reflection and review.

Taken together, these four elements depict learning for transfer as a time-consuming process. From a teaching perspective, it assumes cognisance of what learners transfer in to the learning situation (in terms of their cognitive and affective dispositions), the creation of dissonance between learners' knowledge and the learning challenges they face, and scaffolding of the student so that, incrementally, they develop skills of metacognition and critical inquiry that motivate them to approach unfamiliar tasks with confidence and motivation. From a learning perspective, it assumes active participation in, and responsibility for, personal- and peer-learning, as envisaged in an AfL classroom. In such contexts, teachers and students identify differentiated learning targets that are used flexibly to address identified gaps in learners' knowledge, skills, concepts and attitudes. Such learning becomes possible when teacher-student roles become blurred, when responsibility for learning is actively shared, and when methodologies, such as carouseling – a hybrid of the jigsaw, co-operative method – are used to democratise the learning process and challenge participants to respond creatively to unanticipated challenges.

Adaptive Expertise, Learning Environments and Assessment for Learning

According to Hatano and Inagaki (1986), the nature of learning environments, and the degree to which they encourage and challenge learners to deviate from well-rehearsed and established routines to experiment with novel approaches and alternative solutions, is crucial to the development of adaptive expertise. Such environments are characterised by three tiers or elements: (1) the degree of variability or randomness built into the learning environment; (2) the extent to which it is safe – and the learner is encouraged – to take risks; and (3) the balance between teaching for understanding and teaching for performance. Combining the original traits of adaptive experts identified by Hatano and Inagaki (1986, p. 8) with those added by other researchers (e.g., Wineburg, 1998; Bransford and Schwartz, 1999), Hatano and Oura (2003, pp. 25-27) foreground three core competencies that develop from such educational opportunities which are indicative of adaptive expertise:

1. The ability to articulate explicitly the principles underlying one's skills and, if necessary, arbitrate between conventional and non-conventional versions of those skills;
2. The ability to modify one's skills/schema and/or invent new ones in response to changing contexts and circumstances;
3. The ability to approach new situations with openness and, crucially, a willingness to let go of initial assumptions and tried and tested responses or schema.

In terms of how such skills distinguish adaptive from routine experts, Holyoak (1991, p. 310) suggests that whereas adaptive experts use their expert knowledge to invent new procedures to nuanced challenges, routine experts respond to predictable/anticipated problems with speed and accuracy but are challenged when faced with unfamiliar problems that require novel responses.

Various teaching and learning approaches have been identified that provide such opportunities, amongst them inquiry-based learning that includes project-based, problem-based and design-based learning (Barron et al., 1998). Although there are subtle differences between each one, this family of approaches prioritises learning that involves '…extended construction work, often in collaborative groups, and subsequently demands a good deal of self-regulated inquiry' (Darling-Hammond et al., 2008, p. 13) Moreover, inquiry-based learning approaches assume a systems perspective to classroom activities, curriculum and assessment and, crucially, an ability on the teacher's part to ensure that both formative and summative assessment tools and procedures are optimised to provide timely feedback that is used by teachers and students to drive learning forward.

Expanding on this theme, Darling-Hammond et al. (2008) identify three elements of assessment that are required for meaningful learning of this kind to take place. These are:

1. Designing *intellectually ambitious performance assessments* that define the tasks students will undertake in ways that allow them to learn, and apply the desired concepts and skills in authentic and disciplined ways;

2. Creating guidance for students' efforts in the form of *evaluation tools* such as assignment guidelines and rubrics that define what constitutes good work (and effective collaboration);
3. Using formative assessment to provide feedback to develop students' capacity to assess their own work, so that they internalise standards and become meta-cognitive in their thinking about their own learning. (pp. 63-69)

In light of what we know about the triad of problems facing teachers, coupled with the necessity to develop lifelong skills of adaptability and transfer, such statements challenge us to consider our preparedness in terms of our assessment literacy and practice to advance teaching and learning. Consequently, the final section of the chapter highlights data from recent Irish studies that: (a) shed light on assessment practices in Irish schools; and (b) evaluate students' adaptive expertise by way of judging the nature and extent of the challenges that lie ahead.

Data on Practices and Standards in Ireland

The publication of three reports, two national (Department of Education and Skills (DES), 2010; Eivers et al., 2010) and one international (OECD, 2010), in the closing months of this decade, put paid to any residual illusions that Ireland's *Celtic Tiger* period brought prosperity and equality to all. Reflecting on the OECD report findings that Irish students' performance in literacy has dropped some 13 points, the columnist Fintan O'Toole remarked that 'Ireland is just as outstanding for its illiteracy as for its literary genius. All through the boom about a quarter of Irish adults remained incapable of reading and writing well enough to be able fully to participate in society…' Reflecting on the impact of such an apparent drop in Irish performance, he surmised that we might 'for the first time, be creating a generation that is less literate than the previous one' (O'Toole, 2010, p. 8).

While this bleak perspective would undoubtedly be challenged by many Irish educators, the findings of the DES, Eivers et al. and OECD reports (all published in 2010) cannot be ignored as they cast long shadows over some teaching and learning practices in Irish schools, not least in relation to assessment. Beginning with the national studies, data from the DES (2010) study, *Inspectorate Evaluation Studies,* reported composite findings of incidental (i.e., unannounced) inspections undertaken during the 12-month period October 2009/2010.[1] Eivers et al. (2010) conducted the tenth national assessments of Mathematics and English Reading on behalf of the DES in the same year, in which almost 4,000 sixth class and 4,000 second class pupils participated. In both cases, assessment practices in schools were identified as problematic. Reporting 'particularly serious problems' in relation to assessment (DES, 2010, p. 6), DES inspectors called for 'urgent school improvement' and the provision of continuous professional development (CPD) for teachers and principals focusing on 'aspects of the teaching of literacy and numeracy – and especially the use of assessment to improve learning' (p. 18). In turn, Eivers et al. (2010) urged that principals and teachers 'should ensure that assessment for learning is a feature of every classroom, with good practice shared at school-level' (p. ix).[2]

Coupled with these studies at primary level, in 2009 Irish post-primary students participated in the Programme for International Student Assessment (PISA) which purports to examine the '... knowledge and skills that are essential for full participation in society' (OECD, 2007, p. 16), rather than the outcomes of school curricula. To date, representative samples of 15-year-olds in Ireland have participated in each of the four cycles of PISA (2000, 2003, 2006 and 2009). As reported (Cosgrove et al., 2010), across the OECD Ireland's mean score in reading fell 31 points from fifth place in 2000 to seventeenth place in 2009; the largest reduction among the 34 OECD countries who participated. Likewise, in mathematics, comparing PISA results from 2003 with those of 2009, Ireland's rating dropped from seventeenth to twenty-sixth, which represents a statistically significant decline in achievement of 16 scale score points – the second largest decline among participating countries. In science, no change in achievement was reported since 2006 (Cosgrove et al., 2010).

In interpreting these data, acknowledgement is also made of commentary from a range of respected sources cautioning that the apparent drops in performance may be explained, at least partially, by extenuating factors ranging from changing demographics to examination fatigue to changes in the format of questions (see, for example, Cosgrove et al., 2010). Of particular interest in the context of this chapter is whether the OECD's claim that PISA examines students' capacities for knowledge transfer, critical thinking and problem-solving can be sustained, given its narrow remit. Specifically, Eivers (2010) asks if PISA, which is a pen and pencil test, provides a fair assessment of what education systems accomplish. The author notes that PISA's singular focus on three domains of learning may, in fact, be at odds with PISA's stated intention of providing OECD member states with international comparisons of performance of education systems (OECD, 2011). Acknowledging that the three subjects assessed represent core domains of knowledge, she suggests that the focus is overly reductionist and fails to capture the breadth and scope of what is taught in Irish schools:

> It would be a poor education system that only taught students reading, mathematics, and science. As well as scholastic achievement across a variety of subjects, the traditional view of a 'good' education system encompasses a range of outcomes, often described as 'soft' skills and considered by employers and economists as very important in gaining employment: attitudes, values, motivation, oral presentation skills, the ability to work with others. None of these elements are reflected in PISA (p. 113).

Such criticisms are not new. Indeed, the literature is replete with calls to expand the range and nature of data collected from single to multiple measures (e.g., DuFour, 2004; Goodwin, Englert and Cicchinelli, 2003) in an effort to shift the focus from a reductionist preoccupation with test scores to a more inclusive assessment of the quality of education and learning achievement (e.g., Goodson and Hargreaves, 2003; Hogan, 2003).

One response to this challenge has been to note the absence of appropriate assessment tools to capture and measure the 'soft' skills (e.g., Dwyer, Millett and Payne, 2006), a response which prompted Pellegrino (2006, p. 12) to ask 'if current assessments do not effectively measure the impact of instruction or if they fail to capture important skills and knowledge, how can educators interpret and address gaps in student learning?' In turn, Shavelson (2007) notes that what we measure reflects what we value and suggests that by failing to assess the full range of knowledge and expertise, we may inadvertently lend our support to high stakes accountability regimes that by definition focus on 'a more restricted, easily and less expensively measured subset of learning outputs' (p. 3). In reality, such decisions are part of a much wider debate (flagged previously in this chapter with reference to Shepard, 2000) that has been ongoing internationally for many years in relation to the alignment – or, perhaps more correctly, the lack of alignment – between learning theories, teaching practices and assessment. As has been urged for many years now, if such alignment is to be achieved, the form and content of classroom assessment must change to 'better represent important thinking and problem solving skills in each of the disciplines' (Shepard, 2000, p. 7) and teachers and students need to view and use assessment information differently so that its formative potential is prioritised and optimised.

Conclusion: Implications for Teacher Education

By way of conclusion to this chapter, three questions are posed that are intended to speak to key issues raised previously, notably, the triad of problems peculiar to teaching identified by Hammerness et al. (2007) and the need for teachers to develop adaptive expertise in order to embrace the responsibility of preparing the next generation of students with confidence and creativity.

The first question relates to the need to challenge the mental models of assessment pre-service teachers develop during their apprenticeship of observation years. Assuming, on the basis of the data introduced in the previous section, that the assessment practices to which current entrants to initial teacher education programmes were exposed as school-going students may not consistently have represented best practice, the question arises as to how teacher educators can encourage critical reflection and review of ingrained perspectives on, and approaches to, teaching, learning and assessment, so that they are not perpetuated in future teaching.

The fact that it is not possible currently to disaggregate data derived from studies undertaken on behalf of the DES on teaching and learning in Irish schools (including those reviewed in the previous section), raises other questions such as how we ensure that school placements for pre-service teachers will serve to extend and embed best practice in assessment, as advocated and modelled in college courses and programmes. In turn, this reintroduces the vexed question of the need for classroom deprivatisation, as described by Lortie (1975), across all sectors of the system. Moving forward, we need to ensure that there is increasing alignment between what we purport to believe, how we teach, and how, what, when and why we assess. One of the most challenging questions this presents is how we can make explicit the teaching and learning paradigms underpinning our work and, crucially, how we will assess progress towards the development of adaptive expertise and knowledge – across the system from college courses, through teaching practices to student achievement – in the absence of appropriate assessment tools. In attempting to address these challenges systematically at pre-service level, one thing is clear: if, as teacher educators, we are serious about exploiting the well documented evidence-based potential that AfL offers all students, not least perennial low achievers (Black and Wiliam, 1998), then, increasingly, we will have to openly challenge – in voice and deed – teaching, learning and assessment practices and beliefs that are not complementary to and/or compatible with AfL philosophy.

An immediate and very challenging first step towards achieving this aim is to consider how we can redesign our pre-service learning environments and interactions to encourage the democratisation of teaching, learning and assessment, thereby allowing us to model the practices we want to develop in our graduates. At its core, AfL is a pedagogy of contingency that presupposes the ability to adapt teaching in response to students' individual and collective knowledge, skills and understanding in real time by employing a range of strategies and techniques (e.g., questioning, peer- and self-assessment) to close the gap between students' current performance and desired learning goals (Sadler, 1998). As such, it demands, not only considerable content knowledge and pedagogical skill, but, crucially, an ability to 'adapt the teaching work to meet the learning needs' of students in real time (Black et al., 2003, p. 2), something recent studies on teaching and learning in Irish schools suggest is not currently pervasive.

Given this reality, if initial teacher education is to effect any real change in understanding and use of AfL, teacher educators must model best practice and, in doing so, engage with student teachers to challenge beliefs and practices about how 'teachers teach and students learn.' A key element of this work will involve frank public acknowledgement of the challenges such a pedagogy presents for both teachers and students and a willingness to use AfL to work collaboratively to identify and optimise creative learning opportunities. In conclusion, it is suggested that by re-imagining pre-service teacher education in this way, we will, in effect, be providing our students with what Barbara Ragoff (1990) termed an 'apprenticeship of thinking' which will aid them as they attempt to battle the triad of challenges with which they must wrestle if they are to attain the gold standard of teacher education (Darling-Hammond, 2006) that is adaptive expertise.

Endnotes

[1] Information regarding the sampling frame employed to determine how schools were identified for inclusion in this study was not made explicit in this report [DES, 2010]).

[2] For a detailed review of these reports, the reader is referred to Lysaght, 2011.

References

Barron, B. and Darling-Hammond, L. (2008). *How can we teach for meaningful learning.* In L. Darling-Hammond, B. Barron, D. Pearson, A., Schoenfeld, E., Stage, T., Zimmerman, G., Cervetti and J. Tilson (Eds.), *Powerful learning: What we know about teaching for understanding* (pp. 11-70). New York: Jossey-Bass.

Barron, B., Schwartz, D.L., Vye, N.J., Moore, A., Petrosino, T., Zech, L. and Bransford, J.D. (1998). Doing with understanding: Lessons from research on problem and project based learning. *The Journal of the Learning Sciences*, 7, 271-311.

Berry, A. (2004). Self-study in teaching about teaching. In J. J. Loughran, M. L. Hamilton, V. K. LaBoskey and T. Russell (Eds.), *International handbook of self-study of teaching and teacher education practices* (pp. 1295-1332). Dordrecht: Kluwer Academic Publishers.

Black, P., Harrison, C., Lee, C., Marshall, B. and Wiliam, D. (2002). Working inside the black box: Assessment for learning in the classroom. *Phi Delta Kappan 86*(1), 8-21.

Black, P., Harrison, C., Lee, C., Marshall, B. and Wiliam, D. (2003). *Assessment for learning: Putting it into practice*. New York: Open University Press.

Black, P. and Wiliam, D. (1998). Inside the black box: Raising standards through classroom assessment. *Phi Delta Kappan, 80*(2), 139-148.

Borko, H. (2004). Professional development and teacher learning: Mapping the terrain. *Educational Researcher, 33*(8), 3-15.

Bransford, J. (2001). Thoughts on adaptive expertise. Unpublished Manuscript. Retrieved from Vanderbilt University website: http://www.vanth.org/docs/AdaptiveExpertise.pdf

Bransford, J. D., Brown, A. L. and Cocking, R. R. (1999). *How people learn: Brain, mind, experience, and school.* Washington, DC: National Academy Press.

Bransford, J., Darling-Hammond, L. and LePage, P. (2007). Introduction. In L. Darling-Hammond and J. Bransford (Eds.), *Preparing teachers for a changing world: What teachers should learn and be able to do* (pp. 1-39). San Francisco, CA: Jossey-Bass.

Bransford, J. and Schwartz, D. (1999). Rethinking transfer: A simple proposal with multiple implications. *Review of Research in Education*, *24,* 61-100.

Cochran-Smith, M. and Lytle, S. L. (1999). Relationships of knowledge and practice: Teacher learning in communities. *Review of Research in Education, 24*, 249-305.

Cochran-Smith, M. and Lytle, S. L. (2002). *Teacher learning and the new professional development*. Retrieved from The StateUniversity.com website: http://education.stateuniversity.com/pages/2483/Teacher-Learning-Communities.html

Cosgrove, J., Shiel, G., Archer, P. and Perkins, R. (2010). *Comparisons of performance in Ireland on PISA 2000 and PISA 2009: A preliminary report to the Department of Educational and Skills.* Dublin: Educational Research Centre.

Darling-Hammond, L. (Ed.). (2006). *Powerful teacher education.* San Francisco: JosseyBass.

Darling-Hammond, L., Barron, B., Pearson, D., Schoenfeld, A., Stage, E., Zimmerman, T., Cervetti, G. and Tilson, J. (2008). *Powerful learning: What we know about teaching for understanding.* New York: Jossey-Bass.

Darling-Hammond, L. and Bransford, J. (Eds.). (2005). *Preparing teachers for a changing world: What teachers should know and be able to do.* New York: Jossey-Bass.

Department of Education and Skills (DES). (2010). *Incidental inspection findings 2010: A report on the teaching and learning of English and Mathematics in primary schools.* Dublin: The Stationery Office.

DuFour, R. (2004). Are you looking out the window or in the mirror? *Journal of Staff Development, 25*(3), 63-64.

Dwyer, C. A., Millett, C. M. and Payne, D. G. (2006). *A culture of evidence: Postsecondary assessment and learning outcomes.* Princeton, NJ. ETS.

Eivers, E. (2010). PISA: Issues in implementation and interpretation. *The Irish Journal of Education, 28,* 94-118.

Eivers, E., Close, S., Shiel, G., Millar, D., Clerkin, A., Gilleece, L. and Kiniry, J. (2010). *The 2009 national assessments of Mathematics and English Reading.* Dublin: The Stationery Office.

Fairbanks, C., Duffy, D., Faircloth, B., He, Y., Levin, B., Rohr, J. and Stein, C. (2010). Beyond knowledge: Exploring why some teachers are more thoughtfully adaptive than others. *Journal of Teacher Education, 61*(1-2), 161-171.

Feiman-Nemser, S. (1983). Learning to teach. In L. Shulman and G. Sykes (Eds.), *Handbook of teaching and policy,* (pp. 150-170). New York: Longman.

Flavell, J. H. (1976). Metacognitive aspects of problem solving. In L. B. Resnick (Ed.), *The nature of intelligence* (pp. 231-235). Hillsdale, NJ: Lawrence Erlbaum.

Flavell, J. H. (1979). Metacognition and cognitive monitoring: A new area of cognitive-developmental inquiry. *American Psychologist, 34*, 906 - 911.

Flores, B., Cousin, P. and Diaz, S. (1991). Transforming deficit myths about learning, language, and culture. *Language Arts, 68,* 369-379.

Goodson, I. and Hargreaves, A. (Eds.). (2003). *Leading learning*. UK: Open University Press/ McGraw-Hill.

Goodwin, B., Englert, K. and Cicchinelli, L.F. (2003). *Comprehensive accountability systems: A framework for evaluation* (rev. ed.). Aurora, CO: Mid-continent Research for Education and Learning.

Hammerness, K., Darling-Hammond, L. and Bransford, J. (with Berliner, D., Cochran-Smith, M., McDonald, M. and Zeichner, K.). (2007). How teachers learn and develop. In L. Darling-Hammond and J. Bransford (Eds.), *Preparing teachers for a changing world: What teachers should know and be able to do* (pp. 358-389). San Francisco: Jossey-Bass.

Hatano, G. (1982). Cognitive consequences of practice in culture specific procedural skills. *The Quarterly Newsletter of the Laboratory of Comparative Human Cognition, 4*, 15–18.

Hatano, G. and Inagaki, K. (1986). Two courses of expertise. In H. Stevenson, H. Azuma and K. Hakuta, (Eds.), *Child development and education in Japan* (pp. 262 – 272). New York: Freeman.

Hatano, G. and Oura, Y. (2003). Reconceptualizing school learning using insight from expertise research. *Educational Researcher, 32*(8), 26 – 29.

Hattie, J. (2005). *What is the nature of evidence that makes a difference to learning?* Research conference: Using data to support learning, Melbourne (11-21). Retrieved from the Australian Council for Educational Research website: http://www.acer.edu.au/documents/RC2005_Hattie.pdf

Hogan, P. (2003). Teaching and learning as a way of life. *Journal of Philosophy of Education, 37*(4), 207-221.

Holyoak, K. J. (1991). Symbolic connectionism: Toward third-generation theories of expertise. In K. A. Ericsson and J. Smith (Eds.), *Toward a general theory of expertise: Prospects and limits* (pp. 301-335). UK: Cambridge University Press.

Kennedy, M. (1999). The role of preservice teacher education. In L. Darling-Hammond and G. Sykes (Eds.), *Teaching as the learning profession: Handbook of teaching and policy* (pp. 54-86). San Francisco: Jossey Bass.

Lampert, M. (2001). *Teaching problems and the problems of teaching.* New Haven, CT: Yale University Press.

Leahy, S., Lyon, C., Thompson, M. and Dylan, D. (2005). Formative assessment: Minute by minute, day by day. *Educational Leadership, 63*(3), 19-24.

Lin, X., Schwartz, D. and Bransford, J. (2007). Intercultural adaptive expertise: Explicit and implicit lessons from Dr. Hatano. *Human Development, 50*(1), 65-72.

Lortie, D.C. (1975). *Schoolteacher.* Chicago: The University of Chicago Press.

Loxley, A., Johnston, K., Murchan, D., Fitzgerald, H. and Quinn, M. (2007). The role of whole-school contexts in shaping the experiences and outcomes associated with professional development. *Journal of In-Service Education, 33*(3), 265-285.

Lysaght, Z. (2011). Assessment for learning in Irish schools: A window into current practice. *InTouch, 116*, 38-39.

O'Toole, F. (2010, p. 9). Culture shock. *Irish Times Newspaper,* December, 8.

Organisation for Economic Co-operation and Development (OECD). (2007). *PISA 2006: Science competencies for tomorrow's world* (Vol. 1). Paris: Author.

Organisation for Economic Co-operation and Development (OECD). (2010). *PISA 2009 results: What students know and can do.* Retrieved from http://www.pisa.oecd.org/document/61/0,3746,en_32252351_32235731_46567613_1_1_1_1,00.html

Organisation for Economic Co-operation and Development (OECD). (2011). *OECD Programme for International Student Assessment (PISA).* Retrieved from http://www.pisa.oecd.org/pages/0,2987,en_32252351_32235731_1_1_1_1_1,00.html

Pajares, M. F. (1992). Teachers' beliefs and educational research: Cleaning up a messy construct. *Review of Educational Research, 62*(3), 307-332.

Pellegrino, J. W. (2006). *Rethinking and redesigning curriculum, instruction and assessment: What research and theory suggests.* Washington, DC: National Center on Education and the Economy.

Ragoff, B. (1990). *Apprenticeship in thinking. Cognitive development in social context.* New York: Oxford University Press.

Sadler, D. R. (1998). Formative assessment: Revisiting the territory. *Assessment in Education, 5*(1), 77-84.

Schwartz, D. L., Bransford, J. D. and Sears, D. A. (2005). Efficiency and innovation in transfer. In J. Mestre (Ed.), *Transfer of learning from a modern multidisciplinary perspective* (pp. 1-52). Greenwich, CT: Information Age Publishing.

Shavelson, R. (2007). *Assessing student learning responsibility: From history to a bodacious proposal.* Retrieved from the Council for Aid to Education website: http://www.cae.org/content/pdf/ABriefHistoryOfAssessingUndergrad.pdf

Shepard, L. (2000). The role of assessment in a learning culture. *Educational Researcher 29*(7), 4-14.

Shulman, L.S. (2004). *The wisdom of practice: Essays on teaching, learning, and learning to teach.* Jossey-Bass, California.

Tharp, R. and Gallimore, R. (1988). *Rousing minds to life: Teaching, learning, and schooling in social context.* Cambridge: Cambridge University Press.

Wiliam, D. (2007). *Five 'key strategies' for effective formative assessment.* Retrieved from the National Council of Teachers of Mathematics website: http://www.nctm.org/uploadedFiles/Research_News_and_Advocacy/Research/Clips_and_Briefs/Research_brief_04_-_Five_Key%20Strategies.pdf

Wineburg, S. (1998). Reading Abraham Lincoln: An expert/expert study in the interpretation of historical texts. *Cognitive Science, 22*, 319-346.

Section Three:

Navigating Ideological Spaces in Initial Teacher Education

Chapter 8

Bridging Being and Becoming: Teacher Education Programmes in the Republic of Ireland

James G. Deegan
Mary Immaculate College, Limerick

> In the Brothers Limbourg's depiction of *The Fall and Expulsion from Paradise* (1415), a serpent with a human face passes the fruit of the tree of knowledge to a curious Eve... What appears is that as Eve, and then Adam, gain access to this troubling knowledge, their world changes around them... They are unceremoniously moved on by a rather forbidding scarlet angel and ushered firmly through an imposing gateway, a threshold, into a different kind of space (Meyer and Land, 2006, xiv).

> For being understood as being-possible, opens up the idea of becoming. Being cannot be understood without a sense of its unfolding, of its becoming (Barnett, 2011, p. 2).

In my response to the enduring question of re-imagining initial teacher education in the primary sector, I bring forward memories, or in Joycean terms, 'fragments', that serve as illuminative epiphanies in my journey as a teacher educator. Influenced by Heidegger's

([1927] 1998) phenomenological writings, *Being and Time*, where 'being' is 'being possible' (p. 183) and 'becoming' is 'its unfolding' (p. 183), in combination with Barnett's (2007; 2011; 2012a) stream of conceptual translations for higher education contexts, *Being a University*, where 'being' is cast in the context of time and space as contending concepts, I describe these epiphanies as 'Bridging Being and Becoming in Teacher Education Programmes'. In this chapter, I explore some possibilities and potentials of being a student teacher across the full scope and sequence of a complex teacher education programme. What I describe complements and elaborates what is currently underway in teacher education programmes, nationally and internationally. In Barnett's (2011) terms, what lies before us is the challenge of re-imagining 'being' in the here and now and also 'becoming' as a 'feasible utopia' (p. 4) or 'glimpse' of some positive signs for the future of teacher education in the twenty-first century in Ireland.

The proposed exploration of time and space in teacher education is operationalised here in its hybridised form as a 'spatio-temporal reality' that is anticipatory, robust and adaptive to change (Aaltonen, 2009) and, *inter alia,* a never-ending project. In essence, I am writing about 'a dynamical system or ecology' (Mason, 2008), best regarded in its entirety as a whole or web of complex, interrelated and contingent factors. Those becoming teachers who are themselves in a becoming teacher education programme share 'vital simultaneities' with teacher educators (Davis, 2008). Together they meet the challenges of 'imposing gateways', cross 'conceptual thresholds' and move into 'different kinds of spaces' (Meyer and Land, 2006, xiv). These illuminative epiphanies, 'leavened by empirical claims' (Luke, 2011, p. 367), invoke deep structures and improvisational responses and yield a set of postulates for mutually transforming self and system.

Evidence of paradigmatic shifts in teaching and teacher education is replete in leading and seminal handbooks, reports and other publications, internationally (for example, Cochran-Smith et al., 2008). In comparison there have been no big bang theories about teaching and teacher education as 'a technical problem' in the fifties, 'a problem-solving problem' in the eighties, and 'a policy problem' in the nineties, nationally (Deegan, 2004, p. 16). There have been no paradigm wars about constructivism, reflectivity, diversity and communication, notwithstanding their integration in curriculum innovations and programme renewals. In this chapter, the emphasis is on how elaborated ideologies like these are 'refashioned' into everyday ideologies (Gramsci, 1971) about being and becoming a learner, teacher, researcher and leader in Bachelor of Education (BEd) degree programmes. In this way, being and becoming a student teacher is not an essentialist or singular phenomenon but a catalytic element in a constellation of key constitutive elements such as becoming a learner, researcher and leader.

A Short Sociohistorical Review of Teacher Education Policy Planning and Production

The ways in which we re-imagine teacher education is contested terrain in the second decade of the twenty-first century (Harford, 2010) in Ireland. Renewal and change can potentially become a motivating context for subverting traditional and dominant orthodoxies in historically and conservative hidebound institutions and, paradoxically, a regressing one for socially, culturally and institutionally reproducing the status quo, business-as-usual, familiar ways of doing things, and conventional wisdom. In his seminal analysis of educational programme development and developers as 'a community of practice', Land (2004) illustrated differing orientations in organisational cultures as analogous to an old-fashioned political barnstorming with a big cast of players including 'modeller-brokers', 'political strategists', 'discipline-specific provocateurs', 'internal consultants', 'programme managers' and 'ecological humanists' (pp. 12-96), among other orientations. The backcloth for our present drama goes wider and deeper than the educational development of any particular programme, however, to the developmental seam between national and international policy discourses, identities and practices. The present developmental seam is characterised by what Ball (1998) describes as cycles of influence, production and power surrounding agency, consultation and partnership, by what Taylor (2004) describes as the interplay of context, text and consequences surrounding statutory, governmental and policy frameworks, and by what Apple (2006) describes as the pitched 'political battlefield[s]' (p. 198) of standards, religion and inequality surrounding pluralism and patronage.

The origins of teacher education as a programme development project lie, specifically, in cycles of influence and contexts of policy planning and frameworks that go far back, at least ninety years, to the National Education Programme Conferences of 1925 and 1926. These conferences inscribed an elaborated ideology of cultural nationalism and religion with a focus on 'gaelicisation' into an everyday ideology of fluency and competence in the Irish language and catechetical and devotional practices in Catholic teaching. By 1933, a three-part programme of studies, including a professional course in educational studies, a general education in academic subjects, and an optional course, set the seal for a forty year period of gradual incrementalism or near-stasis in educational policy planning, development and production. Coolahan (2004) describes the broad swathe of policy planning, development and production beginning again thirty years later through the 'creditable [policy] work' in the mid-sixties to the mid-eighties, followed by '[policy] slowdown' and 'policy wobbles' in the late eighties, and then the unprecedented surge of statutory and policy production in the last decade of the twentieth century. The present era retains a residual focus on gaelicisation and religion but is increasingly located in the widening landscape and generic problems of massification, marketisation and consumerism, new pedagogies and epistemic changes, standards and accountability, collaborations and partnerships, and new managerialism (Lingard and Rawolle, 2011).

The landmark production and publication of statutory and policy frameworks in teacher education has historically been evidenced in two bellwether or highly developed incidences which have produced what could be described as the first and second generations of the BEd degree programme. The first bellwether took place with the introduction of the BEd three year degree programme in September 1974 and the second almost forty years later with the introduction of the BEd four year degree programme in September 2012. A notable exception to these two bellwether developments was the short lived impetus for renewal and change generated by Kelleghan's (2002) report on *Preparing Teachers for the 21st Century* which called for a reconceptualisation focused on helping students assume responsibility for their own learning through critical and enquiring methods. In an era where structures and agencies are linked and integrated with social, personal, professional and institutional borders and boundaries, the launch of the long overdue BEd four year degree programme is especially vulnerable to the new legitimacies of the 'audit culture' (Nield, 2002). The threat lies in the focus on 'measured and measurable' outcomes or arithmetic reasoning in the context of shifting political-economic agendas.

The refashioning of elaborated ideologies in teacher education into enacted and lived everyday realities of implementation and consolidation is fraught with uncertainty in the prevailing context of debilitating fiscal austerity and limiting resources. Like its predecessor, the epoch-making significance of the BEd four year degree programme is one of those rich and rare opportunities for developing the hidden potential of renewal and change. Unlike its predecessor, the present opportunity is, in large measure, conceptually and politically moored in what Luke (2011) critiqued as the phenomenon of 'policy export' or generalising 'scientific and policy rationales for transnational standardization' (p. 367) across geopolitical borders and epistemological boundaries. The recent 'mixing' of national and international policy achievement discourses in literacy and numeracy is an object example of policy export for transnational standardisation and the 'generalising' of purported systemic wholeness with reference to ranking countries in new elite subject areas such as literacy, numeracy and science. What is noteworthy is that these developments have taken place with little reference to contextual, cultural and human variables of analysis and their consequential collateral losses for social capital as a producer of 'civic engagement' and a broad societal measure of communal health (Putnam, 2000).

In an era where economic sovereignty has become just another tradable commodity and where the quotidian of austerity is unrelenting, the concept of educational sovereignty, and by extension teacher education sovereignty, is at risk of becoming 'subdiarized' and a casualty of hegemonic politics and multi-scalar educational policy decision-making, planning and analysis (Lingard and Rawolle, 2011).

These developments are integrally related to the increasing influence of aggregate analyses of achievement, without reference to individual and small group differences, in the circulating grand narratives of PISA's star countries such as Finland, Japan, Singapore and South Korea. Indeed the conflation of recent literacy and numeracy planning, decision-making and policy with teaching and teacher education planning and policy in circulating official discourses was one of the striking features of how 'a part', albeit a fundamental one, of a teacher education programme can be overrepresented and exploited as 'the whole' of teacher education.

In this way, arbitrary and convenient epistemological proofs can become privileged over exploratory and difficult ontological inquiries. One of the potential casualties of this reasoning is a focus on making and doing in teacher education as opposed to being and becoming. The fledgling BEd four year degree programmes currently underway are premised on the fusing of conceptual understandings as the bases of operational practices and can potentially redress the recent slide from conceptual towards operational frameworks. An indicative example of this sliding is the tendency to omit or consign to appendices conceptual frameworks in new programme approval and accreditation processes.

Key Questions Underpinning a Different Kind of Teacher Education

How we seize the hidden potential of a different kind of teacher education well suited for the twenty-first century will crystallise in the new BEd four year degree programme between 2012 and 2016. In postmodern terms, we are currently deep in a 'flow' of things. For the first time, official accreditation is assured for teacher education programmes that meet national and international quality criteria. The teacher continuum from initial through induction and then in-career phases, originally inscribed in a statutory and policy context more than a decade ago, is now part of an elaborated official policy discourse. Whether an essentialist or privileged focus on literacy and numeracy will help students acquire the analytical, reasoning and communication skills necessary for full participation in a knowledge society is hotly contested terrain across different knowledge claims and practices in teacher education, the social sciences and the liberal arts.

Whether you take the view that the recent outgrowth of policy planning, decision-making and production is more stratagem than strategy and a ruse for gathering all of us blithely into a national moral panic about literacy and numeracy, analogous to the 1983 US Department of Education report, *A Nation at Risk: The Imperative for Educational Reform,* which sparked a dystopian legacy of 'schools as failing', or an opposing view that holds it is a response to a national educational crisis, current debates and controversies are helping to move teacher education from the margins to the mainstream of policy agendas. These developments, separately and together, represent the hidden potential of our re-imaginings, not least, the re-inscribing of what it means to be a learner, a teacher, a researcher and a leader in the contemporary lexicon and grammar of teacher education. Herein may lie the most enduring development in this memorable period of policy planning, decision-making and production in teacher education – how we conceptualise the interrelated and irreducible link between being and becoming a teacher across the full scope and sequence of teacher education progammes in the context of the present social, cultural, educational and economic realities of the second decade of the twenty-first century. Towards this challenge, we might begin to organise our thinking ontologically and then epistemologically by thinking about the essences of what we understand as teacher education and then how these essences could potentially become embedded in a relevant and responsive teacher education programme development project? The following questions arise in the context of essences and responses in contemporary teacher education:

- How does re-imagining teacher education fit into the grand narrative of educational development in higher education in the Republic of Ireland?
- How is teacher education a complex, self-organising and emergent phenomenon?

- How is teacher education programme development an interactive outcome of discourses, identities and practices?
- How does 'spatio-temporal' reasoning serve as a plausible and explanatory framework for connecting learning, teaching, researching and leading?
- How does the transformation of learner, through the portals of teacher and researcher, and leader intersect with the conceptual axes of anticipatory, adaptive, democratic and innovative change?
- How does re-conceptualising teacher education as a 'feasible utopia' (Barnett, 2011, p. 4) or possible future fit the emergent broader higher education context?

As part of the answer to this clutch of questions, I believe that we should turn towards a 'radical, relational, conceptual and complex paradigm' as a project of choice – a project designed to be greater than the sum of the parts – one situated in the structural conditions of higher education broadly and, more specifically, the flourishing of human relationships across colleges, schools, communities and broader society. Such a project recognises that amid the flow of political, ideological and economic tides nationally and internationally, there are still choices open to us in re-conceptualising what is a teacher education programme and how we can continually re-imagine it as a 'fully becoming' (Barnett, 2011, p, 2) endeavour.

Selected Re-imaginings of Things Being Otherwise in Teacher Education

Re-imagining teacher education as project of choice towards transformation is a hard, stubborn and enduring question. By 'project of choice' I mean the will that precedes the way and it includes both dispositions and qualities oriented towards a cluster of forms of knowing embedded in a set of practices (Barnett, 2007). Re-imagining things being otherwise through the harsh light of policies, frameworks and programmes and the soft lens of discourses, identities and practices is a naturally occurring phenomenon in the journeys of student teachers, classroom teachers and teacher educators. 'Imagining things being otherwise', Greene (1995) states in her writings on education, the arts and social change, 'may be the first step toward things becoming different – a space of freedom to move before we choose in the light of possibility' (p. 22). We are currently in one of those rich and rare spaces in re-imagining our teacher education programmes. Whereas space connotes coordinates, boundaries and borders, albeit borders that can be traversed, the act of re-imagining is not prescribed in the same way. The act of re-imagining space comes periodically to a close with every new programme but it should not come to an end. Failure to re-imagine what it means to begin has engendered the overweening influence of hidebound conservative thinking, attitudes and behaviours and has historically yielded near-stasis in teacher education programme development in Ireland.

Adherence to becoming a teacher as defined within the space of teaching alone is somewhat analogous to Putnam's (2000) influential writings on 'bowling alone' and occludes the linked and integrated concepts of learning, researching and leading. Being and becoming in learning communities and networks are prerequisites for what Barnett (2012b) describes as becoming 'ecologically professional'. By ecologically professional is understood a student teacher who is aware of her 'ecosophy' or place in the local and global ecologies of teaching and learning in their own and other contemporary societies. Learning to teach as only teaching in these terms, or indeed only researching, is only partially becoming ecologically professional.

The act of re-imagining teacher education assumes anterior imaginings from classical to present times. Indicative examples of 'collective imaginings' from Spinoza, through Rorty, to Lacan address whether imagining should be individual, collective or combined, past and/or present-centred, or indeed if the idea of a coherent unity is an illusion (Gatens, 1999). Influential contemporary imaginings include Taylor's (2004) political writings on rules that do not contain the principles of their own application, Castells' (2009) communication writings on the net as the replacement for vertical hierarchies, and Castoriadis' (1997) philosophical writings on change involving radical discontinuities.

While it was difficult to map national or inherited imaginings on to a broader social, economic, cultural and political international landscape until the advent of 'generalising [policies] across borders' (Luke, 2011), the twin imaginings of cultural nationalism and religion have largely endured as unexhausted influences in schools, colleges and universities and broader society for almost two centuries. An indicative example is the 'great desideratum, a good moral education for the whole community' (Blake, cited in Akenson, 1970, p. 1) proposed at the time of the foundation of the Irish national system of education in 1831 with its notions of popular sovereignty, civic engagement and moral enterprise. It has taken a cyclical turn of almost two hundred years before the present metamorphic developments on pluralism and patronage (Coolahan, 2012). Indeed, O'Sullivan (2005) in his seminal publication, *Cultural Politics and Irish Education Since the 1950s*, provides one of the most sustained critiques of policy paradigms and power in what is arguably the zeitgeist of our times, the shift from 'a theocentric to a mercantile paradigm' (pp. 101-203), with the compelling subheading, 'the erosion of doxa' (p. 103), albeit with only tacit reference to the cultural politics of teacher education.

For a short period during the economic boom of the last decade of the twentieth century, there were a number of significant efforts to re-imagine futures scenarios for education using futures studies methodologies or polyvalent social science methodologies that were markedly different from 'more traditional modes of mystical prophecy, grand ideologically inspired utopias and mechanistic predictive models' (Miller, 2004, p. 30). Indicative examples of this orientation included the Government of Ireland publications, *Information Commission's Report - Learning in the 21st Century: Towards Personalisation* (2004) and *Futures Ireland Project Report* (2009), which argued for the individualisation of learning needs as a core of educational transformation and a more experimentalist, participative and socially dynamic society, respectively. What this selective sampling of imaginings and re-imaginings across times and tides yields is the importance of what Aaltonen (2009) describes in the following fourfold set of cautions as adherence to: (1) the legacy of efficient cause or single causes for problems that arise from the interactions of multiple; (2) underlying and interrelated causes which render many real-world problems intractable; (3) sense-making and decision-making reduced to a single element or a few elements, if any, and blind to complex chains of causality from the top-down and bottom-up; and (4) the classical idea of a fixed, permanent and absolute which is simultaneously an acontextual truth as opposed to a spatio-temporal approach that necessitates new ways of understanding epistemology, methodology and leadership and helps produce better futures (pp. 1-2).

Greene's (1995) signature educational philosophy of 'imagining things as if they could be otherwise' similarly reminds us that re-imagining is not only a dialectical tick-tacking between elaborated and time-honoured ideologies, paradigms and theories about constructivism, reflectivity, diversity and communication (Cochran-Smith et al., 2008) but also, recursively, everyday ideologies and realities 'that are continually shaped and reshaped via, discourse, embodied sensations, memory, personal biography and interactions' (Lupton, 1988, p. 2). In this way, conceptually hyphenating space and time as a spatio-temporal phenomenon is not only a matter of critically engaging with subject knowledge and pedagogical content knowledge (Shulman, 2004) but also with [student] learning spaces' (Savin-Baden, McFarland and Savin-Baden, 2008) that often lie beneath the surface of things in subterranean channels across classrooms, schools, colleges, communities and broader society.

Conceptualising the Whole as Greater than the Sum of the Parts in Teacher Education

Two key possibilities underlie the theoretical, conceptual and methodological underpinnings of re-imagining being and becoming a teacher in a teacher education programme. Complexity theory has its origins in the fields of physics, biology and chemistry and is recently beginning to insinuate itself into the social sciences and education where, as Mason (2008) states, its appeal lies in its focus 'with wholes, larger systems or environments, and the relationships among their constituent elements or agents, as opposed to the often reductionistic concerns of mainstream science with its focus on the essence of the *ultimate particle*' (p. 2). In complement and counterpoint, Meyer and Land (2006) in their seminal writings on threshold concepts discuss how concepts can be used to advance student learning not only within a discipline but between disciplines and can enable learners to grasp a deeper understanding and mastery of their discipline. Their potential has been identified for the development and improvement of teaching skills, undergraduate research, the first year experience, and flexible course provision incorporating inquiry based learning.

Potential of Complexity Theory for Teacher Education

One of the cardinal principles of 'complexity theory and education' (Mason, 2008) is a focus on generating and conceptualising solutions to multi-step problems that arise in philosophy, systems theory, science and art, and in areas such as non-linear dynamics, evolution and adaptation, collective behaviour and pattern formation. At the heart of complexity theory are questions of continuity and change in particular environments or dynamical systems, for example, a teacher education programme – a cauldron for the emergence of new properties and behaviours which are not necessarily contained in the essences of constituent elements or able to be predicted from a knowledge of initial conditions. In this way complexity theory shifts the focus from a concern with de-contextualised and universalised essences to contextualised and contingent complex wholes. It is argued that educational and institutional change is less a consequence of effecting change in one particular factor or variable, and more a case of generating momentum in a new direction by attention to as many factors as possible. Complexity theory suggests, in other words, what it might take to change a teacher education programme from an ethos of 'times of space' where metaphorically the pail is the academic year and the liquid is the subject knowledge and pedagogical content knowledge, with all the consequential problems of 'time compression', to 'spaces of time' where the space is a clutch of linked and integrated sensitising themes related to being and becoming a learner, teacher, researcher and leader across classrooms, schools, neighbourhoods and communities.

Davis (2008) identifies a number of simultaneities that are often presented as coincidental in teacher education literature but are rarely co-implicated. These simultaneities need conceptual unpacking to show their markings on the teacher education terrain. A selection of these dualisms as opposed to dualities includes the following:

- 'knower and knowledge', where complexity theory, by considering both simultaneously, aims to move beyond the common distinction between teachers' representing the established and objective knowledge of the curriculum while pedagogically fostering subjective knowing in learners;
- 'transphenomenality', where complexity theory offers insights that can be had only by the simultaneous consideration of factors normally associated with quite different phenomenal levels of explanation;
- 'transdisciplinarity', where, similarly, complexity theory offers insights that can be had only by the simultaneous consideration of factors normally associated with quite different disciplinary perspectives;
- 'interdiscursivity', where, similarly, complexity theory offers insights that can be had only by the simultaneous consideration of factors normally associated with quite different discursive perspectives' (p. 4).

What these perspectives highlight is the motivating salience of working to ensure that the whole is always greater than the sum of the parts, knowledge lies in the intersections of 'knowing-for-itself, knowing-in-itself, knowing-for-the-world, and knowing-of-the-world' (Barnett, 2011, pp. 31-32) and, by interrogating various knowledge claims and wisdom across colleges, schools, communities and broader society, there is a greater opportunity for holism through 'a process of cross-fertilisation, pollination, [and] catalytic ideas' (Doll, 2008, pp. 181-203).

Potential of Threshold Concepts for Teacher Education

The second potential for re-imagining teacher education are 'threshold concepts', 'akin to a portal, opening up a new and previously inaccessible way of thinking about something … [representing] a transformed way of understanding, or interpreting, or viewing something without which the learner cannot progress' (Meyer and Land, 2006, xiv). These serve as a useful conceptual metaphor for accomplishing a transformational approach to learning across the full scope and sequence of a teacher education programme. By highlighting threshold concepts as a way of transforming a student's internal view of subject matter, subject landscape, or even world view across time and space in the context of troublesome knowledge, threshold concepts provide a complement and counterpoint to complexity theory and education. A selection of transforming as opposed to transmitting concepts includes the following:

- 'transformative', where a threshold concept, once understood, changes the way in which the student views the discipline;
- 'troublesome', where a threshold concept can be troublesome, counter-intuitive, alien or seemingly incoherent for the student;
- 'irreversible', where threshold concepts, given their transformative potential, are also likely to be irreversible, or they are difficult to unlearn;
- 'integrative', where threshold concepts, once learned, are likely to bring together different aspects of the subject that previously did not appear, to the student, to be related;
- 'bounded', where a threshold concept will probably delineate a particular conceptual space, serving a specific and limited purpose;
- 'discursive', where crossing of a threshold will incorporate an enhanced and extended use of language;
- 'reconstitutive', where understanding a threshold concept may entail a shift in learner subjectivity, which is implied through the transformative and discursive aspects already noted which is, perhaps, more likely to be recognised initially by others, and also to take place over time;
- 'liminality' – which has been likened to the crossing of the pedagogic threshold, to a 'rite of passage' or a transitional or liminal space – has to be traversed often as a difficult, messy journey back, forth and across conceptual terrain.

What these perspectives highlight is that threshold concepts are central to student learning and can be optimised through a discrete and permeated focus that allows for recursive and conceptual looping back and forth across spatio-temporal contexts. Two significant cautions regarding the otherwise developmental power of threshold concepts lie in their inherent liminality. They are not only conceptually troublesome and difficult but can be emotionally counterintuitive, unsettling and potentially involve a sense of loss. In the words of Palmer (2001), they can induce 'a pleasant awakening or rob one of an illusion' (p. 4) and, in this way, they assume a responsibility to respond to student learning that goes beyond subject matter and pedagogical content knowledge. Specifically, they assume a responsibility for emotional understanding and empathy in terms of what Hargreaves (2001) describes as patterns of closeness and distance in the human interactions we experience about relationships to ourselves, each other and the world around us and what he describes as 'emotional [physical, moral, professional, political, and sociocultural] geographies of teaching' (p. 1056).

Another caution suggested by Meyer and Land (2006) lies in the potential skewing of thresholds as part of a 'totalising' or colonising view of teacher education where, for example, learner, teacher, researcher or leader separately or in some restricted combinative way could become the normalising function of a teacher education programme. In this context, cultural reproduction could reassert itself and being and becoming a teacher would operationally regress to an essentialist or singular variable of becoming, for example, being a teacher, without reference, recursively and interactively, to being a learner, researcher and leader.

Teacher Education as an Educational Programme Development Project

Few would argue that the BEd three year degree programme had long passed its shelf date and had become a Procrustean exercise of super stretching and pulling in a maelstrom of curriculum innovations and changes in Ireland. As Kelleghan (2002), writing about the role and relationship between educational foundations and educational pedagogies, competences and learning outcomes, standards and accountability, and education and arts, humanities and social science subjects at a time of near-stasis or policy limbo, stated, 'the delay may in part be due to the extreme pressure to increase teacher supply in recent years, though that, while it might affect implications, should not necessarily have affected planning' (p. 25). To this day, however, we know little about 'the substantive attitudes, values, beliefs, habits, assumptions and ways of doing things' (Hargreaves and Fullan, 1992, p. 219). What has long been evident is that a radical overhaul of the *complexus* or embrace, where the whole is greater than the sum of the parts, is a national imperative.

One of the threats to the challenge of re-conceptualising a new teacher education programme is also a hazard for educational developers in all fields, namely that the four year baccalaureate degree can potentially induce a simple dicing and cutting of single or essentialist variables of measured time defined by duration, rates and intervals across 'times of space' as opposed to the, hitherto, neglected and largely forgotten response of 'spaces of time' (Gibbons, 2005, p. 71). This can induce a situation where a temporal calculation (or a quantitative judgement about how much time is available) overrides a thematic conceptualisation (or qualitative judgement about how to use the time available). Re-imagining the BEd four year programme into a responsive and relevant form of spatio-temporal reasoning represents a significant 'conceptual turn' in programme development. One of the ways proposed for making sense of complexity is through a four-fold clutch of spatially patterned transformations or 'learning spaces' (Savin-Baden, McFarland and Savin-Baden, 2008) described in terms of four sensitising space-time couplets: Learner/Year1; Teacher/Year 2; Researcher/Year 3; and Leader/Year 4. While a full and comprehensive exploration of these themes does not fall within the scope of this chapter, there is a rich corpus of positive signs for transformation regarding what it means to be a learner, teacher, researcher and leader in the international teaching and teacher education literature and discourse (Cochran-Smith et al., 2008).

Quite simply, being a student teacher and becoming a teacher from Learner in Year 1 to Leader in Year 4 is a non-linear journey that goes back and forth and loops recursively between personal and professional experiences on college campuses and school settings. It does not necessarily move from theory to practice, from one subject to the next, from novice to advanced or easy to hard but is a personal and professional messy business that sees the student teacher growing from learner to teacher, from teacher to researcher and researcher to leader. Being a student teacher is a complex project of the heart and the mind where the programmatic goal is ensuring that when students pass through the college gates into the world beyond, we can confirm that the whole of their learning is greater than the sum of the parts. We will have some justification in doing so if the 'in-between' or liminal years have rendered some of the hallmarks of international teaching and teacher education discourse, for example, problem-based learning in real world contexts, writing autobiographical understandings and inquiries, self and collective reflexive reasoning, knowledge of learning theories and metacogntive strategies, rules of argumentation and reasoning, practising new media and communication technologies, using democratic decision-making, distributed and sustainable leadership, and working with minorities and marginalised groups in an increasingly diverse society, among a slew of other problematic and fluid experiences.

Conclusion: Bridging as an Animating Metaphor for Re-imagining Teacher Education

> Of all the things that are man-made, bridges are, with dams, the most 'structural', single-minded, and imposing. As connectors at a breaking point, they have a heroic force that is aided by challenging structuralism. As a strand of continuity in a non-continuum, the bridge is full of implied meanings. It is the opposite of divisiveness, separation, isolation, irretrievability, loss, segregation, abandonment. To bridge is as cogent in the psychic realm as it is in the physical realm. The bridge is a symbol of confidence and trust. It is a communications medium as much as a connector (Soleri, 1971).

In his architectural *Sketchbooks* (1971), Soleri uses the metaphor of 'bridge' as structure and agency and as 'a strand of continuity in a non-continuum', 'a connector at a breaking point', and as 'a symbol of confidence and trust'. His bridges allow for a long span between bearing points, a minimum of vertical dimensions in relation to span, and pulsate with the rhythms of naturally occurring events around them in streets, neighbourhoods and communities. His physical and cultural bridges are a useful heuristic and interpretive device for re-imagining teacher education as linking the long span of four years with the vertical dimensions of learner, teacher, researcher and leader and the pulsating rhythms of naturally occurring events in an increasingly ecological and complex world around them. In this chapter, I have attempted not only to re-imagine a different kind of teacher education at the bridge points or entrances and exits but also in the in-between years and interstitial spaces, and in doing so to re-imagine teacher education differently – as a complex, self-organising and self-renewing project.

In terms of teaching and teacher education as a self-renewing project into the future, Harford's (2010) caution that 'while structurally, teacher education in Ireland has undergone significant reform in order to conform to a wider European agenda, significant gaps remain in existing teacher education policy particularly in relation to continuous professional development which will, if not addressed, impede Ireland's capacity to adequately prepare teachers for the challenges of the twenty-first century' is a significant clarion for extending the bridging metaphor across the teacher development continuum (p. 349). The proposed conceptual ideas in this chapter assume a dynamical, ecological and complex system with theories of self, a range of social epistemologies, a portfolio of pedagogical principles and practices, and innovative ideas for civic engagement. While these variables of epistemology, pedagogy, practice and engagement are moored conceptually, operationally and contextually in particular years and semesters, they are also naturally occurring phenomena across the full scope and sequence of programmes and experienced recursively across classrooms, schools, communities and broader society, and into the teaching continuum. In this way teacher education programmes can be conceptualised as a responsive and relevant bridging for being possible and its becoming or unfolding in the twenty-first century in Ireland.

References

Aaltonen, M. (2009). *Robustness: Anticipatory and adaptive human systems.* Litchfield Park, AZ: Emergent Publications.

Akenson, D. H. (1970). *The Irish education experiment: The national system of education in the nineteenth century*. London: Routledge and Kegan Paul.

Apple, M. (2006). *Educating the 'right' way: Markets, standards, god, and inequality* (2nd ed.). New York: Routledge.

Ball, S. J. (1998). Big policies/small world: An introduction to international perspectives on educational policy. *Comparative Education*, *34*(2), 119-130.

Barnett, R. (2007). *A will to learn: Being a student in an age of uncertainty.* Maidenhead: McGraw-Hill/Open University Press.

Barnett, R. (2011). *Being a university*. London: Routledge.

Barnett, R. (Ed.). (2012a). *The future university: Ideas and possibilities*. London: Routledge.

Barnett, R. (2012b). Towards an ecological professionalism. In C. Sugrue and T. Dyrdal Solbrekke (Eds.), *Professional responsibility: New horizons of praxis*. Abingdon: Routledge.

Castells. M. (2009). *Communication power*. Oxford: Oxford University Press.

Castoriadis, C. (1997). *World in fragments: Writings on politics, society, psychoanalysis, and the imagination*. (Translated and edited by David Ames Curtis). Stanford: Stanford University Press.

Cochran-Smith, M., Feiman-Nemser, S., McIntyre, D. J. and Demers, K. E. (Eds.). (2008). *Handbook of research on teacher education: Enduring questions in changing contexts* (3rd ed.). New York: Routledge.

Coolahan, J. (2004). The historical development of teacher education in the Republic of Ireland. In A. Burke (Ed.), *Teacher education in the Republic of Ireland: Retrospect and prospect* (pp. 7-30). Armagh: Centre for Cross-Border Studies.

Coolahan, J. (2012). *The school patronage report: Context, issues and way forward.* Paper presented at Mary Immaculate College, Limerick, Ireland.

Davis, B. (2008). Complexity and education: Vital simultaneities. In M. Mason (Ed.), *Complexity theory and the philosophy of education* (pp. 46-61). Oxford: Wiley-Blackwell.

Deegan, J. (2004). Challenging, confronting and choosing *new appraisal* in initial teacher education in the primary sector in the Republic of Ireland. In A. Dolan and J. Gleeson (Eds.), *The competences approach to teacher professional development: Current practices and future prospects* (pp. 15-24). Armagh: SCoTENS.

Doll, W. E. (2008). Complexity and the culture of curriculum. In M. Mason (Ed.), *Complexity theory and the philosophy of education* (pp. 181-203). Oxford: Wiley-Blackwell.

Gatens, M. (1999). *Collective imaginings: Spinoza, past and present.* London: Routledge.

Gibbons, L. (2005). Spaces of time through times of space: Joyce, Ireland and colonial modernity. *Field Day Review*, *1*, 71-86.

Government of Ireland. (2004). *Learning in the 21st century: Towards personalisation* (Information Society Commission). Dublin: The Stationery Office.

Government of Ireland. (2009). *Ireland at another turning point: Reviving development, reforming institutions, and liberating capabilities* (NESDO, Report No.1.). Dublin: The Stationery Office.

Gramsci, A. (1971). *Selections from the prison notebooks.* London: Lawrence and Wishart.

Greene, M. (1995). *Releasing the imagination: Essays on education, the arts, and social change.* San Francisco: Jossey-Bass.

Harford, J. (2010). Teacher education policy in Ireland and the challenges of the 21st century. *European Journal of Teacher Education*, *33*(4), 349-360.

Hargreaves, A. (2001). Emotional geographies of teaching. *Teachers College Record*, *108*(6), 1056-1080.

Hargreaves, A. and Fullan, M. (Eds.). (1992). *Understanding teacher development.* New York: Cassell.

Heidegger, M. ([1927] 1998). *Being and time.* Oxford: Blackwell.

Kelleghan, T. (2002). *Preparing teachers for the 21st century: Report of the working group on primary pre-service teacher education*. Dublin: The Stationery Office.

Land, R. (2004). *Educational development: Discourse, identity and practice.* Maidenhead: Open University Press/McGraw-Hill.

Lingard, B. and Rawolle, S. (2011). New scalar politics: Implications for education policy. *Comparative Education*, *47*(4), 489-502.

Luke, A. (2011). Generalizing across borders: policy and the limits of educational science. *Educational Researcher*, *40*(8), 367-377.

Lupton, D. (1998). *The emotional self: A sociocultural exploration*. London: Sage.

Mason, M. (Ed.). (2008). *Complexity theory and the philosophy of education.* Oxford: Wiley-Blackwell.

Meyer, J. and Land, R. (2006). *Overcoming barriers to student understanding: Threshold concepts and troublesome knowledge*. London: Taylor and Francis.

Miller, R. (2004). Imagining a learning intensive society. In *Learning in the 21st century: Towards personalisation* (Information Society Commission). Dublin: The Stationery Office.

Nield, R. (2002). *Public corruption: The dark side of social evolution*. London: Anthem.

O'Sullivan, D. (2005). *Cultural politics and Irish education since the 1950s: Policy paradigms and power*. Dublin: IPA.

Palmer, R.E. (2001). *The liminality of Hermes and the meaning of hermeneutics*. Retrieved from MacMurray College website: http://www.mac.edu/faculty/richardpalmer/liminality.html Last modified May 29, 2001.

Putnam, R. (2000). *Bowling alone: The collapse and revival of the American community*. New York: Simon and Schuster.

Savin-Baden, M., McFarland, L. and Savin-Baden, J. (2008). Learning spaces, agency and notions of improvement: What influences thinking and practices about teaching and learning in higher education: An interpretive meta-ethnography. *London Review of Education*, *6*(3), 211-227.

Shulman, L. S. (2004). *The wisdom of practice: Essays on teaching, learning and learning to teach*. San Francisco: Jossey-Bass.

Soleri, P. (1971). *The sketchbooks of Paulo Soleri*. Boston: MIT Press.

Taylor, C. (2004). *Modern social imaginaries*. Durham: Durham University Press.

US Department of Education. (2004). *A nation at risk: The imperative for educational reform*. Washington DC: Author.

Chapter 9

Teaching Ethics and Religion from 'Within' and 'Without' a Tradition – From Initial Teacher Education to the Primary School Context

Jones Irwin
St Patrick's College, Drumcondra

Introduction

> ... a school is engaged in a practical enterprise of great complexity which calls for many forms of practical knowledge (McLaughlin, 2008b, p. 204).

Ethos in schools is a multilayered concept and reality which, as McLaughlin suggests in the epigraph above, calls for subtle educational understanding and practice. Some school ethoi define themselves, for example, in relation to language and culture (one prominent instance being the gaelscoileanna in Ireland which teach through the Irish language), while other schools may be defined in terms of their theory of learning or epistemology (for example, Steiner schools). We might further speak of there being multiplied layers of ethos in schools, which can extend from issues of curriculum and teaching to issues of organisation and administration to the complex of what Norman calls the 'expressive culture' of a school, its various interpersonal levels and relationalities (Norman, 2003). This chapter focuses, however, on the specific connections between ethos and the teaching of religion and ethics, as this problematic extends from initial teacher education (ITE) to schools. Recent commentators on Irish primary education, even from within a Catholic tradition, have pointed to a certain problematicity with regard to the teaching of ethics and religion (Williams, 2003; Norman, 2003). In this chapter, I will explore some of the key tensions in this debate, focusing especially on the paradigmatic distinction between teaching ethics and religion, whether to student teachers or primary school children, from 'within' and 'without' a tradition (McLaughlin 2008b). Within a dramatically changing context of Irish education, it is imperative that we explore different alternatives to ethical and religious pedagogy.[1] Traditionally in Ireland, the latter has been characterised by a rather top-down or nondemocratic philosophy, which has tended to foster, in Norman's phrase, a 'culture of compliance' amongst children and educators (Norman 2003).[2]

However, the possibility of significant transformation is now being foregrounded within the Irish system. For example, the Forum on Patronage and Pluralism[3] (Coolahan, Hussey and Kilfeather, 2012) made its final recommendations in April 2012 and, alongside the significant implications for all schools, these recommendations also have specific things to say about the need for change in initial teacher education in an Irish context. Moreover, in March 2012, the Minister for Education and Skills, Ruairí Quinn, requested the Higher Education Authority (HEA) to undertake a review of the structure of such ITE provision in Ireland. This follows on from the significant changes in the content of ITE programmes detailed in the Teaching Council's *Initial Teacher Education: Criteria and Guidelines for Programme Providers* (Teaching Council, 2011), as well as the decision to extend the three year Bachelor of Education (BEd) programme for primary school teachers in Ireland from three to four years, beginning in September 2012.

The ramifications of these respective processes and reviews extend to all areas of education, but here my focus will be on their potential bearing on the specific problematic of the teaching of ethics and religion in schools and colleges of education. The predominance of denominational education in the state sector of Irish primary education has meant that ethical and religious education has become synonymous with a certain type of religious formation, a policy of fostering in young people a commitment to a particular faith position. This involves (at least in Ireland) the teaching of religion as faith-formation in school time, preparation for sacraments by the class teacher as well as a foregrounding of the symbolism of the particular religion throughout the school (Norman, 2003; Williams, 1997). Whatever about the respective merits of this approach taken in itself, there has also been a noticeable lack of focus on the spectrum of different approaches to the teaching of ethics and religion (Alexander and McLaughlin, 2003) which can be adopted in schools, whether denominational or otherwise. This question also bears on the relation between religion and ethics *per se*, whether we can sketch out respective territories belonging to both genres which then might be seen as intersecting (and dividing) at certain key points. These two intersecting questions will constitute my first problematic in this chapter, which might be described as *meta-pedagogical* in orientation. In the second case, employing some foundational theoretical resources, I will address some issues which must be looked at when approaching the content of such an ethico-religious course. Here, my concern is what might be termed *meta-ethical* (Noddings and Slote, 2003), insofar as it is focused on different approaches to the nature of ethics and ethical practice in education. I will thus look in brief at *four distinctive paradigms of the ethical*, and the contrast between their perspectives will allow us to develop some key philosophical and practical-political issues.[4]

Meta-Pedagogical Issues – Teaching Religion and Ethics 'From Inside' or 'From Outside'?

Firstly, however, I want to focus on the meta-pedagogical issue of how to teach ethical and religious content to students. This is a highly contested problematic and one of the most fruitful approaches, in my view, is to foreground the inherently ideological dimension of this debate. In other words, there can be no value-neutral approach to the relation between religion and ethics, much as Freire says that 'education is never a neutral process in itself' (1992). Thus, a constructive approach seems to be to present the conflicting ideological readings of the relation between religion and ethics as one moves from, for example, a secularism on the one side to a more theocentric or theistic view on the other, with all the varied permutations in between. Looking at the problem in this way, one also becomes increasingly aware of the inherently *political* dimension of these questions. Discussion of ethical and religious education in schools is, amongst other things, a political-philosophical issue. It is connected to the wider question of how our society and political system, in this case in an Irish context, must engage with the increasingly urgent and intense questions of diversity, in whatever myriad and complex forms the latter can manifest themselves in, for example, language, religion, ethnicity, gender, class, sexuality, disability, etc. As political philosophers such as Callan (Callan and White, 2003) have pointed out, contemporary philosophy of education has much to build on in relation to such questions from the recent (and not so recent) history of international political thinking and philosophy, for example, in terms of the conflict between liberalism and communitarianism. One point which seems important to prioritise here is the sense in which each national context has its own peculiarities and this is also true of Ireland. Thus, while we can learn much from comparative contexts, we should also bear in mind the specificity of the Irish educational and political-social context (Seery, 2008; O'Sullivan, 2005).

Here, my question is not so much 'what is ethical?' as 'what is the most appropriate way, or rather what are the most appropriate ways, in the plural, to teach ethics and religion in educational contexts, most especially in contexts of significant ethical or religious diversity?' Both of these questions are complex in their own right, but it is perhaps the second one which is the most pressing contemporary issue, both theoretically and practically, in Irish education, both at primary level in schools and at third-level, in terms of teacher education. What I will explore here is intended as a kind of provisional sketching out of some of the most insistent problems faced in this context, alongside a delineation of some of the options available here to construct a different approach to the one currently available (as such alternatives seem to become increasingly desirable) moving into the future. In making decisions about the overall pedagogical approach, we will also have to make decisions about ethical content to be taught. Again, we shall see this is also a highly contentious area of debate, with significantly different approaches in each case.

Education 'From Within' and 'From Without'

The study of ethics as a discipline in itself, as we shall see below, raises all kinds of problems with regard to the contestation of what might be seen as the best approach to ethics and moral thinking. Simply put, we can describe these issues as *intra-ethical.* However, when we come to look at ethical education on a more meta-level, it is clear that while there are very significant intra-ethical issues, both practical and philosophical, these issues become particularly acute when we introduce the topic of the relation between ethics and religion, and especially the question of how ethics and religion might be taught to children and/or student teachers. For some kinds of thinking, of a more traditionalist sort, ethics must always be subsumed under religion as a sub-category, while for the opposite extreme, associated with secularist approaches, ethics must be somehow divorced from religion completely. We will look at both these perspectives in more detail below, but first, it is helpful to clarify a key pedagogical distinction in terms of approaches to the teaching of ethical and religious education, which, following Hanan Alexander and Terence McLaughlin, we can refer to as follows: 'in the context of this focus, it is useful to draw a distinction between two broad conceptions of education in religion and spirituality, which we shall label 'education in religion and spirituality from the outside' and 'education in religion and spirituality from the inside' respectively' (2003, p. 361).

In the context of Irish primary schools, it is clear that the first model is employed in denominational schools, where faith-formation is seen as integral, including sacramental preparation. The situation of Irish teacher education is more complex, where one could argue that the religious education which is taught in teacher education colleges is not seeking to be a kind of faith-formation, but is rather simply professional preparation. This is a complex issue but it is at least clear that Catholic education in teacher education colleges is 'ethical and religious education from within', that is from within a Catholic perspective, even if it is not exactly faith-formation. At present, there is no 'ethical and religious education from without' available to student teachers, with the exception of the Ethics and Education course which is offered as an alternative at St Patrick's College, having begun in the academic year 2010/2011.[5]

The Intricate Relationship between the Religious and the Civic in Liberal Democratic Societies

McLaughlin and Alexander begin by foregrounding some of the complex issues which face educationalists in religion and spirituality, for example in contexts of liberal democratic societies and education systems. First, while most contemporary educational approaches emphasise the value of critical rationality and epistemological knowledge, it is arguable that what Alexander and McLaughlin call the 'domain' of religion (2003, p. 356) is often in tension with this emphasis, due to a contrary emphasis on faith or a critique of the limits of rationality through religious faith. Second, education often involves a notion of liberation or flourishing at its heart, but as Alexander and McLaughlin suggest, while there are visions of liberation also at the heart of religious movements and approaches, the distinctive visions of liberation and flourishing embodied in religious and spiritual traditions 'may be seen as widely contested and as in conflict with educational values [per se]' (2003, p. 356). Thirdly, and this is a point which has become increasingly important in recent times, education is often linked to the values and principles of liberal democratic societies, founded in a conception of universal human rights, and affirming pluralism and multiculturalism (Taylor, 1994). However, 'education in religion … is often seen as addressing beliefs that are not held in common by the wider public and which are significantly controversial' (Alexander and McLaughlin, 2003, p. 356). With regard to this last point, we can say that it *specifically* has become the contemporary socio-political point of contestation. From a liberal perspective, for example in Sweden or Denmark, Islamic practices and beliefs of a traditionalist sort are seen as inimical to democracy and human rights. From the other side, for example with regard to multiculturalism in the UK (including, crucially, multi-religiosity), the argument has been made that liberal democracy is far too assimilationist and difference-blind (Taylor, 1994).

Consequently, we can speak of the 'intricate relationship between the religious and the civic in liberal democratic societies' (Alexander and McLaughlin, 2003, p. 357) and the ensuing tensions with regard to political and educational policies as complex ones. Some of the key problems to be faced in such societies concern the status of what is called *common schooling* and its relation to religious and ethical education but also the issue of *faith-schools* or denominational schooling, and the extent to which the state should support such schools (ibid., p. 356). The peculiarity of the Irish context is clear when one realises that the question in Ireland is rather the very opposite, in the measure to which the state already supports 96 per cent of its primary schools as denominational or faith-based (Irwin, 2010). *In Ireland, one of the key questions is rather to what extent the state is prepared to support common schooling, and what kinds of approach to common schooling should be taken*? Additionally, there are recalcitrant issues in relation to the type of denominational schooling which should remain; whether, for example, in Norman's terms, Catholic education should be more liberal or traditionalist (Norman, 2003)? And indeed, whether there are viable alternatives to the either faith-school or common school binary opposition, such as mixed models combining faith-formation and comparative religion and ethics? Or whether, finally, more radical types of school which opt out of ethics and religious education completely on philosophical grounds, such as nondenominational or secularist schools, should be possible in an Irish context?

This question of the peculiarity of the problems in the Irish context also raises concerns about the exact nature of the Irish political system in its relation to the school system. To what extent is Ireland a *unique case* in the evolution of liberal politics in the West, particularly from the point of view of church/state relations?[6] If Ireland is a peculiar case, this also raises issues about the possible solutions which might be proposed. Following Freire, we can warn against the importation of models from other countries in this regard (Freire, 1977). Freire's discussion of the specificity of post-colonial societies (as opposed to 'director' societies) is also very relevant to this discussion, not least because the Brazilian experience (as described by Freire) has significant affinities with the Irish case (Freire, 2005).

Let us return to the paradigmatic pedagogical distinction which Alexander and McLaughlin make between 'education in religion and spirituality from the outside' and 'education in religion and spirituality from the inside' (2003, p. 361). This distinction itself needs to be problematised somewhat but it does serve a useful function in foregrounding a choice between two fundamental models of pedagogy (we will also see in the discussion of ethics that different ethical approaches will tend to favour one or other of these pedagogical models). Alexander and McLaughlin make clear that they are not trying to hold to this distinction in any absolutist way and describe the difficulty in finding the 'best vocabulary' in relation to this distinction, citing categories other than 'inside' and 'outside' such as 'common and open' versus 'distinctive and tradition-supporting', 'educating about' and 'educating within', and finally 'educating for understanding' and 'educating for faith commitment' (2003, p. 372). But for Alexander and McLaughlin, it is clear that there is no *either/or* choice to be made here but rather what is being sought is a 'more complex picturing of contrasting elements' (ibid., p. 372). Ultimately, those who seek to 'educate about' must also seek, in some measure, to 'educate from within' in order to truly capture what is going on in such traditions and practices and, by the same token, education which fosters 'faith commitment' cannot focus simply on its own faith tradition but should seek to also offer some form of 'comparative' analysis with other faiths and belief-systems (ibid., p. 372).

For Alexander and Mc Loughlin, consequently, our liberal-democratic societies are obliged to recognise both kinds of approach to education, recognising the distinctiveness of each, while also recognising that there is much intersection between the two models (2003, p. 362). They seem to summarily dismiss the claims of what are often called nondenominational schools, which they describe as 'deeply problematical' (ibid., p. 362), insofar as the latter do not allow one to educate children concerning religion whatsoever, and will thus run the risk of causing misinformed prejudices to develop in the population concerning religion.[7] For Alexander and McLaughlin, then, the discussion must take place in terms of a debate between the value of 'openness' on the one hand and the value of 'rootedness' on the other (ibid., p. 362). This pedagogical distinction is also a distinction of ethical significance. In what measure should the study of ethics foster an 'openness' and to what extent should it be encouraging a rootedness in the values of a well-tested tradition? This discussion can take place at a meta-level but it also, we will now see, is a debate which has taken place right at the very heart of the history of more substantive ethical thinking.

Four Paradigms of Ethical Enquiry – Character Formation, Moral Development, Care Ethics and Genealogical Critique

The history of philosophy is the history of the contestation of one ethical paradigm after another. At the same time, many ethical approaches, while distinct, often share significant elements of commonality. Some perspectives, which we have associated with Nietzschean thought and postmodernism (Nietzsche, 1967), can be critical of the ethical *per se* or in principle, although this does not outrule their right to still make some claim to the ethical (insofar as they often judge previous ethical claims to be based on deception or a misinterpretation of the semantics of ethics). In a significant article, entitled *Changing Notions of the Moral and of Moral Education* (2003), Nell Noddings and Michael Slote contextualise three key paradigms of ethical thinking which are influential on current debates within moral education. I will add a fourth paradigm of ethical thinking which Noddings and Slote do not discuss, but which I think must also be taken into account.

The Kantian Paradigm of Morality

Noddings and Slote begin with the foregrounding of the 'Kantian paradigm of morality' which they describe as having 'come under fire ... in recent years' (2003, p. 342). The ideology doing the targeting is identified as 'communitarianism' and here we have two of our ethical paradigms. In the first case, the Kantian paradigm of morality is exemplary of a liberal or modernist approach to ethics, which stresses the individual as primary and the value of moral autonomy (Callan and White, 2003). With regard to ethical education, this approach has been most associated with Kohlberg's (Kohlberg, 1981) work on the moral development of children, which also exemplifies the rationalism and universalism of this paradigm. We might also associate this philosophical perspective with the emphasis on a more child-centred education, which connects liberalism to what has become known as progressivism, or progressivist education or pedagogy (Darling and Nordenbo, 2003). These affiliations and alignments are not without their complexities and tensions and I will return to an analysis of some of these tensions later in the chapter. The critique of this liberal approach, a critique which is both political and pedagogical, raises questions about 'the Kantian emphasis on the autonomous individual, individual rights and universal principles' (Noddings and Slote, 2003, p. 342). This critique develops from the philosophical approach known as 'communitarianism', which is associated with philosophers such as Alasdair MacIntyre and Charles Taylor (Taylor, 1994), amongst others. The approach of communitarianism is to stress the 'moral centrality of communities, social contexts, webs of interlocution and different ways of life' (Noddings and Slote, 2003, p. 342).

One of the key points of contestation here relates to the question of how significant cultural difference is for the formation and maintenance of moral and societal norms and values, and of course we know that this has been a central issue in Irish education in more recent years (Irwin, 2010). The liberal perspective presents the basis for ethical education as a moral universalism which is, or at least should be, independent of cultural differences. This is the view which Charles Taylor refers to in his 1994 essay, *The Politics of Recognition*, as 'difference-blind liberalism'. As Noddings and Slote observe:

> Kantianism has its roots in the enlightenment belief in the universal power of human reason, in the possibility of coming up with rational social rules and institutions that take no sustenance or brook any interference from the religious, cultural, and ethnic differences that have historically divided one community from another (2003, p. 342).

Whereas Kant and the modernist project in philosophy claims that such rules can be constituted rationally by a society, in a self-conscious operation, *ex nihilo* as it were, for theorists such as MacIntyre and Sandel, this is to vastly underestimate the extent to which these moral norms are 'given' (Noddings and Slote, 2003, p. 342), that is, pre-formed and socialised by the traditions in which individuals and societies find themselves embedded. This issue becomes especially acute in multicultural societies where some groupings can arrive in a society with a whole set of norms and values from their own tradition, completely distinct (and often at odds) with the analogous values of the indigenous culture. On Kantian terms, this is not such a problematic situation, as we should be able to test whichever values at the tribunal of universal reason. For communitarianism, however, when different cultures find their moral values at odds, the hermeneutic issues of interpretation and evaluation are much more acute. As Taylor suggests, in such situations, what he calls 'difference-blind' liberalism (or 'procedural liberalism') runs into crisis, as it overestimates the universalisability of reason and of moral norms which are themselves culture-specific (for example, so called Western liberal values, which he suggests should be seen as very much derived from and influenced by Christianity in the West) (Taylor, 1994). For Taylor, then, so called universal morality and universal reason is really neo-Christian orthodoxy, which has been formed and developed through cultural traditions which are specific and historically rooted. Thus liberalism commits a ruse when it seeks to present such moral criteria and standards as 'value-neutral'. Liberalism is rather for Taylor a 'fighting creed' and must own up to being so (Taylor, 1994; Guttman, 1994).

From the point of view of ethical education, then, liberalism would present a picture of a pedagogy which sought to foster above all else individual and rational autonomy and, as I have suggested, the most famous example of this approach to the education of children has been that of Kohlberg (1981). For Noddings and Slote:

> Kantian/Rawlsian rationalism and liberalism would seemingly encourage moral education to take the form of developing certain capacities for moral reasoning and certain very general principles that can be applied to different moral dilemmas or decisions (2003, p. 249).

As noted earlier, if we are looking for empirical examples of such an education in practice, we might point to the approach of child-centred curricula, which have been associated with progressivism (Darling and Nordenbo, 2003).

Character Education and an Ethic of Care

Much as we might think of such approaches to education as dominant in our time, what Noddings and Slote want to suggest is that such an approach to ethical education has often been historically marginalised, not just in the West but also in the East: 'the history of moral education – not only in Western cultures but in most Eastern ones as well – has been dominated by character education' (2003, p. 350). This latter kind of pedagogy, then, becomes the second main paradigm of ethical education, and it is identified with the philosophy of 'communitarianism' and also 'virtue ethics', although this is a complex grouping, with significant internal differentiation. As Slote and Noddings comment, 'virtue ethics and mainstream communitarianism would naturally encourage a form of moral education in which schools would seek to inculcate good character in the form of specific (labelled) habitual virtues' (ibid. p. 349).

The third approach to ethical education which Noddings and Slote foreground is what they term 'an ethic of care':

> … an ethic of care would see naturally moral education as a matter of children's coming to an intelligent, emotional understanding of the good or harmful effects of their actions on the lives of other people as well as deepening understanding of defensible ways to live their own lives (ibid., p. 349).

Again, if we are looking for a philosophical home for this kind of pedagogy, we might associate it with more postmodern approaches to education, which tend to critique the cognitivism of liberalism and simultaneously the political conservatism of character education. This 'ethic of care' is especially associated (although not exclusively) with feminist approaches, for example, the work of Noddings herself, or that of Carol Gilligan.

How are we to understand such an ethic of care in relation to the aforementioned ethical models? First, we can say that care theory agrees with character education or communitarianism/virtue theory that the liberal Kohlbergian (1981) emphasis on reasoning is overstated and too cognitivist. However, standing alongside the Kohlbergians, care theorists simultaneously have concerns about the 'perceived lack of careful reasoning in some character education programs' (Noddings and Slote, 2003, p. 353). But, by the same token, some character educators have argued that care theory 'lacks moral content'. One can see that this truly is a matrix of affinity and disaffinity between the three models of ethical education. The slight about the moral content of care theory education relates to the fact that 'care theorists rely more heavily on establishing conditions likely to encourage goodness than on the direct teaching of virtues' (ibid. p. 355), although they agree with character educators that the way to a more ethical world is more likely to depend on better human beings than on simply better principles in education.

The Approach of Genealogical Critique

There is a fourth model of ethics which I would like to foreground, although it is missing from most discussions of the topic, and Noddings and Slote do not cite its relevance to the issue of moral education. This model might broadly be defined as *the approach of genealogical critique*, particularly associated with the work of the German philosopher Friedrich Nietzsche (1967) and the developers of his legacy in postmodernism, for example Michel Foucault and Jacques Derrida. A key difference between the genealogical critique and other forms of ethical education is that the former attacks the emphasis on virtue, characteristic of the latter. Nietzsche's critique of morality and virtue as a social construction with negative psychological effects for individuals in *On the Genealogy of Morals* (1967) is set up in opposition to the contrary assumption, for example, in Aristotelianism, that 'being good' actually makes people happy. For Nietzsche, then, there is a need to move 'beyond good and evil.' This critique of morality is also a critique, according to the neo-Nietzscheans (Drolet, 2003) of the power structures which lie hidden behind the veneer of altruism. Often, so-called 'virtue' can be a front for the maintenance of the status quo and a protection of vested interests. Paul Ricoeur refers to this aspect of Nietzsche's work as emblematic of his being a 'master of suspicion' (Ricoeur, 1970, p. 32).

This last point pushes us towards a more positive possibility within the genealogical critique which, in its most developed form, has become identified with postmodernist philosophy. Rather than such a philosophy being a recipe for nihilism, it may also be seen as offering the possibility of a critique of the blind spots within the discourse of more conventional ethical education. It is this dimension of postmodernism which has led to its importance for figures such as Giroux and McLaren, critical thinkers on culture and politics associated with the movement of Critical Pedagogy (Giroux, 2000; McLaren and Leonard, 1993). To this extent, postmodernism may be arguing less for an end to well-being than for the advent of a more authentic well-being (Irwin, 2008).

Given these four models of ethical education, it is clear that it is character education which is by far the most predominant model in education, although its content and nature can vary considerably from country to country. The other two main models of ethical education, whether they refer to the liberal Kantian/Kohlbergian (Kohlberg, 1981) model or the ethics of care, are used less commonly and often they are not so much used as a stand-alone model but more as a supplement to the model of character education. The fourth model of ethical education, that of genealogical critique associated with Nietzsche's work (1967) and his successors in postmodernism, is never used as a stand-alone model in schools, but we might argue that its influence on the wider societal values since the nineteenth century is immense, perhaps (it could be argued) the greatest in influence of all the four models. Additionally, certain aspects of this Nietzschean approach (Nietzsche, 1967), such as its avowal of atheism and its radical critique of metaphysics, can be seen as increasingly relevant to comparative ethics and religious programmes, which are often very weak on 'nonreligious' ethical perspectives most especially, for example, atheism, agnosticism or humanism (Irwin, 2010).

However, although character education remains significantly dominant in terms of educational approaches, Noddings and Slote also point to its more recent decline:

> … the decline of character education in the USA can be traced in part to studies which showed that it was not working well; but the diversity of American society also put stumbling blocks in the way of character education. There are problems about whose values and whose traditions should form the basis for public moral education, and these very problems have encouraged the development of other models (2003, p. 350).

But if character education had become associated with traditionalism and regression, for example in the USA, then liberal progressivist education (Darling and Nordenbo, 2003), associated more with the Kantian philosophical ideal, in turn ran into difficulties with the development of a more explicitly diverse society. Child-centred education of a liberal progressivist model itself remained, in Charles Taylor's terminology, excessively difference-blind (Taylor, 1994).

Conclusion

If character education and the liberal moral development model have both run aground in different ways in more recent times, it perhaps shows that our other two models of ethics, whether that of the ethics of care or of ethics as genealogical critique, may play a much more significant role in ethics education in years to come. From the point of view of the meta-pedagogical issues we have addressed, this also has significant implications. Both of the ethical models described have links to a more postmodernist approach to ethics and politics, and, as such, call into question the distinction which Alexander and McLaughlin (2003) foreground, while themselves also seeking to go beyond it – that is, the distinction between an ethics 'from within' and an ethics 'from without'.

From such a point of view, in Ireland, then, the questions at the heart of our educational system become more complexified. The central question remains: should we favour ethics and religion from 'within' or from 'without', or *common schools* versus *faith schools*, or at least have a fairer distribution of each type? A second question is: would it be possible to develop a model of school which can avoid the binarism of either or both of these approaches to schooling and values-education? This at least would seem to be the question developing from a more postmodernist approach to ethical and religious education (Noddings and Slote, 2003; Nietzsche, 1967). However, we should not underestimate how many parents, teachers and students might still value an *either/or* model, whether that is in terms of a faith-school approach *or* a multi-denominational system of education. We should additionally note that secularist models of education would reject both of these pedagogical models in favour of simply not teaching religion in any fashion (or perhaps additionally not teaching any ethical curriculum or content as such). The American and French pedagogies, in terms of existing state models for example, teach religion *neither from 'within' nor from 'without'*.[8]

It is in just such a context of contested ideological positions, then, that the education debate will take shape in the months and years to come. It has been precisely the lack of such a debate in the past, in an Irish context, that has marked out our education system as peculiar and, for some, rather backward. For many, the key issues will take place in relation to primary education, at the level of the patronage of the primary schools, and the ensuing implications for ethos on both a formal level but also on a ground level (Norman, 2003). But, in terms of teacher education, we have an analogous if not more acute situation. As Donnelly has shown (Donnelly, 2011), the politics of education as they relate to the governance of the colleges of education and teacher education are anachronistic. Already, there is a disparity between the primary schools and the colleges of education, with 96 per cent of primary schools being denominational while 100 per cent of state-funded colleges are (Donnelly, 2011). However, this issue will become intensified with the planned development of more multi-denominational (Rowe, 2000) and state VEC[9] inter-denominational schools. In such a context, the problems become more than simply theoretical or philosophical but also increasingly professional. More and more, it is becoming clear that we are not educating, in effect *we are seriously failing to prepare*, our student teachers to teach in an increasingly diverse Ireland.

Endnotes

1. At the time of writing, 96 per cent of state schools are denominational, with 90 per cent being Catholic and 6 per cent Church of Ireland (Protes-

tant). To put this in historical context, 100 per cent of state primary schools were denominational up until the late 1970s and, even by 2001, only 1 per cent of schools were multidenominational (Irwin, 2010). On the one side, a denominational religious ethos aims as a matter of policy to foster in young people a commitment to a particular religion. In multidenominational education, on the other hand, the truth claims of religion and other belief systems are explored as part of the school's ethos but truth is not associated with a particular view. Students study a comparative religious and ethics programme, where belief systems are critically explored without the assumption of any one faith. Sacramental preparation does not take place in school time and the symbolism of the school must represent a diversity of perspectives (Rowe, 2000).

2. This reactionary theological position can be contrasted sharply with a more open-minded and pluralistic philosophy from a denominational perspective, notable in Ireland in the works of Joseph Dunne (1991), Padraig Hogan (Hogan and Williams, 1997), Andrew Burke (2009) and Dermot Lane (1997) amongst others, or internationally in the work of thinkers such as Richard Pring (2008) or Terence McLaughlin (2008a; 2008b). McLaughlin most especially has addressed the issue of educational ethos throughout his work. He has consistently argued for a form of denominationalism (what he calls 'the separate school' [McLaughlin, 2008b]) which remains, on his terms, wholly compatible with democratic values and the values of reason and autonomy.

3. The Forum on Patronage and Pluralism was set up by the Government in 2011 and consulted widely with the various educational lobby groups. The idea of the forum was originally suggested by the Catholic Archbishop of Dublin, Diarmuid Martin, as a response to a growing diversity in the population (Coolahan, Hussey and Kilfeather, 2012).

4. For a discussion of the ethical paradigms, see the section titled *Four Paradigms of Ethical Enquiry*. Education from 'within the tradition' is usually associated with character education and thus is also close to virtue ethics and communitarianism (Taylor, 1994). Education 'from outside' the tradition tends to be associated with a more liberal approach to pedagogy and thus is usually more connected to the 'moral development' model of ethics (Callan and White, 2003). In terms of philosophical paradigms, we might associate 'education from within' with more pre-modern or metaphysical approaches, while 'education from without' is more associated with modernist,

rationalist-universalist perspectives or human rights perspectives (Waldron and Ruane, 2010). In the postmodern perspective (Nietzsche 1967), the very distinction between 'education from within' and 'education from without' becomes more complex and there is greater possibility for a mixed-model approach. In practical terms, the new VEC state school primary model in Ireland could be seen as enacting just such a 'mixed-model', including both 'faith-formation' and 'comparative ethics and religion.'

5. Since 2011, a curriculum course in Ethics and Education has been offered at St Patrick's College, Drumcondra. This course has been taught primarily by Dr Philomena Donnelly, Brian Ruane and I (St Patrick's College) and Fionnuala Ward (Educate Together). This curriculum course has offered a 'multi-denominational' alternative to student teachers on an either/or basis with Catholic religious education. This curriculum course is the first of its kind to be offered in the history of the state.

6. For a seminal discussion of the complex issues surrounding the development of the Irish education system and culture, see O'Sullivan, 2005.

7. This latter is a highly contestable claim and, without dealing in detail with it here, one can argue that such nondenominational or secularist schools have every much as right to be part of the public dialogue for change as either of the other two models of denominational or multi-denominational.

8. In terms of our distinctions between different paradigms of thinking on ethics and religion, it would seem that the 'secularist' approach is probably best described as a radically modernist view of values education, which brooks no compromise with alternative perspectives.

9. The new so-called community national or VEC primary schools propose to dedicate 20 per cent of religion/ethics teaching time to faith formation and 80 per cent of the time to a more comparative programme of ethics and religion. These schools are currently (after some discussion) referring to themselves as 'multi-faith' schools and represent a relatively new and distinctive type of school in the Republic.

References

Alexander, H. and McLaughlin, T.H. (2003). Education and Spirituality. In N. Blake, P. Smyers, R. Smith and P. Standish (Eds.), *The Blackwell guide to philosophy of education*. Oxford: Wiley-Blackwell.

Burke, A. (2009). The BEd degree: Still under review. *Oideas*, *Sep,* 1-43.

Callan, E. and White, J. (2003). Liberalism and communitarianism. In N. Blake, P. Smyers, R. Smith and P. Standish (Eds.), *The Blackwell guide to philosophy of education*. Oxford: Wiley-Blackwell.

Coolahan, J. Hussey, C. and Kilfeather, P. (2012). *The forum on patronage and pluralism in the primary sector: Report of the forum's advisory group*. Dublin. DES.

Darling, J. and Nordenbo, D. (2003). Progressivism. In N. Blake, P. Smyers, R. Smith and P. Standish (Eds.), *The Blackwell guide to philosophy of education*. Oxford: Wiley-Blackwell.

Donnelly, P. (2011, June). *Fit for purpose? The governance and control of primary teacher education in Ireland: Time for change.* Paper presented to the Re-imagining Initial Teacher Education Conference, St Patrick's College, Dublin.

Drolet, M. (2003). *The postmodernism reader*. Routledge: London.

Dunne, J. (1991). The Catholic school and civil society: Exploring the tensions. In N. Brennan et al. (Eds.), *The Catholic school in contemporary society*. Dublin: CMRS.

Freire, P. (1977). *Cultural action for freedom* (J. da Veiga Coutinho, Trans.). London: Nicholls.

Freire, P. (1992). *Pedagogy of hope: Revisiting pedagogy of the oppressed.* London: Continuum.

Freire, P. (2005). Education as the practice of freedom. In *Education for critical consciousness*. London: Continuum.

Giroux, H. (2000). *Breaking in to the movies*. New York: Routledge.

Gutmann, A. (Ed.). (1994). *Multiculturalism: Examining the politics of recognition.* New Jersey: Princeton University Press.

Hogan, P. and Williams, K. (Eds.). (1997). *The future of religion in Irish education*. Dublin: Veritas.

Irwin, J. (2008). Philosophical questioning of the normativity of well-being. In M. O'Brien (Ed.), *Well-being and post-primary schooling: A review of the literature and research* (NCCA Research Report No. 6).

Irwin, J. (2010). Interculturalism, ethos and ideology. Barriers to freedom and democracy in Irish primary education. *REA: A Journal of Religion, Education and the Arts, 6.*

Kohlberg, L. (1981). *The philosophy of moral development.* London: Harper Collins.

Lane, D. (1997). Afterword: The expanding horizons of Catholic education. In P. Hogan and K. Williams (Eds.), *The future of religion in Irish education.* Dublin: Veritas.

McLaren, P. and Leonard, P. (Eds). (1993). *Paulo Freire: A critical encounter.* London: Routledge.

McLaughlin, T.H. (2008a). The burdens and dilemmas of common schooling. In D. Carr, M. Halstead and R. Pring (Eds.), *Liberalism, education and schooling: Essays by T.H. McLaughlin* (pp. 137-174). Exeter: Imprint.

McLaughlin, T.H. (2008b). The ethics of separate schools. In D. Carr, M. Halstead and R. Pring (Eds.), *Liberalism, education and schooling: Essays by T.H. McLaughlin* (pp. 175-198). Exeter: Imprint.

Nietzsche, F. (1967). *On the genealogy of morals.* (W. Kaufmann and R.J. Hollingdale, Trans.). London. Vintage.

Noddings, N. and Slote, M. (2003). Changing notions of the moral and of moral education. In N. Blake, P. Smyers, R. Smith and P. Standish (Eds.), *The Blackwell guide to philosophy of education.* Oxford: Wiley-Blackwell.

Norman, J. (2003). *Ethos and education in Ireland.* New York: Peter Lang.

O'Sullivan, D. (2005). *Cultural politics and Irish education since the 1950s: Policy, paradigms and power.* Dublin: IPA.

Pring, R. (2008). Introduction. In D. Carr, M. Halstead and R. Pring. (Eds.), *Liberalism, education and schooling: Essays by T.H. McLaughlin* (pp. 95-98). Exeter: Imprint.

Ricoeur, P. (1970). *Freud and philosophy: An essay in interpretation* (2nd ed.) (D. Savage, Trans.). New Haven: Yale University Press.

Rowe, P. (2000). Educate Together schools: Core values and ethos. In C. Furlong and L. Monahan (Eds.), *School culture and ethos: Cracking the code.* Dublin: Marino.

Seery, A. (2008). Slavoj Žižek's dialectics of ideology and the discourses of Irish education. *Irish Educational Studies*, *27*(2).

Taylor, C. (1994). The politics of recognition. In A. Gutmann (Ed.), *Multiculturalism: Examining the politics of recognition*. NJ: Princeton University Press.

Teaching Council. (2011). *Initial teacher education: Criteria and guidelines for programme providers*. Dublin: Author.

Waldron, F. and Ruane, B. (Eds.). (2010). *Human rights education: Reflections on theory and practice*. Dublin: The Liffey Press.

Williams, K. (1997). Religion in Irish education: Future trends in government policy. In P. Hogan and K. Williams (Eds.), *The future of religion in Irish education*. Dublin: Veritas.

Williams, K. (2003). Foreword. In J. Norman, *Ethos and education in Ireland*. Peter Lang.

Chapter 10

Care, Relationality and a Humanising Education: The Significance of the Affective Context in Initial Teacher Education

Maeve O'Brien

St Patrick's College, Drumcondra

> I do not mean to suggest that the establishment of caring relations will accomplish everything that must be done in education, but these relations provide the foundation for successful pedagogical activity (Noddings, 2005).

Introduction

In the current economic and social context, given the increasing dominance of overly rationalistic and technicist views of the human, it is ever more difficult to speak of and give recognition to the affective domain of life and its significance to human flourishing.[1] Social commentators and educationalists have highlighted the dominance of economic perspectives in shaping our view of the human as *homo economicus*, and how that relates to our understandings and experiences of affective relations of care, connection and moral life.

Although there has been a long tradition of valuing care in practice in Irish education (Drudy and Lynch, 1993), particularly at primary level where the national curriculum has, since the 1970s, articulated the importance of the holistic development of the child, teaching and teacher education are now under increasing pressure from trends towards instrumentality and a pervasive economic metrics. Indeed critical educational scholarship suggests that educators' professional practices may be shaped by discourses of accountability and performativity that undermine their passion for teaching, relationality and the very soul of their pedagogy (Ball, 2003; Prosser, 2006; Wetz, 2010). Critical and feminist scholars writing on the affective context and its significance for education are concerned that anti-humanist, overly rational paradigms and monetarist conceptions of the 'good' (Gomberg, 2007) can infiltrate education through policy and ideology (Freire, 1970, 1998; Noddings, 1999, 2005; Lynch, Baker and Lyons, 2009; O'Brien, 2011) shaping the nature of student-teacher relations, curricula and assessment, and often failing to recognise and appreciate the importance of a holistic and humanising education.[2]

Despite such trends in the social world, which put pressure on relationships and view affect as non-productive, diverse scholarship on well-being suggests that care and relationality are the very glue of social life and fundamental to our capacity to thrive in a postmodern globalised world (Sevenhuijsen, 1998; Bauman, 2003).[3] More recently, perspectives on teaching and teacher identity have taken seriously issues around affect and emotional life and their significance for the construction of teacher and student identities that are liberating and not essentially fixed through policy discourses and managerial practices (Zembylas, 2003). This growing scholarship also critiques the marginalisation and systematic neglect of affect, as distinct from normalised emotions, and it challenges a focus on *cognitive* approaches to emotional education in western schooling (Boler, 1997a).[4] Meanwhile, international educational research indicates that students' positive perceptions of their school experiences and of their learning are strongly related to the affective and relational aspects of school life (Opdenakker and Van Damme, 2000; Smerdon, 2002). Qualitative research carried out in Ireland with adults who failed to acquire literacy throughout their schooling suggests an absence of care, conceptualised as 'learning care', and indicates that the emotional and care contexts in which teaching occurs have lifelong effects on literacy learning and on well-being (Feeley, 2009).

On the international stage, economistic and neoliberal ideologies persuade that high quality educational products (technical rational knowledge and skills that are visible, measurable and deliverable) are a priority, essential for global competitiveness and for the maintenance of particular forms of culture and development, often at the cost of less privileged and marginal peoples (Scatamburlo-D'Annibale and McLaren 2009; Apple, Au and Gandin, 2009). Currently, in Ireland, a landscape of austerity casts a shadow over educational programmes, threatening their future and regulating the imagined possibilities of what is deliverable and even permissible. Threats that are both ideological and material lend a rationale to decision-makers to privatise what is considered no longer publicly affordable. Thus, education becomes more commodified and vulnerable to market forces (see Lynch, 2006), shaping its value as a market good in ways that may block a more holistic development. In this challenging context, it is critical that initial teacher education (ITE) resists these pressures from without and continues to scaffold strongly the capacity of 'becoming' teachers to engage with diverse populations of students, recognising the affective context and the embedded relational nature of teaching and learning (Kelthchermans, 2005; Hall et al., 2012).

This chapter draws on a growing interdisciplinary and largely feminist literature on care, affect and well-being to elaborate the traditional and continuing marginalisation of care and relationality within the social world and the problems this poses for justice and development. Within this frame it explores some of the challenges this creates for educators in primary education and in ITE. As well as exploring the problem of sustaining caring and affective relations in education today, it hopes to make explicit the relationship between care and an education that promotes *social justice* and well-being. Taking care and relationships seriously in education and teacher education means recognising the pressures from managerialist discourses on emotional expression (Hochschild, 1983), and what Amsler (2011) has called the biopolitics of some forms of pedagogy around emotions, which can be more regulatory than liberating. Even within the small pool of empirical research on emotions in teaching, there has been little attention given to the connection between emotions and just actions (see Gilligan, 1982, 2011), or to the relationship between emotions and how they are core to an ethic of care and caring practice (Boler, 1997b). In order to discuss the issue of care and affect and its implications for ITE, it is necessary to explore this within the continuum of education and to consider the significance of caring and affect to society more generally. This broader landscape frames current movements and pressures in ITE and provides a context for the discussion of the significance of care and transformative praxis. The final section of the chapter draws out what a commitment to care means for teacher educators and for their students and explores some of the implications of humanising care praxis in ITE.

The Significance of Care and Emotions to Holistic Development and Well-Being

The *Code of Professional Conduct for Teachers* developed by the Teaching Council of Ireland (2012), which guides teachers' ethical practice, names *care* as one of the core values which underpin the code (trust, respect and integrity being the other three). Moreover, the core value of care is articulated not only as a legal 'duty of care' expected of teachers, but also in terms of something more substantive which suggests that teachers' caring means looking out for 'the best interests' of their students. Under this code of conduct, teachers' duty of care can be interpreted as an aspect of their role concerned with fostering students' capacities in a holistic way for their own flourishing.[5] However, the adequacy of such codes in ensuring ethical practice is contested. Campbell (2000), for example, suggests that there is widespread agreement in the literature on educational ethics that 'ethical codes, in and of themselves, are by no means an adequate resource for preparing and sustaining moral professionals' (p. 204). Campbell also observes the views expressed by Soltis (1986, p. 2) that, although codes of professional practice 'do not offer a philosophical justification of fundamental ethical principles', they do contribute to conceptualising teaching as an ethical activity.

There has been a long tradition within humanistic education that the development of the whole person is fundamental to their flourishing and to their education as citizens. More recently a happiness or an 'enhancement agenda' in education has been debated, and an over emphasis on happiness rather than subject learning and academic achievement has been critiqued (see Cigman, 2008). Others argue that flourishing, happiness *and* achievement should not be mutually exclusive. However, there are continuing tensions in the literature as to how teachers' classroom practices can facilitate meeting immediate emotional and care needs alongside promoting students' academic achievements (Sumsion, 2010), particularly among 'disadvantaged' students (Noddings, 1992; Farrelly, 2009). Moreover, within liberal educational traditions, understandings of flourishing (coming to us from Aristotle's *eudaimonia*) have been informed by holism and by an idea of well-being that is concerned not just with the individual but with the 'good of society'. Within this view, affect and emotions are not dismissed as irrelevant, but are understood as aspects of the human which can be problematic and that need to be tamed and educated in order to lead to just thinking and action. This perspective on a moral praxis that is at once rational and also infused by affect and a concern with appropriate emotional responsiveness is evident in the work of feminist care scholars, including educationalists. Nussbaum's philosophical work on human development highlights the significance of emotions and affect to caring relationships, moral action, our capacity to be fully human and to fostering a 'good society' (1995).

Feminist interdisciplinary discourses on care emphasise the necessity and inalienability of emotional/affective effort and attunement for the development of certain types of caring. The problem recognised by many care scholars is that the traditional dichotomisation of care as 'love' or 'labour' facilitates misrecognition of the significance of emotions. Feminist care discourse draws attention to the role of emotional engagement within caring, albeit to varying degrees, in both 'hands on' *caring for* face-to-face relationships and in *caring about*, a less physically embodied care. Caring about is characterised by a disposition or attitude that keeps the object of care in mind/heart over time, even when we are not in the presence of the 'object of care'. This disposition is predicated on an emotional engagement, one that motivates us to feel and think about an *other* and act to support their good or interests (Noddings, 1992; Hollway, 2006). While the degree of emotional engagement in caring is relative to both the specific context and to the nature of the relationship between the cared for and the care giver, and although definitions of care differ according to context and disciplinary positioning, care scholars generally acknowledge that the continuum of care/love relationality inalienably involves our emotional selves:

> In caring for others, we act to meet their needs in a way that involves an attitude of concern or even love. Love involves acting for those we love and care for, not just feeling for them. Solidarity involves active support for others, not just passive empathy. (Lynch, Baker and Lyons, 2009, p. 1)

Here, Lynch et al. suggest a continuum of caring that may extend to loving or not, but they also point out that even within solidarity relations – relations which are associated with a more public space of relationality and less intimate care contexts – meaningful care still requires both emotional connection *and* activity or action, what we might call a *care praxis* (O'Brien, 2011). While the degree of emotional connection in caring relations, as many policy and theoretical care writers have suggested, varies across private and public care contexts, it is wrong to assume that 'paid for' caring work (as in teaching for example, see Hargreaves, 2000) does not involve one's emotions, as there are emotional dimensions to all care work (and indeed to work that is not care work, see Hochschild, 1983).

Feminist scholarship on care across the disciplinary areas of critical psychology and sociology, political science and law suggest that what is most significant in a world that reifies and worships 'rationality' are those *emotional* capacities and their expression which enable us to care and to love, capacities that are thus fundamental to our own well-being and that of others. Carol Gilligan's (1982) work has been seminal in bringing human emotions, their relational dimensions and expression into the discourse on moral development. Her work suggests that for many women (and indeed for men, though to a lesser extent) orientations to moral action are based in a language and valuing of relationships and particularly in *feelings* of empathy that we learn from our earliest encounters in the social world.[6]

In challenging an overly rational 'malestream' view of the human being, feminist care scholarship has posited a strong counter position to a prevalent view of the human as a detached rational actor, rootless and self-interested. This scholarship on the significance of emotions and relational life to human development and well-being supports the significance of caring as an ethical practice and as a form of experience and knowledge to be sustained within teaching and teacher education programmes. The discourses on relationality and the moral significance of emotions suggest that as teachers and teacher educators, 'as carers', we will feel responsible for and encouraged to develop emotional connections with colleagues and students. In our daily work as teacher educators and teachers, despite limited resources, changing demands for relevance and newly ordered priorities within a complex educational landscape, we feel the need to respond to that other (Sumsion, 2010), to follow a moral imperative to care within a complicated nexus of relationality (Noddings, 1992).

Affect and Caring in Educational Contexts

In this section I argue for the importance of the emotional and affective context within education for students' own well-being and holistic flourishing. Caring education necessitates making well-being an explicit aim of education or at least naming it as a universal good to which education as a humanising process can contribute. Against the grain of a global capitalism, which is often focused on education as a supplier of human capital for the 'knowledge economy', a holistic humanising education will include a focus on cognitive development and skill development, but it will not do so at the cost of other aspects of learning and development.[7] Taking relational life seriously in terms of development means that as educators we need to explore how care and affect, and indeed their embodiment, can be brought more centrally and explicitly into pedagogy and classroom praxis.

While there is little recognition of the significance of care and affect within the discourse of educational policy, feminist and social justice approaches to education offer a starting point. From a critical perspective, theorists have explored new approaches and pedagogies that are concerned with emotions and their contribution to radical transformation through caring for students *and* a commitment to social justice (Ellsworth, 1989; Weiler, 1994; Boler, 1997b). In addition, while there has been a sustained feminist interest in the caring dimensions of teaching and of teachers' responsibilities for care, little of the scholarship and research on care and well-being has been adapted in any systematic and applied way to explore the relation between well-being, schooling and teachers' professional responsibility for caring. While there are countless international studies on school reform and school effectiveness, student achievement and satisfactions, few have looked at the question of overall or holistic well-being of students, teachers or school communities, and the contribution of caring to well-being. Finnish research on well-being and schooling has led the way in this regard. In a series of research studies, the Quality of Life model of well-being/welfare developed by Erik Allardt was adapted for the school context (Konu and Rimpela, 2002; Konu, Lintonen and Rimpela, 2002; Konu, Alanen, Lintonen and Rimpela, 2002). Allardt's model is useful because it includes both objective and subjective categories of well-being and recognises and includes the significant area of *affect and relationships* within a three dimensional model (Allardt, 1993). The dimensions of well-being outlined are *having, loving and being*. *Having* includes resources and services and impersonal needs; *loving* refers to the need for social relationships; while *being* is about agency, choices, opportunities, personal growth and participation. The model is holistic in that it also takes account of the wider home and community context as part of a broader teaching and learning ecological landscape in which teachers, as professionals, care for their students.

The adaptation of this model for promoting and assessing well-being in schools raises questions about the nature and extent of teachers' responsibilities towards their students and, in terms of the 'loving dimension' specifically, their duties of care in respect of affective life and relationality within the school community. The prioritising of student achievement as a measure of school reform, however, can mean that teachers' responsibility for the holistic care and well-being of students is *not* recognised as primary. International research on students' feelings of liking school suggests that 'liking' does not necessarily correlate with high student achievement. In the child well-being research carried out by UNICEF (2007), for example, Finland scored very highly on school achievement but very low on students' 'liking school'. Recently, in Sweden there has been a move to re-conceptualise their model of education to encompass what is termed 'social pedagogy' which includes a holistic focus on integrating education, personal development and care (which is also reflected in their ITE practice). This change expresses a pedagogy/praxis that is about 'bringing up the whole child' through an integrated services delivery rather than in a pedagogy that is didactic and through a curriculum delivered solely by teachers. At the heart of this approach is a valuing of relationality and significant caring attachments, which enable a secure basis for engagement of all children in school (Wetz, 2010).

Teachers' Caring and Emotions as Making a Difference in the World

In this section I consider what it means for teachers to see care as part of their professional praxis and integral to the role of the critical educator for social justice and transformation (Freire 1998; Boler, 1997b; Apple, 2011). Given the threats to affectual life and to the emotional caring relations that sustain it (Lynch, Baker and Lyons, 2009), there is a need to explore the costs, understandings, satisfactions and indeed extensive work, involved for teachers in caring about students and the world in their daily practices, relative to the particular contexts in which they are working. Building on feminist care scholarship and the radical humanising practice elaborated by Freire, this section considers care as a form of dialogic relationship in which teachers engage with their students, with ideas and the larger society in order to transform themselves and their world, through the process of humanisation and the overcoming of oppression.

In recent times, Noddings (2003) has argued that caring is a fundamental aspect of being an educator. She suggests that schooling and teaching without care are not education but rather a technical exercise with deeply unequal effects on individuals and groups. She argues that educators have responsibilities which include: caring *for* oneself and intimates; caring *about* strangers, the planet and ideas and culture (the *manmade* world). Noddings' work embraces the multidimensionality of caring in education. It indicates that some aspects of teachers' daily praxis demand a stronger emphasis on *caring for* (in the sense of relational emotional connection and attunement to the affective state of the other), while other aspects of their caring are more cognitively articulated and shaped in and through attitudes, dispositions and thinking (caring about).

A holistic educational practice needs to take seriously the various dimensions of caring, which include both *caring for* and *caring about*, the relational *emotional* aspects of care that vary in emotional intensity relative to particular situations, and also a care that is expressed in and through *critical thinking*. Although care discourses explore these dimensions of care, and the emotional and normative aspects of caring, there still is a need in teacher education discourses to theorise the relation between the emotional and more cognitive dimensions of teachers' caring practices and students' development. It would be foolish to underestimate the care challenges that teachers and teacher educators experience in trying to balance such a holistic perspective with demands for measurable learning outcomes that are generically stated and perhaps irrelevant, or even worse, damaging and not in the interests of some students (see Noddings, 1999, on challenges for teachers and Maguire, 2000, on teacher educators). Radical critical approaches to education, such as found in the work of Freire, name didactic 'banking education' as deeply unjust/uncaring and against the interests of the people it purports to serve. Freire suggested that the transformation of self and society through a humanising education must be brought about through deep feeling, through a 'revolution in love'. This is an orientative principle of love for the people (a caring about), a love without sentimentalisation or manipulation and not based in some abstract principle of justice (Freire, 1970, p. 70). Over time, Freire acknowledged the dangers – as well as the power – of deep feeling and emotions to education, and in his last work, *Pedagogy of Freedom* (1998), he states most strongly that we must overcome the dichotomising of teaching and emotional expressiveness. True education, he states, cannot be treated as something cold, without feeling or desire, as something merely technical; true education is of necessity relational and dialogical.

Noddings' work is also concerned with an approach to education premised on *an ethic of care that can bring about justice*, in what she perceives to be a deeply unequal and exclusionary formal schooling system. Building on Noddings, Falkenberg (2009) suggests that the distinction between *natural* care and *ethical* care can be helpful to educators in trying to understand the nature of person-to-person caring encounters between teachers and students, and more cognitive and critical aspects of caring that require thinking and imagination in order to care at a distance (for example about justice issues). We need to be mindful, however, that the distinction between these two aspects of care does not become too forced (although I am not suggesting that this is what Noddings intends). The categorisation of natural and ethical care in this way can undermine the ground hard-won by feminist care theorists. They have argued that the activity of person-to-person care, which has largely been assigned to and undertaken by women, has been 'constructed' as natural although it demands effort. If teachers' considerable efforts of care are constructed as something natural (particularly as primary teaching and teacher education are increasingly feminised professions), and therefore as effortless, this devalues care as an aspect of their professional work. In caring, the effort it takes, the very fact that we choose to, and go that extra mile, makes it valuable in an often careless world. Furthermore, the categorisation of care as natural *or* ethical may promote the dichotomisation of care as either love *or* labour, and a view of a *natural* love as *not* ethical, falling into the traditional 'malestream' view of the moral challenged by Gilligan (1982). This framing of care has implications for those involved in caring professions including teacher education, and it has consequences for how some aspects of their labour may be either devalued as 'natural', or stripped of their affectual dimensions to emphasise a moral *rationality* of care.

A further challenge in valuing and doing caring relational work is that teachers themselves may be somewhat uncomfortable with the term *care* in relation to their professional status as educators. They may not want to be categorised as 'educarers' (Lynch, Lyons and Cantillon, 2007). The body of literature on the care aspects of teachers' work and identities, and on teaching as a caring profession, reflects diverse perspectives. In feminist sociological research, for example, Skeggs (1997) has discussed how feminised professions, and particularly feminised care work with children, is seen as low status and misrecognised. In ITE, recent research suggests that caring can be marginalised within the academy more generally, while still held as a key value and motivator by teacher educators (Maguire, 2000; Murray, 2006). Care, because it has been, and still is, associated with the feminine and mothering, is seen as natural and not given the same value as other forms of work/effort, thereby threatening the professional status of those for whom caring is a significant aspect of their professional practice. Currently, to emphasise caring in teaching, particularly beyond primary level, can be seen as a process of de-professionalisation, leading to a further marginalisation of teacher educators within the academy. As Ball (2003) remarks, in a globalised capitalist world, teachers are professionalised in response to markets and a new ethic and discourse of self-interest. Teachers and teacher educators face these ideological and political challenges when they choose to value care, and to meet real needs and foster the diverse talents of students.

Within the landscape of Irish education, particularly at primary level, but also within all-girls second-level schools (Lynch and Lodge, 2002) care has traditionally been a valued aspect of schools' missions or ethos. However, this commitment to care may be undermined by the spread of the care*less* 'religions' of fast capitalism and secular individualism (Sennet, 2006; Taylor, 1991). These ideologies are increasingly dominant in a cultural and economic context in which teachers and teacher educators are fighting for relationships and struggling for the time and space to foster the emotional engagement and dialogue that are necessary to keep *caring for* daily practices and *caring about* projects of justice on the educational agenda. In changing institutional landscapes of higher education, further challenges may be experienced by teacher educators, and although the Irish context for teacher education has been quite different from the UK and US, changes afoot within the global context affect us. This is significant for caring and well-being, particularly at a time when instrumental and 'fitness for purpose' thinking narrows the possibilities for more holistic approaches and perspectives that might create and sustain school and teaching environments sensitive to care and affectual life, thereby threatening the possibilities for a full humanising and transformative education.

Conclusion

I have argued that to develop holistic approaches to human development and education, teachers and teacher educators need to be radical and critical caring professionals. Through various dimensions of caring and a dialogic relational praxis which recognises and embodies the emotional/affective dimensions of the human, they can facilitate student and societal well-being. Objections might be raised that this view is too normatively fixing in ways that are oppressive to teachers and their professional identities, or that 'over' emphasising care and affect runs the risk of marginalising the cognitive and professional dimensions of teaching. But if we accept that education is about human flourishing in the holistic sense, and not about reproducing cycles of oppression and exploitation, then embodied feelings, responsiveness and relationality provide us as educators with pedagogies of caring possibility. Those teachers who from day-to-day and year-to-year meet their students in dialogic caring practice are the heroes and heroines of the profession and of the communities they serve. They compare to what Lynch and McLoughlin (1995, p. 259) call the silent invisible armies of women in the community, carers who put bread on the table of emotional life and ensure that communities and society thrive and function.

The implications of conserving a relational caring approach within ITE are multifaceted, particularly in a decade of austerity when economic rationality seems to fill the vision of what it is to create improvement in society and education. The trend in much international education policy and discourse is towards greater performative, managerialist and bureaucratic rationality which affects pedagogy, curricula and relationships. In such a climate, as Keltchermans (2005) has pointed out, understanding and reflecting on our emotions in teaching relationships and on developing pedagogies of critical emotional literacy (Weiler, 1994) provides the possibility to reflect on both the political and personal dimensions of education, and how particular agendas are encroaching on what educators most value. It has been argued that experiences and feelings are sources of knowledge which enable us to name our world and to question what needs to be radically transformed. Thus, as pressures within the market and global capitalist ideologies squeeze the holistic view of the human, and as new rhetorics of professionalism proliferate the cultural space, programmes and processes in ITE need to take account of the possibilities for the undermining and marginalisation of what is seen as 'soft' – the 'caring' and the 'emotional'. Likewise, the radical nature of a relationality and dialogue which includes emotional care can be eroded under managerialist approaches within education. Thin engagement with developing individuals' emotional intelligences (often in an overly cognitive fashion) may replace emotional and critical approaches to developing truly caring citizens. There is considerably more to be discussed vis-à-vis the relation between a pedagogy of care and a curricular praxis in ITE, but for now suffice it to say that efforts of care and ethical work can be easily undermined if left unrecognised, taken for granted as natural, and if the costs of caring are denied (O'Brien, 2007).

A final thought however, Noddings warns us that many things have been done in the name of care, and that systematic solutions which *seem* just or fair, and that are not tempered by care, often merely introduce new forms of inequality in education. Care thinking and affective relational practice help us to move closer to transformative praxis and to get beyond the reproduction of traditional and new forms of oppression. The development of creative programmes of critical emotional literacy in ITE will enable and nourish becoming teachers and help them care for themselves on their journey into being, as caring professionals. This may be easily written into the ITE discourse, but we should not underestimate the courage, hope and commitment required to engage in holistic and humanising teacher education.

Endnotes

[1] The affective context can be understood as the domain of relationality and emotional life, a domain which has traditionally been relegated to the *private* space of the home and assigned to the 'natural' and the feminine.

[2] In an Irish context, for example, state policy emphasises the need to shape higher education in ways that create closer relations with the economy (see the *National Strategy for Higher Education to 2030*, Department of Education and Skills, 2011, p. 32).

[3] For a discussion of caring as productive work, see Lynch and McLoughlin, 1995.

[4] Boler (1997a) draws a distinction between emotions and affect. She argues that while emotions are more amenable to disciplining and rationality, to categorisation and expression in verbal language, affect is a more radical expressive state of being, expressed through aspects of embodiment and attunement and not necessarily through verbal language.

[5] In an earlier draft of the code (2011), the value of care extended explicitly to educating their students to develop as citizens who would have a critical awareness of issues of justice and equality. The latest document is more general and refers to teachers' practices around inclusion rather than any remit to educate students explicitly in relation to justice and citizenship. Nonetheless, the tenor and emphasis in the professional code on care and holism is welcomed.

[6] Gilligan (1982, 2011) is not suggesting an essentialist gendered predisposition to care but a socialised one.

[7] Gardner's (1987) work on multiple intelligences, for example, suggests that there are eight intelligences which warrant development and Goleman (1995) makes the case for the significance of emotional intelligences and the need for education of this intelligence for the good of individuals and society. Damasio's work (2003) contends that the quality of cognitive functioning is interdependent on affective moderation.

Acknowledgements

I am indebted to Dr Andrew O'Shea of Human Development in St Patrick's College for his helpful, insightful and critical comments on the final draft of this paper, particularly in relation to holistic education and care.

References

Allardt, E. (1993). Having, loving, being: An alternative to the Swedish model of welfare research. In M. Nussbaum and A. Sen (Eds.), *The quality of life* (pp. 88-94). Oxford: Oxford University Press.

Amsler, S. (2011). From therapeutic to political education: The centrality of affective sensibility in critical pedagogy. *Critical Studies in Education, 52*(1), 47-63.

Apple, M. (2011). Paulo Freire and the tasks of the critical educator/scholar/activist. In A. O'Shea and M. O'Brien (Eds.), *Pedagogy, oppression and transformation in a post critical context.* London: Continuum.

Apple, M., Au, W. and Gandin, L. (Eds.). (2009). *The Routledge international handbook of critical education.* New York, NY: Routledge.

Ball, S. (2003). The teacher's soul and the terrors of performativity. *Journal of Educational Policy, 18*(2), 215-228.

Bauman, Z. (2003). *Liquid love: On the frailty of human bonds.* Cambridge: Polity.

Boler, M. (1997a). Taming the labile other: Disciplined emotions in popular academic discourses. *Philosophy of Education Archive*, 416-425.

Boler, M. (1997b). Disciplined emotions: Philosophies and educated feelings. *Educational Theory, 47*, 203-227.

Campbell (2000). Professional ethics in teaching: Towards the development of a code of practice. *Cambridge Journal of Education, 30*(2), 203-220.

Cigman, R. (2008). Enhancing children. *Journal of Philosophy of Education, 42*(3-4), 539-557.

Damasio, A. (2003). *Looking for Spinoza: Joy, sorrow and the feeling brain,* London: Vintage.

Department of Education and Skills (DES). (2011). *National strategy for higher education to 2030: Report of the strategy group.* Dublin: The Stationery Office.

Drudy, S. and Lynch K. (1993). *Schools and society in Ireland.* Dublin: Gill and Mcmillan.

Ellsworth, E. (1989). Why doesn't this feel empowering? *Harvard Educational Review, 59*(3), 297-324.

Falkenberg, T. (2009). Starting with the end in mind: Ethics-of-care based teacher education. In F. Benson and Caroline Riches (Eds.), *Engaging in conversation about ideas in teacher education.* New York: Peter Lang.

Farrelly, M. (2009). *Care and performativity: Walking the tightrope: A case study in an educationally disadvantaged setting.* Unpublished PhD thesis, St Patrick's College, DCU, Dublin.

Feeley, M. (2009). Living in care and without love: The impact of affective inequalities on learning literacy. In K. Lynch, J. Baker and M. Lyons (Eds.), *Affective equality.* London: Palgrave.

Freire, P. (1970). *Pedagogy of the oppressed.* New York: Continuum.

Freire, P. (1998). *Pedagogy of freedom: Ethics, democracy and civic courage.* Maryland: Rowan and Littlefield Publishers.

Gardner, H. (1987). *Frames of mind: The theory of multiple intelligence.* London: Fontana.

Gilligan, C. (1982). *In a different voice: Psychological theory and women's development.* Cambridge, MA: Harvard University Press.

Gilligan, C. (2011). *Joining the resistance.* Cambridge: Polity.

Goleman, D. (1995). *Emotional intelligence.* New York: Bantham Books.

Gomberg, Paul (2007). *How to make opportunity equal: Race and contributive justice.* Oxford: Blackwell.

Hall, K., Conway, P., Murphy, M., Long, F., Kitching K. and O'Sullivan, D. (2012). Authoring oneself and being authored as a competent teacher. *Irish Educational Studies, 31*(2), 103-118.

Hargreaves, A. (2000). Mixed emotions: Teachers' perceptions of their interactions with students. *Teaching and Teacher Education, 16*, 811-826.

Hochschild, A. (1983). *The managed heart.* Berkley: University of California Press.

Hollway, W. (2006). *The capacity to care: Gender and ethical intersubjectivity*. Sussex: Routledge.

Kelthchermans, G. (2005). Teachers' emotions in educational reforms: Self-understanding, vulnerable commitment and micropolitical literacy. *Teaching and Teacher Education, 21*, 995-1006.

Konu, A., Alanen, E., Lintonen, T. and Rimpela, M. (2002). Factor structure of the School Well-being Model. *Health Education Research: Theory and Practice, 17*(6), 732-742.

Konu, A., Lintonen, T. and Rimpela, M. (2002). Factors associated with schoolchildren's general subjective well-being. *Health Education Research: Theory and Practice, 17*(2), 155-165.

Konu, A. and Rimpela, M. (2002). Well-being in schools: A conceptual model. *Health Promotion International, 17*(1), 79 – 87.

Lynch, K. (2006). Neoliberalism and marketisation: The implications for higher education. *European Educational Research Journal, 5*(1), 1-17.

Lynch, K., Baker, J. and Lyons, M. (2009). *Affective equality: Love, care and injustice*. London: Palgrave.

Lynch, K. and Lodge, A. (2002). *Equality and power in schools*. London: Routledge Falmer.

Lynch, K., Lyons, M. and Cantillon, C. (2007). *Breaking silence: Educating citizens for love care and solidarity*. Invited paper for the International Studies in Sociology of Education Journal.

Lynch, K. and McLoughlin, E. (1995). Love labour. In P. Clancy et al. (Eds.), *Irish society: Sociological perspectives* (pp. 250-292). Dublin: Institute of Public Administration.

Maguire, M. (2000). Inside/outside the ivory tower: Teacher education in the English academy. *Teaching in Higher Education, 5*(2), 150-165.

Murray, J. (2006). Constructions of caring professionalism: A case study of teacher educators. *Gender and Education, 18*, 381-397.

Noddings, N. (1992). *The challenge to care in schools: An alternative approach to education*. New York: Teachers College Press.

Noddings, N. (1999). Care, justice and equity. In M. Katz, N. Noddings and K. Strike (Eds.), *Justice and caring: The search for common ground in education.* New York: Teachers College Press.

Noddings, N. (2003). *Happiness and education.* Cambridge: Cambridge University Press.

Noddings, N. (2005). *Caring in education.* Retrieved from The Encyclopaedia of Informal Education website: www.infed.org/biblio/noddings_caring_in_education.htm.

Nussbaum, M. (1995). *Women, culture and development: A study of human capabilities.* Oxford: Clarendon Press.

O'Brien, M. (2007). Mothers' emotional care work in education and its moral imperative. *Gender and Education, 19(*2), 159-178.

O'Brien, M. (2011). Professional responsibility and an ethic of care: Teachers' care as moral praxis. In C. Sugrue and T. Dyrdal Solbrekke (Eds.), *Professional responsibility: New horizons of praxis.* London: Routledge.

Opdenakker, M. and Van Damme, J. (2000). Effects of schools, teaching staff and classes on achievement and well-being in secondary school education: Similarities and differences between schools and outcomes. *School Effectiveness and School Improvement, 11*(2), 166-196.

Prosser, B. (2006, November). *Emotion, identity, imagery and hope as resources for teachers' work.* Paper presented at the Australian Association for Research in Education Annual Conference, Adelaide.

Scatamburlo-D'Annibale, V. and McLaren, P. (2009). The reign of capital: A pedagogy and praxis of class struggle. In M. Apple, W. Au and L. Gandin (Eds.), *The Routledge international handbook of critical education* (pp. 96-109). New York: Routledge.

Sennett, R. (2006). *The new culture of capitalism.* New Haven: Yale University Press.

Sevenhuijsen, S. (1998). *Citizenship and the ethics of care: Feminist considerations on justice, morality and politics* (E. Savage, Trans.). London/New York: Routledge.

Skeggs, B. (1997). *Formations of class and gender.* London: Sage.

Smerdon, B (2002). Students' perceptions of membership in their high schools. *Sociology of Education*, *75*, 285-305.

Soltis, J. (1986). Teaching professional ethics. *Journal of Teacher Education*, *37*(3), 2-4.

Sumsion, J. (2010). Caring and empowerment: A teacher educator's reflection on an ethical dilemma. *Teaching in Higher Education*, *5*(2), 167-179.

Taylor, C. (1991). *The ethics of authenticity*. MA: Harvard University Press.

Teaching Council (2012). *Code of professional conduct for teachers*. Dublin: Author.

UNICEF (2007). *Child poverty in perspective: An overview of child well-being in rich countries* (Report Card 7). Florence: Innocenti Research Centre.

Weiler, K. (1994). Freire and a feminist pedagogy of difference. In P. McLaren and C. Lankshear (Eds.), *Politics of liberation: Paths from Freire* (pp. 12-40). London: Routledge,.

Wetz, J. (2010). *Is initial teacher training failing to meet the needs of all our young people?* Retrievable from the CfBT Education Trust website: http://www.cfbt.com/evidenceforeducation/pdf/itt.pdf

Zembylas, M. (2003). Emotions and teacher identity: A poststructural perspective. *Teachers and Teaching; Theory and Practice*, *9*(3), 213-2.

Section Four:

Language, Teaching and Learning in Initial Teacher Education

Chapter 11

Learning Autonomy: Irish Language Education in Initial Teacher Education

Ríóna Ní Fhrighil

Coláiste Phádraig, Droim Conrach

Introduction

Described as the 'buzz word' of the 1990s in the field of language education (Little 1991, p. 2), the concept of 'learner autonomy' is still the dominant paradigm in current theories of language acquisition. This shift of emphasis in the area of language learning from teacher-led pedagogical paradigms to learner-centred models has been mirrored by developments in the area of computer assisted language learning (CALL) and research into the potential of information and communication technology (ICT) to promote learner autonomy. Learner autonomy as an educational goal and its application to theories of second-language acquisition and educational technology inevitably entails a reassessment of the role of both language teacher and language learner.

This chapter discusses the main facets of learner autonomy and explores its implications for Irish-language teaching and learning in initial teacher education (ITE) programmes. This is timely given the emphasis placed on the teaching and learning of Irish in the Teaching

Council's[1] publication, *Initial Teacher Education: Criteria and Guidelines for Programme Providers* (Teaching Council, 2011), as well as developments in Irish-language syllabus design and implementation at third level since 2009.[2] In a wider context, it is in line with the Council of Europe's goal of promoting democratic citizenship through plurilingualism and pluriculturalism.[3] The potential of ICT to develop language learner autonomy, especially in relation to oral language skills, will also be discussed. In particular, some of the practical considerations of integrating technology into language teaching and learning in order to promote language learner autonomy will be examined through findings of a case study based on the introduction of Wimba Voice Tools to an Irish-language curriculum as part of an ITE degree programme.

Learner Autonomy

The proliferation of publications and commentary on 'learner autonomy' has resulted in a certain amount of uncertainty as to what exactly this term means. Indeed, some discussion about the misconceptions regarding the nature of the concept and its implementation appear to be standard in publications on the topic.[4] Although its application to language education is associated with the Council of Europe's Modern Language Project of the early 1970s,[5] as late as 1997 Benson and Voller lamented the lack of theorising on the fundamentals of learner autonomy and contended that the ambiguity surrounding concepts such as 'autonomy' and 'independence' would lead to conflicts over their practical implementation (1997, p. 2). David Little's numerous articles and publications on the subject of learner autonomy have teased out the various aspects of the concept, particularly in relation to language learning, and have examined the implications these have for pedagogical theory and practice.[6] Little asserts that success in second-language teaching 'is governed by three interacting principles: learner involvement, learner reflection and target language use' (2007, p. 23).

The emphasis on learner choice and learner responsibility can lead to theorists ignoring or minimising the role of the language teacher. As Voller notes, teachers' roles risk being oversimplified when they are portrayed as highly responsive to learners' needs but not highly didactic (1997, p. 98). In addition, the introduction of ICT to language learning settings has sometimes led to the further marginalisation of the teacher as the computer software is deemed the unerring source of knowledge. In relation to CALL, Milton (1997), Kaltenböck (2001), Corbel and Gruba (2004), and Levy and Stockwell (2006), among others, have highlighted the limits of technology, especially where feedback is concerned. They recognise the important role of the teacher in setting tasks that encourage students to exploit the affordances of learning technologies, in developing learners' digital literacy skills, especially in their second or third language, and in providing expert feedback. Murray (2005) correctly points out that, as with all forms of instruction, 'the teacher needs to support learners' progress towards autonomy; that is, teachers need to scaffold instruction using technology' (p. 196).

The interdependence of teacher and learner autonomy is particularly relevant in ITE programmes. If students are to be reflective teachers they must first be reflective learners. The learning and teaching discourse of which they are part must be one based on the principles of autonomy and it must be facilitated and nurtured by practitioners who lead by example.

Learner Involvement

The principle of learner involvement requires a reconceptualisation of the learning process for both teachers and students alike. It is widely acknowledged among researchers and practitioners, however, that 'few learners will arrive at their first class ready to take complete charge of their own learning' (Little, 2007, p. 23). 'Learning how to learn' has thus become a catchphrase in literature on language learner autonomy. The *Common European Framework of Reference for Languages* (CEFR) explicitly emphasises the need for learners to learn languages proactively, rather than reactively, and contends that 'even within the given institutional system they can then be brought increasingly to make choices in respect of objectives, materials and working methods in the light of their own needs, motivations, characteristics and resources' (Council of Europe, 2001, p. 141).

A natural consequence of learner-centred approaches to language teaching is the necessity of identifying learner needs. Both Brindley (1989, p. 65) and Berwick have pointed out that the definition of learner needs is by nature subjective and is often an ideologically loaded term:

> Our perceptions of need develop from what we believe is educationally worthwhile … needs are not simply 'out there' waiting to be counted and measured with the latest innovations of educational technology (Berwick, 1989, p. 56).

Brindley (1989), following Richterich (1980), refers to objective needs analysis and subjective needs analysis. Objective needs could be classified as product-oriented needs, that is, they are based on language skills, on real-life communicative contexts, and are therefore relatively easy to identify. In many respects, the objective needs of student teachers of Irish can be predicted by researching the classroom setting and the Irish-language primary curriculum which they will have to implement. Clearly language syllabi in ITE should incorporate relevant topics and communicative contexts and focus adequately on oral, aural and writing skills.

Due recognition must be given, however, to the linguistic reality of implementing a task-based communicative curriculum in the primary classroom, especially for students for whom Irish is not their first language. A notional-functional syllabus, i.e., a corpus of language 'for the classroom', would not, from a linguistic viewpoint, prepare student teachers adequately for the reality of the language classroom, even at primary level. As Betáková (2000, p. 183) has noted in relation to English-language teaching in the Czech Republic, the requirements of a learner-centred communicative curriculum place much greater linguistic demands on teachers as there are no set answers or rehearsed conversations. Teachers must be proficient enough to respond to learners' varied and unpredictable communicative needs. Research by Harris et al. (2006, pp. 127-8) seems to substantiate this claim regarding the linguistic demands of learner-centred curricula; 60.7 per cent of sixth class Irish pupils in ordinary schools in 2002 were taught by teachers who indicated that they would like to attend a course to improve their Irish.[7] Surprisingly, this was also the case among a substantial number of teachers in Gaeltacht schools[8] and gaelscoileanna[9] (48.6 per cent of pupils in Gaeltacht schools were taught by teachers who wished to improve their Irish and 42.3 per cent of pupils in gaelscoileanna).

The CEFR 'can do descriptors' aim to assist curriculum designers in identifying learners' needs while also encouraging students to reflect on and to identify their own needs as language learners and as language users. It is also envisaged that these 'can do descriptors' will provide guidance to those designing language activities as well as those involved in language assessment. Little (2009) concludes, 'the CEFR offers to bring curriculum, pedagogy and assessment into a closer relation to one another than has traditionally been the case, challenging us to rethink each from the perspective of the other two' (p. 1).

Learner Reflection

Learner involvement in the planning, monitoring and assessing of his/her learning encourages learners to take greater responsibility for their learning. Reflecting on this process, one would imagine, would be a natural progression by the learner. However, this deduction is a gross simplification of a process which is actually gradual and complex, one which, as Little correctly explains, will most likely begin as teacher-learner collaborative reflection and will only eventually develop into 'an individual and wholly internal phenomenon' (2002, p. 51).

Learner reflection is closely related to questions of language awareness, which James defines as:

> LA [language awareness] is broadly constituted of a mix of knowledge of language in general and in specific, command of metalanguage … and the conversion of intuitions to insight and then beyond to metacognition (1999, p. 102).

He further asserts that language awareness 'implies redressing, not reinforcing, the bias towards intuitive, expressive, communicative modes that has been established in education over the last three decades, and reinstating the formal and technical aspects' (ibid., p. 101).

Interestingly, in discussing their experience as Irish-language learners heretofore, the group of students involved in the case study detailed below indicated that in secondary school the emphasis was predominantly on written language skills, while much less attention was paid to the spontaneous use of language. The bias towards communicative modes of which James speaks does not appear to have been a feature of these students' learning experience even though a communicative syllabus for Irish-language teaching was introduced at Leaving Certificate[10] level in post-primary schools in 1995. Indeed research by Ní Thuathail (2003) and Ní Ghothraigh (2003) indicates that there are major discrepancies between curriculum guidelines and actual implementation in the classroom.

James' (1996; 1999) discussion of 'language awareness' in language teaching has some significant methodological implications. In the context of ITE programmes in Ireland, I believe that his proposals regarding cross-linguistic awareness deserve further attention. He advocates the use of contrastive analysis between one's mother-tongue and one's additional languages and contends that 'an integrated language education policy would systematically do in the classroom what bilinguals do socially and spontaneously' (James, 1996, p. 144). Given that the vast majority of student teachers have all studied at least three languages to Leaving Certificate level, including Irish and English, I contend that cross-linguistic awareness should form an integral part of their initial teacher education, both in their study of languages and in their study of literacy, including mother-tongue literacy. As bilingual or indeed multilingual individuals, student teachers should be encouraged to utilise the transferable competencies and linguistic skills they possess.

Finally, reflection should lead the learner to acknowledge that formal instruction is only one facet of the learning process and that it can ultimately only lead to limited success. Refining competencies in contexts other than school or university and engaging in intercultural activities is a central aim in learner-centred curricula and is underscored in the CEFR (Council of Europe, 2001, p. 9-13) and the European Language Portfolio (ELP). The proposal by the Teaching Council that ITE programmes should 'provide for an extended and reconceptualised *Gaeltacht* residency' attests to the importance of the

Gaeltacht as both a linguistic and cultural entity (Teaching Council, 2011, p. 10).

Target Language Use

The principle of target language use posits that all classroom activities – organisational, communicative and reflective – should take place through the medium of the target language. Learner-centred curricula encourage the learner to communicate meanings that emanate from the learners themselves, i.e., language use that is relevant to the learner's own context. This principle pertains to learners at all levels. Action research by Dam and Legenhausen (1996), Dam (2000) and Thomsen (2003) documents how they successfully used the target language, English, in learning activities with young primary school learners of limited proficiency. CEFR promotes an action-oriented approach and therefore deems language learning as a form of language use (Council of Europe, 2001, p. 9).

Language proficiency, however, does not necessarily result in language use. In the case of the Irish language, the discrepancy between language proficiency and language use in the wider population is well documented.[11] In the context of primary education, research by Harris et al. (2006) indicates that in the Republic of Ireland in 2002, 65.2 percent of sixth class pupils were taught by teachers who felt that they did not have sufficient opportunities to *practice* their Irish. Surprisingly, teachers of a substantial number of Gaeltacht pupils (24.2 per cent) and pupils in gaelscoileanna (38.6 per cent) also felt this to be the case. It is clear that identifying opportunities to use the language and to acquire further language skills must be an integral part of the student teachers' learning experience if they are to be effective language users after their initial teacher education.

Although to date there is no definitive alignment between the CEFR and the National Framework of Qualifications,[12] in practice language experts assume that those achieving honours grades in language subjects at Higher Level Leaving Certificate have achieved outcomes corresponding to B1 on the CEFR. There is a working assumption among language experts in higher education that Bologna first cycle degrees, i.e., bachelor's degrees, correspond to level C1 on the CEFR. In this regard, it is important to note that the Common Reference Level B2 and higher represents a level of competence which exceeds the level of competence that could reasonably be expected to result from general language classes. That is to say, B2 is closely related to content and language integrated learning (CLIL).[13] CLIL essentially seeks to teach two subjects at once – a content subject and a language. The development of CLIL is especially important in Ireland given that ITE graduates may wish to teach in Gaeltacht schools or in gaelscoileanna. At present, there is no ITE programme in the Republic of Ireland which is taught exclusively through the medium of Irish at primary level. Indeed, if the goal of democratic citizenship is truly to be an aim of language education in Ireland, then the importance of facilitating students at all levels whose first language is Irish must be one of the priorities of ITE programmes.

Case Study: *Wimba Voice Tools*

Given the importance of oral Irish in the primary classroom and in light of the findings by Harris et al. (2006), I decided to undertake a small-scale exploratory case study that focused on oral language skills and the use of *Wimba Voice Tools* to facilitate and to encourage oral interaction between language learners. The length of time involved was relatively short – one semester – and therefore I focused on learner experience rather than learning outcomes. Two aspects of students' experience were of particular interest, namely the level of metalinguistic reflection by students and their use of the target language. Descriptive statistics were used to examine user patterns as reported by students and as evidenced from their postings to the voice board. Data collected in a written survey distributed to participants at the end of the six weeks were also analysed to provide an overall view of students' opinions of *Wimba* and how its incorporation into the syllabus affected their learning processes. The written survey was based on a similar questionnaire used by McIntosh et al. (2003) who investigated the effectiveness of the combination of *Wimba* and oral learning activities with 41 third-level students of English for Academic Purposes. This allowed for some comparison between the two case studies.

Wimba Voice Tools is essentially an online forum which is based on oral messages as opposed to written messages. It is an asynchronous voice technology. Students record their messages and post them to a communal voice board where they can be accessed by other participating students. Students have the opportunity to listen to each other's messages and then to post a reply. In the traditional language classroom, once an utterance is made, it is gone. With this technology, however, oral texts are available to both teacher and student after the utterance is made – allowing for further reflection or comment. Unlike the traditional classroom setting where some students opt not to participate vocally or where students only interact with classmates sitting next to them, *Wimba Voice Tools* affords all students an opportunity to participate in classroom discussion and to listen to each other.

The participants were a group of 16 Bachelor of Education students in St Patrick's College who were in the final semester of their three year degree course and who were studying Professional Irish.[14] None of the participants were native Irish speakers or students who had been educated through the medium of Irish. Before the case study commenced, oral language classes were traditional classroom-based conversational classes. Students had one 50 minute class per week which involved very little, if any, use of technology. For the duration of the case study, these conversational classes were held in a computer room where all 16 students had individual access to a computer and headsets. All participants reported that they had no previous experience of oral activities online, and indeed, had little experience of, or knowledge about, online Irish-language resources in general.

Students undertook four activities during the course of this research. Three activities were based on constructivist approaches to language learning which, in brief, build on prior knowledge and seek to integrate language, content and process. These activities included problem solving and creative tasks. Particular emphasis was placed on group and pair-work. The tasks were so designed to accommodate linguistic scaffolding. From a linguistic perspective, Little advocates peer collaboration on the grounds that:

> ...social speech can also enable learners to compensate interdependently for an underdeveloped capacity for inner speech. This is one of the reasons why collaborative written tasks often yield texts that are vastly superior to anything any one member of the group could produce individually (2000, p. 13).

Summary of Results

The extent to which *Wimba Voice Tools* encouraged and/or facilitated metalinguistic reflection by students was judged based on information provided in 12 user surveys submitted at the end of the semester and by an analysis of the content of students' messages posted to the voice board throughout the semester.

Table 1 summarises respondents' accounts of their preparation before recording a message and compares them to user patterns reported by McIntosh et al. (2003). Remarkably, no respondent in the present study recorded directly without some form of written preparation. In contrast, 49 per cent of participants in McIntosh et al. recorded directly with only 17 per cent writing everything down before recording.

Table 1: Comparison of Processes Used by Respondents in Preparing a Message

When Posting a Message I:	Present Case Study (n=12)	McIntosh et al. (2003) (n=41)
Wrote everything down and then recorded	42%	17%
Wrote points down and then recorded	42%	29%
Wrote in the online text box and then recorded	16%	n/a
Recorded directly without any written text	0%	49%

There were, however, striking similarities between user patterns in both case studies in relation to the number of times participants recorded their message before they felt ready to post it to the general voice board.

Table 2 below, shows the number of recordings made by respondents before they posted their message to the voice board, and compares this with findings by McIntosh et al.

Table 2: Comparison of Number of Recordings Made by Respondents Before Posting a Message

How Often Did You Record Your Message Before Posting It?	Present Case Study (n=12)	McIntosh et al. (2003) (n=41)
One to three times	82%	80%
Four to six times	18%	17%
Seven to ten times	0%	2%

A further question, posed only in the present case study, pertained to pre-recording preparation. Sixty-four per cent of respondents practiced their message between one and three times before recording it, while 36 per cent never practiced before recording. These results indicate that the majority of participants in the present case study took advantage of the lack of time pressure involved in asynchronous communication when formulating their response. The fact that all respondents prepared some form of written response before recording and that the majority of respondents then practised their answer before actually recording it, implies a certain degree of metalinguistic awareness. It also suggests a certain lack of confidence with regards to oral Irish – unlike a substantial percentage of participants in the study by McIntosh et al., all participants in this case study clearly felt that they needed the help of some form of written script to make an oral recording. With reference to the data collected, it is impossible to determine whether students prepared and practised their answers before posting them out of an intrinsic desire for greater accuracy, or because they wished to be positively evaluated by peers and/or by the teacher.

The property of *Wimba* which compels reflective behaviour is the actual recording of one's own voice, a self-conscious act that obliges students to consider how to formulate their answers. Other properties, though not compelling, afforded students the opportunity to reflect upon their postings. These included the asynchronous nature of the medium which meant that students could prepare and practice their answers; the opportunity to re-record messages before posting them to the voice board; the opportunity to listen to other postings; the opportunity to listen again to one's own message when it appeared on the voice board. The distinction by O'Rourke and Schwienhorst (2003) between 'incidental reflection' and 'deliberate reflection' is relevant in this regard. They contend that 'learners are more inclined to local, expedient, tactical exploration of metalinguistic affordances than to displaced, strategic, considered exploitation' (p. 53). They conclude that language students who are not autonomous learners will only exploit the affordances of ICT applications if learning activities require them to do so or as a result of positive pressure from the teacher.

Target Language Use

Student participation involved listening to a message or messages and recording a reply and posting it to the voice board. A total of 104 student postings were recorded. All postings made to the voice board and all class pair and group work observed was through the medium of Irish.

Following Hew and Cheung (2008), the depth of the threads was analysed in order to determine the extent of student interaction. The depth of the thread includes the initial posting and the number of replies. Hew and Chung considered a level of six postings optimal 'because such a level not only suggests that a discussion is taking place but also the possibility that the discussion is sustained or extended' (2008, p. 1,114). Given that there were no facilitators in this present study encouraging further student participation, and taking account of other factors such as access to computer laboratories, I deemed that in this instance, a depth of four upwards could be considered an optimal level of student interaction. This level of interaction was not evident in any of the threads; in fact none of the threads exceeded an initial posting with one or two replies.

Before concluding that *Wimba* did not encourage or facilitate sustained interaction between students outside of the classroom setting, some mitigating factors need to be considered. Firstly, as teacher-researcher I had no experience in designing oral activities suitable for *Wimba* and did not anticipate that students would succeed in completing each task with minimum interaction. Secondly, students' access to computer facilities outside class time was limited given that the case study was undertaken in the final semester of the academic year when computer rooms tend to be busy as students prepare end of term essays and projects. Thirdly, and arguably most significantly, these students were required to undertake the same performance-based end of term assessment as their peers. This assessment, based on 'general conversational skills', would not specifically assess the communicative tasks that this particular group of students were required to perform, both in class and outside of the formal class setting.

This issue highlights a major challenge in the area of digital innovation in teaching and learning – that of appropriate valid assessment. If language assessments are to have content and face validity then they must take due cognisance of the range of skills required of language students in such CALL settings, the language-learning strategies that digital technologies promote and foster, as well as the prospective use that students will make of these technologies in L2 interactions. If the integration of tools such as *Wimba* is to be effective, or indeed transformative, then assessment procedures must be appropriately revised so that they will be in accordance with, as well as a continuation of, the learning process itself.

Limitations

The principal limitations of this study pertain to the small number of participants and the relatively short period of time in which learning activities were carried out. This weakens the generalisability of findings. Holland and Reeves (1996, p. 259), following McGrath (1990), note that synchronic studies which focus on tasks rather than on longer processes such as projects miss important historical processes. This is also true of much research on CALL, including the present case study. Such research fails to include a diachronic aspect such as the development of the learner over a sustained period of time and the long-term integration of technology in a particular educational setting.[15] Another limitation relates to the selection of participants which was restricted due to timetable constraints. Ideally, participants would not be part of a convenience group and would have been more evenly balanced from the point of view of gender.

A large part of this study was based on qualitative analysis. Qualitative analysis is by nature limited to the specific research in question, and although it undoubtedly gives invaluable insights, its generalisability is also weak. Nonetheless, Breen et al. (2001, p. 99) argue convincingly that small scale focus groups often produce more useful information than large scale surveys. Valuable insights in relation to students' learning experiences and their use of learning technologies, gained from this present case study, have informed subsequent larger scale case studies, as well as classroom practice.

Conclusion

As the foregoing discussion indicates, language learner autonomy is not developed in isolation or independently of other areas of learning. Learner involvement and learner reflection involve management skills and competencies which are equally applicable to other areas of the ITE curriculum. Likewise, language use, especially in CALL settings, develops not only literacy skills in the traditional sense, but also digital literacy skills. The case study detailed above demonstrates the potential of ICT to expand opportunities for language use, both geographically and temporally. This is particularly important in the Irish-language context as many students and teachers have limited access to communities of Irish-speakers and often regret the lack of opportunities to actually speak the language. Notwithstanding the opportunities afforded by technologies like *Wimba Voice Tools*, however, the research presented here highlights the fact that educational and language technologies will not succeed in developing and promoting student autonomy if this is not already a feature of the language learning discourse to which students have been exposed.

The development and introduction of a new Irish-language syllabus at third level, based on the CEFR, is a welcome development, especially in ITE programmes. Irish-language students, whether native speakers or second-language learners, who become familiar with the concepts of the CEFR and the principles upon which it is based, are better placed to continue to develop their own linguistic skills as they progress as teachers and also to encourage their own pupils to be autonomous language learners from an early age. The CEFR is context-free and can be interpreted in an age-appropriate manner, and as such can inform curricula, lesson plans and assessments at all levels. As reported earlier, action research in other countries in Europe has shown how the principles of language learner autonomy can be successfully implemented at primary level, provided that children's learning is effectively scaffolded by the teacher. In the Irish-language context, it is crucial that those entrusted with the implementation of the learner-centred communicative curriculum at primary level have both the linguistic competency and the requisite understanding of the principles of language learning autonomy to implement the curriculum effectively.

This last point once again underlines the inextricable link between learner autonomy and teacher autonomy. Teachers must be reflective practitioners if they are to respond effectively to the socio-cultural, personal and vocational needs of their students. The increasing use of ICT in language education will continue to change our understanding of learning and teaching. Language education at all levels should therefore be research led.

The importance of CLIL in the Irish context has already been outlined. From a linguistic point of view, it is necessary if student teachers who are second-language learners of Irish are to develop productive skills which would enable them to speak and to write competently about topics related to the Irish-language primary curriculum or other fields of interest. From an ethical and professional point of view, it is essential for students who will teach in Gaeltacht schools and in gaelscoileanna – teachers who will be expected to teach all aspects of the primary curriculum through the medium of Irish. Given that all students entering into ITE programmes in Ireland are at least bilingual, ranging from those who are native Irish speakers to those who have the minimum required competency in Irish, and given the range of linguistic contexts in which these students will potentially teach in the future, ITE programmes in Ireland are well positioned and should strive to be leaders in the area of CLIL research. This is of utmost importance if language education in Ireland aims to be truly inclusive and to recognise the plurilingual and pluricultural realities of twenty-first century Ireland.

In the final analysis, as researchers and educators, it is our duty to ensure that our initial teacher education programmes are based on the most progressive educational and civic goals and exhibit best research-led pedagogical practice.

Endnotes

1. The Teaching Council is the professional body for teaching in Ireland and was established on a statutory basis in 2006.

2. The new Irish-language syllabus for third level is available at www.teagascnagaeilge.ie. For an account of its development and implementation see Walsh (2010).

3. The Common European Framework of Reference for Languages explains the plurilingual approach as follows: [It] emphasises the fact that as an individual person's experience of language in its cultural contexts expands, from the language of the home to that of society at large and then to the languages of other peoples (whether learnt at school or college, or by direct experience), he or she does not keep these languages and cultures in strictly separated mental compartments, but rather builds up a communicative competence to which all knowledge and experience of language contributes and in which languages interrelate and interact (Council of Europe, 2001, p. 4).

4. See Benson, 2001; Benson and Voller, 1997; Esch, 1997; Little, 1991.

5. For a detailed account of the history of the concept of autonomy in European language education see Benson (2001, pp. 7-21); Gremmo and Riley (1995).

6. See Little, 1991; 1996; 1997; 2000; 2007.

7. 'Ordinary schools' is the term used by Harris et al. (2006) to refer to mainstream English-medium primary schools.

8. The statutory definition of 'Gaeltacht' is as follows: specified areas, being substantially Irish-speaking areas and areas contiguous thereto which, in the opinion of the Government, ought to be included in the Gaeltacht with a view to preserving and extending the use of Irish as a vernacular language (Section 2(2), Ministers and Secretaries (Amendment) Act, 1956). In popular use, it refers to geographical areas where a greater part of the population speaks Irish daily, as a community language.

9. 'Gaelscoileanna' is the Irish term used to refer to Irish medium schools.

10. The Leaving Certificate, popularly referred to as the 'Leaving Cert', is the final examination in the secondary school system in the Republic of Ireland.

11. See Ó Gliasáin,1996; Ó Riagáin 1993; 1997.

12. The National Framework of Qualifications was introduced in 2003. It is the single structure through which Irish qualifications can be defined and compared. A report on the alignment of the National Framework of Qualifications and the Common European Framework of Reference for Languages is available at http://www.nqai.ie/documents/reltionshipbetween-CommonEuroF-W.doc

13. See Little, 2009, p. 8.

14. Professional Irish is a course consisting of language modules for those who have not chosen Irish as an academic subject to degree level. It is a requirement of the Department of Education that students obtain a pass in this course before being fully recognised as primary-school teachers.

15. This is one of the recommendations made by Charle Poza (2005) who calls for more longitudinal studies on educational technologies and their integration into language curricula. Belz (2007) also notes, with regret, that learner corpora has attracted little attention among second-language acquisition researchers who tend to take a synchronic approach and do not investigate how L2 competence changes over time.

References

Belz, J. (2007). The role of computer mediation in the instruction and development of L2 pragmatic competence. *Annual Review of Applied Linguistics, 27*, 45-75.

Benson, P. (2001). *Teaching and researching autonomy in language learning.* Harlow: Pearson Education/Longman.

Benson, P. and Voller, P. (Eds.). (1997). *Autonomy and independence in language learning.* London: Longman.

Berwick, R. (1989). Needs assessment in language programming: From theory to practice. In R. K. Johnson (Ed.), *The second language curriculum* (pp. 48-62). Cambridge: Cambridge University Press.

Betáková, L. (2000). The importance of using the target language in the classroom. In D. Little, L. Dam and J. Timmer (Eds.), *Focus on learning rather than teaching? Why and how?* (pp. 175-191). Dublin: Trinity College, Centre for Language and Communication Studies.

Breen, R., Lindsay, R., Jenkins, A. and Smith, P. (2001). The role of information and communication technologies in a university learning environment. *Studies in Higher Education, 26*(1), 95-114.

Brindley, G. (1989). The role of needs analysis in adult ESL programme design. In R.K. Johnson (Ed.), *The second language curriculum* (pp. 63-78). Cambridge: Cambridge University Press.

Charle Poza, M. I. (2005). *The effects of asynchronous computer voice conferencing on learners' anxiety when speaking in a foreign language.* Department of Advanced Educational Studies: West Virginia University.

Corbel, C. and Gruba, P. (2004). *Teaching computer literacy.* Sydney: Macquarie University, AMEP Research Centre.

Council of Europe (2001). *Common European framework of reference for languages, learning, teaching, assessment.* Cambridge: Cambridge University Press.

Dam, L. (2000). Why focus on learning rather than teaching? From theory to practice. In D. Little, L. Dam and J. Timmer (Eds.), *Focus on learning rather than teaching: Why and how?* (pp. 18-37). Dublin: Trinity College, Centre for Language and Communication Studies.

Dam, L. and Legenhausen, L. (1996). The acquisition of vocabulary in an autonomous learning environment – the first months of beginning English. In R. Pemberton, E. Li, W. Or and H. Pierson (Eds.), *Taking control: Autonomy in language learning* (pp. 265-280). Hong Kong: Hong Kong University Press.

Esch, E. M. (1997). Learner training for autonomous language learning. In P. Benson and P. Voller (Eds.), *Autonomy and independence in language learning* (pp. 164-176). London: Longman.

Gremmo, M.J. and Riley, P. (1995). Autonomy, self-direction and self access in language teaching and learning: The history of an idea. *System, 23*(2), 175-181.

Harris, J., Forde, P., Archer, P., Nic Fhearghaile, S. and O'Gorman, M. (2006). *Irish in primary schools: Long–term national trends in achievement.* Dublin: The Stationary Office. Retrieved from http://www.linguae-celticae.org/dateien/Irish_in_Primary_Schools.pdf

Hew, K.F. and Cheung W.S. (2008). Attracting student participation in asynchronous online discussions: A case study of peer evaluation. *Computers and Education, 51,* 1111-1124.

Holland, D. and Reeves, J. R. (1996). Activity theory and the view from somewhere: Team perspectives on the intellectual work of programming. In B. Nardi (Ed.), *Context and consciousness: Activity theory and human-computer interaction* (pp. 257-281). London: MIT Press.

James, C. (1996). A cross-linguistic approach to language awareness. *Language Awareness,* 5(3 and 4), 138-149.

James, C. (1999). Language awareness: Implications for the language curriculum. *Language, Culture and Curriculum, 12*(1), 94-115.

Kaltenböck, G. (2001). Learner autonomy: a guiding principle in designing a CD-ROM for intonation and practice. *ReCALL, 13*(2), 179-190.

Levy, M. and Stockwell, G. (2006). *CALL dimensions: Options and issues in computer assisted language learning.* Mahwah, New Jersey: Lawrence Erlbaum.

Little, D. (1991). *Learner autonomy I: Definitions, issues and problems.* Dublin: Authentik.

Little, D. (1996). Freedom to learn and compulsion to interact: Promoting learner autonomy through the use of information systems and information technologies. In R. Pemberton, E. Li, W. Or and H. Pierson (Eds.), *Taking control: Autonomy in language learning* (pp. 203-218). Hong Kong: Hong Kong University Press.

Little, D. (1997). Language awareness and the autonomous language learner. *Language Awareness, 6*(2-3), 93-104.

Little, D. (2000). Why focus on learning rather than teaching? In D. Little, L. Dam and J. Timmer (Eds.), *Focus on learning rather than teaching: Why and how?* (pp. 3-17). Dublin: Trinity College, Centre for Language and Communication Studies.

Little, D. (2002). We're all in it together: Exploring the interdependence of teacher and learner autonomy. In L. Karlsson, F. Kjisik and J. Nordlund (Eds.), *All together now* (pp. 45-56) (Papers from the 7th Nordic Conference and Workshop on Autonomous Language Learning September 2000). Helsinki: University of Helsinki Language Centre.

Little, D. (2007). Language leaner autonomy: Some fundamental considerations revisited. *Innovation in Language Learning and Teaching, 1*(1), 14-29.

Little, D. (2009). *The European language portfolio: Where pedagogy and assessment meet.* Retrieved from the Council of Europe website: http://www.coe.int/t/dg4/education/elp/elp-reg/Source/Publications/ELP_pedagogy_assessment_Little_EN.pdf

McGrath, J.E. (1990). Time matters in groups. In J. Galeher, R. Kraut and C. Egido (Eds.), *Intellectual teamwork: Social and technological foundations of cooperative work* (pp. 23-61). Hillsdale, NJ: Lawrence Erlbaum Associates.

McIntosh, S., Braul, B. and Chao, T. (2003). A case study in asynchronous voice conferencing for language instruction. *Education Media International, 40*(1), 63-74.

Milton, J. (1997). Providing computerized self-access opportunities for the development of writing skills. In P. Benson and P. Voller (Eds.), *Autonomy and independence in language learning* (pp. 237-248). London: Longman.

Murray, D. (2005). Technologies for second-language literacy. *Annual Review of Applied Linguistics, 25*, 188-201.

Ní Ghothraigh, P. (2003). *Siollabas an Teastais Shóisearaigh sa Ghaeilge agus a oiriúnaí atá sé don chur chuige chumarsáideach.* Unpublished M.Ed. Thesis, National University of Ireland, Maynooth.

Ní Thuathail, A. (2003). An reitric i gcoinnean réalachais maidir le modhanna múinte na Gaeilge sna hiar-bhunscoileanna. *Teagasc na Gaeilge, 8,* 27-47.

Ó Gliasáin, M. (1996). *The language question in the Irish census of population.* Dublin: Institiúid Teangeolaíochta Éireann.

Ó Riagáin, P. (1993). Stability and change in public attitudes towards Irish since the 1960s. *Teangeolas, 32*, 45 – 49.

Ó Riagáin, P. (1997). *Language policy and social reproduction: Ireland 1893-1993.* Oxford: Oxford University Press.

O'Rourke, B. and Schwienhorst, K. (2003). Talking text: Reflections on reflection in computer-mediated communication. In D. Little, L. Dam and J. Timmer (Eds.), *Focus on learning rather than teaching? Why and how?* (pp. 47-60). Dublin: Trinity College, Centre for Language and Communication Studies.

Richterich, R. (1980). *Identifying the needs of adults learning a foreign language.* Oxford: Pergamon Press.

Teaching Council (2011). *Initial teacher education: Criteria and guidelines for programme providers.* Dublin: Author.

Thomsen, H. (2003). Scaffolding target language use. In D. Little, J. Ridley and E. Ushioda (Eds.), *Learner autonomy in the foreign language classroom: Teacher, learner, curriculum and assessment* (pp. 29-46). Dublin: Authentik.

Voller, P. (1997). Does the teacher have a role in autonomous language learning? In P. Benson and P. Voller (Eds.), *Autonomy and independence in language learning* (pp. 164-176). London: Longman.

Walsh, J. (2010). Siollabas nua Gaeilge don chéad bhliain ollscoile. In M. Ó Laoire (Ed.), *Teagasc na Gaeilge, 9*, 13-24.

Chapter 12

Irish-medium Initial Teacher Education: Lessons from Self-evaluation

Eibhlín Mhic Aoidh, Jill Garland, Gabrielle Nig Uidhir, John Sweeney
St. Mary's University College Belfast

Introduction

When the first Irish-medium (IM) primary school to open in Belfast was established by parents in 1971, one of the most challenging tasks undertaken by these parents was the appointment of a teacher. The necessary qualities included all the regular requirements associated with a qualified primary teacher in addition to competence in the Irish language, as Irish was the mother tongue (L1) of these first Irish-medium pupils. For the next thirty years, the recruitment of qualified teachers for IM schools would continue to be one of the key issues for debate in this sector.

As the network of IM schools developed and extended throughout Northern Ireland, the issue of specialist, qualified teachers became more critical. The demand for teacher education for the IM sector gained momentum as the number of Irish-medium schools and units increased and awareness of the advantages experienced by immersion pupils also grew. Initial teacher education (ITE) had become a priority for the IM community by the early nineties. St Mary's University College, Belfast, responded to this need in 1995 by establishing an Irish-medium Postgraduate Certificate in Education Programme (PGCE). This chapter outlines the development of this programme. Locating it within international research and practice, it describes the immersion approach implemented in St Mary's. Aspects of a self-evaluation process that shaped the development of the programme are highlighted, including the findings that collaborative critical self-evaluation processes can promote cross-institutional collective ownership and innovation, while affirming existing good practice. Finally, two critical issues have been selected for exploration: promoting the linguistic competences of students; and developing partnerships with schools and other agencies.

Immersion Teacher Education: The International Context

The literature on immersion education consistently refers to challenges relating to initial and continuing teacher education (Baker, 2006; Day and Shapson, 1993; Mac Corraidh, 2008, McKendry, 2006, Nig Uidhir, 2006). Erben (2004, p. 324) identifies an increase in immersion teacher education programmes worldwide and notes that over 50 faculties of education were offering some type of immersion education by 2003. Internationally, models of immersion teacher education programmes have been introduced in response to teacher shortage in immersion schools. The same issues that present challenges in the immersion school system, such as recruitment, funding and resources, are also pertinent to immersion teacher education providers. Robertson described recruitment as the highest profile issue in Gaelic-medium education, explaining that this shortage of teachers can prevent the growth of Gaelic-medium education in some areas (Robertson, 2002; Nicolson and MacIver, 2003, p. 70).

The need for research is another key issue. In immersion teacher education, research is needed to inform practitioners and policy-makers and to provide a theoretical basis for immersion teacher education principles and practices. Lapkin, Swain and Shapson (1990) called for a focus on immersion teacher education as an area of research in the 1990s. Erben (2004) considered the trends in immersion teacher education research and identified three areas of interest: (1) reviews mapping current models; (2) descriptive studies that include analysis of stakeholders' views that aim to identify the characteristics of good practice; and (3) research investigating the immersion teacher education process. Provision for immersion teacher education reflects the variety found in models of immersion and bilingual education from nursery through to post-primary schools throughout the world, although Ó hAiniféin (2008, p. 14) states that the limited range of immersion models in Ireland is a disadvantage. In Wales, where Welsh-medium education is well established, research has been carried out on bilingual education in ITE courses. The concept of bilingual education embraces a broad spectrum of patterns of delivery and structures. In the ESCalate project, *Bilingual Teaching in Initial Teacher Education and Training Courses* (Roberts, 2002), it was noted that there was a scarcity of international research measuring the effectiveness of various methods of bilingual teaching within higher education.

In current teacher education provision, a range of contextual factors differentiate each immersion situation, including sociocultural, economic and political considerations. Programmes are planned to take cognisance of factors such as the prior experience of the student teachers in the target language (native speakers or second language learners), the resources available to support learning and teaching (including lecturing staff with target language competence), funding and student recruitment (Nig Uidhir, 2002, p. 66). Provision may take the form of an add-on element in the degree programme or it can be integrated into the teacher education experience in a more holistic way where immersion pedagogies are modelled by staff and the curriculum is delivered through the target language.

There is some consensus with regard to the competences required of immersion teachers. These extend beyond language skills and some knowledge of appropriate pedagogies to embrace an understanding of how children learn in an immersion environment, the role of the teacher and the integral role of parents and community, along with other important perspectives (Nig Uidhir, 1996; Mac Corraidh, 2008). Bartlett and Erben (1995) carried out a study of a four year Bachelor of Education (BEd) programme through Japanese immersion in Australia. The authors extend debate beyond the linguistic and sociolinguistic interpretation of immersion education:

> Far from being merely a linguistic bath, however, their study shows teacher education through immersion to be a multidimensional dialectic phenomenon (Bartlett and Erben, 1995, cited in Erben, 2004).

An awareness of the competences required of immersion teachers and an understanding of the developmental needs of student teachers are key factors influencing the structure, content and pedagogical approaches that are introduced to initial teacher education programmes. These factors had an impact upon the design of provision for Irish-medium students at St Mary's University College. As Nig Uidhir (2006) recounts, while the initial plan was to offer a module focused on immersion education which also fostered high standards in Irish:

> … the College community realised that … [I]t is not sufficient to learn about immersion education only. The basic philosophy and educational science of immersion education would have to be experienced by the students in a practical way. In order to give students, especially those who had not been through the Irish-medium system themselves, a meaningful Irish-medium experience, the curriculum would have to be studied through Irish (p. 152).

The Irish-medium PGCE Programme: An Overview

The first cohort of five PGCE students joined their English-medium peers at St Mary's in 1995 in a range of lectures and workshops within a multilingual environment and with a separate group focus on immersion and IM issues. Since then the PGCE provision in the College has changed, so that now the full cohort of students on the PGCE primary programme (currently 20 students) has an IM focus. The supportive linguistic and cultural environment at St Mary's was identified as a significant factor in the introduction and development of IM provision (Nig Uidhir, 2006). IM education at St Mary's is integrated into all College structures, involving the input of an extensive range of staff, both teaching and non-teaching. Since September

2005, the course has been aligned with the National Qualifications Framework and has been organised in a modular structure, offering three modules, two of which are assessed at M-level (Quality Assurance Agency for Higher Education (QAA), 2000). The PGCE IM primary programme has been complemented by the introduction of an IM post-primary PGCE project, funded by the Department of Employment and Learning (DEL), which commenced in August 2007 as a collaborative project between St Mary's University College, Queen's University, Belfast and the University of Ulster to address the shortage of qualified teachers with subject specialisms other than Irish in the IM post-primary sector.

Approaches to teaching and learning on the IM PGCE course have reflected and modelled the theoretical underpinnings and the teaching methodologies that are considered to be characteristic of effective immersion education (Johnson and Swain, 1997; Baker, 2006) and have also reflected international research on immersion teacher education as outlined above. Opportunities for researching and debating immersion issues are incorporated into the course. The philosophy and pedagogies of immersion education are experienced by students in practical ways, in the context of workshops and practical activities, with language planning centrally placed in all teaching and learning experiences. Close partnerships with schools and other related bodies are given a high level of priority, adding a vital dimension to IM initial teacher education at St Mary's University College and ultimately enhancing the students' experience and reflecting the shared values of the wider community.

The nature of the IM PGCE primary programme is both progressive and developmental in nature and is aligned with the framework for competence development outlined by the General Teaching Council for Northern Ireland (GTCNI) (2007) which is:

> ... predicated upon the notion that the achievement of competence is a developmental process which, of necessity, transcends early teacher education and continues throughout a teacher's career (p. 11).

Term 1 is regarded as a foundation phase in which student learning is scaffolded, building competence with particular reference to the IM context. Term 2 focuses on developing effective practice and meeting pupil needs, and Term 3 is concerned with extending professional understanding and moving towards the induction phase of teacher education. Planning for language and literacy (in both Irish and English) is central to the structure, content and implementation of the programme. Numeracy (through the media of both Irish and English) and Irish and English literacy have a high priority which is consistent with the Department of Education's strategy for raising achievement in literacy and numeracy (DE, 2008a). The strong focus on literacy and numeracy complements rather than detracts from the other areas of learning, which are part of the Northern Ireland Curriculum for Irish-medium schools (Council for Curriculum Examinations and Assessment (CCEA), 2009).

One of the essential features of the programme is that immersion education pedagogies are embedded in course content. PGCE students have the opportunity to experience directly the immersion approach from the perspective of the learner as well as the perspective of the student teacher. Much of the programme content is delivered through the medium of Irish and this, coupled with the use of English medium teaching, accords with the theoretical principle of linguistic and academic transfer of skills across languages (Cummins, 2000). Students experience a range of learning and teaching methodologies which reflect best practice in bilingual and immersion education (Gibbons, 2006; Mac Corraidh, 2008; Mac Éinrí, 2008; Cenoz, 2009). Learning and language acquisition are realised through a practically-oriented, collaborative, interactional process (Mercer, 1995; Creese, 2005; Gregory 2008). Key features of this approach include modelling and scaffolding of learning of the target language and the modelling and scaffolding of a range of learning and teaching approaches.

The Self-evaluation Process

There are a number of procedures to systematically self-evaluate and review the quality of learning and teaching in St Mary's University College programmes, many of which are standard procedures for higher education institutions. There is annual evaluation and review of all modules and programmes, as well as a periodic review of all teaching and learning in the College. In addition to these procedures, which are similar to quality assurance procedures in other UK universities, there are specific procedures for the evaluation of initial teacher education programmes in Northern Ireland. These are required for the programmes to be accepted by the Department of Education. Originally ITE programmes were simply inspected by the Education and Training Inspectorate (ETI) as and when they saw fit. However, over the past three years a more structured approach to the inspection process has been agreed and introduced. During the same period, the accreditation process conducted by GTCNI has also been piloted. The respective roles of these two organisations are defined in the DE Circular 2010/03 (DE, 2010). In both instances, the ITE provider evaluates the quality of its own provision, providing evidence to support conclusions.

The College engaged with ETI and other initial teacher education providers in Northern Ireland over a two year period in the development of an agreed framework for self-evaluation and inspection including key questions and quality indicators (ETI, 2009). The self-evaluation took place in autumn 2009 and the College was visited by an inspection team in spring 2010. The self-evaluation tool proved to be extremely useful and effective. Indeed, the benefits of the actual process and the usefulness of the self-evaluation tool itself became apparent during the preparatory phase and during later reflections, leading to the anticipated outcomes outlined by the ETI:

> Self-evaluation is not an end in itself. The process and the action which follows, when implemented effectively, will help to bring about important improvements in the quality of teaching and learning, the experiences of the pupils and the standards they attain (2005).

The following sections outline the key areas of inquiry that were investigated during the self-evaluation process, which drew upon a wide range of evidence sources.

A College-wide Collaboration

Although there is a small core team of IM specialists, a large number of academic staff in the College play a significant role in the initial teacher education of IM PGCE students, and all who contribute to the programme are members of the PGCE course team. In preparation for the self-evaluation process, the core IM team planned and delivered a college-wide staff development workshop which had the aim of increasing understanding of developments in the IM sector with all College academic staff, both those who are members of the PGCE course team and other staff who do not contribute to the PGCE programme. In recognition of the importance of developing and maintaining strong and effective partnerships with schools, pupils from an IM post-primary school and a newly qualified teacher in an IM primary school also contributed to this workshop. This staff development workshop was a great success on many levels and was evaluated positively. Participants identified a range of outcomes. As a result of the workshop, a shared sense of purpose in preparation for the self-evaluation process was created and the profile of IM education within the College was enhanced. The workshop highlighted the role of all College staff in promoting the positive environment that supports the IM provision, along with the relevance of the self-evaluation exercise to the whole College community.

The collaborative approach to self-evaluation was a distinct feature of the process. A planning team, which included staff with particular skills such as ICT, was set up and chaired by the College Principal. Students were informed of the evaluation and were consulted as part of the process; two student representatives attended some of the planning meetings. The parameters for discussing aspects of provision were clarified at the outset so that the sensitivities of individuals with responsibilities in particular areas did not constrain critical debate and reflection.

One of the early tasks carried out by the planning team was the production of the Big Picture, an overview of the structural framework for the PGCE programme and the key components therein. This demonstrated the values and principles which underpinned the programme, as well as detailing elements of the three constituent modules. An important characteristic of the programme that was highlighted in the Big Picture was the interconnectedness of the modules and the content within the modules. This overview was very useful for all staff to appreciate the strong links across, as well as within, modules.

Coordinators and other lecturers were asked to formalise certain areas of provision in the PGCE programme by writing position papers which were posted electronically on the self-evaluation site on the College intranet and discussed by the team. This phase of the exercise required close team work, collaboration and consultation to agree the position papers and contextualise them within existing policy documents relating to the BEd and the PGCE. This writing task was also contextualised by the recent or ongoing experience of staff as representatives on external bodies, for example the Phonics Steering Group, the IM Literacy and Numeracy Working Group, the Review of IM Education Working Group and the POBAL steering group on a Special Educational Needs research initiative. The work of the planning team benefited from the range of expertise and experience that was brought to the task by lecturers.

Both the planning team and the broader programme team convened on a regular basis from September 2009 to January 2010 and the responses by the programme team to the agreed framework of key questions and quality indicators (ETI, 2009) were developed to provide a structure for reflection, debate and analysis throughout the semester. Notes on the work of both teams were posted on the self-evaluation site where all staff could access them and contribute to discussion. The planning team took responsibility for writing the self-evaluation document, uploading drafts onto the intranet site as part of the writing process. The requirement to produce evidence that supported statements in the self-evaluation document also challenged staff to reflect meaningfully on the quality indicators, providing a varied range of examples of good practice. During this process of collaborative critical reflection, key characteristics of the PGCE programme were identified, and the team was encouraged to identify creative and innovative action points that could enhance the programme further.

Evaluating against the Quality Indicators

As a result of the rigorous and systematic process of self-evaluation of the PGCE IM, the programme team was able to identify and recognise the strengths of the program, to celebrate and take pride in these strengths and to ensure that appropriate systems were in place to maintain and further enhance them. Important objectives, when embarking upon a process of self-evaluation, are not only to identify our strengths but also to be prepared to be critical, to be made aware of areas that require development, and to devise a plan of action to address these areas in need of development. The quality indicators for self-evaluation were organised around three headings: leadership and management; achievements and standards; and quality of provision for learning. This involved the scrutiny of key questions related to each heading and the gathering of evidence in support of claims made.

Leadership and Management

The team identified the impact leadership and management had on raising achievement, supporting the student teachers, and enhancing quality on the PGCE programme. During critical reflections, staff and students commented on the collegial nature of leadership and management, whereby staff at all levels interact and exchange views on a regular basis. The strong sense of community and mutual respect that is integral to the College ethos was identified and evidence was provided that showed a leadership focus on ensuring that students receive the highest quality of learning experiences and were enabled to reach their full potential. As the evaluative process facilitated debate and analysis of such observations, the educational vision demonstrated by leaders and managers was discussed. This communication exercise was considered positive and useful by the broader team. It was decided that an area for further development under the theme of leadership and management was to investigate ways in which the PGCE programme could benefit from closer links with An tÁisaonad, the Irish-medium resource unit based in St Mary's. The implementation of this action required further planning and monitoring so that closer links with An tÁisaonad were formed. One action involved staff from An tÁisaonad being invited to deliver workshops with students in the area of IM literacy and resources. Ultimately, this action provided benefits for the student teachers. However, it is anticipated that this closer connection with newly qualified teachers will also benefit An tÁisaonad, which relies on the expertise of practising teachers in the creation of new resources.

Achievements and Standards

A range of evidence was gathered from quality enhancement procedures which indicated a focus on the quality of student attainment on the PGCE course. In so doing, the programme team considered a wide range of sources, including oral and written reports by external examiners. The College also monitors student attainment through student performance in assessment, observations made by staff, consideration of students' views and self-assessments, consideration of formative assessment and reports by host teachers and by principals in host schools. This wide range of evidence was considered in the evaluation of how well the students achieve and numerous strengths were identified, including the dedication and commitment of students to the promotion of IM education and the high regard expressed by schools for the enthusiasm shown by students and their demonstration of appropriate professional values. The team concluded that student teachers on the IM PGCE programme achieve at a very high level across the full range of professional and educational areas that might be expected in a high quality initial teacher education programme. It was felt that this is in no small measure due to the dedication and commitment of the students and the excellent working relationships between students and staff.

The self-evaluation recommended an aspect requiring development related to achievements and standards. This was the continued exploration of the use of electronic portfolios for student self-evaluation and reflection. One of the main approaches used in St Mary's University College to support reflective practice is Personal Development Planning (PDP) through an e-portfolio, the Teacher Electronic Portfolio Northern Ireland (TePNI) system. This encourages students to reflect on their own practice and to consider ways to develop this and provides a structured and supported process for critical self-reflection and planning for further improvement. In 2008/09 PGCE students took part in a pilot of this e-portfolio. A crucial aspect of the PDP process is to encourage students to take ownership and become independent in their ability to self-evaluate critically. In order to further explore the use of an electronic portfolio, the current cohort of students is using the system very effectively by adding evidence of planning, teaching activities and the work of pupils to demonstrate their developing competences.

Quality of Provision for Learning

The process of self-evaluation provided the means through which strengths were identified in the area of quality of provision for learning. A variety of evidence demonstrated that teaching, learning and assessment on the IM PGCE programme is highly effective. The feedback from schools and comments made in reports from external examiners, who have consistently praised the high level of student achievement and the high quality of teaching on the course, were important sources of evidence. Evidence was collated which demonstrated strengths including: the expertise of core staff in the field of IM education; the good practice in immersion education demonstrated by tutors; and the quality of student support, guidance and pastoral care provided. An aspect identified as requiring further development in quality of provision for learning was the need to develop the use of the Gaeltacht to enhance students' language skills. As a result of additional funding from the Department of Education, the College was able to take action in this area and the students received two highly structured Gaeltacht experiences, one at the outset of their PGCE year and another during the second semester. These Gaeltacht experiences provided the students with the opportunity to develop their knowledge of immersion education pedagogies and to develop their individual competences in the Irish language in a naturally linguistic environment.

Issues Specific to Immersion Teacher Education

Many issues were raised and explored as part of the self-evaluation process, some issues relevant to all postgraduate programmes, others specific to immersion teacher education. We have chosen two issues which we consider to be central to immersion teacher education programmes to explore in more detail: the promotion of students' linguistic competence and the importance of partnerships with schools and other IM organisations.

Promoting Linguistic Competence of Students

The Irish language is usually the target language of IM PGCE students. However, the linguistic profile of students is becoming more diverse and includes students who are native speakers of Irish, students who have attended Irish-medium schools, students who are graduates with honours degrees in Irish, and students with degrees in other disciplines. The PGCE programme aims to improve standards in literacy by setting high expectations of student teachers, supported within a positive, developmental model of learning and a creative, challenging learning environment. The ongoing development of the students' competence in the Irish language during the course of the year is regarded as crucial. The College approach consists of four strands:

1. The immersion approach ensures the use of the Irish language 'naturally' in different curriculum and educational contexts, supported by a variety of good quality learning resources;
2. There is a discrete approach through the provision of dedicated language classes on a weekly basis;
3. A Gaeltacht experience is now part of the PGCE programme and this is being developed as funding is made available by the Department of Education;
4. Students are directed in self-evaluating and reflecting with regard to their Irish language skills and supported in developing these through a range of methods including consultations with tutors, peer assistance, Writing Centre support and help from the Royal Literary Fund sponsored College Writing Fellow.

The approach to the PGCE students' developing linguistic competence, as evidenced by the description above, reflects an appreciation of the social nature of learning through guided participation and interaction (Rogoff, 2003). The IM PGCE programme aims to improve linguistic competence by setting high expectations of student teachers, supported within a positive, developmental model of learning and a creative, challenging learning environment. This aspect of provision is considered to be innovative and successful; it also reflects current strategic developments in the IM sector (DE, 2008b;

ETI, 2008). Nevertheless, linguistic competence is but one important aspect of students' achievement and represents one of a range of professional competences that contribute to students' and teachers' performance as effective practitioners.

Developing Partnerships with Schools and Other Agencies

Strong and effective partnerships with schools have been central to high quality teacher education and many professional competences can be developed and extended most effectively through practical experience of working in schools. The partnerships developed with IM schools and with Comhairle na Gaelscolaíochta, in particular, as well as other IM support groups, are a major strength of the PGCE programme. IM tutors have recent classroom teaching experience and also engage in research in schools and extensive outreach work supporting schools and other Irish-medium agencies. They have recently been involved in the review of IM education (DE, 2008b), the revised curriculum for Irish-medium schools (CCEA, 2009), a cross-border research project on pupils' language development (Ó Duibhir and Garland, 2010) and the Irish-medium literacy and numeracy strategy (DE, 2011).

PGCE students have experience of teaching in all phases of primary education during three blocks of school experience. Students are encouraged to seek placement in a variety of school contexts including urban and rural schools and units, and most students gain experience in composite classes. They also have the option of electing to take a one week placement in a nursery or a special school (i.e., school for children with special educational needs). In schools, host teachers and principals are encouraged to observe students teaching and provide constructive feedback to enable students to develop their professional practice. It is part of College procedures that College tutors discuss students' progress with teachers and this allows the host teacher the opportunity to input their view of student progress and be part of the assessment process. This two-way conversation between host teacher and College tutor enables a consensus of judgement to be reached and can lead to richer feedback and 'feed forward' for students from both parties concerned. In addition schools complete a summative report on the student's progress which is taken into account in arriving at a student's final grade. This input from host schools contributes to the consistency and reliability of grades awarded.

Partnerships with schools are enhanced by the IM Schools' Partnership Committee which was set up following an ETI recommendation to strengthen partnership arrangements (ETI, 2000). Membership is rotated on a biannual basis and has recently been extended to include a newly qualified teacher and a host teacher. All principals of IM schools and units are informed of the agenda for meetings, are encouraged to contribute items for the agenda, and receive minutes of meetings. Meetings include discussion of current issues in the sector, school experience procedures and mechanisms for enhancing the students' experience, both at St Mary's and as newly qualified teachers. This committee is a valuable mechanism for improving communication with schools and seeks to engage partners in enhancing provision and improving course design.

Our partnerships extend beyond schools to other IM organisations. School principals, teachers and Comhairle na Gaelscolaíochta officers are involved directly in the selection of new PGCE student teachers. All applicants are interviewed and external members of interview panels work alongside College tutors. In many aspects of the PGCE programme, partners, including IM teachers, provide a useful input into the teaching of courses through lectures, review of materials to be used in classes and modelling good practice to small groups of student teachers in their classrooms. This interaction ensures that College staff have a good understanding of current school priorities and developments and helps ensure that the initial teacher education in St Mary's is highly relevant to the needs of schools as well as being professionally appropriate for the learners.

Conclusion

The experience of developing and reviewing this programme has been very positive and rewarding on many levels. The self-reflection process, described above, required a rigorous and structured approach to programme review. Opportunities for extensive consultation with stakeholders and debate about the provision for literacy, numeracy and special educational needs, in particular, were planned over a period of months. Unexpected outcomes to this collaborative work arose from the need to clearly articulate strengths and areas for development and to provide concrete evidence to support observations. Ultimately, this scrutiny exercise inspired confidence in the programme team and reinforced the connections within and across all areas of provision. It was also unanticipated that a focussed, intense, critical reflection, within a structured framework, would enhance the programme as a resource that is valued within the broader community. Arising out of the analysis, the team considered further ways to support the students' language competence and one strategy was an extended field trip to a Gaeltacht area. This experience did indeed enhance the students' use of Irish. However, interestingly, observations about the students' enthusiasm and openness to learning, communicated to the College on behalf of local residents, indicated that the students had made a positive contribution to life in the local area. This wider understanding of professionalism and an appreciation of their role as members of a larger community was also reinforced by an action planned as part of the self-evaluation process.

In this chapter, we have endeavoured to share information regarding the development of an initial teacher education programme for Irish-medium student teachers that represents one model for supporting student teachers to become effective and inspiring teachers in Irish-medium schools. In the future there may be an opportunity to establish a formal forum where providers of immersion initial teacher education in Ireland can disseminate outcomes of research, share insights gleaned from professional experience and resources produced for teacher education within a collaborative, supportive context.

Endnotes

1. 'Gaeltacht' refers to those regions of Ireland which are substantially Irish-speaking.

2. The organisation set up by the Department of Education in Northern Ireland to promote IIM education following the Good Friday Agreement.

References

Baker, C. (2006). *Foundations of bilingualism and bilingual education* (4th ed.). Clevedon: Multilingual Matters.

Bartlett, L. and Erben, T. (1995). *An investigation into the effectiveness of an exemplar model of LOTE teacher-training through partial immersion.* Canberra: Australian Government Printing Service.

Cenoz, J. (Ed.). (2009). *Towards multilingual education: Basque educational research from an international perspective.* Bristol: Multilingual Matters.

Council for Curriculum Examinations and Assessment (CCEA). (2009). *The revised NI curriculum: Primary Irish-medium.* Belfast: CCEA/PMBNI.

Creese, A. (2005). *Teacher collaboration and talk in multilingual classrooms.* Clevedon: Multilingual Matters.

Cummins, J. (2000). *Language power and pedagogy: Bilingual children in the crossfire.* Clevedon: Multilingual Matters.

Day, E. M. and Shapson, S. M. (1993). French immersion teacher education: A study of two programs. *The Canadian Modern Language Review, 49*(3), 446–465.

Department of Education (DE). (2008a). *Every school a good school: A strategy for raising achievement in literacy and numeracy.* Bangor: Author.

Department of Education (DE). (2008b). *A review of Irish-medium education.* Bangor: Author.

Department of Education (DE). (2010). *Circular 2010/03 initial teacher education: Approval of programmes.* Retrieved from http://www.deni.gov.uk/ite_approval_of_programmes_circular_-_english_version-2.pdf

Department of Education (DE). (2011). *Count read and succeed: A strategy for improving outcomes in literacy and numeracy.* Retrieved from http://www.deni.gov.uk/crs_strategy_literacy_and_numeracy_english.pdf

Education and Training Inspectorate (ETI). (2000). *Report of a survey on teacher education partnerships.* Retrieved from http://www.etini.gov.uk/report-of-a-survey-on-teacher-education-partnerships-st-marys-university-college-a-college-of-the-queens-university-belfast.pdf

Education and Training Inspectorate (ETI). (2005). *Together towards improvement.* Bangor: Author.

Education and Training Inspectorate (ETI). (2008). *Chief Inspector's report.* Retrieved from http://www.etini.gov.uk/index/support-material/support-material-general-documents-non-phase-related/the-chief-inspectors-report/the-chief-inspectors-report-2006-2008.htm

Education and Training Inspectorate (ETI). (2009). *Self-evaluation and inspection of initial teacher education provision.* Retrieved from http://www.etini.gov.uk/index/inspection-reports/inspection-reports-higher-education-initial-teacher-education/inspection-reports-higher-education-initial-teacher-education-2010/self-evaluation-and-inspection-of-initial-teacher-education-provision.pdf

Erben, T. (2004). Emerging research and practices in immersion teacher education. *Annual Review of Applied Linguistics, 24*, 320-388.

General Teaching Council of Northern Ireland (GTCNI). (2007). *Teaching: The reflective profession*. Belfast: Author.

Gibbons, P. (2006). *Bridging discourse in the ESL classroom.* London: Continuum.

Gregory, E. (2008). *Learning to read in a new language: Making sense of words and worlds* (2nd ed.). London: Sage.

Johnson, R. and Swain, M. (Ed.). (1997). *Immersion education: International perspectives.* Cambridge: Cambridge University Press.

Lapkin, S., Swain, M. and Shapson, S. (1990). French immersion agenda for the 90's. *Canadian Modern Language Review, 46*(4), 638-674.

Mac Corraidh, S. (2008). *Ar thóir an deachleachtais*. Belfast: Cló Ollscoil na Banríona.

Mac Éinrí, E. (2008). Teagasc teangacha; teoiric, taighde agus dea-chleachtas. *Taighde Agus Teagasc, 6*, 229-234.

McKendry, E. (2006). An tumoideachas/Immersion education. Belfast: Comhairle na Gaelscolaíochta.

Mercer, N. (1995). *The guided construction of knowledge: Talk among teachers and learners.* Clevedon: Multilingual Matters.

Nicolson, M. and MacIver, M. (2003). Contexts and futures. In M. Nicolson and M. MacIver (Eds.), *Policy and practice in education. Gaelic medium education* (pp. 63-73). Edinburgh: Dunedin Academic Press.

Nig Uidhir, G. (1996). *Teacher training for Irish-medium schools: A report on the introduction of a new Irish-medium pathway into St Mary's College*. Belfast: St Mary's College.

Nig Uidhir, G. (2002). Initial teacher training for Irish-medium schools. In J. Kirk and D. Ó Baoill (Eds.), *Language planning and education: Linguistic issues in Northern Ireland, the Republic of Ireland, and Scotland* (pp. 65-75). Belfast: Cló Ollscoil an Banríona.

Nig Uidhir, G. (2006). Coláiste Ollscoile Naomh Muire agus túsoideachas do mhúinteoirí lán-ghaeilge. In D. Ó Riagáin (Ed.), *Voces diversae: Lesser-used language education in Europe* (pp. 145-156). Belfast: Cló Ollscoil na Banríona.

Ó Duibhir, P. and Garland, J. (2010). *Gaeilge labhartha na bpáistí i scoileanna lan-Ghaeilge in Éirinn*. Armagh: SCoTENS.

Ó hAiniféin, D. (2008). *An tumoideachas in Éirinn. Immersion education in Ireland*. Dublin: Coiscéim.

Quality Assurance Agency for Higher Education (QAA). (2000). *Code of practice for the assurance of academic qualifications and standards in higher education: Section 6: Assessment of students*. Mansfield: Author.

Roberts, G. (2002). Bilingual teaching in ITET courses. *Welsh Journal of Education, 11*(2), 109-115.

Robertson, B. (2002). Teacher training in Gaelic in Scotland. In J Kirk and D Ó Baoill (Eds.), *Language planning and education: Linguistic issues in Northern Ireland, the republic of Ireland and Scotland* (pp. 76-81). Belfast: Cló Ollscoil na Banríona.

Rogoff, B. (2003). *The cultural nature of human development*. New York: Oxford University Press Inc.

Chapter 13

Irish and Modern Languages: A Collaborative Journey in Initial Teacher Education

Áine Furlong, Brendan MacMahon and Sinéad Ní Ghuidhir

Waterford Institute of Technology and NUI Galway

Introduction

Content and Language Integrated Learning (CLIL) is a dual-focused educational approach in which an additional language is used for the learning and teaching of both content and language (Mehisto, Marsh and Frigols, 2008). While the integration of language and content teaching is well established in Irish language immersion programmes, there is an acknowledged lack of acquaintance with the variety of theoretical approaches that are available to other language teachers, a dearth of Irish language CLIL materials, and a lack of teacher education programmes to prepare language and subject teachers for CLIL (McKendry, 2007). This chapter presents the outcome of collaboration between two communities of practice which traditionally may have been perceived as distant cousins. While both are concerned with the role and place of language/s in the curriculum, neither until recently had exchanged knowledge and experience for the benefit of teachers, student teachers and, ultimately, learners. Since 2009, the National University of Ireland (NUI) Galway, through *An Dioplóma Gairmiúil san Oideachas,* the sole initial teacher education course for second-level teachers through the medium of Irish in Ireland, and Waterford Institute of Technology (WIT), through its expertise in Content and Language Integrated Learning, have collaborated in ways that have expanded the perspectives of both communities. This chapter outlines the background, rationale and context for this collaboration, which led to change and innovation in initial teacher education (ITE). Moreover, it points to the benefits that can be gained from interdisciplinary collaboration as a result of common concerns for the future of language education in Ireland, including language issues experienced in English, the dominant language. While these concerns are real, they also present opportunities for change and the development of interdisciplinary mind-sets within teacher education and the teaching world at large. New avenues are opened when the potential of placing language along with content as joint curricular objectives is considered and when the relationship between language and learning is re-asserted. In this respect, Content and Language Integrated Learning has much to contribute.

Background

The teaching and learning of the Irish language remains both a national and a conventional educational issue (Harris, 2007). This is reflected in the manner in which public debate on the low proficiency levels achieved by many students and, more recently, the compulsory status of Irish in the curriculum, tends to mire consideration of Irish language pedagogy in reductionist debates on the future of the language. This in turn obscures the many issues involved in teaching through the language and the opportunities that exist for innovative approaches to learning the language itself. That consideration of the Irish language should be associated so closely with education is unsurprising, given that many students experience prolonged exposure to the language within the school system alone. Problems with regard to the teaching and learning of Irish are also well documented. What must be further acknowledged, however, is the reliance of the language on the education system to reproduce at least a basic level of competence in Irish in each new generation to compensate for low levels of natural transmission (Mac Gréil, 2009; Ó Laoire and Harris, 2006; Ó Riagáin, 1997). Furthermore, Ó Laoire (2007) argues that, unlike learning a foreign language, which can prepare students for communication in the country of the target language, the lack of social contexts within which to use Irish outside the classroom poses challenges for teachers and learners alike. Among the many long-standing difficulties associated with Irish in the context of education are issues related to teaching resources and curriculum content, as well as the initial education of teachers (Ó Flatharta, 2007). However, the common curriculum for Irish at both primary and secondary level obscures the fact that the language is at present taught and studied in three distinct contexts nationally, and that each has its own concerns.

In English-medium schools, attended by the majority of the school population, Irish is taught as a second language (L2). Harris et al. (2006) report on the difficulties faced by this sector in sustaining its traditional language maintenance role in the face of declining standards in spoken Irish, in particular at primary level. At second level, Murtagh (2007) attributes students' failure to attain the speaking proficiency levels set out in curriculum objectives to both the limited instructional time for Irish and the limited opportunities for real communicative use. Furthermore, an analysis of the teaching of Irish at Junior Cycle (Department of Education and Science, Inspectorate, 2007) makes reference to the fact that very little use is made of ICT and that lesson content is frequently unrelated to the experiences or interests of students, which in turn leads to reduced personal investment in learning the language. Irish is taught as L2/L1 within immersion or semi-immersion contexts in Irish-medium schools, and concern has been expressed about the lack of teaching resources and textbooks, the inadequate supply of teachers at primary-level (Máirtín, 2006), and the standards of written Irish at second-level (Walsh, 2007). In Gaeltacht schools[1], where Irish is taught principally as L1, research by Mac Donnacha et al. (2005) points to a crisis in teaching through the language because of the steady encroachment of English as the medium of instruction.

At a wider curriculum level, the Council of Europe Expert Group, in their language education policy profile for Ireland, note the disconnection between Irish and modern languages in post-primary schools (Council of Europe, 2007). A similar point is made in the review of languages in post-primary education, which notes that while revised curricula for languages have been subject to continuing discussion and monitoring since their introduction, Irish has been treated in isolation to this debate (National Council for Curriculum and Assessment (NCCA), 2005). The compartmentalisation of Irish is evident also at a methodological level, and despite having a well-established network of Irish-medium schools, it is argued that teachers working in immersion contexts lack acquaintance with the various theoretical and methodological approaches that are available in the literature to other language teachers (McKendry, 2007). Little (2003) for example, makes the point that Irish medium education has remained almost entirely untouched by the upsurge of international interest in Content and Language Integrated Learning.

Demands for an adequate response to these issues invariably focus on what Harris (2008, p. 184) refers to as the question of 'methods and materials' and on the issue of teacher education. Calls have been made for 'a nationally coordinated teacher education programme' to 'improve the supply of well-trained teachers… sufficiently at ease in the language' (Council of Europe, 2007, p. 16), and for adequate training in language methodology to prepare pre-service teachers to teach in immersion situations (Mac Donnacha et al., 2005; Ó Duibhir, 2006; Ó Flatharta, 2007; Walsh, 2007). Given the place of Irish in immersion and non-immersion contexts, the onus therefore is on initial teacher education programmes to equip Irish language teachers with the theoretical and methodological approaches which enable them to both teach the language and teach through the language. This in turn means utilising the good practice, new methodologies and strategies which have been successful in the teaching and learning of other languages.

CLIL as an educational approach offers many possibilities. In the first instance, it places equal emphasis on language and content, providing a pedagogy for teachers working in immersion situations and also a pedagogy for teachers wishing to work in a language other than the dominant language. Secondly, the focus on subject content gives a context and immediate relevance to language learning which can be lost in purely communicative approaches. The emphasis that is placed on both language as a medium and as a learning outcome makes CLIL adaptable for new approaches to teaching Irish in English-medium schools. As teacher educators, we believe that much of CLIL methodology is not specific to language teaching but must be considered part of educational best practice generally. Coyle (2007) makes the point that more traditional transmission models of content delivery which conceptualise disciplinary subjects as bodies of knowledge to be transferred from teacher to learner are no longer appropriate. CLIL pedagogy therefore, offers an innovative educational approach which emphasises real engagement and interactivity through the social construction of knowledge. Engaging with the CLIL community of practitioners provides a means also of forging what Little (2003) refers to as methodological links between Irish-medium education and the teaching of other languages both in Ireland and Europe.

The rise of English as a global *lingua franca* has led many learners to question the relevance of learning a second language (L2). This is despite initiatives such as the *Modern Languages in Primary Schools Initiative* introduced in Ireland in 1998, the *Post-Primary Languages Initiative* in 2000, as well as efforts to articulate a language policy for Ireland in light of decreasing numbers of L2 learners at post-primary and third-level (Ó Dochartaigh and Broderick, 2006). Difficulties experienced by modern languages and Irish are in essence similar in that they touch on issues of relevance and language use. And it is these difficulties that lead us to reflect on the role and place of language(s) in education since the educational context, and more specifically the classroom, is often the only context where such languages are experienced.

A Rationale for a Language-sensitive Approach to Every Subject in the Curriculum

If Irish shares commonalities with modern languages so too does English. These do not simply apply to socio-linguistic/cultural factors but to the manner in which we use language in the learning process. As educators, we must consider whether the potential of language itself, during the learning process, is fully utilised. Focusing on the relationship between thought and language and, more specifically, on the relationship between thought and word, we realise that awareness of the word is in fact awareness of ourselves and of what we know (or don't know). Vygotsky (1986) concludes that:

> Consciousness is reflected in a word as the sun in a drop of water. A word relates to consciousness as a living cell relates to a whole organism, as an atom relates to the universe. A word is a microcosm of human consciousness (p. 256).

If we accept the relation between a word and consciousness, then we must also accept that learning is its outcome. Consequently, in this light, language becomes central to the process of mediation (Wertsch, 1991; Lantolf, 2000). While this may be stating the obvious, educationalists have felt the need to remind teachers and subject specialists of the multiple functions of language (NCCA, 1999, p. 15). These include the use of language to understand, to communicate, to think, to create, to explain, to use, to make, to recall, and to memorise.

Notwithstanding the opportunities for authentic L2 exposure afforded by technology, over-emphasis on the communicative function of language in second language teaching and learning has led to the removal of meaningful content that, in the past, typically took the form of literature. The language experience in this context becomes impoverished, acted out and memorised within the sole context of the classroom for the purpose of passing an exam. As Vygotsky points out, 'a word devoid of thought is a dead thing' (1986, p. 255). Consequently, because of the gradual erosion of the communicative approach to limited, essentially oral, transactional communication (Dalton-Puffer, 2009), the Council of Europe has urged language learning circles to focus on the transformation of the language *learner* into a language *user*. In other words, the learner is viewed from a wider perspective, as a 'social agent' who may work on tasks where the language learning objectives are subsumed under the aims associated with the completion of the task. These aims may relate 'to a specific environment, within a particular field of action' (Council of Europe,

2001, p. 9). This new emphasis in L2 learning has led to the promotion of task-based learning and/or CLIL as suitable teaching and learning approaches because the communicative function of language is embedded in these frameworks. In this case, the content objectives and/or the purpose of the task precede the language objectives. Consequently, the communicative dimension of language becomes one of the many facets of language fostered during the learning experience. Hence, language is used to understand content, to think and solve problems, to make or construct objects, and to communicate.

The multiple dimensions of language in the learning experience are not just a concern of L2 specialists. They are also a matter of concern for those who rely on the L1 to communicate and co-construct knowledge. Recent publications in a subject such as mathematics highlight the need for teachers to consider language as a crucial dimension of the learning process. McMurry (2010) proposes that 'learning to use maths is not about rote memory' (in this case, language to memorise), 'it is much more like becoming fluent in a language. Once you know the vocabulary and structure of the subject' (language to understand), 'you can start to express yourself' (language to communicate) (in Ahlstrom, 2010, p. 5). The many perspectives on the role of language in the learning of mathematics have been broadly categorised by Solano-Flores (2010) as 'functional', in which the dynamic aspect of mathematical communication is emphasised and 'formal' in which there is a focus on linguistic features. Jamison (2000), who concentrates on the latter aspect, argues that learning the language of mathematics involves the development of critical linguistic awareness by, for example, studying the syntax of mathematical definitions: are the definitions concise yet comprehensive? Are they clear or ambiguous? Are they grammatically correct? L2 specialists will immediately identify with these examples because a language teacher's main focus is to transform content into *Comprehensible Input* (Krashen 1985). In this light, L1 content teachers and L2 practitioners will realise that much is to be gained when content and language are perceived and treated as joint curricular objectives as opposed to compartmentalised units of expertise. How then are we to reconcile content and language or, in Vygotsky's terms, 'thought and word'? How can we create a language-sensitive approach to the curriculum? How can a second language, such as Irish, be used to further emphasise the centrality of language to the learning of any subject?

First, as mentioned above, we note the similarities between the approach of the mathematics teacher and that of a CLIL teacher. CLIL is dually focused on both content and a second language and within this view, teachers and learners must consider all the dimensions of language, that is, language for communication as well as language for learning. At the heart of the approach lies the process of *scaffolding* knowledge and language, which implies that the learner's existing knowledge of the content acts as a foundation upon which to build. Therefore, prior knowledge, background building, the identification of key vocabulary/terminology, sensitisation to useful language and relevant structures are identified by the teacher and learners. Learners are also encouraged to further develop and reformulate the concepts in a multiplicity of contexts by relying on the five language skills, that is, listening, reading, writing, speaking, including verbal production and interaction. The skills may be activated during activities such as transcribing, for example through: dictation; summarising and reformulating; making verbal presentations of and/or mind-mapping one's understanding; debating and questioning. For many language specialists the process can be perceived as daunting because the focus is on what they (the teachers) do not necessarily know well – the content. For content teachers, the process is equally daunting as the content is delivered through another language. However, in both cases, well established L2 principles such as learner autonomy (Dam, 2001; Little, 2007) and task-based learning (Willis and Willis, 2007), combined with the tools of the trade, can be used to achieve this aim. These include graphic organisers (GO), internet resources, Web2.0 technology and numerous pedagogical ideas developed in the field of second language learning and teaching. Strategies developed for reading in a foreign language (Jiang and Grabe, 2007) show how *scaffolding* language encourages learners to develop an awareness of patterns of discourse organisation such as those associated with definitions, cause and consequence, comparison and contrast, or sequencing. Jiang and Grabe (2007) point out that there is a relatively small number of text structures (12 to 15 in total) which can help to represent the interrelationships between ideas and patterns of discourse organisation. In an L2 context, GOs help comprehension and can be used as pre-reading and post-reading tasks (Järvinen et al., 2009). Because the language of learning is a second language (L2), learners gain an additional perspective on the subject in question. The perspective acquired through the medium of another language opens a door to consciousness, because in the words of Huston (2003), '[I]n a foreign tongue, no places are common; all are exotic' (p. 64).

In a CLIL context, the centrality of language to all learning is explicit since the experience is about learning *in* and *through* another language *for* the acquisition of content. It is by restoring the function of language as a means to acquire knowledge of the world (formal and informal), that an environment which is immediately relevant and meaningful to the learner is created. While the European CLIL landscape is predominantly associated with English as an L2, successful examples of multilingual CLIL experiences are emerging, most notably from Spain where minority languages such as Catalan and Basque have occupied a central role in the school curriculum for more than 20 years (Lasagabaster and Ruiz de Zarobe, 2010). Additional initiatives include the work of the ground-breaking project ConBaT+, housed at the European Centre for Modern Languages, where plurilingualism is a feature of CLIL tasks, leading to the active integration of the languages of the class (and their speakers) (Bernaus et al., 2012). The common thread in all these initiatives is the quality of teacher education and the integration of materials development as a pedagogical learning device for initial teacher and in-service teacher education (Ball and Lindsay 2010). Much can be gained from current developments in the field of L2 learning and teaching. Against this background, it is possible to re-imagine the curriculum, or at the very least, aspects of the curriculum, through Irish or other languages. In this light, it is also possible to transform initial as well as in-service teacher education. Moreover, the Irish teaching context lends itself to CLIL developments, in part, because teachers at post-primary level qualify in two subjects and because teachers of Irish seek to integrate the language into meaningful events or learning opportunities. It is in this way that CLIL can be described first and foremost as a mind-set.

The Context: Teaching through Irish in Collaboration with Modern Languages

The *Dioplóma Gairmiúil san Oideachas* (DGO) was established over ten years ago in the School of Education, NUI Galway, in response to the demand for a second-level ITE programme through the medium of Irish. Since inception, the programme has been delivered entirely through Irish and students complete their teaching practice component in Irish-medium schools. From a yearly intake of 40 students, on average 50 per cent come from Gaeltacht areas, 90 per cent have two degree subjects, and in the case of 88 per cent of DGO students, one of these subjects is Irish (latest figures from 2011-12 cohort). The number of new second level Irish-medium schools (gaelcholáistí) continues to grow in response to demand from parents who wish their children to progress from Irish-medium primary schools (gaelscoileanna). Between 1996 and 2010, the number of gaelcholáistí increased from 24 to 40, with a concomitant rise in the number of students from 4626 to 8620. Such growth indicates a clear need for well-trained teachers who are fluent in the language and who are also prepared to teach other subjects through Irish. As the DGO programme developed, it became increasingly evident that, while emphasis was placed on the theoretical and methodological issues relating to the teaching of Irish as a curriculum subject, the issue of supporting pre-service teachers to teach the range of second level subjects through Irish needed to be addressed. Teachers in Irish-medium secondary schools must display competence in the dual role of subject and language teacher and develop learning outcomes for both. Translation is not enough. Language use must be defined, vocabulary and core language structures need to be identified, and teachers must be familiar with the terminology relevant to the subject in order to contextualise language. Consequently, a module called *Teagasc trí Ghaeilge* (Teaching through Irish) was devised and introduced to the programme in 2007-08. The aim of this module was to address the specific issues that arise when using Irish as the language of instruction and to raise awareness of the CLIL mind-set in pre-service teachers. In a CLIL class, engagement with language and with the subject knowledge, skills, concepts and attitudes occurs simultaneously. The challenges posed by content, combined with the linguistic demands of the language of instruction, affect the quality of learning for the student. Teachers, therefore, need to monitor if a student's failure to understand is because the language demands are too high, and/or because the level of cognitive demand is too challenging; otherwise, the student may be discouraged and the learning opportunity lost.

Figure 1 below, adapted from the CLIL Matrix Project (European Centre for Modern Languages 2004 – 2007), identifies the upper left quadrant as the desired working area in the CLIL classroom. Here the cognitive demand of material is both challenging and engaging for the student, but is presented in language that is accessible and does not hinder comprehension. In other words, content is turned into Comprehensible Input (Krashen, 1985).

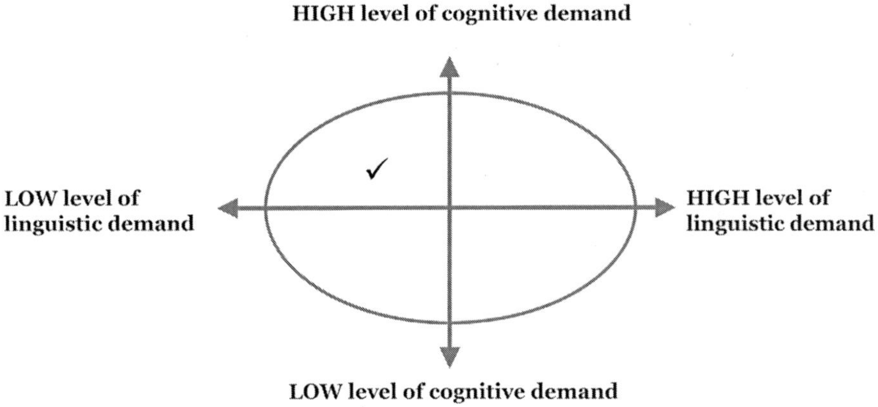

HIGH level of cognitive demand

LOW level of linguistic demand

✓

HIGH level of linguistic demand

LOW level of cognitive demand

Figure 1: Combining cognitive and linguistic challenges (CLIL Matrix project – ECML 2004 – 2007).

Furthermore, the importance of language production, referred to by Swain and Lapkin (1995) as the Output Hypothesis, must also be taken into account, so that learner awareness through Focus on Form and confidence in language proficiency may be improved. Focus on Form encourages the development of 'noticing', 'understanding' and 'awareness' processes. 'Noticing' may happen voluntarily or involuntarily, while 'understanding' and 'awareness' relate to more explicit input in the form of a specific grammar rule or generalisation. According to Schmidt 'more noticing leads to more learning' (1994, p. 18). In the case of Irish-medium schools, and in the Irish language classroom in English-medium schools, the aim is for Irish to become the language of communication as well as the language of instruction. With these considerations in mind, the new module, *Teagasc trí Ghaeilge*, was developed to include multiple perspectives reflecting the complexities surrounding the learning and teaching of subjects through Irish. The course outline below shows how the module was initially developed, with input on:

1. Language and identity
2. Models of immersion / submersion
3. First and second language acquisition theories
4. Language Planning
5. The Irish Context – schools, sociological issues
6. European Language Portfolio
7. The centrality of language to learning (CLIL).

The four key dimensions of CLIL, characterised by the four Cs of Content, Cognition, Communication and Culture (Coyle, 2007), provided a blueprint for the CLIL component of the module. However, once the syllabus was defined, a knowledge gap became apparent which emphasised the need for collaboration with practitioners in the field of CLIL and modern languages. CLIL in Ireland was at that time mainly confined to modern languages, principally in primary schools with the *Modern Languages Primary Schools Initiative* (MLPSI) and, to varying degrees, in third-level courses around the country, one example being Waterford Institute of Technology (WIT). A CLIL research group had already been established in WIT and was actively involved in a number of European programmes. Pooling experience and expertise, a collaboration was formed between the DGO programme in NUIG and the CLIL group in WIT. Through this collaboration, students were introduced to the concept of a language-sensitive approach to content teaching. By considering Irish within the European context, the potential sense of isolation experienced by many who teach through Irish was addressed in a real and practical manner. The module was delivered in a series of seminars over the first term of the DGO to the 2007-08 cohort. Students were made aware of the significance of languages and of their place in the individual's personal, social and professional dimensions. The availability of teaching and learning resources was also addressed. However, it was apparent from the beginning that Irish language resources were scarce and that much time-consuming adaptation of English language resources would be necessary. Although there is a wealth of teaching materials and resources freely available online through organisations such as CLIL Cascade Network (CCN), there is no central data bank of free CLIL Irish language digital resources available to teachers in Ireland.[2] As a means of contributing to the development of new materials, it was decided that DGO students would use available technology to plan and prepare lessons, which could be shared with other practitioners and used as classroom resources. In the process, they would contribute to a growing international data bank of resources, placing Irish learning materials alongside modern languages. On the basis of this new direction for the module, the form of assessment also took a new direction.

Assessment

Initially, assessment during the first two years of the module was by essay-style written exam. While this allowed students to demonstrate theoretical understanding it did not afford them the opportunity to integrate this theory into their practice and to demonstrate a CLIL mind-set. Traditional approaches to assessment are based on selection of a response, take place in a contrived situation, rely on recall and recognition, and are teacher led. On the other hand, authentic assessment in a CLIL classroom is student led, based on real life situations, relies on construction and application, and is focused on performing a task (Barbero, 2009). Consequently, assessment of the module itself gradually placed more emphasis on CLIL in practice, in the Irish language context, through the development of materials and resources to better reflect the nature of assessment in the CLIL classroom. During 2008-09, the second year this module was included in the DGO programme, the students worked in groups according to their own subject areas and developed lesson plans based on the 4Cs of CLIL (Coyle, 2007). Each group gave a short presentation of their ideas and shared their rationale and thinking with the wider group. They then reflected individually about this experience in their end-of-year essay. In 2009-10, further developments included lesson plans of a standard that could be published on the internet and the development of posters which were exhibited at the first International CLIL conference in Ireland, *CLIL – Teagasc Trí Ghaeilge Conference*, which took place in NUI Galway on 27 February 2010.

Further developments have since taken place. Funding has been secured from An Chomhairle um Oideachas Gaeltachta agus Gaelscolaíochta (COGG) for the purchase of Multimedia Mediator Software which allows students to develop sophisticated lesson plans and teaching aids aimed at establishing a DGO-based web resource bank for CLIL materials in Irish.[3] Recent developments in technology include the availability of the iTunesU platform for the DGO. By reconceptualising the purpose of materials development, both as an assessment tool and as a resource for future use, students are motivated to succeed and are empowered in their practice.

Conclusion

Some 20 years ago, Singleton (1992) referred to the situation of languages in the Irish curriculum as one of apartheid and called for an end to it. The current crisis in language use, that is, language for communicating in Irish and modern languages as well as language for learning in English, forces us to reconsider all the dimensions of language in education, thereby creating new interdisciplinary synergies. In this regard, Ireland is particularly well positioned to embark on this journey. And, encouragingly, this journey has begun.

Ireland has a pool of teachers and teachers-to-be who, through their education at primary and post-primary levels, are intellectually disposed, at the outset, to consider the integration of a language-sensitive approach into at least two subjects. With regard to Irish specifically, the rationale for a revision of teacher education, and of materials and resources, is well articulated among academics, practitioners and policy makers. In respect of modern languages, the past 15 years in Europe have seen unprecedented developments and investment in language teaching and learning, including the growth of CLIL, plurilingualism/culturalism, the use of communication technology as well as student mobility. To ignore their potential for the Irish education system is indefensible. In respect of English as L1, much is to be gained through interdisciplinary collaboration, e.g., the formal development of bilingual modules in Transition Year to revise or even introduce important aspects of the subjects examined in the final year of second-level schooling.

We can say that, for some, the journey towards re-imagining initial and in-service teacher education has already begun, as evidenced by the collaboration between NUI Galway and Waterford Institute of Technology. This collaboration has grown from workshops, through conferences, to materials development and seminars. It also places the work of young pre-service teachers on a European platform. It is continued by increasing the visibility of this work in this chapter, as well as by the forthcoming creation of a CLIL Community of Practice at the National Digital Learning Repository (NDLR).[4] The development of a joint teacher education CLIL module to be delivered simultaneously at NUI Galway through Irish, and online at Waterford Institute of Technology, is also under way. These developments are of their time for two reasons: first, they respond to the need for collaboration in order to better understand and tackle the challenges associated with language learning; second, they also address the fundamental role of language/s in our education system. In the words of Van Lier (as cited in Cots and Tusón, 1994, p. 52), 'it is impossible to separate education and language. You cannot do pedagogy without language and language learning is the essence of pedagogy'.

Endnotes

1. Schools within geographical areas where the State recognises Irish as the predominant language.

2. CCN: the CLIL Cascade Network is an online community of CLIL prac-

titioners and their professional partners who share ideas, experiences, and resources. More information is available at http://www.ccn-clil.eu/index.php?name=ContentandnodeIDX=345.

3. COGG: an Chomhairle um Oideachas Gaeltachta agus Gaelscolaíochta, (COGG) was founded in 1998 to cater for the educational needs of Gaeltacht schools and of gaelscoileanna. The Comhairle's role relates to both primary and post-primary education and one of its main areas of work is to provide teaching resources and support services in the sector. However, many of these resources are available only in print form.

4. NDLR: the National Digital Learning Resources platform aims to support greater collaboration in developing and sharing digital teaching resources and associated teaching experience across all subject disciplines and communities of academics and to promote good practice use and re-use of existing resources (http://www.ndlr.ie/services/ndlrabout).

References

Ahlstrom D. (2010, December 1). Book uses vocabulary of maths to teach. *Irish Times,* 5.

Ball, P. and Lindsay, D. (2010). Teacher training for CLIL in the Basque country: The case of the Ikastolas – an expediency model. In D. Lasagabaster and Y. Ruiz de Zarobe (Eds.), *CLIL in Spain: Implementaion, results and teacher training* (pp.162-187). Newcastle upon Tyne: Cambridge Scholars Publishing.

Barbero, T. (2009, September). *Authentic assessment in CLIL.* Paper presented at LINC Conference, Turku, Finland. Retrieved from http://linc.utu.fi/Sivusto/LINC_Barbero.pdf

Bernaus, M., Furlong, A., Jonckheere, S. and Kervran, M. (2012). *Plurilingualism and pluriculturalism in content-based teaching.* Graz: ECML.

CLIL Matrix Project. (2004-2007). ECML's second medium term programme of activities. Retrieved from http://archive.ecml.at/mtp2/CLIL-matrix/

Cots, J.M. and Tusón, A. (1994). Language in education: An interview with Leo Van Lier. *Sintagma 6,* 51-65.

Coyle, D. (2007). Content and language integrated learning: Towards a connected research agenda for CLIL pedagogies. *International Journal of Bilingual Education and Bilingualism, 10*, 543-562. doi: 10.2167/beb459.0

Council of Europe. (2001). *Common European framework of reference for languages: Learning, teaching and assessment.* Strasbourg: Language Policy Division. Retrieved from http://www.coe.int/t/dg4/linguistic/Source/Framework_EN.pdf

Council of Europe. (2007). *Language education policy profile: Ireland.* Strasbourg: Language Policy Division. Retrieved from http://www.coe.int/t/dg4/linguistic/Source/IrelandCountry_report_EN.pdf

Dalton-Puffer, C. (2009). Communicative competence and the CLIL classroom. In Y. Ruiz de Zarobe and R.M. Jiménez Catalán (Eds.), *Content and language integrated learning. Evidence from research in Europe* (pp. 197-214). Bristol: Multilingual Matters.

Dam, L. (2001). Introduction. *AILA Review, 15*, 1 Retrieved from http://www.aila.info/download/publications/review/AILA15.pdf

Department of Education and Science, Inspectorate. (2007). *Looking at Irish at junior cycle: Teaching and learning in post-primary schools.* Dublin: Department of Education and Science.

Harris, J. (2007). Bilingual education and bilingualism in Ireland North and South. *The International Journal of Bilingual Education and Bilingualism, 10*, 359-368. doi: 10.2167/beb449.0

Harris, J. (2008). Irish in the education system. In C. Nic Pháidín and S. Ó Cearnaigh (Eds.), *A new view of the Irish language* (pp.178-190). Dublin: Cois Life.

Harris, J., Forde, P., Archer, P., Nic Fhearaile, S. and O'Gorman, M. (2006). *Irish in primary school: Long-term national trends in achievement.* Dublin: Department of Education and Science.

Huston, N. (2003). The mask and the pen. In I. de Courtivron (Ed.), *Lives in translation: Bilingual writers on identity and creativity* (pp.147-156). New York: Palgrave Macmillan.

Jamison, R.E. (2000). Learning the language of mathematics. *Language and Learning Across the Disciplines, 4* (1), 45-54. Retrieved from http://wac.colostate.edu/llad/issues.htm#4.1

Järvinen, H., Furlong, Á., Corsain, M., Barbero, T., Liubiniene, V., Sygmund, D., Parvainen, H. and Pakozdi, M. (2009). *Language in content instruction.* Turku: University of Turku. Retrieved from http://lici.utu.fi/

Jiang, X. and Grabe, W. (2007). Graphic organizers in reading instruction: Research findings and issues. *Reading in a Foreign Language, 19*, 34-55. Retrieved from http://nflrc.hawaii.edu/rfl/April2007/

Krashen, S. (1985). *The input hypothesis: Issues and implications.* New York: Longman.

Lantolf, J.P. (Ed.). (2000). *Sociocultural theory and second language learning.* Oxford: Oxford University Press.

Lasagabaster D. and Ruiz de Zarobe, Y. (Eds.). (2010). *CLIL in Spain: Implementaion, results and teacher training.* Newcastle upon Tyne: Cambridge Scholars Publishing.

Little, D. (2003). *Languages in the post-primary curriculum: A discussion document.* Dublin: NCCA.

Little, D. (2007). Language learner autonomy: Some fundamental considerations revisited. *Innovation in Language Learning and Teaching, 1,* 14–29. doi: 10.2167/illt040.0

Mac Donnacha, S., Ní Chualáin, F., Ní Shéaghdha, A. and Ní Mhainín, T. (2005). *Staid reatha na scoileanna Gaeltachta.* Dublin: An Chomhairle um Oideachas Gaeltachta agus Gaelscolaíochta.

Mac Gréil, M. (2009). *The Irish language and the Irish people.* Survey and Research Unit: NUI Maynooth, Department of Sociology.

Máirtín, C. (2006). *Soláthar múinteoirí do na bunscoileanna lán-Ghaeilge: Bunachar sonraí agus tuairimí príomhoidí i leith gnéithe den staid reatha sa Ghaelscolaíocht.* Dublin: An Chomhairle um Oideachas Gaeltachta agus Gaelscolaíochta.

McKendry, E. (2007). *An tumoideachas/Immersion education.* Retrieved from http://www.comhairle.org/

McMurry, S. M. (2010). *Mathematics as a language: Understanding and using maths.* Dublin: Living Edition.

Mehisto, P., Marsh, D. and Frigols, M.J. (2008) *Uncovering CLIL: Content and language integrated learning in bilingual and multilingual education.* Oxford: Macmillan Education.

Murtagh, L. (2007). Out-of-school use of Irish, motivation and proficiency in immersion and subject-only post primary programmes. *International Journal of Bilingual Education and Bilingualism, 10,* 428-453. doi: 10.2167/beb453.0

National Council for Curriculum and Assessment (NCCA). (1999). *Primary school curriculum.* Dublin: Author

National Council for Curriculum and Assessment (NCCA). (2005). *Review of languages in post-primary education: Report of the first phase of the review.* Dublin: Author.

Ó Dochartaigh, P. and Broderick, M. (2006). *Language policy and language planning in Ireland.* Dublin: Royal Irish Academy.

Ó Duibhir, P. (2006). *Oideachas agus forbairt ghairmiúil leanúnach múinteoirí i scoileanna Gaeltachta agus lán-Ghaeilge.* Dublin: An Chomhairle um Oideachas Gaeltachta agus Gaelscolaíochta.

Ó Flatharta, P. (2007). *Struchtúr oideachais na Gaeltachta.* Dublin: An Chomhairle um Oideachas Gaeltachta agus Gaelscolaíochta.

Ó Laoire, M. (2007). An approach to developing language awareness in the Irish language classroom: A case study. *International Journal of Bilingual Education and Bilingualism, 10,* 454-470. doi: 10.2167/beb454.0

Ó Laoire, M. and Harris, J. (2006). *Language and literacy in Irish-medium primary schools: Review of literature.* Dublin: NCCA.

Ó Riagáin, P. (1997). *Language policy and social reproduction: Ireland 1893-1993.* Oxford: Clarendon Press.

Schmidt, R. (1994). Deconstructing consciousness in search of useful definitions for applied linguistics. *AILA Review, 11,* 11-26. Retrieved from http://www.aila.info/download/publications/review/AILA11.pdf

Singleton, D. (1992). Languages in the schools: The limits of iconoclasm. *Oideas, 38*, 62-75.

Solano-Flores, G. (2010). Function and form in research on language and mathematics education. In J. N. Moschkovich (Ed.), *Language and mathematics education: Multiple perspectives and directions for research* (pp. 113-149). Charlotte, NC: Information Age.

Swain, M. and Lapkin, S. (1995). Problems in output and the cognitive processes they generate: A step towards second language learning. *Applied Linguistics, 16*, 371-391. doi: 10.1093/applin/16.3.371

Vygotsky, L. (1986). *Thought and language* (A. Kozulin, Trans.). Cambridge, Mass: MIT.

Walsh, C. (2007). *Cruinneas na Gaeilge scríófa sna hiar-bhunscoileanna lán-Ghaeilge i mBaile Atha Cliath.* Dublin: An Chomhairle um Oideachas Gaeltachta agus Gaelscolaíochta.

Wertsch, J.V. (1991). *Voices of the mind: A sociocultural approach to mediated action.* Cambridge, MA: Harvard University Press.

Willis, D. and Willis, J. (2007). *Doing task-based teaching: A practical guide to task-based teaching for ELT training courses and practicing teachers.* Oxford: Oxford University Press.

Section Five:

Responding to Student Voices: Programme Reform and Transformation

Chapter 14

Student Teacher Voice and School Placement: What We Can Learn if We Listen

Bernadette Ní Áingléis, Paula Murphy and Brian Ruane

St Patrick's College, Drumcondra

Introduction

This chapter presents an exploration of the voice of student teachers in the context of school-based experiences set within a school-university partnership approach and premised on a democratic participative model of school placement. Semi-structured interviews with Bachelor of Education (BEd) student teachers revealed the significance of the student teacher/class teacher relationship in how and what student teachers learned on school placement. Where the relationship was mutually respectful and dialogic, student teachers experienced school placement as being conducive to learning how to teach in a happy, open, confident frame of mind. Cognisant of the wider context within which this fundamental relationship operates and the various other roles with which the student teacher/class teacher relationship interacts, this chapter points to the importance of creating and maintaining the conditions whereby a positive learning-oriented partnership can flourish.

The school placement[1] dimension of initial teacher education (ITE) programmes offers an ideal context in which to explore the possibilities of partnership in ITE given the involvement of at least three parties – student teachers, ITE tutors and school-based staff. Historically, in Ireland, a spirit of volunteerism and goodwill and an enduring professional commitment within schools to providing placements for student teachers have created and sustained partnerships between schools and teacher education providers (Coolahan, 2003, 2007). Over the years, the nature of these partnerships may have been relatively informal and unstructured (Department of Education and Science (DES), 2002; DES, 2006). More recently, however, school placement has become the context for re-imagining structured engagement by schools on a collaborative basis with ITE providers (Teaching Council, 2011a; Conway et al., 2009). The systematic involvement of schools in school placement in partnership with ITE providers is now a formal requirement for the accreditation of all ITE programmes in Ireland (Teaching Council, 2011b). Interestingly, school-university partnerships in the context of school-based experiences have been part of the ITE landscape in England since 1992 (Department for Education, 1992).

Whilst conceptualisations of learning to teach and ITE partnerships with schools vary according to the partnership (Day, 2007), typological configurations of democratic partnership assume that there are 'spaces' for the constituent voices to be heard (Furlong et al., 2000). The perspectives of staff in schools and tutors in ITE institutions involved in school-university partnerships are frequently articulated and analysed (McLaughlin et al., 2006; Edwards et al., 2002; Taylor, 2008). Less well-documented, however, are the lived experiences of student teachers in respect of school-based experiences which are underpinned by a commitment to partnership. This raises the critical question as to whether the voice of student teachers has been afforded due space or influence in determining the quality of key processes and structures which impact student teacher learning on placement. Student teachers have a great deal to say about what helps them learn to teach and what switches them off (Allen, 2011; Stanulis and Russell, 2000). Significantly, the quality of relationships between student teacher, host teacher,[2] and the university placement tutor features strongly in what student teachers say about school-based work. In Martin's (2011) evaluation of a school-university partnership, student teachers speak candidly about their experiences on placement. Their narratives (detailed more fully in Ní Áingléis, 2007) make a compelling case for the inclusion of the student teacher voice in re-imagining university-school partnerships. In the process, the student teacher voice spotlights the 'unforgiving complexity of teaching' (Cochran-Smith, 2006, p. 70) and the interplay between relationship, power and agency in learning to teach and consequently in teacher professional development.

Notwithstanding the contestability of professional knowledge coupled with the deeply problematic nature of 'partnership' as both a process and a concept, this chapter sets out to explore and document the voice of student teachers in relation to their school-based experiences during a structured ITE-schools partnership. The research is underpinned by a conceptualisation of learning to teach as a distributed situated cognition within a learning community framework and draws heavily on sociocultural and activity theories (Vygotsky, 1978; Engeström, 2001; Lave and Wenger, 1991). Use is made of an adaptation of Lundy's (2007) four-pronged conceptualisation of 'voice', based on Article 12 of the United Nations Convention of the Rights of the Child, as a frame to explore what student teachers experienced and valued during their school-based experiences. Whilst student teacher voice is at the heart of this chapter, invariably the multi-voice nature of a university-schools partnership, comprising overlapping communities of practice, makes it impossible to disregard the perspectives of other key participants who were involved in the partnership, namely teachers and university placement tutors.[3] Some time is given therefore to listening to the latter voices insofar as they help to deepen understandings of what it is to be a learner teacher and to illuminate further the complexities of getting to grips with 'partnership' in a learning to teach context. The chapter concludes with some recommendations in respect of schools-university partnerships and specifically in terms of student teacher voice in democratising policy and practice in this area.

Research Context

The action research project, *Partnership with Schools*, explores new ways of involving schools more systematically in school placement, for example by engaging cooperating teachers in professional development and training in the area of student teacher mentoring. The Dublin-based project has been in operation since 2005. Participants include primary schools, selected groups of student teachers and university tutors. The professional development modules were designed by university staff in collaboration with student teachers and schools and were research-informed (Furlong and Maynard, 1995). The school-based activity involved a range of structures which aimed to deepen the student's learning process by providing more consistent opportunities for feedback and shared reflection. These included dedicated one-to-one feedback sessions between the student teacher and class teacher based on teacher observation of a number of specific lessons chosen by the student during any one week. Feedback forms generated by the teacher for these sessions were included in a section of the student's folder which was perused by the supervisor during his/her visits. Indeed, increased communication between the class teacher, principal and supervisor was a key feature of the model. Significantly the overall experience was also framed within a whole-school context by the introduction of 'The Wednesday Experience'. This represented a 'non-teaching' afternoon for student teachers during which they were facilitated to observe the wide range of relations and activities which take place in a school outside the formal teaching of lessons. Examples of such experiences might include an observation of a learning support session, accompanying a class group on a school tour, or sitting in on a planning session related to whole school planning.

The rationale underpinning the project centres around the promise of learning in a community of practice - which is deeper than that which can occur if one is learning on one's own (Lave and Wenger, 1991). The type of student teacher learning emphasised is one which prizes opportunities for student teachers on placement to develop classroom competency, reflective dispositions and the skills required to engage successfully and incrementally in professional learning opportunities beyond one's assigned placement classroom. The gradual introduction of students to increased professional responsibilities over the course of the placement affords a legitimacy to the 'peripheral participation' of students in their school-based learning community, encouraging risk-taking in what students planned and taught.

The action research project was founded firmly on trust and mutual respect for relationship, for roles and responsibilities, and on a strong commitment by all involved to learning and to remaining open to new thinking about pedagogy, about student teacher learning, and ultimately about how to 'do' partnership better. Whilst the individual concepts of 'partnership' and 'voice' require careful critique given their complexity and inherent assumptions, we hold the view that 'partnership' is essentially process-centred, scaffolded by structures and arrangements which accommodate interrelated roles and responsibilities. Lundy (2007, pp. 932-33) provides us with a useful model to conceptualise student teacher 'voice' comprising four inter-nestled elements: space, voice, audience, influence. If student teachers are to be viewed as active creative agents in their own professional development during school-based work, they require multi-layered contexts (space) in which to articulate (voice) what they are learning in addition to skilful facilitation of their views to ensure a sense of being listened to (audience). In addition, they must have their views acted upon, as appropriate (influence). In the action research project, for example, through structured mentoring conversations with their cooperating teachers and in their post-lesson evaluation interactions with university tutors, student teachers had access to structures and processes which were, we suggest, more 'sensitive' to student voice than those in the non-partnership project schools. School staff and university staff involved in the project had engaged in professional development modules around working with student teachers, including opportunities to consider what it means and feels like to be a student teacher on placement. Three key questions therefore underpinned the research for this paper: Firstly, how do student teachers interpret relationship in school-based partnership processes? Secondly, what structures and processes facilitated student teacher voice? And finally, what implications arise for structures (including roles and responsibilities) and processes in the context of improving school-based learning for student teachers?

Philosophical Perspectives

In the context of teacher education, the notion of school placement in itself exemplifies a long tradition of philosophical discourse on education which values experiential learning and the inherent good to be derived from the honing of a 'practice' (Dunne, 1995). In the early twentieth century, philosophers from the pragmatic tradition, such as John Dewey, gave particular attention to the nature and quality of experiences which might be considered to encourage the authentic apprehension of knowledge. In an attempt to distinguish an 'educative' from a 'mis-educative' experience, Dewey characterises the former as one which 'takes up something from those which have gone before and modifies in some way the quality of those which come after' (Dewey, 1938, p. 35). In terms of the progression implicit in this trajectory, more recent analysis has revisited the early Greek notion of 'praxis' and the particular role of reflection in the success of the 'learning by doing' approach. The practice of 'dialogue', re-examined and extended by educationalists such as Paulo Freire and Martin Buber, continues to pose stimulating challenges to teachers in this regard, as it confronts a range of suppositions concerned with the nature of knowledge itself and especially with the significance of 'relationship' in the learning process (Buber, 1947; Freire, 1970).

While the *Partnership with Schools* project borrowed much from the preceding approach to teaching practice in terms of an emphasis on situated learning (Lave and Wenger, 1991), in this venture it was the nature and quality of subsequent reflection on that experience that became a particular focus for consideration. Always a challenging area for students in our experience, the previous practice, which in emphasis tended to locate much of the reflective activity in individual written documentation, seems to have procured a limited impact on subsequent performance. As this project evolved however, it began to explore the merits of a wider approach to reflection which acknowledges the inherent values of a more consistent dialogical approach involving two or more perspectives on the experience. In particular, it gave recognition to the rich interaction which began to emerge between the student teacher and classroom teacher. Indeed, the role of the classroom teacher was reviewed and extended on the recommendation of all participants from the very early exploratory stages of the project (Martin, 2011, p. 39).

Martin Buber bases much of his philosophical discourse in education and theology on what he refers to as 'the sphere between' (1973, p. 72). In his conviction regarding the centrality of relationship in all human endeavour, he asserts that 'all real living is meeting' (1947, p. 24). While Freire may be better remembered for the significance he gives to the structural conditions of a productive dialogical process, he also shares much with Buber in terms of the value he places on the qualitative aspects of the learning relationships in question (O'Shea and O'Brien, 2012).

> Founding itself on love, humility and faith, dialogue becomes a horizontal relationship of which mutual trust between the dialoguers is the logical consequence. It would be a contradiction in terms if dialogue – loving, humble and full of faith – did not produce this climate of mutual trust, which leads dialoguers into ever closer partnership in the naming of the world (Freire, 1970, p. 74).

As the notion of relationship was highlighted as one of the most distinctive features of the evolving partnerships within this project (Martin, 2011, p. 39), the particular conditions which led to such an influence became a significant aspect of subsequent research and will be discussed later in this chapter.

The question of power is of course an inevitable concern within all learning situations and should be given due cognizance in the design of any process of this kind. In the case of student teachers, it should be remembered that hanging in the balance of the learning process for them is the formation of an identity which can be thwarted by concerns with risk, judgement and failure. Such a reality can leave the learner vulnerable to a range of reactions which can effect motivation, confidence and personal conviction. While Freire acknowledges the essential difference which necessarily exists between teacher and student in terms of their roles in the process (1997), he is at pains to negate the presumed vertical relationship of authority which tends to exist in traditional learning encounters. In this regard, even the more experienced party is not to be considered 'all knowing', but rather one who provides a particular perspective on a dialogue to which both contribute. Knowledge, from this perspective, 'emerges only through invention and re-invention, through the restless, impatient, continuing, hopeful inquiry human beings pursue in the world, with the world and with each other' (Freire, 1970, p. 53). The notion of educating student teachers towards becoming 'beings for themselves' rather than 'beings for others' (ibid., p. 55) would seem to be a particularly important priority in the context of a career which will inevitably involve an ongoing negotiation between the changing demands of curricular and political reform, and the needs of the child.

It would be important to remember at this juncture that 'the sphere between' in this project was not confined to the relationship between the student and the classroom teacher. While clearly central to the experience, it was also deemed necessary that this fundamental relationship would be held and supported in the context of the wider community from which it takes its meaning. In their seminal research on situated learning and communities of practice, Lave and Wenger (1991) revisit the more traditional notion of 'apprenticeship' in the context of a range of learning situations which tend to be more associated with the functioning of a living community than with the formal school setting. While this research acknowledged the central importance of the 'master-apprentice' relationship, it also posits that 'mastery resides not in the master but in the community of practice of which the master is part' (ibid., p. 94). In their recognition of the generational contribution to such processes, they acknowledge the value of 'a diversified field of relations among old-timers and new comers', which includes contributors at various levels of competence on the continuum, and warn against an exclusively dyadic focus in the learning process (Lave and Wenger, 1991, p. 57). In our view, we would also emphasise the additional emotional support provided by such communities and the extent to which they facilitate essential ingredients to the learning process such as mutual respect, honesty, encouragement and truth.

This does not mean however, that the communities of practice are immune from conflict, tensions or contradictions. On the contrary, a community of practice, given its multi-voiced membership, is fertile ground for positive conflict (Foucault, 1980) in which a student teacher can work through some of the puzzles of practice and knots in thinking which arise during the course of school-based work. Indeed, Engeström (2001, p. 137) would argue that 'expansive learning', in which student teachers need to engage in order to teach well and learn well, is possible in contexts where contradictions are plentiful, e.g., in communities of practice in which student teachers are required to cross the safety of their own boundaries of knowing through inquiry, critique and supportive scaffolding. Learning to teach is, in many respect, a process of boundary-crossing on many levels (the personal, the political, the professional) 'brokered' (Wenger, 1998) substantially by cooperating teachers, university placement tutors, and by agentic student teachers. Giroux's (1992) image of 'border-crossings' seems somewhat edged and acute for process-based learning to teach.

Research Process

This chapter draws primarily on qualitative data collected from semi-structured interviews with focus groups of students who participated in the partnership project. The research participants were selected by the research team, having responded positively to a general invitation issued to all students who had participated in the project. The interview schedules were based on research in mentoring, school-university partnerships, and on findings of research on earlier phases of the project (Ní Áingléis, 2008). The data was supplemented by submissions from students in the form of reflective diaries, conversations with cooperating teachers and semi-structured interviews with university placement supervisors involved in the project. The student teachers who participated in this research were all final year students who had recently completed their final graded four week school placement (teaching practice) in different schools in the greater Dublin area. For the purposes of this chapter, the names of the students, all female and aged 20-22, have been anonymised as follows: Anne, Deirdre, Kate, Julie and Sue.

A constructivist grounded theory approach to data analysis is adopted in this research (Charmaz and Mitchell, 2001). Grounded theory tools – the constant comparative method (Glaser and Strauss, 1967) – are used as guiding principles. It must be pointed out also that it is the focus of inquiry and the interpretative process which form the theorising activity at the heart of grounded theory, rather than the methods (Miller, 2000). The key task, as Charmaz asserts, is 'to develop an integrated set of theoretical concepts from their empirical materials that not only synthesise and interpret them but also show processual relationships' (2005, p. 508). This approach was particularly important given the process-centred nature of learning to teach.

Findings

How do student teachers interpret relationship in school-based partnership processes?

As noted above, the student teachers who participated in the study had just completed their final teaching practice. They all recognised that, in comparison to other teaching practices, they had become more knowledgeable and more confident in their own role as teachers in the classroom. They also acknowledged their status as learner teachers who required respect, support, encouragement and challenge in order to learn. Teaching practice was described as a time when 'a lot of people worry' (Sue), 'feel uneasy' (Kate) and a process 'you put so much work into' (Anne).

In this pressurised context, the participants in this study highlighted the supportive role played by their classroom teachers during their teaching practice. This sense of trust was fostered through students' knowledge of previous participants' experience of feedback from teachers on partnership placements and clear articulation by the classroom teacher of the student's status as the teacher of the class for the period of the teaching practice. This acknowledgement of the student's status by the classroom teacher sets the foundations for Freire's (1970) horizontal learning space.

> I was worried that she would be watching my every move but she wasn't like that at all. My first day there she told the class 'this is Miss Murphy and she is teaching you for the next weeks, so if you need anything you must go to her. I am having nothing to do with it.' So, that was cool. (Deirdre)

The role of the classroom teacher, realised through active observation of a specific lesson followed by a feedback session and the production of an observation report, was to mentor and advise the student in a clear and focused context. The consistency of feedback which this process facilitated was clearly appreciated by the students in this study.

> Just on the reports on a Friday, she (the classroom teacher) would tell you something to improve on for the next week, on the next Friday it was great that she would notice that you have improved and that you had picked up on what she had said. Then she could move onto something else and you could improve on that. (Sue)

This dynamic process enabled a praxis cycle of action, reflection and action (Freire, 1970). It was clear from students' feedback that the teacher's observation of lessons and resulting dialogue created the space for them to be critical and give feedback 'without interrupting lessons' (Anne) or harming their relationship with the student. This was in contrast to previous teaching practices where it was perceived that classroom teachers were afraid to be critical. The creation of a structured dialogue between the teacher and the student enabled the student to express an opinion and express a view on their own learning and progress. The clarity which the partnership brought resulted in an increased focus on the actual practice of the student. As Sue reported, 'we kind of talked more on this TP about what my lessons were doing and where we were going.'

Lundy (2007) understands 'voice' as the right to express such views freely. This sense of voice was experienced differently by participants in this study and these differences emerged most strongly in relation to differing perspectives on teaching approaches and strategies in the class. The findings also demonstrate the ways in which the issue of voice can be affected by the emphasis on assessment which is characteristic of the teaching practice experience generally. While Kate and Deirdre felt that their status and experience as final year students made it possible for them to disagree with a supervisor's comments if required, others in the group asserted that they would never disagree with a supervisor as 'in the end of the day, they are going to judge you' (Julie).

Whether students feel safe to voice a view to a teacher was in the first instance dependent on the disposition of the classroom teacher. All of the participants in this study acknowledged the openness, encouragement, guidance and advice of their teacher, which enabled them to express their own views and implement their own approaches in the classroom.

> My teacher was very open to me changing things around. He had different ways about going about reading groups and I had my own way. He was fine with that – he was very open. (Sue)

Another advantage of the classroom teacher's feedback was related to its specificity in relation to the context and children in question.

> She knew the children better and she would know who should be in which group and could help me pitch my work better for the children. She showed me test results from last year so that I could aim different things for them. (Kate)

In light of the above, when questioned on the necessity of the college supervisor within the process, all of the students strongly identified the need for such a role on teaching practice. Despite their own generally positive relationships with their classroom teacher, all were conscious of the impact a negative relationship could have within the process.

> I think the supervisor is needed. I know people who have had bad experiences with teachers and it would go downhill from there. You need someone higher up … definitely the supervisors are needed. (Kate)

Anne in particular was concerned that the classroom teacher may not be familiar with her 'new teaching methods' that she had learned in college. Kate agreed with this and felt that the supervisors would share the student teachers' knowledge of these methods. What emerges strongly from the participants is the sense that the partnership project provided the necessary balance to ensure that student teachers were adequately and fairly supported on a number of levels and that a variety of perspectives are required to ensure that this is the case.

> Well, you have three supervisors so it's three different people. You might not get on with one but you probably will with the other two – the balance is good whereas if you had just one teacher that would be … there's no one else to give their opinion. (Sue)

The supervisors' focus group too welcomed the enhanced role of the teacher in the partnership project and recognised that the teacher can gain an holisitic view of the student which is not possible for the supervisor. The supervisors also recognised the power imbalance between them and the students due to their assessment role and acknowledged the role of the teacher in mediating this power imbalance on behalf of the student. As Lundy points out in asserting the need for a right of audience for children, 'there is no guarantee that views will be communicated to or taken on board by those adults who are in a position to give them effect' (2003, p. 937). It is in this context that the classroom teacher can ensure the right of audience for student teachers by articulating views which the student teachers are unwilling to express to the supervisor.

> I think it is because some supervisors – they might notice something that went wrong in a lesson but through other lessons the teacher might have given you advice and you took it on board. It's just that in that lesson it kind of went wrong. So that's the thing supervisors pick up on in lessons but then your teacher has seen you do it properly. Your teacher needs to tell the supervisor that. (Julie)

> Students find it very hard to talk on a par with a supervisor whereas a classroom teacher would be very open if a supervisor is out of line in some way in pointing it out and it does need to be pointed out. (Bob)

There was consensus however that while the teacher can usefully mediate the power imbalance between the teacher and the student through fulfilling the audience role envisaged by Lundy (2007), this should be done through dialogue. All parties agreed that this issue would not be addressed by giving the classroom teacher a shared responsibility in grading the student. Grading was seen as a specialist task, requiring special training and opportunities to compare the students with others, both of which are available to supervisors.

> I think in the project school that the way the supervisor talks to your teacher is good – like it would be more beneficial towards your grade because the teacher sees all your hard work that you are doing – if you had the teacher on their own they wouldn't know exactly how to grade, if you weren't getting on great with your teacher you wouldn't get a good grade. (Kate)

What structures and processes facilitated student teacher voice?

The creation of spaces in which participants can speak and be heard has been identified as a prerequisite for an inclusive process (Furlong et al., 2000; Lundy, 2007). The extent to which the partnership schools in this process created an environment in which, in the first instance, student teachers felt safe, welcome and supported was noted by the student and lecturer respondents. Participating schools had made an extra commitment to supporting teaching practice by volunteering to participate in the partnership process, and this self-identification as sites which were committed to the process is borne out in student teacher experiences. In this regard, the role of the principal in setting the tone for the partnership process is central and was highly valued by the student teachers. Each of the students spoke of the availability of the principal. This availability was not perceived however as intrusive or onerous.

> This principal was really involved with the students… even on the first day, the observation, he was like, 'Oh, you have so and so in your class, and this is how I deal with him in differentiation. And it *really* (student emphasis) helps. (Sue)

The positive disposition of the school community towards teaching practice was reflected in an apparent awareness by members of the school community of the needs of student teachers. The inclusion of the Wednesday Experience (a period when student teachers immersed themselves in the wider work of the school) helped students develop relationships with other teachers in the school community, a holistic understanding of the work of the school, and indeed 'a sense of belonging more' (Kate) to the school community, thus creating an active community of practice (Lave and Wenger, 1991). In comparison to other teaching practices, Anne identified:

> More of a willingness in the staff. If we weren't doing the project, we wouldn't have got to see the teachers in the Autism Unit. (Anne)

It appears that the creation of a positive atmosphere in which student teachers are welcomed and teaching practice as a broad learning process is valued, creates the necessary conditions in which students will feel safe to express anxieties and opinions or seek help if required. This helps to avoid the exclusive dyadic focus between master and apprentice identified by Lave and Wenger (1991). This is best exemplified by Kate's response to a question regarding how difficult situations were handled.

> The thing is that there was always someone to go to if you had problems. You felt much more confident to go to someone to ask them. (Kate)

In the partnership project, the clear understanding of teachers regarding their role on teaching practice and the creation of dialogical spaces to engage with students removed such tensions. Regarding the critical feedback which project teachers engaged in the students observed that:

> they didn't feel they had to keep apologising for saying things to us. It was a safe environment. It was ok to do so. (Anne)

The students were conscious too of the abilities of the teachers to listen to what they were saying, to identify their needs, and to identify specific skills and dimensions of teaching practice which would be emphasised by the college. Anne presumed this was as a result of training they had received. The need for training for those who are required to listen to the views of others is highlighted as a special dimension of supporting voice (Lundy 2007).

> I know that you (the college) worked with the schools' training and talking to teachers and I felt they took into consideration what you mentioned to them, like planning for the lessons, objectives, resources you used because they mentioned them in their reports. (Anne)

What are the implications for structures and processes in the context of improving school-based learning for student teachers?

A number of key recommendations have evolved from the experience and research emanating from this project which give life to the fourth component of student voice – the idea of influence. Firstly, student perspectives (and those of others) support the understanding that 'teaching practice' cannot be viewed as an isolated event; rather, it represents a complex web of interaction between a range of participants who act and are acted upon as the process evolves. The concept of community is therefore central to its success, and the meaningful integration of all of its participants should be a key priority of its design.

Secondly, one of the strongest outcomes of the research is its validation of the augmented role of the class teacher within the process. Time and again students referred to issues of consistency, justice, relevance and relationship in terms of the benefits which accrue to such a central and immediate partnership. This has been acknowledged by all participants to facilitate a more comprehensive view of the student teacher's progress and to enable interventions which may be required on his or her behalf. Possible tensions were also recognised, however, and participants from all quarters, including students, have pointed to the centrality of training and support for this learning relationship, both before and during the practice.

This leads to the third recommendation which proposes a review of the role of the supervisor in light of the significant shifts in role which have been referred to thus far. The student teachers in the focus group understood the class teacher to be uniquely placed to guide them in terms of the particularity of the context in question and they recognised the richness of understanding which working closely with a particular practitioner can afford. However, it was also seen as important that the student teachers at some level would remain conscious of the fact that they are engaging with a *particular* perspective which may influence, contradict or confirm his or her evolving identity and practice as a teacher. The development of such independence of thought and practice is understandably a challenging task for student teachers given significant factors which may militate against it, such as their age and status within the situation, alongside their awareness of the strong assessment component of the overall process.

Figure 1 Illustrative Model for Partnership-based School Placement

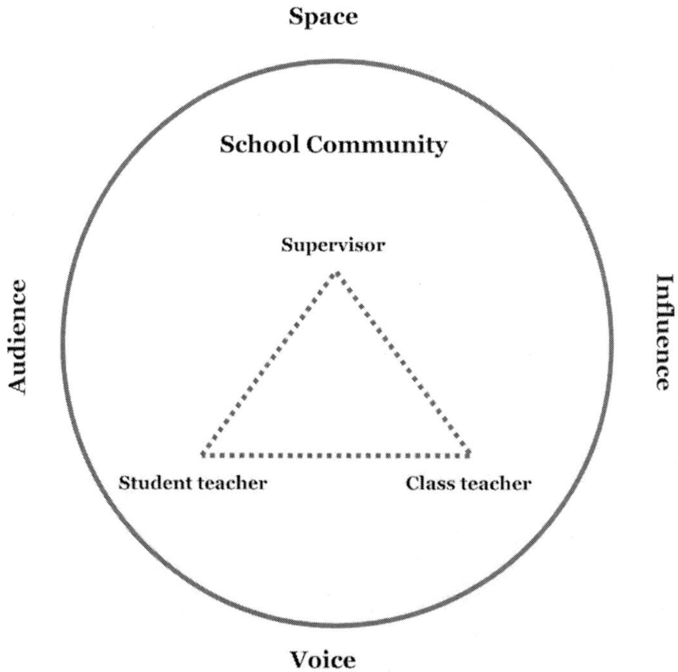

While student teachers recognised the context-sensitive professional and affective support provided by the class teacher, they also cited the significance of the supervisor's role in terms of the broader perspective which they can provide on the macro dimensions of the process. In their view, these related to their knowledge of the overall standard of performance typical of student teachers at this level of experience and their ongoing engagement with new developments in research and practice within the field. While the feedback from the majority of participants was generally very positive regarding the benefits of a closer class teacher/student teacher collaboration, all parties also expressed an awareness of the capacity for this collaboration to be open to the hazards inherent in all working relationships such as clashes of personality, breakdowns in communication and significant perspectival differences. It is in the light of all of the above that the supervisor's role as 'a facilitator of a process' might be further acknowledged and developed in future elaborations of the project. The notion of a more conscious development of a triadic relationship, which acknowledges and exploits the various roles, areas of expertise, and perspectives which are present, is therefore a key recommendation for exploration (See figure 1)

However, there is evidence in the students' responses to suggest that the strong emphasis which is currently placed on the final teaching practice grade may inevitably colour the open communication, independent thinking and balance of power which any amended structure would seek to progress. It is therefore the view of the researchers that this research and its recommendations should be considered in conjunction with the wider discussion on the issue of assessment in teaching practice which is currently taking place in other fora. Finally, while the benefits of the enhancement and expansion of such a model now seem undeniable, the financial and human resource implications for bringing it into the mainstream of teacher education should not be underestimated.

In conclusion, premised as it is on the interactive process of relationship-building and dialogue, the research supports the claim that this approach to partnership provides an ideal space where student teachers' voices can be listened to and where their agency and ownership of the process of learning to teach can be acknowledged. Moreover, the research also underlines the value of providing research-based spaces for listening to student voices, ensuring that the valuable contribution which student voices can make to re-imagining the process of school placement is realised.

Endnotes

[1] School placement is frequently referred to as teaching practice or school-based work.

[2] The host teacher is understood to be the cooperating teacher with whom the student teacher is placed (Teaching Council, 2012).

[3] University placement tutors have traditionally been referred to as teaching practice supervisors (usually university staff or staff with experience of teaching and working with student teachers who are contracted by the university).

References

Allen, J.M. (2011). Stakeholders' perspectives of the nature and role of assessment during practicum. *Teaching and Teacher Education*, *27*(4), 742-750.

Buber, M. (1947). *Tales of Hasidim: Early masters* (O. Marx, Trans.). New York: Shocken.

Buber, M. (1973). *Meetings* (M. Friedman, Trans.). Illinois: Open Court Publishing.

Charmaz, K. (2005). Grounded theory in the 21st century: Applications for advancing social justice studies. In N.K. Denzin and Y.S. Lincoln (Eds.), *The Sage handbook of qualitative research* (pp. 507-535). Thousand Oaks, CA: Sage.

Charmaz, K. and Mitchell R. G. (2001). Grounded theory in ethnography. In P. Atkinson P, A. Coffey, S. Delamont, J. Lofland and L. Lofland (Eds.), *Handbook of ethnography* (pp. 160-174). London: Sage.

Cochran-Smith, M. (2006). *Policy, practice, and politics in teacher education: Editorials from the Journal of Teacher Education*. Thousand Oaks, CA: Corwin Press.

Conway, P.F., Murphy, R., Rath, A. and Hall, K. (2009). *Learning to teach and its implications for the continuum of teacher education: A nine-country cross-national study* (Report commissioned by the Teaching Council). Cork: University College Cork.

Coolahan, J. (2003). *Attracting, developing and retaining effective teachers: Country background report for Ireland*. Dublin: The Stationery Office.

Coolahan, J. (2007). *A review paper on thinking and policies relating to teacher education in Ireland* (Paper commissioned by The Teaching Council). Dublin: The Teaching Council.

Day, C. (2007). *Collaborative approaches to (continuing to) develop effective teachers: An account of the Joint UCET/HMI/STEC Symposium held in Glasgow.* London: The Universities Council for the Education of Teachers (UCET).

Department for Education (1992). *Initial teacher training (secondary phase) circular 9/92.* London: Author.

Department of Education and Science (DES). (2002). *Preparing teachers for the 21st century: Report of the working group on primary pre-service teacher education.* Dublin:

Department of Education and Skills (DES). (2006). *Learning to teach: Students on teaching practice in Irish primary schools.* Dublin: The Stationery Office.

Dewey, J. (1938). *Experience and education.* New York: Collier.

Dunne, J. (1995). What's the good of education. In P. Hogan (Ed.), *Partnership and the benefits of learning.* Maynooth: Educational Studies Ireland.

Edwards, A., Gilroy, P. and Hartley, D. (2002). *Rethinking teacher education. Collaborative responses to uncertainty.* London: RoutledgeFalmer.

Engeström, Y. (2001). Expansive learning at work: Toward an activity theoretical reconceptualization. *Journal of Education and Work, 14*(1), 133-156.

Foucault, M. (1980). *Power/Knowledge: Selected interviews and other writings 1972-1977.* New York: Pantheon.

Freire, P. (1970). *Pedagogy of the oppressed.* London: Penguin.

Freire, P. (1997). *Pedagogy of hope; reliving pedagogy of the oppressed.* New York: Continuum.

Furlong, J., Barton, L., Miles, S., Whiting, C. and Whitty, G. (2000). *Teacher education in transition: Re-forming professionalism?* Buckingham: Open University Press.

Furlong, J. and Maynard, T. (1995). *Mentoring student teachers: The growth of professional knowledge.* London: Routledge.

Giroux, H. (1992). *Border crossings.* London: Routledge.

Glaser, B.G. and Strauss, A.L. (1967). *The discovery of grounded theory: Strategies for qualitative research.* Chicago: Aldine.

Lave, J. and Wenger, E. (1991). *Situated learning: Legitimate peripheral participation.* New York: Cambridge University Press.

Lundy, L. (2007). 'Voice' is not enough: Conceptualising Article 12 of the United Nations Convention on the Rights of the Child. *British Educational Research Journal, 33*(6), 927-942.

Martin, M. (2011). *Teacher professional development partnership with schools project: An evaluation report* (Report commissioned by St Patrick's College). Dublin: St Patrick's College.

McLaughlin, C., Black-Hawkins, K., Brindley, S., McIntyre, D. and Taber, K.S. (2006). *Researching schools: Stories from a schools-university partnership for educational research.* Oxon, England: Routledge.

Miller, R. (2000). *Researching life stories and family histories.* London: Sage.

Ní Áingléis, B. (2007, September). *Unpacking a pedagogy of 'Partnership' in initial teacher education in Ireland: What student teachers have to say.* Paper presented at BERA National Conference, Institute of Education, London.

Ní Áingléis, B. (2008). *The constitution and the dynamics of learning to teach* (Unpublished doctoral dissertation). Institute of Education, Manchester Metropolitan University, Manchester.

O'Shea, A. and O'Brien, M. (Eds.). (2011). *Pedagogy, oppression and transformation in a 'post-critical' climate.* London: Continuum.

Stanulis, R.N. and Russell D. (2000). Jumping in: Trust and communication in mentoring student teachers. *Teaching and Teacher Education, 16*(1), 65-80.

Taylor, A. (2008). Developing understanding about learning to teach in a university-schools partnership in England. *British Educational Research Journal, 34*(1), 63-90.

Teaching Council (2011a). *Policy on the continuum of teacher education.* Dublin: Author.

Teaching Council (2011b). *Initial teacher education: Criteria and guidelines for programme providers*. Dublin: Author.

Teaching Council (2012). *Guidelines on school placement* (1st ed.).

Vygotsky, L. S. (1978). *Mind in society: The development of the higher psychological processes*. Cambridge, MA: Harvard University Press.

Wenger, E. (1998). *Communities of practice: Learning, meaning and identity.* New York: Cambridge University Press.

Chapter 15

Developing 'Good' Post-primary Teachers and Teaching in a Reform Era: Cultural Dynamics in a Programme Level Study[1] of the PDE

Paul F. Conway, Rosaleen Murphy, Michael Delargey, Kathy Hall, Karl Kitching, Fiachra Long, Jacinta McKeon, Brian Murphy, Stephen O'Brien and Dan O'Sullivan

School of Education, University College Cork

Introduction: Policy Context and the Quest for the 'Good Teacher' and 'Good Teacher Education'

Most discussions about the quality of schooling quickly turn to the quality of teachers, reflections and memories of individual teachers who 'made a difference', whether good or not so, in a person's school biography. The quest for the 'good teacher' is important to parents, interleaves itself into a community's conversations about its schools, animates children's and adolescents' reflections on a central feature of their lives and increasingly is the protagonist in policy debates on teacher education. Almost everyone has certain convictions about the characteristics and importance of a good teacher, borne out of schooling as a shared and typically vivid experience. But these convictions tend to foster three misleading assumptions: that quality teaching is only about individuals, that it is innate, and that it is immutable. There is a strong tendency to centre on the individual teacher and ignore the school and community context. The belief that the teacher (again the emphasis is typically on the individual) is born, not made, is often stated, thereby rendering invisible the powerful developmental, cultural and institutional dynamics leading to 'good' teachers and teaching. Kennedy (2010) argues '…that researchers as well as laymen tend to overestimate the influence of personal traits and underestimate the influence of situations on observed behavior' (p. 591). Thus, in comparing differences across classrooms, there is a strong tendency to focus on differences in student learning as a function of the 'characteristics of teachers themselves, overlooking situational factors' (ibid., p. 591). The implications of this for understanding the role of initial teacher education in fostering quality teaching are two-fold: first, what are the relevant situational factors? And second, what are the dynamics and impact of initial teacher education on becoming a good teacher?

To illuminate these issues, this chapter draws on findings from the *Learning to Teach Study* (LETS), a study of initial teacher education. The study, funded by the Department of Education and Skills (DES), was undertaken in the context of the Postgraduate Diploma in Education (post-primary) (PDE) in the School of Education, University College Cork. Its findings on the key cultural dynamics that shape the learning to teach experience are particularly relevant in the context of the current move from a one to a two-year Professional Diploma in Education (DES, 2011; Teaching Council, 2011a, 2011b) as the modal programme for education of post-primary teachers in Ireland, which will necessitate a rethinking and a restructuring of these programmes.[2] Within an overall framework that explored how student teachers develop their skills, competences and identity as teachers, LETS focused in particular on curricular competences in mathematics, science and language teaching, and on the cross-curricular competences of reading and digital literacy and the development of inclusive teaching practices. LETS also sought to understand the dynamics of good teacher education within the context of the expanding literature on this theme over the last fifteen years (e.g., Korthagen et al., 2001; Darling-Hammond, 2006; Kennedy and Barnes, 1994; Tatto, 1999; Korthagen, Loughran and Russell, 2006).

Conceptions of competence are theory-laden and interwoven with the pedagogical, psychological and political aspects of teacher education. Among the dimensions of competence highlighted in LETS are how: (i) classic and contemporary views of competences reflect significant changes in assumptions about the development of human competence; (ii) research on competences should not be seen as separate from other aspects of teacher education; and (iii) current policy discourse neglects much of the complex interwoven nature of pedagogy, psychology and politics associated with competence, for example, in its over-reliance on learning outcomes in a manner that typically eschews both the initial and ongoing opportunities for learning. We highlight in the LETS report (Conway et al., 2011a) how the current rhetorical appeal and widespread uptake of the learning outcomes concept has short-circuited the complexity of understanding, fostering and evaluating both good teaching and good teacher education.

Consequently, the LETS study adopts a sociocultural approach to learning and to becoming competent as a teacher during initial teacher education (ITE). This emphasises the situated, relational and political dimensions of competence and the centrality and nature of assisted practice in learning to teach (Penuel and Werstch, 1995; Lave and Wenger, 1998; Claxton and Wells, 2002; Sawyer, 2006; Hall, Murphy and Soler, 2008; Korthagen, 2010). It enables us to address the teacher archetypes, supports and challenges that are part of the 'learning to teach' process. Drawing upon these key issues, we framed the study in terms of the opportunities to learn to teach available to student teachers, encompassing material and symbolic resources as well as social supports.

For the purposes of this chapter, we focus on three overarching findings at the programme level rather than the wide range of findings within the various sections of the larger LETS study. The three claims are:

- *Mentoring without access to observation of others and the 'invisible learner' phenomenon:* The prevalence in school settings of mentoring as a support structure for student teachers but without opportunities to observe experienced teachers at work in the classroom was bound up with the relative 'invisibility' (Long et al., 2012) of student teachers as learners.
- *Inherited 'good teaching' cultural scripts dominate over reform-oriented images of teaching:* A strong strand theme through the data was student teachers' reliance on inherited cultural scripts about 'good' teaching in their subject areas.
- *Ready to teach but not ready to 'do' inclusion:* Students' perceptions that by the end of the programme they are 'ready to teach' but that they are not yet ready to 'do' inclusion; i.e., inclusion is an add-on rather than an intrinsic characteristic of their teaching.

Research Design

LETS was an empirical research project, funded by the Department of Education and Science (now Department of Education and Skills) and undertaken over three years (2007-10). It involved the participation of an experienced research team from the School of Education, UCC, and the 2008-2009 cohort of PDE students. The principles of the interpretive research genre (Mertens, 2010; Borko, Liston and Whitcomb, 2007) informed the project. Seventeen student teachers were interviewed on three occasions over the course of an academic year. The timing of these interviews was designed to capture opportunities to learn to teach at crucial points in the PDE programme. The study also included analysis of documents and a survey questionnaire completed in March 2009 by 133 of the 212 students of the 2008-2009 PDE cohort (a response rate of 63 per cent). No student was interviewed by his/her own teaching practice supervisor, all were assured of anonymity, and consent was understood to be ongoing, that is, they were free to withdraw at any time from the study.

Finding 1. Student teachers had limited access to the pedagogy of others despite support from mentors

> *Kevin*: …the first two weeks we went into the school we were more or less *told that you would be sitting in the class watching your class teacher* and I mean *I thought that was brilliant* because not only do you get to know the class from sitting at the back of the room but you just get a small bit more confident. I mean this particular day *I saw what the teacher was doing and I thought, yes I can do that. It helped me just to build my confidence more than anything else…* even though there was a drawback in terms of you were *recognised as a student going back to the classroom, that kind of wore off.* (Kevin, learning to teach English, Interview 1, emphases added)

Kevin's story was exceptional in the context of LETS. Under the prevailing system, most of the students surveyed went straight into classroom teaching without a prior period of observation in their teaching practice school. Underpinning contemporary reforms in teacher education is an assumption that access to the pedagogy of accomplished teachers is a key feature of teacher education programmes. A central mechanism for this is through student teachers' experience on field placements where opportunities to observe and be observed, as well as to engage in professional conversations, are assumed to be a staple aspect of learning to teach. In LETS, a contradiction emerged: the vast majority of student teachers surveyed had support within their schools from mentors but this mentoring did not include, except in a small minority of notable cases, access to observing these same teachers' pedagogical practice or to discussions on pedagogical practice. Some students in our study reported that there was little opportunity for professional dialogue in their schools:

> *Fiona:* I don't think I actually learned too much about teaching in the school I am in. They would talk about students and their marks but they wouldn't talk about methodologies that they use, it wasn't the done thing. (Fiona, learning to teach Irish and History, interview 3)

Over 90 per cent of PDE students in our survey had one or more of the three kinds of mentor we identified (an overall school coordinator of teaching practice, an individual mentor assigned by the school, or a mentor whom they sought out or with whom they formed a mentoring relationship within the school), and many of them had more than one mentor within the school. Effective mentoring could really make a difference to the student teacher:

> *Caron*: When I went to the school I was assigned mentor teachers because I was taking over their classes, they were incredibly helpful and incredibly supportive and I really appreciated the work that they did for me. (Caron, learning to teach science and maths, interview 3, p. 15)

It is noteworthy however that a minority of the survey participants had no mentor at all within their teaching practice school.

By comparison with the general availability of mentoring, however, opportunities to observe in the classroom were rare. Only two in five (40 per cent) were enabled either to observe experienced teachers or be observed by these same teachers during teaching practice, and almost half of these had observed on fewer than four occasions. Four out of five (82 per cent) of those who did not have an opportunity to observe another teacher stated that they would have valued the opportunity had it been available. The interviews helped to shed some light on the minority who would not have welcomed the opportunity to observe: some saw it as automatically labelling them as student teachers and thereby having the capacity to undermine the highly sought-after sense of independent authority and discipline deemed necessary to function as a teacher in schools.

Maeve (who at 23 was one of the younger participants in the study and whose teaching practice school was located in the small town where she herself went to school) was initially glad that her school did not insist on student teachers observing before beginning to teach a class on their own, but later changed her mind:

> *Maeve*: Because I felt that if you were sitting at the back of the classroom of another teacher, they (the students) know straight away that you are a student teacher and you are leaving yourself open. But now I feel that it is good to observe be-

> cause you do forget your own school days … (Maeve, teaching Irish and English in a Gaelscoil, interview 1)

The LETS study characterises the student teachers' appetite for isolation in terms of their 'invisibility' as learners and finds that students are less successful at negotiating curriculum or assessment issues in those schools when no one in the school takes responsibility for their learning as novice teachers (Long et al., 2012; Hall et al., 2012).

> *Siobhán*: The teachers in my school in general are very helpful, but there's no specific person and at the start I wouldn't have felt comfortable maybe asking for help because like that you were afraid you would be seen as weak and things like that. Maybe you don't want to draw the extra attention on yourself... and again you are not that confident within the school structure at that stage and you don't know where you fit in (Siobhan, teaching French, interview 1)

In summary, for students in LETS, opportunities for deep professional engagement about pedagogy during school placement were significantly constrained, in spite of the widespread availability of mentoring of some kind (Conway et al., 2011a). These findings are entirely consistent with the recent OECD Teaching and Learning International Survey (TALIS) study (Gilleece et al., 2009) which found that professional collaboration in second-level schools is typically focused at the level of exchange and coordination rather than deeper levels of collaboration centred around activities such as team teaching, observation and co-planning.

Gradual and supported assumption of responsibility

A fundamental assumption guiding this study is that learning to teach is best undertaken in a context in which student teachers experience gradual and supported entry into full classroom responsibility. This assumption is based on research on learning as assisted performance (Vygotsky, 1978; Tharp and Gallimore, 1988) and on more recent teacher education studies (Moore-Johnson, 2004; Mewborn and Stinson, 2007). These suggest that the 'sink or swim' model of learning to teach ultimately undermines teaching; it provides far fewer opportunities to develop a wide repertoire of skills, and the pressure to survive consigns student and beginning teachers to an over-reliance on their 'apprenticeship of observation' (Lortie, 1975). In this regard, how can we characterise the experiences of these PDE students?

In order to address this question and to expand on the concept of support in schools for learning to teach in the context of different subject specialities, we drew on both survey and interview data. A five-item *Support in School* scale (Cronbach Alpha = 0.70) was constructed; this was a subset of the questions in the survey. Given the modest number of items in this scale the reliability can be seen as adequate. The five items used were

1. Got a lot of help planning lessons from school staff
2. Had chances to talk daily about lesson progress with teachers
3. Felt supported by staff in school
4. Had access to resources in school, textbooks, etc.
5. Felt supported in my main subject

The last item reflects the fact that student teachers in general have two teaching subjects, one of which is their major subject for purposes of the PDE. The maximum possible score on the scale was 20 and the minimum was 0. There were significant differences in support for students in different subjects (see Table 1).[3] Overall, the mean scores suggest that a low to moderate degree of support was available to student teachers in both their main and second subjects. Multiple comparisons were run on the different means for the subjects, that is, ANOVAs followed by a posthoc test, i.e. Tukey. There was a statistically significant difference (Tukey posthoc, p=0.05) between the degree of support in schools for student teachers of Maths (mean=14.2, sd 2.8) compared to teachers of French (mean=8.5, sd 3.9). We are unable to suggest a reason why this might be so; no other two-way comparison of mean scores on the 'Support in School' scale – between Maths, Science, French, or Other Languages – was significant.

Table 1: 'Support in Schools' for main and second PDE subject

PDE Subject: Main and Second	*Mean (as a main subject)*	*n*	*Mean (as a second subject)*	*n*
Maths	14.2	10	9.9	31
French	8.5	9	7.7	5
Other language	12.6	3	11.0	5
Science (including Biology)	11.2	25	12.3	9

(Score scale: min = 0 and max = 20)

The LETS study reflects other studies (Britzman, 2007; Moore-Johnson, 2004; Mewborn and Stinson, 2007) in finding that isolation is a constraining factor in learning to become a competent teacher and that school-level collaboration is the only sustainable option. In conclusion, the phenomenon of mentoring that typically does not include observation or associated opportunities to discuss pedagogy is bound up with what we termed the 'invisible learner' phenomenon (Long et al., 2012). A significant implication of the limited opportunities to engage with the pedagogy of others in schools is the consequent foreclosure on opportunities to reconsider dominant cultural scripts about what constitutes good teaching.

Finding 2. Inherited 'good teaching' cultural scripts dominate over reform-oriented images of teaching

In the absence of opportunities to observe experienced and skilled teachers at work, Lortie's (1975) classic concept, the 'apprenticeship of observation', calls our attention to the ways in which those learning to teach draw on their own experiences at school as a way of framing what it means to be a good teacher. Not surprisingly, there was consistent evidence that this was the case among all LETS participants, especially near the beginning of the year:

> *Aisling*: At the beginning of the year... I was doing too much lecture style, teacher talking, students listening ... I suppose in the first few weeks I went in thinking that was the way to teach.

While university supervisors and tutors might give advice on alternative ways of teaching, the lack of opportunities to observe subject teachers at work in their teaching practice school meant that some student teachers looked elsewhere for role models. Julie (teaching science) spoke of how she trawled YouTube for resources, especially as a means of expanding observation opportunities for herself on how to manage scientific investigations (these, we presume, were also being taught in her teaching practice school):

> *Julie*: Well I copy the videos on YouTube on my own computer and then bring it into the school. There is a school in Dublin and we have videos of the entire junior cert and Leaving Cert physics experiments, which is really handy to see other boys and girls... (Julie, Interview 2)

Julie's experience draws attention to a number of important factors in learning to teach: the need for role models, the appeal of observing others' practice, the absence of opportunities to do so within the school, and the way in which accessing others' pedagogy, in this case via YouTube, was a means of engaging with 'new' and other scripts of teaching. Julie's quest to do so highlights the natural reliance on role models that is an inescapable feature of becoming a teacher. In an era in which many subjects are undergoing significant reform and innovation, a reliance on 'good' teachers from the past as models may foreclose on ways of thinking about what it means to be a good teacher in the context of reform-oriented images of teaching in various curriculum areas.

Crucially, core issues to the teaching of any subject are conceptions of knowledge, assumptions about learning, teaching and assessment in the domain, and the role of curriculum resources. Inherited cultural scripts regarding what constitutes good teaching are typically challenged by reforms in these areas. For example, in their university-based mathematics methods module, student teachers are expected to acquire new ways of thinking about teaching and learning maths, that is, a vision of mathematics that is different from the traditional exposition and practice model of practice that they themselves experienced as students of mathematics (Conway et al., 2011c). There were issues for the student teachers of mathematics in our study in trying to put this new vision of mathematical education into practice and to develop resource-rich environments in schools.

> *Emma*: Before, my idea of a good teacher of maths would have been quite traditional, *like the good teachers that I had who went up to the board, they did examples, and then we did examples*. So now I wouldn't have that image of a good maths teacher. I would think it is somebody who gets the kids active so they are sitting up rather than just slouching ... *who looks for resources and tries to relate the material to the students.* (Emma, teaching maths and French, interview 2, emphases added).

Changes in other subject areas bring similar challenges; some student teachers of languages, for example, found that there was now a greater emphasis on the communicative approach (McKeon, 2007) in contrast to the more didactic way in which they themselves were taught. In Kevin's school, the procedure was for all student teachers to observe for the first two weeks before taking on classes themselves. Kevin therefore was one of the few (approximately 10 per cent) of the PGDE student teachers who observed more than once or twice. The observations he undertook prompted considerable reflection:

> *Kevin*: It was very interesting to see him teaching, how he managed the class and how he interacted with the class... He used group work (teaching an English literature class) and I thought that was particularly strange because I didn't have any group work with my teachers when I was in secondary school... I was very surprised about it. (Kevin, teaching English, Interview 1).

These three examples show how student teachers typically seek out and interpret observation opportunities that are available to them in light of their own experience of schooling or apprenticeship of observation, the input from their methodology classes, and their own current experience of teaching. Typically, teaching, especially at second level, has been 'closed' and not open to observation by others, except in very limited circumstances. The LETS findings in relation to the nature of the support afforded student teachers provide an important insight into a powerful cultural dynamic within the teacher education arena, namely the very limited opportunities for deep collegial engagement with pedagogy and the learning opportunities afforded when these do occur.

This is one of the fundamental dilemmas of teacher education and for the re-imagining of the PDE: how should the next generation of teachers be educated and assessed in a reform-oriented era? How can they become flexible and adaptive learners and teachers? While advances in technology mean that it may be easier to access the practice of others in the future – with bodies such as the National Council for Curriculum and Assessment and others making examples of what is considered good practice available online, for example – changes in the structure of the PDE, which allow more time for a gradual induction into the practice of teaching, should also allow more time for observation, discussion and reflection. A more generative learning environment will only be provided by a synergy between university and school which provides an environment for growth and development.

Finding 3. Ready to teach but not yet ready to teach for inclusion

Despite survey results indicating that 84 per cent of the participant cohort 'feel ready to teach' as they neared the end of their PDE programme, many student teachers expressed genuine uncertainty and apprehension in relation to their role in facilitating more inclusive learning practices. Nevertheless, the participant students in LETS typically displayed evidence of feeling responsible for the whole range of abilities and motivations present in their classroom. This genuine care ethic matched, or was a part of, their developing competence in the classroom. Initially, the focus was on classroom control and on showing care in this context. As Maeve states, 'at the start of the year you are trying to get to grips with the teaching, never mind things like inclusion and things like that as well' (Interview 2, p. 5). This view of inclusion as a separate issue was not uncommon, and perhaps the timing of lectures was a factor:

> *Padraig*: I sat in on an in-service in the school in differentiation and learning with special needs and I'm having a look at that at the moment and I like the way that is going. We haven't covered it in lectures yet but it sounds quite doable and I am very, very open to it. So I have started to try and introduce differentiation into my lessons and just appeal to the different learning styles of the students and I am just starting it but I can't say that I have found it a success, obviously it is very early days (Padraig, teaching maths and science, interview 1).

As the year went on, a great sense of self-efficacy and competence meant that they could express their genuine care ethic with more conviction. They began to situate differentiation in the context of curriculum delivery:

> *Interviewer*: What part of your teaching experience do you find the most interesting and rewarding?
>
> *Aoife*: I think the girls in my class who have learning difficulties, even if they are not recognised ones, probably the most rewarding for me is of course when they get something and when they get good marks in a test or, you know, will I be able to pick on them to explain it to the rest of the class... I do some support classes as well as regular classes so it is nice to see them coming on (Aoife, teaching science and maths, interview 1).

For another respondent, inclusion meant democratic engagement in the classroom. This, in turn, demanded a pupil-centred pedagogy where individuals' values, opinions and needs mattered. However, such an enlightened view did not appear as a typical feature of reports of practice.

It is worth considering that the very notion of differentiation as a cornerstone of an inclusive pedagogy is something that can be unexpected by those learning to teach or by those who have little experience of being outside the traditional teacher-learner norm in school work. Padraig's thinking suggests that differentiation in teaching is something that is not necessarily out of reach of those learning to teach, at least in aspirational terms. Yet regardless of the specific nature of learning difficulties encountered, notions of good teaching and particular labels can become, and remain, compartmentalised. Differentiation, student behaviour and 'activity-based learning' may be divided as separate things the teacher must 'learn to manage', rather than wholly integrated features of a learning community.

Discussion

In presenting some key findings from LETS, three questions emerge that ought, we think, to be generative in re-imagining teacher education at post-primary level in Ireland:

- How can teacher education support deeper engagement with and sharing of pedagogy with others as part of the learning to teach experience in schools, in tandem with enhancing the visibility of student teachers as learners?
- In what ways can teacher education engage with both inherited cultural scripts and reform-oriented images of good teaching?
- How can initial teacher education foster a broader conception of readiness to teach so that it encompasses teaching for inclusion?

In addressing these three core challenges, we recognise that the scope of teacher competence is broad, and always has been, as teachers are expected at once to be academically knowledgeable, capable of planning learning in order to share their own and others' knowledge, to act as caring and moral persons, and to represent and act within societies as civic and cultural persons (Darling-Hammond and Bransford, 2005). None of this makes learning to teach easy. In our discussion, we draw upon seven principles summarising Korthagan, Loughran and Russell's (2006) review of research on good teacher education in the last twenty years. These principles are: (i) Learning about teaching involves continuously conflicting and competing demands; (ii) Learning about teaching requires a view of knowledge as a subject to be created rather than as a created subject; (iii) Learning about teaching requires a shift in focus from the curriculum to the learning; (iv) Learning about teaching is enhanced through (student) teacher research; (v) Learning about teaching requires an emphasis on those learning to teach working closely with their peers; (vi) Learning about teaching requires meaningful relationships between schools, universities and student teachers; and (vii) Learning about teaching is enhanced when the teaching and learning approaches advocated in the program are modelled by the teacher educators in their own practice.

Thus, many of the findings in LETS are not unique to the PDE or to UCC but reflect some perennial dilemmas and emerging challenges in teacher education.

How can teacher education support deeper and collegial engagement with pedagogy as part of the learning to teach experience in schools?

The LETS study found that the development of competence during the PDE is typically characterised by a 'sink or swim' model of learning to teach, in schools where there is very significant professional exchange and coordination to support ITE, but very little deeper and more complex professional collaboration centred on the practice of teaching in classrooms. As such, learning to teach is, in many respects, a relatively private personal experience, with infrequent and short public moments when visited by a tutor or very infrequently (and not typically across schools) by another teacher. We need, therefore, to develop new models of interaction and partnership between the schools who offer teaching practice placements and the university-based teacher educators. There are a variety of ways in which this might be done; see Conway et al. (2011b) for an exploration of this topic.

In what ways can teacher education engage with both inherited cultural scripts and reform-oriented images of good teaching?

Within subject domains, the student teachers in our study were all grappling with images of good teaching from their own apprenticeship of observation, seeking opportunities to observe or be observed and forming new identities. While all teachers have a shared interest in understanding how to best build on and integrate students' out of school experiences to make learning in school more powerful and meaningful, particular subject domains also demand disciplinary-specific knowledge cutting across a range of areas of teacher knowledge (Shulman, 1987; Darling-Hammond and Bransford, 2005). In Ireland, rolling reviews of both subject areas and junior and senior cycle at second-level include a focus on effective pedagogy and ways in which pedagogy might change, meaning that what is considered good teaching within subject domains is not necessarily static (Looney and Klenowski, 2008).

In this respect, collaboration between teachers and teacher educators is again key. There is scope for greater inclusion of student teachers in the development and implementation of new pedagogies, for example by ensuring that they can participate in workshops, seminars and debates held by the relevant subject associations, and that they are given opportunities to observe these new pedagogies being modelled by experienced teachers.

How can initial teacher education foster a broader conception of readiness to teach so that it encompasses teaching for inclusion?

As part of what is called the 'new teacher professionalism', the demands on teachers are becoming increasingly complex. How teachers reconcile and integrate their own emerging sense of professional competence with these is not an easy task. As evidenced in this study, the societal and ideological context impacts on student teachers very significantly. As they neared the end of the PDE, our student teachers felt ready to teach, competent in teaching their subject area, and enjoyed teaching but nevertheless did not think similarly in terms of their competence to teach for inclusion, The challenge of meeting the diverse needs of learners is not one that is unique or particular to student teachers; it extends across the whole school system and has implications for leadership and for resources at school and system as well as classroom level. The challenge to teacher educators is to be inclusive in their own teaching and to make it an integral part of their own practice.

Conclusion

The aim of the *Learning to Teach Study* (LETS) was to identify the individual and contextual dynamics of how student teachers develop curricular and cross-curricular competences during initial teacher education. Based on the LETS study, we have identified directions for future research and teaching in relation to the PDE in UCC, but also we hope more broadly within policy on post-primary teacher education in Ireland as well for contemporary scholarship on initial teacher education and induction in Ireland and internationally.

We hope that the insights we have gleaned, which will inform our own work as we continue to develop the PDE, will also have a wider application.

Acknowledgements

Work on this chapter was funded by a research grant Department of Education and Skills (*Learning to Teach Study*/LETS, 2008-10) and an Irish Research Council Advanced Collaborative Research Award (*Re-imagining Initial Teacher Identity and Learning*/RiITILS, 2012-13). We would like to thank the participating student teachers for their time and thoughtful input into the research detailed in this chapter.

Endnotes

1. The research detailed in this chapter was supported by a research grant from the Research and Development Committee of the Department of Education and Skills. The views expressed in this chapter are those of the authors and do not necessarily reflect the views or policy of the Department of Education and Skills.

2. For second level teaching, the consecutive model of teacher education, comprising a subject-based degree followed by a PDE or similar, is the dominant one. The concurrent model where teaching subjects and education studies are taught side-by-side is more common in specialised degrees such as physical education and at primary level where the three year BEd has been the main teaching qualification for many years, although the consecutive mode is also available.

[3] In the context of teaching their main PDE subject, a one-way ANOVA, with two-way Tukey test posthoc comparisons to assess the differences in means between support for students in different subjects, was significant overall (df 9/123, F=2.64, p=0.008).

References

Borko, H., Liston, D. and Whitcomb, J.A. (2007). Genres of empirical research in teacher education. *Journal of Teacher Education, 58*(1), 3-11.

Britzman, D. P. (2007). Teacher education as uneven development: Toward a psychology of uncertainty. *International Journal of Leadership in Education, 10*, 1-12.

Claxton, G. and Wells, G. (Eds.). (2002). *Learning for Life in the 21st century: Sociocultural perspectives on the future of education*. Oxford: Blackwell.

Conway, P.F., Murphy, R., Delargey, M., Hall, K., Kitching, K., Long, F., McKeon, J., Murphy, B., O'Brien, S. and O'Sullivan, D. (2011a). *Learning to Teach Study (LETS) executive summary*. Cork: School of Education, University College Cork.

Conway, P. F., Murphy, R., Hall, K. and Rath, A. (2011b). Leadership and teacher education. In H. O'Sullivan and J. Burnham-West (Eds.), *Leading and managing schools* (pp. 89-110). London: Sage.

Conway, P.F., Delargey, M., Murphy, R. and O'Brien, S. (2011c). Learning to teach in the context of reform-oriented mathematics. In T. Dooley, D. Corcoran and M. Ryan (Eds). *Mathematics teaching matters: Proceedings of the fourth conference on research in mathematics education, MEI 4.* St Patrick's College Drumcondra Dublin, 22-23 September 2011. Retrieved from http://www.spd.dcu.ie/main/academic/mathematics/documents/MEI4_Proceedings.pdf

Darling-Hammond, L. (2006). *Powerful teacher education: Lessons from exemplary programs.* San Francisco: Jossey-Bass

Darling-Hammond, L. and Bransford, J. (Eds.). (2005). *Preparing teachers for a changing world: What teachers should learn and be able to do.* Washington: US National Academy of Education.

Department of Education and Skills (DES). (2011). *Information note: Literacy and numeracy for learning and life: The National Strategy to improve literacy and numeracy among children and young people*. Dublin: Author.

Gilleece, L., Shiel, G. and Perkins, R. (with Proctor, M.). (2009). *Teaching and learning international survey: National report for Ireland*. Dublin: Educational Research Centre.

Hall, K., Conway, P.F., Murphy, R., Long, F., Kitching, K. and O'Sullivan, D. (2012). Authoring oneself and being authored as a competent teacher. *Irish Educational Studies, 31*(2), 103-117.

Hall, K., Murphy, P. and Soler, J. (2008). *Pedagogy and practice: Culture and identities*. London: Sage Publications and The Open University.

Kennedy, M. (2010). Attribution error and the quest for teacher quality. *Educational Researcher, 39*, 8, 591-598.

Kennedy, M. M. and Barnes, H. (1994). Implications of cognitive science for teacher education. In C. Collins and J. Margieri (Eds.), *Creating powerful thinking in teachers and students* (pp. 195-212). New York: Harcourt Brace.

Korthagen, F. (2010). Situated learning theory and the pedagogy of teacher education: Towards an integrative view of teacher behavior and teacher learning. *Teaching and Teacher Education, 26*(1), 98-106.

Korthagen, F. A. J., Kessels, J., Koster, B., Lagerwerf, B. and Wubbels, T. (2001). *Linking practice and theory: The pedagogy of realistic teacher education*. Mahwah, NJ: Lawrence Erlbaum Associates.

Korthagan, F., Loughran, J. and Russell, T. (2006). Developing fundamental principles for teacher education programs and practices. *Teaching and Teacher Education, 22*(8), 1020-1041.

Lave, J. and Wenger, E. (1998). *Communities of practice: Learning, meaning, and identity*. Cambridge University Press.

Long, F., Hall, K., Conway, P. F. and Murphy, R. (2012, in press). Novice teachers as 'invisible' learners. *Teachers and Teaching: Theory and Practice, 18*.

Looney, A. and Klenowski V. (2008). Curriculum and assessment for the knowledge society: interrogating experiences in the Republic of Ireland and Queensland, Australia. *Curriculum Journal, 19*(3), 177-192.

Lortie, D.C. (1975). *Schoolteacher*. Chicago: University of Chicago Press.

McKeon, J. (2007). The role of reflection in pre-service student teachers' understanding of communicative language teaching. In A.-B. Fenner and D. Newby (Eds.), *Coherence of principles, cohesion of competences: Exploring theories and designing materials for teacher education*. Strasbourg: Council of Europe.

Mertens, D. (2010). *Research and evaluation in education and psychology* (3rd ed.). Thousand Oaks CA: Sage.

Mewborn, D. and Stinson, W. (2007). Learning to teach as assisted performance. *Teachers College Record*, *109*(6), 1457-1487 2007.

Moore-Johnson, S. (2004). *Finders and keepers: Helping new teachers survive and thrive in our schools*. San Francisco: Jossey Bass.

Penuel, W.R. and Wertsch, J.V. (1995). Vygotsky and identity formation: A sociocultural approach. *Educational Psychologist*, *30*, 83-92.

Sawyer, R.K. (2006). *The Cambridge handbook of the learning sciences*. New York: Cambridge University Press.

Shulman, L.S. (1987). Knowledge and teaching: Foundations of the new reform. *Harvard Educational Review*, *57*, 1-22.

Tatto, T. (1999). The socializing influence of normative cohesive teacher education on teachers' beliefs about instructional choice. *Teachers and Teaching*, *5*(1), 95-118.

Teaching Council (2011a). *Degree and teacher education qualification requirements (post-primary)*. Dublin: Author.

Teaching Council (2011b). *Initial teacher education: Criteria and guidelines for programme providers*. Dublin: Author.

Tharp, R.G. and Gallimore, R. (1988). *Rousing minds to life: Teaching, learning, and schooling in social context.* Cambridge: Cambridge University Press

Vygotsky, L. (1978). *Mind in society*. Cambridge: Harvard University Press.

Chapter 16

Inclusive Initial Teacher Education: The Case of Mature Students

Anne M. Dolan
Mary Immaculate College, Limerick

> In terms of the three year BEd programme, if I had known what was involved and what I would have to go through, I would never have done it. But at the same time I'm delighted that I got a chance to do it and I know that in the long run I will have a career out of it. I know that when I am in the classroom that I love teaching and I love the kids (Student interview, Dolan, 2008, p.132).

Introduction

Teacher education policy in Ireland is at a 'critical juncture' (Harford, 2010, p. 357). Initial teacher education programmes are undergoing significant reform in response to revised programme accreditation criteria which require, *inter alia*, the extension of the duration of all initial teacher education programmes, a significant increase in school-based learning and a stronger focus on what have been identified as national strategic priorities, such as numeracy, literacy, special educational needs and early childhood education (Department of Education and Skills (DES), 2011a; Teaching Council,

2011).[1] Reforms in teacher education are also being influenced by a range of national, European and international policies and contexts. In national policy terms, the strategy for higher education states that 'the capacity of higher education will have to double over the next twenty years largely through the provision of more flexible opportunities for larger and more diverse student cohorts' (DES, 2011b, p. 10). In a European context, the Bologna Process has led to a restructuring of higher education programmes in order to make European qualifications more comparable. Simultaneously, the global recession and Irish economic crisis have placed unprecedented pressure on public expenditure at a time when the need for resources to support the reform agenda in teacher education has never been greater. These policy changes and economic challenges collectively have major implications for all higher education institutions, including colleges of education which are the traditional sites of primary initial teacher education in Ireland.[2] Given the current volatility in the sector, the time is also opportune to consider provision for mature students in light of recent government projections (DES, 2011b).

In 2009 almost 14 per cent of students in higher education in Ireland were 'mature students' (i.e., those aged 23 or more years on 1 January of the year in which s/he registers). This represents almost one in every six students in higher educational institutions (Higher Education Authority (HEA), 2010). Becoming a mature student represents a period of great transition for an adult learner and not all groups and individuals are successful in managing that transition (Osborn, McNess and Pollard, 2006). Indeed, returning to formal education after a period of time can be an intensely positive or negative experience depending on individual circumstances and the support systems offered by the institution (Dolan, 2008). In the current economic crisis in Ireland, the demand for places in initial teacher education (ITE) programmes generally remains high despite reduced opportunities for permanent employment for graduates. While a majority of undergraduate places on ITE programmes are reserved for those who apply through the Central Application Office (CAO) system, where allocation is based solely on performance in state examinations, each year approximately 10 per cent of places are reserved for mature students and these are awarded on the basis of competitive interviews in English and in Irish.

This chapter focuses specifically on the needs of mature students who choose to undertake an undergraduate Bachelor of Education (BEd) degree programme in Ireland. It begins by examining issues of access and accessibility in higher-level education in the context of lifelong learning. Drawing on national and international research into the experiences of mature students, the chapter argues for flexible provision for mature students in the context of current reforms of initial teacher education.

Access and Accessibility in the Context of Lifelong Learning

In Ireland, policies to increase wider participation in higher level education have focused on a number of previously under-represented groups, such as those with a disability, socio-economically disadvantaged learners, those from the Travelling community, ethnic minorities and mature students (HEA, 2008). Adults register as mature students for degree programmes in Ireland for many reasons. These can include the quest for a qualification, a desire to return to education, a professional requirement to up-skill, or more commonly for employment reasons (Woodley et al., 1987). According to Inglis and Murphy (1999), the challenge facing higher level institutions with regard to mature students is two-fold: making the institution more accessible on the outside to mature applicants, while also transforming the college on the inside to make it more accessible to those mature students who have managed to gain entry. The distinction made by Wright (1989, p. 99) between access and accessibility is a useful one, with access dwelling on mechanisms for access, such as special access courses, flexible admissions policies and recognition of prior learning, and accessibility characterised by addressing those factors that make third-level education remote from the experiences of non-traditional students. In a study based on the practices of lecturers in the institutes of technology in Ireland, Kelly (2005) highlights the mismatch that exists between access and accessibility. While there are quotas to promote the increase of numbers, she laments the lack of 'practical pedagogical and support measures in place where colleges can ensure successful performance, retention and completion' (p. 209).

Access and accessibility for mature students is informed by the ideology of lifelong learning. The ideals of lifelong learning have been embraced by a range of policy makers at national, EU and international levels, including the United Nations Educational, Scientific and Cultural Organization (UNESCO), the Organisation for Economic Co-operation and Development (OECD), the World Trade Organization and the European Union. The European Commission (2004) defines lifelong learning as 'all learning activity undertaken throughout life with the aim of improving knowledge, skills and competencies within a personal, civic, social and/or employment related perspective' (p. 3).

Lifelong learning embraces all learning, including that which takes place formally and informally within organisations and higher education institutes (Chapman and Aspin, 1997). It is closely aligned to ideals of the learning society and learning organisations (Senge, 1990; Edwards, 1997). Thus, lifelong learning is about learning to be, learning to do, learning to work, and learning to learn (Delors, 1996). The life-wide nature of lifelong learning has also been emphasised in the literature in terms of a 'cradle to grave' approach (Delors, 1996). According to Coolahan (2007, p. 23), a strategy for lifelong learning has been accepted as the '*leitmotif* for education policy for the twenty-first century' while Dolan (2012, p. 53) refers to lifelong learning as 'a new paradigm for teacher education.' However, the development and implementation of concrete measures have lagged substantially behind the language and ambition of the policy community (Field, 2006). While policies of lifelong learning are generally presented in positive terms, the concept itself has been criticised in the literature for being vague, overambitious and unrealistically aspirational. Part of the problem is conceptual in nature. Lifelong learning is such a broad concept that it is difficult to reach a clear uncontested definition (Chapman and Aspin, 1997).

The OECD review of higher education in Ireland highlights the importance of 'giving a high priority to lifelong learning, widening participation, and the encouragement of mature students' (2004, p. 8). One practical strategy to foster lifelong learning is to promote access to a range of non-traditional students, including mature students. While there are immense personal, social and professional benefits for mature students who successfully complete their degree programmes (Kenny et al., 2010), the benefits for host institutions are also considerable. According to the DES, 'mature students add to the richness of the population' in colleges of education (2002, p. 66). Mature students, who often have considerable experience of the world of work, bring a range of diverse and broad perspectives to classroom discussions, assignments and practical work. These rich perspectives enhance classroom experiences for all involved, including lecturers and other students. Tom Schuller (2002) argues that, in addition to the considerable benefits to the higher education system, there are benefits to society in general including enhanced social networks, more intergenerational contacts and greater employment prospects. Other commentators argue that involving more citizens in education endeavours increases opportunities for the learning society to flourish (Kenny at al., 2010).

Despite the commitment to lifelong learning evident in state policy and the general recognition of its benefits as a paradigm, a deficit remains in terms of implementation, particularly in the case of mature students. In recent years ambitious targets have been set in relation to lifelong learning and the widening of participation and access to higher education for non-traditional students (DES, 2011b; Greenbank, 2006; Duke and Layer, 2005; Duke, 2005). Indeed, Ireland has made consistent progress in increasing the numbers of mature students entering full-time higher level educational institutions from 1.6 per cent of students in 1986 to 12.8 per cent by 2006.[3] Furthermore, colleges of education, who are the only providers of initial teacher education at undergraduate level, have enrolled a higher number of mature students than other higher level institutions (Clancy, 1999). Nevertheless, despite recent increases, Irish rates of participation for mature students remain below the EU average (HEA, 2008; OECD, 2006). However, recent projections from the Department of Education and Skills (2011b, p. 44) indicate the demand for places in higher education will increase significantly by 2025 with the bulk of the increased demand coming from mature students.

Notwithstanding Ireland's commitment to lifelong learning in the context of the knowledge society, one of the major obstacles for Irish adults wishing to access higher level education is the limited provision and choice of part-time flexible learning opportunities for National Framework of Qualifications (NFQ) levels 6-8 (HEA, 2009). It is widely acknowledged that these levels of participation need to be further increased (HEA, 2008). The current low levels of opportunities for part-time study limits the accessibility of higher education for working adults with caring responsibilities (HEA, 2009). It is not possible, for example, for mature students to complete a BEd degree programme in Ireland on a part-time basis. Improvements in provision for lifelong learning will require greater flexibility in the delivery of programmes and in continuing progress to expand entry routes. Further targets have been set for the provision of flexible/part-time provision to increase from the current share of 7 per cent of undergraduate entrants to 17 per cent by 2013 (HEA, 2008, p. 61). While flexible provision is key to improving access for mature students, there are other issues – structural, relational and cultural – that need attention.

Factors Affecting the Mature Student Experience

The experience of mature students is directly affected by a number of factors, both within the college structures and procedures (e.g., programmes, courses, timetables and facilities which inform college life) and factors which are external to the college (finance, relationships and other external commitments). Both internal and external factors feature prominently in the literature (Kenny et al., 2010; Dolan, 2008). The effects of these factors are in turn mediated through class, gender and ethnic background.

Finance is a key issue which impacts on the lives of mature students (Woodley et al., 1987; Lynch, 1997). According to Ozga and Sukhandan (1997), one of the main reasons for mature students failing to complete their courses is the greater financial and family pressure they experience. This is further intensified by class and gender (Lynch and O'Riordan, 1998). In a study exploring the experiences of mature students who failed to make the transition to higher education after an access course, Reay identified 'a shortage of money, lack of time and childcare problems as the most common reasons for leaving courses prematurely' (2002, p. 15). The mature students in my own research (Dolan, 2008) endured severe financial restraints due to their loss of income for the duration of the three years. Individual circumstances and varying degrees of financial pressure affect students differently. Some mature students work part-time to fund their time in college while others are supported by family and personal resources. The 'burden of finance' was described in different ways by individual students. This financial pressure is further compounded by course-related expenses such as photocopying and teaching practice expenses. One student believed that mature students take their studies more seriously than school leavers because of the sacrifices they have made, including the financial pressures which are being endured:

> That's a big difference because, because it's my choice, because there's so much money involved in it, because I made sacrifices to do this. Definitely I take it more seriously. I feel more pressure on myself to do well because again after all the burdens of finance I feel I have to make this worthwhile (Student interview, Dolan, 2008, p.120).

In 1995, the Irish Government abolished the payment of fees for students attending university courses. Under the 'Free Fees Initiative', the Government now pays the tuition fees of students who meet relevant course, nationality and residence requirements as set down under the initiative. However, a registration fee is payable at the start of the academic year by students undertaking most courses; this fee is intended to cover student examinations, registration and services. At the time of writing, the re-introduction of fees is being considered, a move which would have a disproportionate impact on mature students (Kenny at al., 2010) and could further marginalise this group. This would be contrary to stated government policy to increase participation rates of mature students.

Researchers who have investigated the status and experience of female mature students in higher education argue that, despite some improvements in regard to access and accommodation issues, the reality of higher education for many women is still incongruent with the reality of their lives (Gouthro, 2005; Bowl, 2003). Edwards (1993) highlights the dilemma of mature women students struggling to satisfy two 'greedy institutions' – universities and families – which compete for women's time and energy. Childcare has been identified as a crucial factor in determining decisions to participate in higher education for potential female students (Russell et al., 2002). This is also true in teacher education as female students are more likely to feel pressures of childcare and home based duties (Dolan, 2008).

> If there was some sort of a crèche I think that would be huge, I really do. I see it with the girls, Rachel [pseudonym] now for example. Rachel drives up here with the kids to drop in essays and things like that and she's dragging the kids around the place. There's no one to look after them. Either one of us has to look after them or else she drags them up to the offices. But there are so many times she hasn't been able to come up if she just can't get someone, or if her parents are away and I think that's crazy. There should be some sort of facility so that you can leave the kids there, even if it's just for an hour or two. There should be a room or some place and even if a person was employed to mind children, someone who just took one of the rooms in a private capacity, because it's not easy on the girls (Student interview, Dolan, 2008, p. 106-107).

The higher education system in Ireland was designed to cater for school leavers who enter university to complete full-time undergraduate degrees. However, an increasingly heterogeneous student body, including increased numbers of mature students, poses a challenge for higher level institutions. Darmody and Fleming (2009) call on higher education institutions to expand opportunities for participation in part-time study in the light of changing demography and provision of resources to facilitate students' participation in higher education. The constraints of full-time study for mature students is fully acknowledged by the *National Strategy for Higher Education to 2030* which states, 'Ireland's current low level of part-time study opportunities limits the accessibility of higher education for working adults and adults with caring responsibilities' (DES, 2011b, p. 46).

Becoming a Teacher – The Perspective of the Mature Student

There is limited research available on mature student teachers and even less on mature primary student teachers. Research conducted by the author demonstrates the instrumental reasons for female mature students deciding to embark on a BEd degree programme. In this research, the BEd was described as 'a means to an end' and the desire to be a primary teacher was described by one student as 'an obsession' (Dolan, 2008). The final outcome, a qualification to teach in primary schools, was considered more important than the process of undertaking the degree programme for its own sake. Students in this research put their lives on hold to complete their degree in teacher education. Therefore, given the motivational factors associated with a degree in teacher education, a consecutive model of initial teacher education consisting of an undergraduate degree followed by a part-time ITE programme would not be considered a viable option.

National and international studies demonstrate the complex web of problems experienced by mature students in an ITE context. Maguire's (1999) work focused on the narrative of a working-class second-level student teacher, highlighting the manner in which class operates in the process of becoming a teacher. A study of mature, second-level student teachers conducted by Priyadharshini and Robinson-Pant (2003) demonstrated that students who were parents felt that insufficient notice was taken of their parental responsibilities. No proper consideration was given to the needs of mature students in assigning schools for teaching practice, timetables were given out late regardless of parents' needs to make suitable childcare arrangements and the Postgraduate Certificate in Education (PGCE) course ran full-time when children were on mid-term breaks, thus making childcare difficult. In this study, many students said they would have appreciated the greater flexibility offered by a part-time programme.

Duncan's (1999) work focused on a series of interviews with female mature student teachers, examining the processes of change and adaptation which take place as they learned to become teachers. Her study examined the uneasy blend of struggle, contestation, guilt and success which became a daily feature of their lives as mothers, wives and full-time student teachers. White's (2008) study in New Zealand focused on mature student teachers who were mothers with young children. In her symbolic interactionist study of student teachers in Ireland, Dolan (2008) examined the identities of mature primary student teachers in colleges of education and how these identities changed over the course of their studies. Both Dolan and White's studies highlighted the strong motivation for wanting to become primary school teachers and the impact this decision had on their extended lives.

Dolan's study explored the everyday reality of widening participation and lifelong learning for mature students, some of whom entered university with family, work and caring commitments. These mature students negotiated daily the inherent contradictions in the Irish system, where, on the one hand, ambitious government targets have been set to increase the participation of mature students, while on the other hand the government has adopted a policy of free fees (excluding registration fees) for full-time students, but not for part-time students. These ongoing and contradictory policies ignore the lived realities of mature students with family, financial and work commitments who are not in a position to return to full-time study. Those who do return to full-time study do so at a significant cost both to themselves and their families (Dolan, 2008; White, 2008). This highlights the 'rather *ad hoc*, piecemeal and muddled policies' on widening participation and lifelong learning (Greenbank, 2006, p. 161).

The complexity characteristic of mature students' lives is reflected also in the range of life experiences they bring with them to their courses, including previous educational experiences, work experience and experiences in the wider community. Yet, George and Maguire's study of women with ages ranging from 33-50 years who were preparing to become teachers found that these women often felt 'patronised and undervalued' (1998, p. 421) whilst in college. They felt their prior experience was ignored. All undergraduates were treated as recent school leavers and were generally expected to 'listen and learn' rather than participate. They also believed there was a contradiction between the manner in which they were educated and the actual theories of learning which they were studying. Mature women were isolated, marginalised and 'rendered invisible by staff and student alike' (ibid., p. 428). Indeed, when mature learners are included in large cohorts of adult students who are primarily school leavers, there is a danger that their uniqueness is not recognised or that their potential development is not realised. This diversity and complexity can differentiate them from younger students. This is demonstrated in one of the comments from a student in Dolan's work:

> We all have our lives outside of college. Whereas you look at the younger ones and it's just, that's their life, its college, you know. And they haven't really built up their own lives outside of it yet, whereas we have, so we're bringing different dynamics to it (Student interview, Dolan, 2008, p. 97).

The reference here to 'bringing different dynamics' to college is something which is recognised by the students themselves and, as noted earlier, it represents a significant potential asset for colleges who are entrepreneurial enough to realise this. It is imperative also for providers to treat all students, and particularly mature students, as adult learners. Consideration, therefore, must be given to the *type* of learning that is experienced by mature students in the context of the extensive literature available on adult education. It is equally important for mature students to view themselves as adult learners and to act accordingly.

Wright's (1989, p. 99) distinction between access and accessibility is useful as it reminds us that efforts to support entry to higher education alone are not sufficient. There is also a need for higher education institutions to change internally in order to make their practices and procedures more accessible for mature students, rather than expecting mature students to make all of the compromises. Currently, the same BEd degree programme is provided simultaneously for mature students and school leavers in Ireland. There is no difference in the content or methods of teaching adopted, although some lecturers try to engage more with mature students (Dolan, 2008). The BEd programme itself is undergoing fundamental reforms. There are opportunities for addressing the specific needs of mature students in the context of this reform. Initially, it is possible for every ITE provider to 'mature student proof' their courses, consulting with mature students to make sensitive adjustments which would seek to address their needs in key areas such as timetabling.

Developing More Accessible Teacher Education Programmes

In light of recent proposals to increase the numbers of both mature students and of flexible and part-time study options (DES, 2011b; HEA 2008, 2009), it is apt for colleges of education to rethink the nature and mode of delivery of their courses. The lengthening of the BEd to a four year programme will make initial teacher education even more inaccessible for mature students. In this context, I believe that, rather than subject mature students to the pressures of a full-time education course designed for school leavers, programme providers should consider the development of a part-time BEd programme specifically for mature students, mirroring the flexibility that already exists at post-graduate level. If programme providers wish to address the promotion of lifelong learning, and specifically the provision of lifelong teacher education, the case for introducing a part-time BEd degree for mature students is compelling. There are many flexible options which could be considered in terms of mode of delivery and timetabling, including blended and independent learning strategies to support on-campus taught courses, intensive teaching periods at appropriate and accessible times, and a flexible and negotiated approach to specific requirements around school placement and Irish immersion provision.

In its report *Attracting, Developing and Retaining Effective Teachers*, the OECD outlined nine key features of flexible and responsive teacher education programmes, including:

- Modular curriculum structures that support part-time or distance education, enabling students to combine teacher education with work or family responsibilities;
- Alternative routes into teaching for those who want to make a mid-career change that allow them to combine on-the-job support with formal study;
- Reducing the length and cost of courses through accreditation of prior learning;
- Opportunities for existing teachers to gain new qualifications, which allow them to teach in different schools or to take on new subject areas that are in high-demand (OECD, 2005, p. 133).

Undoubtedly, care would have to be taken to ensure that such proposals did not run counter to recent policy decisions endorsing high-quality research-driven teacher education programmes which occur in university settings (DES, 2012) by allowing a reductionist training paradigm to replace the complex pedagogy of initial teacher education. Yet, the imperative to provide flexible pathways for mature students is evident.

A number of sticking points remain however, that need to be addressed. Firstly, in Ireland part-time students are not eligible for free fees. This discrepancy in policy between full-time and part-time students has been highlighted by many commentators, including the OECD (2006). There is a strong argument here for the Irish Government to tackle the issue of fees for part-time students. As Greenbank argues 'if the government is to make real progress on widening participation (and the statistics suggest they are not doing this), they need to be more courageous in the policies they adopt' (2006, p. 161). Secondly, while the previous educational experience of mature students is incredibly rich and valuable it does not seem to be acknowledged or valued in any concrete manner. Dolan (2008) observed the lack of Accredited Prior Learning (APL) facilities for mature students. Indeed, research participants noted that few lecturers ever expressed any interest in their previous experience, with the exception of their initial interview to gain entry to the programme. This is an issue which also pertains to higher education in general (Murphy, 2003). There are two elements to consider when addressing the prior experience of the mature student. In the first instance, it is important to include this experience into the ongoing educational development of the student. More importantly, it is essential to value this experience in a formalised, transparent, accredited manner. It is this life experience which differentiates mature students from school leavers, yet the two groups are treated for the most part in an identical manner. Hence, if providers are to re-design their courses for mature students, the issue of prior learning needs to be addressed.

Finally, there is a range of issues that argue for a cultural shift in how academic institutions engage with their students and order their lives. To support government aspirations to increase the numbers of mature students on campus, a multi-layered strategy is required.

While providers differ in relation to their level of provision, there are key areas that can be identified such as the need for a comprehensive review of policy and procedures, targeting of mature students through dedicated information services, access to trained mentors across all institutions and ongoing consultation with mature students themselves. Where publicly-funded providers of teacher education are serious about attracting, recruiting and retaining mature students, they must be prepared to be more flexible in the design, delivery and assessment of courses. Increasingly, private colleges are offering online and distance learning facilities for students. The demand for these options indicates that there is a real need for university-based colleges to explore more flexible options, e.g., part-time degree courses and flexible modular programmes. Assessment options also need to suit the needs of mature students and should be planned carefully in consultation with mature students.

Conclusion

This chapter explores issues of access and accessibility for mature student teachers in the context of lifelong learning policies and practices. In Ireland, the provision of higher education continues to be inflexible for mature students with some exceptions (Kenny et al., 2010). In terms of initial teacher education, there is a need for a greater range of options for accreditation which would be of benefit to mature students who are balancing studies with a wide range of other commitments. Ireland is currently below the EU average of participation in lifelong learning. In recognition of this, the HEA has revised its targets of participation to be reached by 2013. These targets include: an increase in the number of mature students to 20 per cent of full-time students; an increase in the share of mature students to 27 per cent of the total combined cohort of full-time and part-time entrants; an increase in the number of flexible and part-time courses; and an increase in the non-standard entry routes to higher education. These targets have also been endorsed by the *National Strategy for Higher Education to 2030* (DES, 2011b) which predicts that the capacity of higher education will almost double in the next twenty years with most of the growth coming from non-traditional areas such as mature and overseas students.

The lengthening of the BEd programme to four years will pose even more challenges for mature students who are already struggling to meet the demands of a three year programme. While mature adult learners remain on the margins of the higher education system in general and teacher education in particular, there are now many more opportunities to create an educational landscape which places the needs of the learner rather than the institution at the epicentre of the teaching and learning process. There is much here for higher level institutions to consider. In the meantime, it is important to remember that the life of the adult mature student can be greatly enhanced by adopting an 'adult-friendly' policy to teaching and learning. While these recommendations have been specifically constructed for mature students, some recommendations are also applicable for the entire higher-level student population. Teacher education as a sub-section of the broader higher education sector has much to offer in terms of teaching and learning practices. It is therefore important for teacher education to model exemplary inclusive practices with regard to mature students. The time is ripe for change.

> I suppose for me the course could be compared to some kind of white water rafting, definitely a journey that was full of ups and downs. I just didn't know what was going to happen from one minute to the next or if I was going to survive at all or would I be better off pulling out altogether. But then when I came to the end of it.... it's like an adrenaline rush 'I did it' (Student interview, Dolan, 2008, p. 137).

Endnotes

1. The duration of all undergraduate initial teacher education programmes has been extended from three to four years, from September 2012 in the case of the primary sector. Graduate initial teacher education programmes will be extended to two years from September 2014.

[2.] Currently there are five publicly funded providers of initial teacher education programmes in Ireland: Mary Immaculate College, Limerick; St Patrick's College, Drumcondra; Marino Institute of Education; Froebel College of Education; and Church of Ireland College. The sector has recently embarked on a process of structural reform. See http://www.hea.ie/en/node/1477. There is one private for-profit provider of initial teacher education, Hibernia College, which does not offer an undergraduate teacher education programme.

[3.] These figures refer to first time (new) entrants to a full-time undergraduate course (NFQ levels 6-8).

References

Bowl, M. (2003). *Non-traditional entrants to higher education: They talk about people like me.* Stoke on Trent: Trentham Books.

Chapman, J. D. and Aspin, D., (1997). *The school, the community and lifelong learning* (School development series). London: Cassell.

Clancy, P. (1999). Participation of mature students in higher education in Ireland. In T. Fleming and J. Coolahan (Eds), *Higher education the challenge of lifelong learning.* Maynooth: Centre for Educational Policy Studies, National University of Ireland, Maynooth.

Coolahan, J. (2007). *A review paper on thinking and policies related to teacher education in Ireland.* (Report commissioned by The Teaching Council). Retrieved from http://www.teachingcouncil.ie/_fileupload/Teacher%20Education/Continuum_ppr_PositionPaperJohnCoolahan_18feb2009_ck_61560932.pdf

Darmody, M. and Fleming, B. (2009). Irish part-time undergraduate students in higher education. *Irish Educational Studies, 28*(11), 67-83.

Delors, J. (1996). *Learning the treasure within* (Report to UNESCO of the International Commission on Education for the Twenty-first Century). Paris: UNESCO.

Department of Education and Science. (DES). (2002). *Preparing teachers for the 21st century: Report of the working group on primary pre-service teacher education.* Dublin: Government of Ireland.

Department of Education and Skills (DES). (2011a). *Literacy and numeracy for learning and life: The national strategy to improve literacy and numeracy among children and young people 2011–2020.* Dublin: Author. Retrieved from http://www.education.ie/servlet/blobservlet/lit_num_strat.pdf?language=EN&igstat=true

Department of Education and Skills (DES). (2011b). *National strategy for higher education to 2030.* Dublin: Government Publications. Retrieved from http://www.hea.ie/files/files/DES_Higher_Ed_Main_Report.pdf

Department of Education and Skills (DES). (2012). *Report of the International Review Panel on the structure of initial teacher education provision in Ireland* (Review conducted on behalf of the Department of Education and Skills). Retrieved from http://www.education.ie/en/Press-Events/Press-Releases/2012-Press-Releases/Report-of-the-International-Review-Panel-on-the-Structure-of-Initial-Teacher-Education-Provision-in-Ireland.pdf

Dolan, A. M. (2008). *Integrating the experiences and identities of Irish mature student primary teachers.* Unpublished doctoral thesis, Sheffield Hallam University.

Dolan, A. M. (2012). Lifelong learning: A new paradigm for teacher education. In T. G. Grenham and P. Kiernan (Eds.), *Emerging educational trends in contemporary Ireland: Trends and challenges* (pp. 53-71). Bern: Peter Lang.

Duke, C. (Ed.). (2005). *The tertiary moment: What road to inclusive higher education?* England and Wales: National Institute of Adult Continuing Education.

Duke, C. and G. Layer, (Eds). (2005). *Widening participation: Which way forward for English higher education?* England and Wales: National Institute of Adult Continuing Education.

Duncan, D. (1999). *Becoming a primary school teacher: A study of mature women.* London: Trentham Books.

Edwards, R. (1993). *Mature women students: Separating or connecting family and education.* London; Washington, DC: Taylor & Francis.

Edwards, R. (1997). *Changing places?: Flexibility, lifelong learning and a learning society.* London: Routledge.

European Commission. (2004). *Implementation of education and training 2010 work programme. Working group B 'key competences'. Key competences for lifelong learning. A European reference framework.* Retrieved from http://ec.europa.eu/education/policies/2010/doc/basicframe.pdf.

Field, J. (2006). *Lifelong learning and the new educational order* (2nd ed.). Stoke on Trent, UK/Sterling, USA: Trentham Books.

George, R. and Maguire, M. (1998). Older women training to teach. *Gender and Education, 10*(4), 417-30.

Gouthro, P. (2005). A critical feminist analysis of the home-place as learning site: Expanding the discourse of lifelong learning to consider adult women learners. *International Journal of Lifelong Education, 24*(1), 5-19.

Greenbank, P. (2006). The evolution of government policy on widening participation. *Higher Education Quarterly, 60* (2), 141-66.

Harford, J. (2010). Teacher education policy in Ireland and the challenges of the twenty first century. *European Journal of Teacher Education, 33*(4), pp. 349-360.

Higher Education Authority (HEA). (2008). *National plan for equity of access to higher education 2008-2013.* Dublin: National Office of Equity of Access to Higher Education, Higher Education Authority.

Higher Education Authority (HEA). (2009). *Open and flexible learning, HEA position paper.* Dublin: Author.

Higher Education Authority (HEA). (2010). *Mature Students.* Retrieved from http://www.hea.ie/en/older-mature-students on 19/8/2010.

Inglis, T. and Murphy, M. (1999). *No room for adults? A study of mature students in University College Dublin (UCD).* Dublin: UCD.

Kelly, M. (2005). The effects of increasing numbers of mature students on the pedagogical practices of lectures in the institutes of technology. *Irish Educational Studies, 24* (2-3), 207-221.

Kenny, A., Fleming, T., Loxley A. and Finnegan F. (2010). *Where next? A study of work and life experiences of mature students (incl. disadvantaged) in three higher education institutions* (Working Paper 10/02). Dublin: Combat Poverty Agency. Retrieved from http://arrow.dit.ie/cgi/viewcontent.cgi?article=1003&context=beschconart

Lynch, K. (1997). A profile of mature students in higher education and an analysis of equality issues. In R. Morris (Ed.), *Mature students in higher education* (Proceedings of conference at Athlone RTC, March 1996). Cork: Higher Education Equality Unit.

Lynch, K. and O'Riordan, C. (1998). Inequality in higher education: A study of class barriers. *British Journal of Sociology of Education, 19*(4), 445-478.

Maguire, M. (1999). 'A touch of class': Inclusion and exclusion in initial teacher education. *International Journal of Inclusive Education, 3*(1), p. 13-26.

Murphy, A. (2003). Is the university sector in Ireland ready to publicly assess and accredit personal learning from outside the academy? *European Journal of Education 38*(4) (12), 401-11.

Organisation for Economic Co-operation and Development (OECD). (2004). *Review of national policies for education: Review of higher education in Ireland*, examiners' report. Paris: Author.

Organisation for Economic Co-operation and Development (OECD). (2005). *Teachers matter: Attracting, developing and retaining effective teachers.* Paris: Author.

Organisation for Economic Co-operation and Development (OECD). (2006). *Review of national policies for education: Higher education in Ireland.* Paris: Author.

Osborn, M., McNess, E. and Pollard, A. (2006). Identity and transfer: A new focus for home-school knowledge exchange. *Educational Review, 58*(4), 415-33.

Ozga, J. and Sukhandan, L. (1997). *Undergraduate non-completion in higher education in England* (Research Report 97/29). Briston: HEFCE

Priyadharshini, E. and Robinson-Pant, A. (2003). The attractions of teaching: An investigation into why people change careers to teach. *Journal of Education for Teaching, 29*(2) (07): 95.

Reay, D. (2002). Class, authenticity and the transition to higher education for mature students. *Sociological Review, 50*(3), 398-418.

Russell, H., Smyth, E., Lyons, M. and O'Connell, J. (2002). *Getting out of the house: Women returning to employment, education and training.* Dublin: Liffey Press, ESRI.

Senge, P. (1990). *The fifth discipline: The art and practice of the learning organization*. Doubleday.

Schuller, T. (2002, May 14, p. 13). Higher education opinion: Expanding higher education is a laudable target but we must not forget that it is important for those over 30 too, *The Guardian*.

Teaching Council (2011). *Initial teacher education: Criteria and guidelines for programme providers*. Dublin: Author. Retrieved from http://www.teachingcouncil.ie/_fileupload/Teacher%20Education/ITE%20Criteria%20and%20Guidelines%20Final%20July%202011.pdf

White, S. (2008). Mothers who are student teachers: Navigating their dual roles in pre-service teacher education. *Studies in Continuing Education, 30* (2), 159-172.

Woodley, A., Wagner, L., Slowey, M., Fulton, O. and Bowner, T. (1987). *Choosing to learn*. Buckingham: SRHE/Open University Press.

Wright, P. (1989). Putting learning at the centre of higher education. In O. Fulton (Ed.), *Access and institutional change*. Buckingham: Open University Press.